Hands Up Education is a non-profit organization and international community of practice, creating and sharing high-quality teaching resources. The core focus of our work is on Latin and Classics for a modern curriculum.

All income generated by SUBURANI is invested in supporting Classics teaching in schools around the world.

Published by Hands Up Education Community Interest Company.

First published in 2021.
2nd printing 2022.

All papers used in this book have been sourced from sustainable forests.

Library of Congress Cataloguing in Publication Data.
British Library Cataloguing in Publication Data.
A catalogue record for this book is available from the British Library.

Paperback edition ISBN 978-1-912870-05-9
Hardcover edition ISBN 978-1-912870-06-6

Printed in the United Kingdom.

Hands Up Education Community Interest Company, 133-134 Bradley Road, Little Thurlow, Haverhill, CB9 7HZ, United Kingdom.
www.hands-up-education.org, contact@hands-up-education.org

Contents

Caledonia
Oceanus Septentrionalis
Hibernia
Britannia
Camulodunum
Londinium
Aquae Sulis
Germania
Germania Inferior
Oceanus Atlanticus
Gallia Belgica
Gallia Lugdunensis
Germania Superior
Raetia
Noricum
Vesontio
Vindonissa
Pannonia
Dacia
Alpes Poeninae
Gallia Aquitanica
Lugdunum
Alpes Cottiae
Gallia Narbonensis
Alpes Maritimae
Arelate
Dalmatia
Moesia
Italia
Mare Adriaticum
Hispania Tarraconensis
Corsica
Roma
Pompeii
Macedonia
Lusitania
Conimbriga
Baleares
Sardinia
Brundisium
Delphi
Corinthus
Olympia
Athenae
Achaea
Baetica
Sicilia
Syracusae
Carthago
Mauretania Tingitana
Mauretania Caesariensis
Africa
Mare Internum
Lepcis Magna
Gaetulia
Cyrenaica
N
W
E
S
0
250
500
750
1000
MILES
Scale (approximate)

The Roman Empire
AD 64–68

According to legend, Rome was founded as a small village in 753 BC. By AD 64, when our stories begin, Rome had grown into a huge city, and its armies had conquered a vast empire. Rome controlled lands in areas we now think of as North Africa, the Middle East, Asia, and Europe.

Population

Approximately one million people lived in Rome itself, but between 50 and 100 million people lived in the empire it governed. Some of those people lived in cities, but most lived in small towns, villages, and on farms.

Provinces

The Romans organized their empire into provinces, each under the control of a governor. The shape and size of a province was influenced by natural features (such as mountain ranges or large rivers) and by the location of local peoples and cultures.

Mare Internum

Rome's empire centered around the Internal Sea (*Mare Internum*), which we now call the Mediterranean Sea (the sea in the middle of the land). As it was often quicker to travel by sea than by land, the Mare Internum helped to link together the various peoples and goods of the Empire.

Roads and rivers

To help people, goods, and armies move around the Empire more easily, the Romans built a network of over 50,000 miles of roads. Major rivers, such as the Rhône and the Rhine, also played an important part in the movement of goods.

Information

The Romans built a system of staging posts, where riders with government messages could change horses and rest overnight if necessary. In normal situations it was more important that a message arrived safely than that it arrived quickly, and messengers usually traveled about 30 miles in a day. However, if a message was urgent riders could cover over 100 miles in a single day.

Pompeii

In the autumn of AD 79 the volcano Vesuvius erupted, destroying the nearby town of Pompeii. The town was buried in layers of ash and pumice. Archaeologists have gradually excavated about two-thirds of the site. The remarkably well-preserved remains we can see today give us a unique glimpse into the lives of ancient Romans.

Pompeii was about 125 miles southeast of Rome, in the region of Campania. It was located on a low hill of volcanic rock at the estuary of the River Sarno. In ancient times the city was close to the sea, but the coast has since moved further out. The precise site of Pompeii's port is still unknown, but it was likely to have been at the mouth of the River Sarno. There may have been a smaller harbor near the Marine Gate.

The major cities of Campania were Neapolis (modern Naples), Capua, and Puteoli (modern Pozzuoli). Puteoli was the hub for Rome's trade with the East. In comparison, Pompeii was small and unimportant; nevertheless, it was a thriving commercial center. It had a population of roughly 12,000–15,000 with an additional 12,000 or so in the surrounding countryside.

The town can be traced back to at least the sixth century BC, when the city walls were built. It became a Roman colonia in about 80 BC, when veterans were settled there, and the people of Pompeii were given Roman citizenship.

Our story is set just a few years after a severe earthquake in AD 62 or 63 damaged many of the buildings in Pompeii. The historian Tacitus recorded:

> Because of an earthquake, a large part of the busy town of Pompeii in Campania collapsed.

The region was subject to frequent earthquakes, and the inhabitants must have been used to minor earth tremors. Nevertheless, the severity of the AD 62 earthquake meant that at the time of our stories much of Pompeii was a building site, with houses and other buildings being repaired and rebuilt. It was also a time of opportunity for anyone willing to take the risk of investing in the town.

This plan shows Pompeii as it was in AD 79 at the time of its destruction by the eruption of Vesuvius. Many of the streets and buildings would have been unchanged in the interval. Pompeii, like many Roman towns, was laid out on a grid system, dividing it into blocks. The names of the gates and houses are modern. In Roman times most of the streets probably did not have names.

Chapter 17: Pompēiī

prīmā lūce

5 tandem cellam dominī tacitē intrāvit.
6 servus pānem, quem ā pistōre ēmerat, in mēnsā relīquit. aquam, quam in urnā tulerat, in pōculum effūdit. tum pōculum in mēnsā posuit.
urna jug, urn
effundō I pour out
pōnō I put, place
7 salvē, domine. parātum tibi est ientāculum.
8 grātiās tibi agō, Currāx. nunc ī ad tabernam meam. amphoram vīnī optimī domum Oculātiī portā. ille cēnam splendidam crās praebēbit.
ientāculum breakfast
praebeō I provide
stabulum stable
9 vir ientāculum, quod Currāx parāverat, cōnsūmpsit. tum dē cellā dēscendit et per hortum ad stabula ambulāvit.
10 subitō fēmina pulchra eum vocāvit.
11 salvē, Giscō! ubi est fīlius tuus?
12 salvē, Iūlia! Attō in cellā dormit.
13 estne puer sōlus?
14 minimē! Celer eum libenter prōtegit.

domus dēserta
1 Currāx per viās ambulāverat et iam ante domum magnificam stābat. in pavīmentō faucium erat imāgō canis ferōcis, sed neque canis neque iānitor ibi stābat. puer igitur lentē prōcessit per iānuam. amphoram, quam Giscō vīnō implēverat, portābat. Currāx erat lentus quod amphora erat gravissima.
dēsertus *deserted*
faucēs *entrance, entry passage*
neque … neque … *neither … nor …*
iānitor *doorkeeper*
2 puer iam in ātriō stābat atque circumspectābat. impluvium et mēnsās et sellās cōnspexit. sed nēminem Currāx vīdit. puer ānxius sibi dīxit 'cūr nēmō adest?'
3 tablīnum quoque erat dēsertum. Currāx amphoram in ātriō relīquit et ānxiē prōcēdēbat.
atque *and*
impluvium *impluvium (pool for rainwater)*
sella *chair*
tablīnum *tablinum (room next to the atrium)*
4 Giscō dīxit Oculātium cēnam praebēre et vīnum optimum quaerere, sed eum invenīre nōn possum.
5 Currāx trīclīnium intrāvit, ubi imāginem pulcherrimam cōnspexit. in imāgine Thēseus Ariadnam relīquerat et in nāvem ascendēbat. Currāx attonitus imāginem intentē spectābat.
Thēseus *Theseus (Athenian hero)*
Ariadna *Ariadne (Cretan princess)*

6 subitō post Currācem ex hortō 'heus, puer. quis es tū?' senex quaesīvit.
8 dominus, Giscō nōmine, mē hūc mīsit.
7 Currāx Oculātium, quī prope larārium appāruerat, cōnspexit.
quaerō I ask
larārium lararium (shrine to the household gods)
9 senex puerum ad ātrium dūxit, ubi amphoram breviter īnspexit. 'haec amphora est vacua!' inquit. Currāx trīste vīdit amphoram esse vacuam.
10 vīnum nōn amphoram vacuam emere volō. abī, puer!
vacuus empty
11 Currāx cōnfūsus ad Giscōnem trīstissimē reveniēbat. Oculātius duōs servōs, quī vīnum abstulerant, mox valdē laudābat.
cōnfūsus confused

The domus

There were various types of housing in Pompeii, ranging from single rooms, such as the one we see Gisco, Atto, and Currax living in, to grand mansions. Here we are going to look at a town house belonging to a rich, but not enormously wealthy, family. This type of house is known as a ***domus***. Just like houses today, not every domus was exactly the same, but they had some common features.

The story **domus dēserta** is set in a real house which archaeologists have called the House of the Tragic Poet. They chose the name because the house is decorated with wall paintings showing scenes from Greek myth and literature. We don't know who lived in the house; we have imagined the owner as Oculatius because members of his family are known to have supported the theater in Pompeii.

The exterior of the house gave little hint of the size and splendor that lay inside. The entrance was directly on one of the main streets, between two shops, and there were only a few small windows on the upper floor. However, anyone gazing inside from the street would be able to see the magnificently decorated atrium, and, beyond it, the garden with its lararium. The house was arranged around two courtyards, open to the air.

The Roman domus was a workplace as well as a place to live. The owner conducted some of his business affairs at home, and the atrium was often busy with visitors. He would also have private meetings in the smaller rooms, and entertain guests at dinner in the triclinium. Enslaved people would be at work all over the domus. There was very little privacy.

1. tabernae

On either side of the front door were shops open to the street. There were also entrances to the shops from the house, indicating that the house and shops were connected. The owner of the house may have owned the shops and managed them through his freedmen or slaves. When archaeologists were excavating the shop on the left of the entrance they found items of precious jewelry – gold and pearl earrings, necklaces, bracelets, and rings. It is possible that this was a jewelry shop.

Left: gold and pearl earrings of the style found at Pompeii.

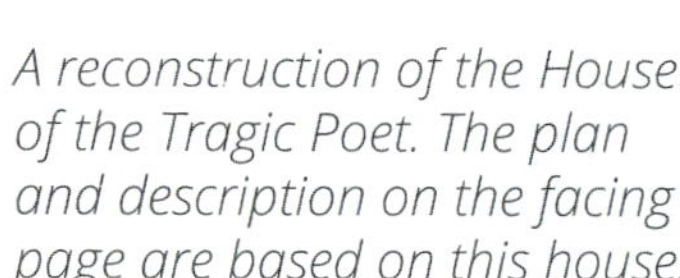

A reconstruction of the House of the Tragic Poet. The plan and description on the facing page are based on this house.

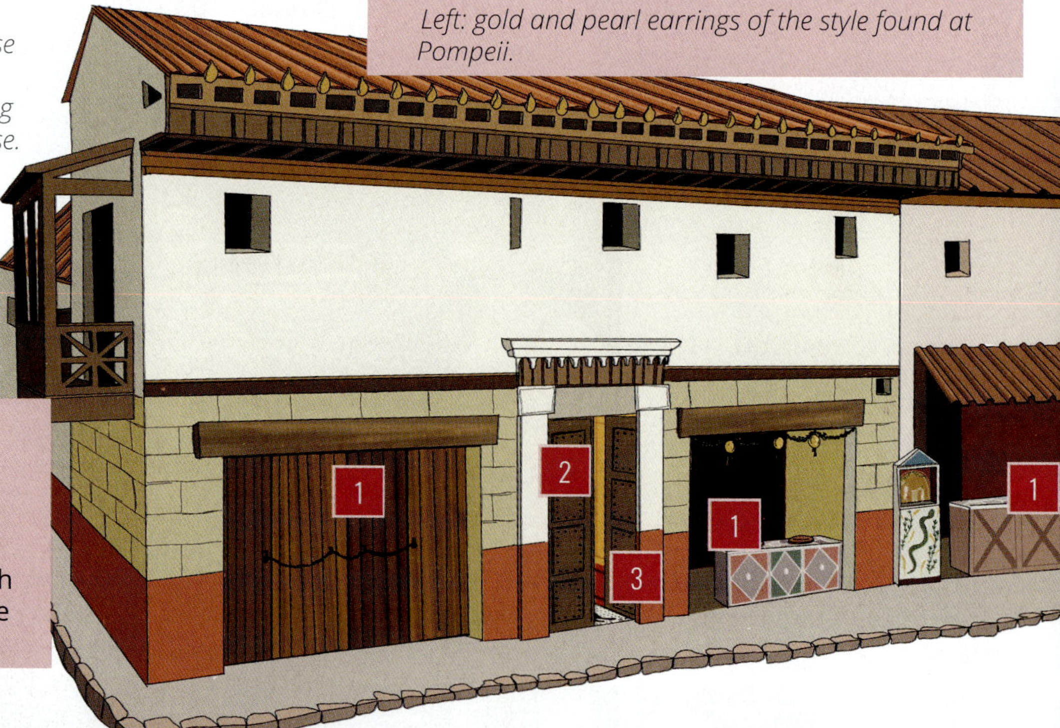

2. iānua

The imposing entrance was more than ten feet high. The double doors were made of wood, with metal fittings and bronze studs.

6. peristȳlium

At the back of the house was a garden (***hortus***), with a colonnade on three sides: this kind of courtyard is known as a peristyle (***peristȳlium***: in Greek this means 'with columns around'). At the back of the garden there was a lararium. Archaeologists found the shell of a tortoise in the garden – possibly a household pet.

5. tablīnum

This room opened off the atrium, from which it could be separated by a wooden partition or curtain. On one side it was open to the garden. It had several functions. The owner may have used it for conducting business and receiving guests more privately. It was also a place for storing records. Sometimes it may have been used for dining.

7. triclīnium

In the House of the Tragic Poet the dining room was at the back of the house, off the peristyle. In some other houses, it was in the front part of the house, next to the atrium. Some houses had more than one triclinium.

8. culīna

The kitchen was a small room next to the triclinium. The bathroom (***lātrīna***) adjoined the kitchen.

cubicula and storerooms

The function of the other, smaller rooms cannot be identified. Some must have been bedrooms (***cubicula***) or storerooms, or used for less formal dining.

4. ātrium

The atrium was the center of the house, a large room where the owner received his guests: friends, business associates, and dependents. There was an opening in the roof (***compluvium***) to let in light, and to allow rain to fall into a marble-lined pool (***impluvium***) directly below. The rainwater was stored in a separate tank under the floor. Some houses in Pompeii also had water piped in.

In the House of the Tragic Poet the walls of the atrium were decorated with paintings of scenes from the Trojan War. In some houses the roof of the atrium was supported by pillars. Often there was a lararium in the atrium.

3. faucēs

The fauces was a passage leading from the door to the main rooms of the house. On the floor, just inside the door, there was a mosaic of a dog, with the words: CAVE CANEM. During the day the front door was probably open. Although there may not have been a real guard dog, there would probably have been a slave stationed near the entrance to check visitors and guard against intruders. The small room on the left behind the shop may have been the doorkeeper's room.

staircases

These led to the upper floor, which has not survived. Upstairs there may have been more storage rooms, or the enslaved members of the household may have slept there. Some rooms may have been rented out.

LANGUAGE NOTE 1: PLUPERFECT TENSE

1. Can you spot the difference between these pairs of sentences?

Currāx duōs servōs cōnspexit. *Currax noticed two enslaved men.*	**Currāx duōs servōs cōnspexerat.** *Currax had noticed two enslaved men.*

And again in these examples?

Pompēiānī aquam portābant. *The Pompeians were carrying water.*	**Pompēiānī aquam portāverant.** *The Pompeians had carried water.*

What is the difference in the form of the Latin verbs? How does that difference affect the meaning of the verbs?

2. The -**era**- in the ending of the Latin verb indicates that the action **had** taken place some time ago. This form of the verb is known as the **pluperfect tense**.

3. Look at the pluperfect tense of the Latin verb **vocō** (*I call*):

vocāveram	*I had called*
vocāverās	*you had called*
vocāverat	*he/she/it had called*
vocāverāmus	*we had called*
vocāverātis	*you had called*
vocāverant	*they had called*

The very end of the verb (-**m**, -**s**, -**t**, -**mus**, -**tis**, -**nt**) tells us *who* had carried out the action, and the -**era**- tells us *when* they had done it.

4. Now look at these sentences and notice how the pluperfect tense is used:

fēmina pānem, quem anteā fēcerat, vēndēbat.
The woman was selling bread, which she had made previously.

Giscō aquam, quam Currāx in mēnsā posuerat, bibit.
Gisco drank the water, which Currax had placed on the table.

In the first sentence, the woman had made the bread before she was selling it. In the second sentence, Currax had placed the water on the table before Gisco drank it. The pluperfect tense is often used to show that one action had taken place before another action.

5. Finally, compare the forms of **vocō** in the following sentences:

Present	**fēmina Giscōnem vocat.**	*The woman calls Gisco.*
Imperfect	**fēmina Giscōnem vocābat.**	*The woman was calling Gisco.*
Perfect	**fēmina Giscōnem vocāvit.**	*The woman called Gisco.*
Pluperfect	**fēmina Giscōnem vocāverat.**	*The woman had called Gisco.*

Note that the pluperfect tense is based on the perfect (**vocāvī**) rather than the present (**vocō**).

in fullōnicā

iterum Currāx amphoram per viās portābat. Giscō enim eum ad virum dīvitem, quī vīnum emere volēbat, mīserat. Currāx tamen fessus erat, et quiēscere volēbat. igitur in viā sedēre cōnstituit. sōl erat calidus, puer cōnfectus. mox Currāx dormiēbat.

prope Currācem erat fullōnica, ubi servī vestīmenta sordida, quae lavāre temptābant, in lacibus calcābant. fullō vestīmenta dīligenter īnspiciēbat. ūna toga erat sordidissima.

'adfer plūs ūrīnae!' clāmāvit fullō.

ancilla amphoram quaerere coepit. nōnnūllās in viā cōnspexit. ancilla ūnam in fullōnicam rettulit. sed haec amphora, quam Currāx extrā fullōnicam innocenter posuerat, nōn erat plēna ūrīnae.

'effunde illam ūrīnam quam celerrimē!' clāmāvit fullō. nēmō putābat amphoram plēnam vīnī esse. ancilla dominō celeriter pāruit. statim multum vīnum erat in lacū.

'stultissima!' fullō clāmāvit. 'haec toga nunc sordidior est quam anteā! est toga Oculātiī, quī īrātissimus erit, quod vīnum vestīmentum eius corrūpit!'

Currāx, quem clāmor excitāverat, fullōnicam intrāverat et verba fullōnis audiēbat. puer rīdēbat et sibi dīxit 'nunc Oculātius certē vīnum Giscōnis habet.'

ē fullōnicā quiētissimē exiit et ad tabernam Giscōnis lentē reveniēbat.

fullōnica *fullery, laundry*

enim *for, because*
dīves *rich*
quiēscō *I rest*
cōnfectus *worn out, exhausted*
lavō *I wash, soak*
lacus *tub, basin*
calcō *I tread*
fullō *fuller, laundry manager*
toga *toga (formal garment)*
adferō *I bring*
ūrīna *urine*
referō *I carry back*
extrā *outside*
innocenter *blamelessly, innocently*
pāreō *I obey*
corrumpō *I spoil, ruin*

The remains of the fullonica of Stephanus in Pompeii.

arca parva

in portū urbis stābat Iūlia. multōs odōrēs maris, piscium, garī, hominum sordidōrum olfaciēbat. laetē rīsit. nāvis, quae multōs diēs ex Aegyptō nāvigābat, nunc ad portum perveniēbat. eam libenter spectābat.

prīmō vēre Iūlia epistulam ad frātrem, quī in Aegyptō habitābat, scrīpserat multaque arōmata petīverat. nunc haec nāvis, quae iter longum trāns mare fēcerat, parvam arcam arōmatum plēnam tandem ferēbat.

in portū parvae undae nāvēs lēniter lambēbant. breviter terra tremuit. stābat tamen Iūlia aequō animō. tandem arcam ā nautīs accēpit et domum quam celerrimē prōcessit.

prope domum Iūlia cōnspexit Giscōnem in popīnā sedēre.

Iūlia salvē, Giscō! vīnum emis aut vēndis?

Giscō hodiē vīnum bibō! quid tū agis?

Iūlia bene! et bene tū cēnābis, mī Giscō, apud mē paucīs diēbus!

Giscō sacculus tuus est plēnus?

Iūlia ita est – plēnus arāneārum! necesse erit tibi, mī amīce, vīnum et cibum ferre!

Giscō ha! quam benigna es!

Iūlia prō vīnō et cibō amīcitiam praebēbō. aut, aliquid melius, unguentum tibi dabō. nam mox unguentum optimum facere poterō. sī tibi deī favent, mūtābunt tōtum tē in nāsum!

illō tempore iuvenis popīnāriam vocāvit ...

iuvenis ohē! ancilla! plūs vīnī! quantī est?

Iūlia ancilla? līberta est. eius est popīna! hic vir eam, quae fīlium eius servāverat, ēmit līberāvitque.

Quārtilla nihilōminus ... est duōbus assibus, amīce.

odor *smell, scent*
garum *garum (fish sauce)*
olfaciō *I smell*
Aegyptus *Egypt*
vēr *spring*
arōma, n. *spice*
lēniter *gently*
tremō *I tremble, shake*
aequō animō *calmly, with a calm mind*
quid? *how?*
cēnō *I dine*
sacculus *purse*
ita *so, in this way*
arānea *cobweb*
amīcitia *friendship*
unguentum *perfume*
nam *for, because*
faveō *I favor, support*
mūtō *I change*
līberta *freedwoman, former slave*
as *as (low value coin)*

Making perfume

corpusque suāvī tēlinō unguimus
and we anoint the body with fragrant telinum

This line of poetry is said to have been composed by Julius Caesar. The ingredients of telinum included olive oil, fenugreek, marjoram, and honey.

Roman towns must have been full of unpleasant smells: vats of urine, waste thrown into the street, animal dung, workshops such as tanneries (where leather was produced), and fullonicae. Therefore Romans liked to surround themselves with the fragrance of flowers and perfumes. Both women and men wore perfume. Men used perfumed hair oil, and Emperor Nero sprinkled the soles of his feet with perfume. The host of a dinner party sometimes provided perfume for his guests.

Ingredients

The Romans used oil, especially olive oil, as the base for perfume. Fragrance was added in the form of resins, flowers, herbs, spices, and rinds. Perfume was produced in Campania, where high-quality ingredients were available locally. Growing flowers, especially roses, was an important business. Other local ingredients included pomegranate rind, coriander seeds, and herbs such as marjoram.

Some expensive perfumes and exotic ingredients were imported, particularly from Egypt and Arabia. These included myrrh and frankincense, and spices such as cinnamon. It wasn't just the rich who enjoyed perfume. Cheap perfumes were made from olive oil scented with flowers such as iris and rose.

The perfume industry

There were perfume-sellers, and it is likely that some sellers also made perfume. Archaeologists have excavated a garden in Pompeii where flowers were grown commercially; these could have been used for making perfume, as well as for garlands.

Below: this wall painting from the House of the Vettii in Pompeii shows perfume being made and sold. The workers are mythological creatures – male Cupids and female Psyches.

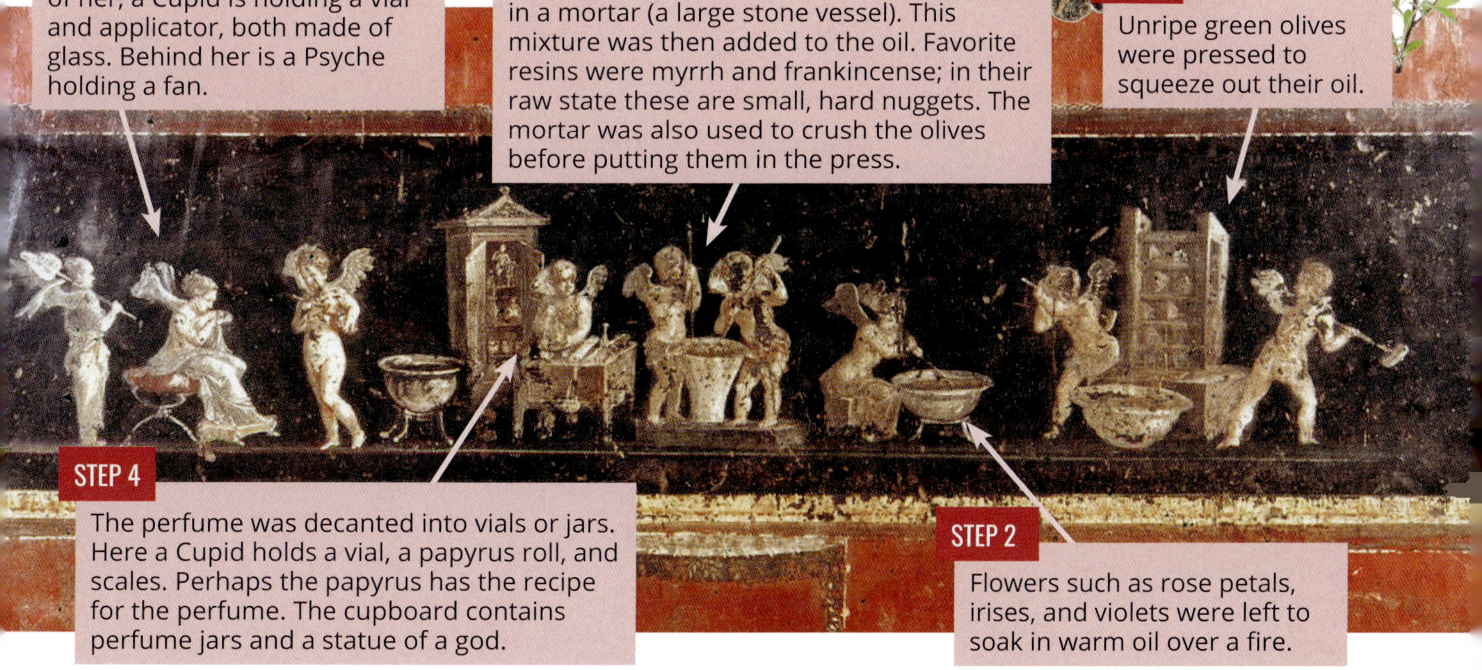

STEP 1

Unripe green olives were pressed to squeeze out their oil.

STEP 2

Flowers such as rose petals, irises, and violets were left to soak in warm oil over a fire.

STEP 3

Resins, spices, herbs, and rinds were ground in a mortar (a large stone vessel). This mixture was then added to the oil. Favorite resins were myrrh and frankincense; in their raw state these are small, hard nuggets. The mortar was also used to crush the olives before putting them in the press.

STEP 4

The perfume was decanted into vials or jars. Here a Cupid holds a vial, a papyrus roll, and scales. Perhaps the papyrus has the recipe for the perfume. The cupboard contains perfume jars and a statue of a god.

STEP 5

The shop: a customer tests the perfume on her wrist. In front of her, a Cupid is holding a vial and applicator, both made of glass. Behind her is a Psyche holding a fan.

LANGUAGE NOTE 2: ADVERBS

1. Study the following sentences. What do you notice about the words in red?

   Currāx per iānuam lentē prōcessit.
   Currax proceeded slowly through the doorway.

   senex amphoram breviter īnspexit.
   The old man briefly inspected the amphora.

2. In the first sentence, **lentē** describes **prōcessit** – it tells us how Currax proceeded. In the second sentence, **breviter** describes **īnspexit**, telling us how the old man inspected the amphora. Words which describe verbs in this way are known as **adverbs**.

3. Many adverbs are formed from adjectives. Most adverbs formed from first and second declension adjectives end -**ē**:

Adjective		Adverb	
laetus	*happy*	**laetē**	*happily*
saevus	*cruel*	**saevē**	*cruelly*
stultus	*foolish*	**stultē**	*foolishly*

4. Some adverbs formed from third declension adjectives end -**e**, others end -**ter**:

Adjective		Adverb	
facilis	*easy*	**facile**	*easily*
trīstis	*sad*	**trīste**	*sadly*
celer	*quick*	**celeriter**	*quickly*
ferōx	*fierce*	**ferōciter**	*fiercely*
fortis	*brave*	**fortiter**	*bravely*

5. Superlative adverbs also end -**ē**:

Superlative adjective		Superlative adverb	
laetissimus	*very happy*	**laetissimē**	*very happily*
celerrimus	*very quick*	**celerrimē**	*very quickly*

6. Note a special use of the superlative adverb with **quam** to mean *as … as possible*:

   soror mea quam celerrimē currēbat.
   My sister was running as quickly as possible.

   tertiō diē quam longissimē iter fēcimus.
   On the third day we traveled as far as possible.

familia Ampliātī

postrīdiē Currāx ad magnam domum antīquam advēnit. iānitōrem exspectābat. subitō servus senex iānuam alteram aperuit.

'hūc venī! haec via servīs est. Cosmus sum.'

senex puerum per ātrium, ubi Currāx cōnspexit multōs servōs labōrāre, dūcēbat, et in culīnā dispēnsātōrem invēnērunt.

Cosmus heus, Nymphī! hic puer vīnum attulit.

Nymphius bene. sed ubi est garum? diū garum exspectō. dominus noster enim garum optimum, quod Umbricia Fortūnāta vēndit, postulāvit.

Currāx quis est dominus vester?

Cosmus nōnne dē Numeriō Popidiō Ampliātō audīvistī? Ampliātus est vir dīvitissimus ac nōtissimus. vīnum optimum vēndit. et templum Īsidis prō fīliō aedificat ...

Nymphius ... garum quoque postulat, ut dīxī!

Currāx dē Ampliātō certē audīvī. sciō eum lībertum esse!

Nymphius tacē, puer! et abī! prō vīnō grātiās dominō tuō agimus.

Cosmus, quī iam Currācem in peristȳlium quiētē dūxerat, laetē dīxit 'spectā hoc emblēma!' ille Currācī imāginem proeliī in pavīmentō ostendit. Alexander Magnus Graecīque hostēs ferōciter oppugnābant.

Cosmus nōnne magnificum est? nōs Graecī Persās vīcimus.

mātrōna ita est, sed vōs servī labōrāre dēbētis!

Cosmus mihi ignōsce, domina.

domina, quae rīdēbat, discessit.

Cosmus mātrōna, nōmine Corēlia Celsa, benignior est quam marītus.

Currāx Ampliātus est dominus dūrus?

Cosmus quamquam ille lībertus est, saepe servōs pūnit. necesse est servīs dominōs semper cavēre, ut bene scīs.

Currāx per viās urbis ambulābat. verba, quae Cosmus dīxerat, cōgitābat.

antīquus *old, ancient*
senex *old*
dispēnsātor *housekeeper, supervisor*
et *even, also*
Īsis *Isis (Egyptian goddess)*
prō *in the name of*
ut *as*
prō *for, in return for*
peristȳlium *peristyle (courtyard surrounded by columns)*
Graecī *Greeks*
Persae *Persians*
vincō *I conquer*

Shops and businesses

The inhabitants of Pompeii were involved in a wide variety of trades and businesses. The streets of the town were lined with shops and bars, catering for the local population as well as visitors and passing traders. Generally, larger workshops were located on the outskirts of the town, but in the city itself there were numerous smaller ones, producing and selling goods. The wealth that some Pompeian business owners amassed from their trade is evident in the decoration of their luxurious houses.

A mosaic from the floor of the House of Siricus in Pompeii shows the words SALVE LUCRU(M) – 'Hello, profit'.

Here is blessed Campania, in whose valley rise hills covered in vineyards with their glorious wine and merriment, famous throughout all the world and, as the old writers say, the site of the fiercest competition between Father Liber and Ceres*. These shores are watered with hot springs and are noted beyond all others in the sea for their prized shellfish and fish. Nowhere is there a more noble olive oil.

Pliny the Elder

*Father Liber is another name for Bacchus, the god of wine. Ceres was the goddess of grain and the harvest.

Local produce

The Pompeians took full advantage of the natural assets of their surroundings, both land and sea. The volcanic soil around Vesuvius was very fertile and heavily cultivated. Pompeii was well known for its figs, onions, and cabbages. This fresh produce was sold in the markets of the town and consumed locally. Other products, such as wine, were exported widely. Amphorae bearing trade stamps from Pompeii have been found as far away as Gaul, Spain, and North Africa.

Pompeii's coastal position provided access to trade across the Empire, and its port became the main gateway to the southern Campania region. Around the port there was also a thriving fishing business, bringing in fresh fish to be sold at market. Some of the catch was used to make garum, the fish sauce for which Pompeii was famed. There were also salt pans, where seawater was evaporated in shallow pools to make salt, an important ingredient in garum.

There were regular market days, when local farmers and traveling merchants would come into town to sell their products. There were also commercial market gardens (growing vegetables and flowers) and vineyards in the city itself.

Right: this wall painting from the House of the Centenary shows Bacchus, the god of wine, wearing a bunch of grapes. Behind him stands Mount Vesuvius, its slopes covered in vineyards. The snake is a symbol of fertility.

Trades in the town

Usually a rich patron provided the initial capital for raw materials and equipment, and a freedman or freedwoman ran the day-to-day business. Often the shop or workshop was attached to the patron's domus. He normally owned the premises and sometimes also the land on which the raw materials were produced. In return for his investment, he received rent for the premises, and interest on the loan or a share of the profits.

Archaeologists have uncovered many shops and workshops in Pompeii, but it is often difficult to identify what was produced and sold in them. Most of what we know about the various trades in the town comes from written inscriptions. These include election notices and advertisements written on walls (graffiti), and tombstones.

Leather

A graffito painted on the outside of a building identifies its purpose: 'Tannery of Xulmus'. Here raw animal hides were treated. After being soaked in a combination of water and urine, the hair and any remaining flesh was scraped off with a knife. The hides were then smeared with animal dung, usually dog or pigeon, and then soaked again until they became soft and supple. They were then left to dry. The stench of such an industry would have been unavoidable, and another tannery in Pompeii was suitably located on the outskirts of the town, near the Stabiae Gate. This large tannery probably supplied most of the shoemakers and leatherworkers in the town.

The Via Mercurio, a street in Pompeii running north from the forum, was lined with shops, workshops, and bars.

Pottery

Archaeologists have identified two pottery workshops. One was located outside the city, near the Herculaneum Gate. Here, archaeologists found unfired amphorae, which had been shaped and were on the ground waiting to be placed in the kiln.

In the southern part of the city, near the Nuceria Gate, another potter's workshop has been excavated. This workshop specialized in the manufacture of oil lamps. The oil lamps were made by pressing the clay into molds. They have been found in large quantities throughout the city.

In both workshops archaeologists have found potter's wheels and kilns. The workshops had shop areas facing onto the street, where customers could browse and buy the products.

Similar workshops with shops have been discovered throughout Pompeii, producing ironware, jewelry, woven mats, and many other items.

Hospitality and services

Many inhabitants of Pompeii worked at one of the numerous bars or inns. Almost 200 small bars providing drinks and food have been uncovered. They would have been filled with people socializing and gambling, eating and drinking, and some would have offered a place to sleep for traveling tradesmen. Many Pompeians did not have kitchens at home and ate out; these bars and cafes were a major part of the local economy. Some also housed brothels.

Other services offered in Pompeii included those of barbers, builders, painters and decorators, pawnbrokers, and architects. The urban elite were involved in businesses such as banking, auctioneering, and the law courts.

LANGUAGE NOTE 3: CONJUGATIONS

1. Look at the infinitive forms of the following verbs:

vocāre	*to call*	**tenēre**	*to hold*
mittere	*to send*	**audīre**	*to hear*

vocāre ends -**āre**, **tenēre** ends -**ēre**, **mittere** ends -**ere**, and **audīre** ends -**īre**. The four infinitives are all slightly different because each verb belongs to a different group of verbs, known as **conjugations**.

2. When you look up a verb in the dictionary, the first two forms enable you to identify its conjugation:

vocō, vocāre	*first conjugation*
teneō, tenēre	*second conjugation*
mittō, mittere	*third conjugation*
audiō, audīre	*fourth conjugation*

In addition to the differences in the infinitive, notice that second conjugation verbs end -**eō** in the present tense, and fourth conjugation verbs end -**iō**.

Cleaning clothes

Most laundry was done at home, often by slaves, but some large woolen items such as togas and cloaks were sent to the fullonica for specialist treatment. Archaeologists have identified twelve fullonicae in Pompeii, which suggests that people, and not only the wealthy, must have used the services of the fullonica regularly. New clothes were also sometimes sent to the fullonica for finishing. The purpose of finishing was to improve the quality of the surface of a woolen garment, making it smooth and even.

A painted pillar showing workers in a fullonica.

Fulling involved the following steps:

1. Workers washed the clothes in a mixture of water, stale urine, and fuller's earth (a kind of clay).
2. The clothes were rinsed in tanks of water.
3. The surface (nap) was brushed and trimmed.
4. Sometimes the garments were bleached or treated with chalk to enhance their whiteness. Bleaching involved stretching the garment over a frame and burning sulfur underneath. White clothes would need to be washed more often, but most people did not wear white. The wealthy elite distinguished themselves by wearing white, and candidates for public office had their togas specially whitened. The Latin word ***candidātus*** (candidate) literally means 'whitened'.
5. The garments were dried, pressed, and folded.

Our story is set in the fullonica of Stephanus, which had been converted from a large domus. The shop was at the front and the laundry at the back, and there were also living quarters. The workers in the fullonica would have been a mixture of slaves, former slaves, and free people. Some of the jobs, such as treading, were labor intensive; others, such as brushing and trimming, required special skills.

LANGUAGE PRACTICE

1. Complete the sentence by choosing the pluperfect tense verb, then translate.

a. Giscō Quārtillam, quae fīlium servāverat, libenter .... (līberāvit, līberāverat, līberābat)

b. vīllam terramque trīste .... (relinquēbāmus, relīquimus, relīquerāmus)

c. frāter Iūliae haec arōmata in Aegyptō .... (ēmerat, ēmit, emēbat)

d. legiōnēs prīncipēs hostium ferōciter .... (oppugnābant, oppugnāvērunt, oppugnāverant)

e. num cibum in hortō stultē .... ? (pōnēbātis, posuerātis, posuistis)

f. domum quam celerrime .... , quod dormīre volēbam. (redieram, redībam, rediī)

g. tū, quī omnia intellegere potes, mihi paene .... (persuādēbās, persuāserās, persuāsistī)

h. alter cōnsul dē cōnsiliō comitis breviter .... (dīxit, dīcēbat, dīxerat)

2. Choose the correct Latin word for the English word in italics.

a. Currax fell asleep *briefly* in the street. (brevis, breviter)

b. My sister overpowered the *fierce* thief. (ferōciter, ferōcem)

c. We caught sight of our *foolish* friends. (stultē, stultōs)

d. You spoke *anxiously* about what had happened. (ānxius, ānxiē)

The Alexander Mosaic from the House of the Faun shows Alexander the Great, king of Macedon, fighting Darius, king of Persia, probably at the Battle of Issos in 333 BC. Alexander, on the left, is on horseback, while Darius is in a chariot. This is the floor mosaic which Currax sees in the story ***familia Ampliātī****. We have imagined Ampliatus living in the House of the Faun. The mosaic measures 8.9 feet x 16.8 feet and over one and a half million tiny tesserae were used.*

Archaeology of Pompeii

This drawing from 1776 by Pietro Fabris shows the discovery of the temple of Isis at Pompeii.

As Vesuvius erupted, many Pompeians fled, taking with them whatever possessions they could. In the weeks and months after the eruption, some inhabitants returned to rescue their property, thieves searched for items to steal, and officials sent by Emperor Titus investigated the site. But then for centuries Pompeii and the neighboring town of Herculaneum were gradually forgotten. Locals may have been aware that artifacts could be found in the vicinity of Vesuvius, but nobody linked such findings to the lost towns. This changed in the eighteenth century, when first Herculaneum (in 1709) and then Pompeii (in 1748) were rediscovered.

Early excavations

The first excavations aimed to find lost treasures to adorn the palaces of the king of Naples, rather than to advance knowledge about the Roman Empire. For this reason, Herculaneum and Pompeii were excavated in an unsystematic manner. Statues, frescoes, and other works of art were removed, usually with no record of where they had been found. Then a large part of the excavated area was covered again to avoid looting. Most of the findings went to the royal collection and visitors from other countries were not permitted to view them.

Systematic excavation (1860–1962)

When Pompeii ceased to be owned privately and became the property of the nation, the first systematic excavations began. Archaeologists introduced a number of scientific methods, which included:

- the development of an accurate plan of Pompeii, dividing the town into regions and insulae (blocks). This made it easy to identify the different buildings and to map where objects were discovered.
- the introduction of stratigraphic (layer by layer) excavation, which helped to show the context of the finds. It also prevented the collapse of buildings.
- the use of plaster of Paris to create casts of the remains of human bodies.

Between 1924 and 1962 archaeologists increased the size of the excavated area almost to its current extent, as a result of considerable government funding. In the Fascist era, Mussolini wanted to use the glories of ancient Rome to promote his own view of Italy, and actively supported the excavations of Pompeii.

Conservation and science

Since so much of the site was unearthed and open to the public, huge problems for conservation and preservation arose. From the late twentieth century, efforts have concentrated on preserving the areas which have already been excavated, and very few new excavations have been undertaken. In 2012 'The Great Pompeii Project', with EU funding, started a major program of works to preserve the exposed buildings and to consolidate the unexcavated area.

Parallel to this field work, new scientific methods, such as DNA analysis and environmental archaeology, have been applied to the Vesuvian cities. For instance, in Herculaneum archaeologists investigated the remains of human excrement found in a sewer in order to understand more about the diet of the people who lived in an apartment building. The human bones found at Pompeii and Herculaneum have been the subject of careful research. This has allowed archaeologists to assess the health, age, gender, and height of some of the people who died in the eruption.

DISCUSSION

1. Pompeii attracts over two million tourists each year from across the world. They both generate money for the site and contribute to its decay. To what extent should ancient sites be open to the public?
2. Some people would like to excavate parts of Pompeii that are still buried. Others think that it is more important to concentrate on preserving and studying what has already been uncovered. What do you think?

Chapter 18: lībertās

salūtātiō

1 prīmā hōrā nōnnūllī cīvēs lībertīque in ātriō Ampliātī stābant. omnēs Ampliātum, multī sportulam, paucī invītātiōnem exspectābant. inter hōs erat Giscō, quī cliēns Ampliātī esse volēbat. Nymphius dispēnsātor nūntiāvit:

2 dominus mox aderit.

3 postrēmō Ampliātus ātrium intrāvit et clientēs salūtābat.

salūtātiō *morning greeting*
sportula *money, little basket*
invītātiō *invitation*
cliēns *client*
postrēmō *at last*

4 'hodiē quārtā hōrā ad forum ībō et ōrātiōnēs audiam. vōs omnēs mēcum venīre volō.'

5 'sextā hōrā cum Numeriō Popidiō Apelle ac Numeriō Popidiō Trogō ad thermās ībō. ibi enim pilā lūdēmus.'

6 'crās cēnam Numeriō Popidiō Victōrī ac Numeriō Popidiō Postumō praebēbō. illī optimē cēnābunt et bibent.'

7 'et crās māne omnēs hūc reveniētis.'

ōrātiō *speech*
sextus *sixth*
pila *ball*

II

Nymphius sportulam clientibus dabat. Ampliātus Giscōnem in tablīnum vocāvit.

Ampliātus mī Giscō, grātiās tibi agō prō vīnō optimō quod servus heri hūc tulit. plūs vīnī tuī emam. servī meī, quōs Nymphius ad tē mittet, multās amphorās auferent. sī cōnsentiēs, tē dīvitem faciam.

cōnsentiō *I agree*

Giscō placet mihi haec verba audīre.

Ampliātus optimē! itaque patrōnus tuus erō.

Giscō maximās grātiās tibi agō. cliēns fidēlis erō. tēcum ad forum hodiē veniam.

Ampliātus bene! et ad salūtātiōnem cōtīdiē veniēs.

Giscō ad tabernam suam laetē reveniēbat. crēdēbat Ampliātum patrōnum optimum esse.

Ampliātus quoque erat laetus. nam sciēbat vīnum Giscōnis melius esse quam vīnum suum. sibi dīxit, 'nunc vīnum optimum vēndam. sīc mē, nōn Giscōnem, dīvitem faciam!'

The atrium of the House of Menander in Pompeii.

Patrons and clients

In the story **salūtātiō** you have read about Ampliatus, a ***patrōnus***, and Gisco, his ***cliēns***. There is no precise English equivalent for these Latin words, but we translate them as 'patron' and 'client'. A female patron was a ***patrōna***. Patrons were richer, more powerful, and of higher social status than their clients. They helped and protected their clients in various ways. In return, clients provided services and loyalty to their patron. In a society without a welfare system, patrons played a crucial part in the lives of the poor.

A patron could help his clients by giving them gifts of food or money, offering legal help and advice, and occasionally inviting them to dinner. He could be particularly useful supporting a client in his business or career, by lending money or making introductions. He could call upon his clients to perform useful services, such as being a witness to a legal document. Clients would also support their patron in his political career and vote for him in elections. If a patron invested in a business run by one of his clients, he would get a share of the profits. Another benefit to the patron was the boost to his prestige. Having a large number of clients paying their respects at the ***salūtātiō*** or accompanying him to the forum or the baths was a sign of a patron's status, and in ancient Rome status was very important.

salūtātiō

One of the obligations of a client was to go to his patron's house at dawn to greet him at the salutatio, 'the greeting ceremony'. The word ***salūtātiō*** comes from ***salūtō***, 'I greet'. Some houses in Pompeii had stone benches outside where clients could sit and wait to be allowed into the atrium. As a mark of respect, it was customary for the client to dress formally in a toga – although we can't be certain how many people adhered to this custom. In return for attending, the client received a gift, the ***sportula***. Originally the sportula was a basket of food (***sportula*** means 'little basket'), but by the time of our stories the gift was usually in the form of a small amount of money.

Patronage

Patronage was a system of mutual favors and obligations, with benefits for both patron and client. Roman society was very hierarchical and personal connections were important. The emperor was at the top: he was the most powerful patron of all, and he didn't have a patron. Beneath him were the senators, then the wealthy citizens. In Pompeii, the local magistrates, who often came from the old aristocratic families, were the most important patrons. It was possible to be both a patron of someone lower in status and the client of someone higher up the social scale. If you were an ordinary working person, it was important to have a patron who could provide advice and protection. Some of the poorest people in society relied on regular gifts of food and money from their patrons to support themselves and their families.

There were other forms of patronage. Sometimes wealthy individuals gave money to their local town. For example, in Pompeii we know of Eumachia who paid for a grand building in the forum. Poets such as Horace, Vergil, and Martial depended on wealthy patrons for financial support and promotion of their work.

Enslaved people who had been freed became clients of their former owners. The relationship between a freedman (***lībertus***) or freedwoman (***līberta***) and their former owner was a special kind of patronage, and you will learn more about it later in this chapter.

A statue of Eumachia from the building on the east side of the forum in Pompeii.

Becoming a citizen

Not every free person who lived in Rome or Pompeii was a Roman citizen. Male and female citizens were protected in law from unjust treatment. In addition a male citizen had certain rights and privileges:

- He could vote in elections.
- He could wear the toga, the formal dress of the male Roman citizen.

Some rights were reserved only for male citizens who were freeborn:

- He could stand for election as a magistrate.
- He could serve in the army as a legionary.

How did you become a Roman citizen?

- If your parents were citizens, you were too.
- By the end of the first century BC all citizens of towns in Italy were also Roman citizens.
- Some towns and individuals in the Empire were given citizenship as a reward for loyalty.
- An auxiliary soldier became a citizen when he was discharged from the army.
- Slaves who were freed became citizens.

In AD 212 Emperor Caracalla granted citizenship to virtually all the free people of the Empire.

A male Roman citizen had three names, e.g. Marcus Oculatius Verus.

praenōmen: a personal name, e.g. Marcus.

nōmen: the name of the 'clan' (***gēns***) to which he belonged, e.g. Oculatius. A clan was a group of families.

cognōmen: sometimes this had originated as a nickname, e.g. Verus, which means 'true'.

A female Roman citizen used a feminine form of her father's nomen (e.g. Oculatia). She might also use a cognomen (e.g. Vera, Verilla) or praenomen (e.g. Secunda, Minor).

Citizens could be known by any one or more of their names.

The toga

Wearing a ***toga*** was a sign of your status: only men who were Roman citizens were allowed to wear a toga. The toga was a large, semicircular piece of woolen cloth that was draped and folded around the body and shoulders, over a tunic. There were various kinds of toga, each reserved by custom for a particular usage or to display one's rank. For example, some senators wore the ***toga praetexta***, a white toga with a wide purple stripe along one edge.

A toga was uncomfortable, impractical, and took a long time to put on, but it was an important symbol of being a Roman citizen, and would have been worn for public events. The poet Vergil refers to the Romans as the ***gēns togāta*** ('toga-wearing race').

This statue, from the late first century BC, shows a Roman citizen wearing a toga. He is proudly holding the carved portraits of his ancestors, a display of the hereditary nature of his citizenship.

lībertī

As you saw in Chapter 6, some enslaved people were freed in a process called manumission, and became freedmen or freedwomen. In Herculaneum, a town near Pompeii, it has been estimated that former slaves made up as much as 30% of the population. In Pompeii many of the craftsmen, shopkeepers, and skilled workers would have been freedmen or descendants of freedmen.

Romans were unusual in freeing so many enslaved people and integrating them into society. Although it was a very unequal society, there was a great deal of social mobility. It was possible for someone to start life as a slave and become very successful and rich. Ampliatus is an example. The Vettii brothers, who owned one of the grandest houses in Pompeii, were also wealthy freedmen.

After manumission a freedman became a Roman citizen, although there were some limitations to his rights. He could not stand for public office in Rome or his local town, or serve in the legions. However, he could marry, and his children were full citizens.

Continuing relationships

Freed slaves had a special relationship with their former master. The libertus or liberta became a client and their former master became their patron. Freedmen were members of their patron's familia and sometimes continued to live in the same house. A freedman or freedwoman had some obligations to their patron. They had to work for their former owner for a certain number of days a year. They also were obliged to offer loyalty and support to him and his family. This meant in practice that the libertus or liberta had to live relatively close to their patron.

The relationship between a freedman or freedwoman and their patron was mutually beneficial. A freedman relied on help from his patron to invest in his business, provide premises, and make introductions to customers, while the patron received rent and/or a share in the profit and also benefited from having clients who were in his debt.

New name

A freed slave added two names of his former owner to his own personal name. A libertus thus had three names, a sign of a male Roman citizen. For example, Numerius Popidius Ampliatus took the names Numerius Popidius from his patron and added them to his own name, Ampliatus. The Popidii families were prominent and active in Pompeian politics.

SOURCE 1

Trimalchio is a fictional freedman in Petronius' novel the *Satyricon*. He is portrayed as vulgar and tasteless in the way he flaunts his wealth. Here he describes how he made his fortune:

> I built five ships. I loaded them up with wine – which was then worth as much as gold – and I sent them to Rome. But all the ships were wrecked. That's fact, not fiction. In a single day Neptune gulped down three million sesterces. Do you think I gave up? I built more ships, bigger and better and luckier. I loaded them up again with wine, bacon, beans, perfume, and slaves. On one voyage I made a million sesterces.

SOURCE 2

Pliny describes a dinner where he was a guest:

> Our host served rich dishes to himself and a few others, while he set before the rest small portions of cheap food. There was one kind of wine for himself and us, another for his less important friends, and a third for the freedmen. The man reclining next to me noticed and asked me whether I approved. I said I didn't. 'What do you do, then?' he said. 'I provide the same for everyone. I treat as equals in every respect those whom I have made equal at my table.' 'Even the freedmen?' he said. 'Yes. For I regard them as fellow guests, not as freedmen.' He continued: 'That must cost you a lot.' 'Not at all,' I replied. 'How's that?' 'Because my freedmen don't drink what I drink; I drink what my freedmen drink.'

QUESTIONS

1. What can you learn from these sources about:
   a. how freedmen saw themselves?
   b. how they were perceived by freeborn Romans?
2. What are the limitations of these sources?

LANGUAGE NOTE 1: FUTURE TENSE (CONTINUED)

1. In Chapter 14, you saw that the future tense is often indicated by **-b-** in the ending of the verb. For example:

Present tense	Future tense
tū ad Lūsitāniam nāvigās. *You are sailing to Lusitania.*	**tū ad Lūsitāniam nāvigābis.** *You will sail to Lusitania.*
illī optimē cēnant. *They are eating very well.*	**illī optimē cēnābunt.** *They will eat very well.*

2. Now study these sentences:

Present tense	Future tense
Giscō vīnum optimum mittit. *Gisco sends excellent wine.*	**mox Giscō vīnum optimum mittet.** *Soon Gisco will send excellent wine.*
ōrātiōnēs audiō. *I am listening to speeches.*	**quārtā hōrā ōrātiōnēs audiam.** *At the fourth hour I shall listen to speeches.*

3. First and second conjugation verbs, such as **vocō** (*I call*) and **teneō** (*I hold*), form their future tense in one way, while third and fourth conjugation verbs, such as **mittō** (*I send*) and **audiō** (*I hear*) form their future tense in a different way.

4. Compare the future tenses of **vocō** and **mittō**:

vocābō	*I shall call*	**mittam**	*I shall send*
vocābis	*you will call*	**mittēs**	*you will send*
vocābit	*he/she/it will call*	**mittet**	*he/she/it will send*
vocābimus	*we shall call*	**mittēmus**	*we shall send*
vocābitis	*you will call*	**mittētis**	*you will send*
vocābunt	*they will call*	**mittent**	*they will send*

LANGUAGE PRACTICE

1. Complete the sentence by selecting the future tense of the verb, then translate.
   - **a.** tūne epistulam ad frātrem tuum crās .... ? (scrībis, scrībēbās, scrībēs)
   - **b.** tanta praemia amīcīs nostrīs .... (prōmittēmus, prōmīsimus, prōmittimus)
   - **c.** nōnnūllī prīncipēs ad vōs mox .... (pervēnērunt, pervenient, perveniunt)
   - **d.** nēminī quī aut malus aut saevus est .... (crēdō, crēdideram, crēdam)
   - **e.** verba dūcis ante proelium .... (audīvistis, audiētis, audītis)
   - **f.** ille senātor dōna ad templum deae .... (mittet, mīsit, mittit)

Daily routine

The Roman day

The Romans divided daylight, the time between sunrise and sunset, into twelve equal hours. As the seasons changed so did the length of the hours. Daylight hours in midsummer were about 1 hour 15 minutes long, in midwinter about 45 minutes.

SOURCE 1

The **first** and **second** hour wearies clients at the salutatio.
The **third** is time for lawyers to work, pleading their cases.
Rome prolongs its various labors into the **fifth** hour.
The **sixth** is rest for the weary.
The **seventh** will be the end.
The **eighth** to **ninth** is for oiled athletes in the palaestra.
The **ninth** tells us to crush cushions piled up on couches.
The **tenth** hour is for reciting my poems.

Martial

In this poem Martial is describing life in Rome hour by hour.

- List the activities which occupy the day, and the hours at which they take place.
- When does the working day finish?
- Who do you think Martial recites his poems to at the tenth hour?

SOURCE 2

Horace, the son of a freedman, became rich and successful as a poet. Yet he did not regret his humble origins and often wrote about his lack of ambition and preference for a quiet life.

Often in the evenings I'll stroll around the Circus and the Forum. I loiter beside the fortune tellers; then I make my way home to a bowl of soup with leeks and peas. My supper is served by three slaves. Then I go off to bed with no worries about having to be up early in the morning. I stay in bed until the **fourth** hour, then walk; or else, after reading or writing something for my private pleasure, I have a massage. When I'm feeling tired and the sun becomes fiercer, telling me it's time for the baths, I finish my game of triangle and leave the park. A light lunch – just enough to save me from having to go through the day on an empty stomach; then I laze about at home. This is what life is like when you are free from the cruel compulsion to get to the top.

Horace

Horace also lived in Rome, but his typical day is very different from that described by Martial.

- How does Horace spend his day?
- At approximately what time do his various activities take place?

This Roman sundial is on top of a column, in front of the temple of Apollo in Pompeii. The location is appropriate as Apollo was the god of the sun.

QUESTIONS

1. Think about some of the characters you have met in our stories. Do you think the way they spent their days would resemble the days described by Martial and Horace?
2. How useful do you think these sources are as evidence for the daily life of ordinary Romans?

Umbricia Fortūnāta

Quārtillae pāx animī erat nūlla. in popīnā eius, multa aqua ē fistulā eam spargēbat. intrāvit Stalliānus, plumbārius vetus.

Quārtilla Stalliāne! placet mihi tē vidēre! nam tanta aqua in popīnam it! ō, pedēs meī!

Stalliānus nōlī dēspērāre! mox enim fistulam reficiam.

sed Stalliānus statim in nōnnūllās amphorās cecidit et eās frēgit.

Quārtilla placuit mihi tē vidēre, sed nunc ...

Stalliānus ecce, Quārtilla! in parte ūnius amphorae sunt multae litterae.

Quārtilla ad amīcam Umbriciam, quae haec verba legere poterit, ībō.

♦ ♦ ♦

Quārtilla ad tabernam Umbriciae iit.

Quārtilla licet mihi intrāre?

Umbricia salvē, amīca! quid agunt vulnera tua hodiē?

Quārtilla nihil est. sed semper trīstis sum. nam Currācem līberāre maximē cupiō. quam pauper sum, Umbricia! et hodiē Stalliānus trēs amphorās meās frēgit. haec fragmenta accipe. tūne verba intellegis?

Umbricia verba lēgit.

Umbricia difficile est verba legere: '... sīc ... faciēs ... gar...' ō, Quārtilla! quam fēlīx es! crēdō hoc esse praescrīptum optimum et veterrimum garī vīnō mixtī. multōs annōs nēmō id cōnsūmit. cōnsilium habeō. crās id ūnā faciēmus. sī tū vīnum optimum quaerēs, ego garum splendidum inveniam. sīc tē, Quārtilla, dīvitem faciēmus!

Quārtilla id facere poterimus?

Umbricia mihi crēde, Quārtilla! ea quae tibi prōmīsī, faciam.

plumbārius *plumber*
pēs *foot*
frangō *I break*
licet *it is allowed, one may*
fragmentum *fragment*
praescrīptum *recipe*
mixtus *mixed*

Garum

Umbricia Fortunata was selling garum, a sauce made from fish. The Romans loved garum. They used it for flavoring many of their dishes, as we would use salt, soy sauce, or Thai fish sauce. Umbricia did not make the sauce herself. It was made in large quantities in a workshop, probably located outside the town, on the coast.

Garum was produced in Pompeii on an industrial scale for both local consumption and export. The town was ideally situated, as the three key ingredients were available locally: fish, fresh water from the River Sarno, and salt.

Salt

Sodium is essential to life. It is found in some foodstuffs, but also in sodium chloride – salt. Salt was very important before the days of refrigeration as a way of preserving food. Since prehistoric times humans have tried to find salt, and it was a rare and valuable commodity. Roman soldiers were partly paid in salt: the word 'salary' comes from ***sal dare*** (to give salt). One source of salt is the sea.

The gate on the north-west side of the town, now known as the Herculaneum Gate, was in Roman times called the Salt Gate (***Porta Salīniēnsis***) because it led to the salt pans on the coast. Here, sea water was drawn into large, shallow basins: the water evaporated in the heat of the sun, leaving the salt.

Making garum

Garum was made from various types of fish. Small fish, such as anchovies, were used whole, while only the guts of larger fish, such as mackerel, were used. The fish, mixed with salt, were left to ferment for about two months, with occasional stirring. The clear liquid that resulted was strained off and bottled. A solid residue, ***allec***, was left; this was also used in cooking.

There were different varieties and grades of fish sauce. One may have been specifically for Jews (kosher garum). Garum could be altered by adding other ingredients, such as wine, olive oil, or water. Some was very expensive. The poet Martial wrote:

> Take this expensive gift, lordly garum,
> made from the first blood of a still breathing mackerel.

But there were also cheaper varieties. Ordinary people in Pompeii would have been able to afford garum to enhance the taste of their food.

The garum trade

The garum business in Pompeii at the time of our stories was dominated by Aulus Umbricius Scaurus. He had a huge mansion on the west side of the town, overlooking the sea. It even had its own private bathhouse. The atrium was decorated with a mosaic, showing four of his sauce bottles, one at each corner of the impluvium. On entering the house, a visitor would see both an advertisement for Scaurus' product and a boast of the source of his fortune.

*Each bottle (**urceus**) has a slightly different label. This one says:*

G. F. SCOM
SCAURI
EX OFFI
NA SCAU
RI

G(ARI) F(LOS) SCOM(BRI) SCAURI
EX OFFI(CI)NA SCAURI

The flower (i.e. best) of the mackerel garum of Scaurus from the workshop of Scaurus. (Scaurus' finest mackerel garum from his workshop.)

Garum for the home market was decanted into amphorae and taken by cart to shops in the town. There, it was stored in the amphorae or transferred to large vessels, then poured into small pottery bottles for sale. Agents of Scaurus – freedmen, freedwomen, and slaves – managed the shops and workshops. Umbricia Fortunata, a freedwoman, was one of these. Urcei have been found with labels painted on them naming Umbricia as the seller of the garum. In the Roman world of the first century AD women like Umbricia Fortunata could be involved in business and be economically independent.

Garum was produced elsewhere along the Mediterranean coast, especially in Spain and Lepcis Magna in North Africa. Huge quantities were shipped all over the Empire, in amphorae which were sometimes labeled with the name of the producer. Pompeii was famous for its fish sauce, and some was probably exported from the port on the River Sarno. A container with Scaurus' name painted on it has been found in a shipwreck off the coast of southern France. Fish sauce imported from Spain, where particularly high-quality garum was produced, was also sold in Pompeii.

LANGUAGE NOTE 2: NECESSE EST, PLACET, LICET

1. Look at the following sentences. How might we translate them more naturally into English?

   necesse est vōbīs discēdere.
   It is necessary for you to leave.

   necesse erat nōbīs Aucissae subvenīre.
   It was necessary for us to help Aucissa.

   The first sentence might more naturally be translated simply as *You must leave*, and the second sentence as *We had to help Aucissa*.

2. Now look at these sentences. Again, how might we translate them more naturally?

   placet mihi haec verba audīre.
   It pleases me to hear these words.

   placuit mihi tē vidēre.
   It pleased me to see you.

   The first sentence can more naturally be translated as *I am glad to hear these words* or *I am happy to hear these words*. The second sentence might be translated as *I was pleased to see you*, or *I was glad to see you*.

3. Similarly, **licet** may be translated in a variety of ways:

licet tibi hoc facere.	Literal:	*It is allowed for you to do this.*
	Natural:	*You may do this.* *You are permitted to do this.* *You are allowed to do this.*

4. When translating, aim to write English that feels natural, while still giving the reader all the information that is in the Latin.

LANGUAGE PRACTICE

2. Translate the following sentences twice, first literally, then more naturally.

   a. Ampliātō placuit cēnam magnificam praebēre.

   b. gladiōs quam celerrimē rapere tibi necesse est.

   c. hīs cīvibus apud senem dīvitem saepe cēnāre licet.

   d. heri eīs necesse erat flūmen altum trānsīre.

   e. omnibus placet bene cēnāre fābulāsque nārrāre.

   f. licuitne illīs līberīs in viīs per tōtum diem lūdere?

pittacia

postrīdiē Currāx in tabernā Giscōnis labōrābat. pittacia, in quibus titulus 'vīnum Giscōnis' erat, amphorīs affīgēbat. mox servī, quōs Nymphius mīserat, advēnērunt et multās amphorās auferēbant.

'heus, puer,' clāmāvit servus quīdam. 'fer illam amphoram et nōbīscum venī!'

Currāx mox per viās longās prōcēdēbat. 'quō hanc amphoram portābō?' sibi susurrāvit.

postrēmō servī ad cellam vīnāriam Ampliātī pervēnērunt, ubi plūrimae amphorae erant. Nymphius in pittaciīs novīs titulum scrībēbat.

'illa pittacia dīmovēbimus,' dīxit Nymphius servīs, 'et haec affīgēmus. deinde nēmō alius sciet hoc esse vīnum Giscōnis!'

servī pittacia mūtāre coepērunt. subitō Nymphius Currācem cōnspexit. 'necesse est tibi tacēre, puer,' inquit. 'sī dominus tuus dē hīs rēbus audiet, poenās dabis. abī ac tacē!'

Currāx capite nūtāvit et ē cellā vīnāriā exībat.

fūrtim pittacium novum ab amphorā, quae prope portam stābat, dīmōvit. sibi dīxit: 'hoc ad dominum adferam. crēdō enim Ampliātum aliquid malum Giscōnī parāre.'

pittacium *label*
titulus *description*
affīgō *I fasten*
quīdam *one, a certain*
vīnārius *wine (adjective)*
dīmoveō *I remove*
alius *else*
nūtō *I nod*

A section of painted wall from a cubiculum in the Villa of Publius Fannius Synistor, in the countryside just outside Pompeii.

condiciō

Currāx dominum nusquam invenīre poterat. nam extrā moenia Pompēiōrum, in umbrā arboris prope flūmen Sarnum, stābat Giscō. iterum epistulam, quam amīcus scrīpserat, lēgit. in animō verba diū volvēbat. tandem eques eī appropinquāvit.

'salvē, Giscō,' inquit eques.

'salvē, comes. mēcum venī, nam omnia nova audīre volō.'

dē equō dēscendit Indus. mox duo comitēs prope flūmen sedēbant. Indus, quī in cohorte Batāvōrum merēbat, rettulit plūrimōs senātōrēs Nerōnem interficere velle. tum Indus rem magnī mōmentī nārrāvit.

condiciō *proposal*

nusquam *nowhere*
moenia *town walls*
arbor *tree*
Sarnus *Sarno (river near Pompeii)*
volvō *I turn, roll*
cohors Batāvōrum *Batavian cohort (private guard of Nero)*
mereō *I serve*
referō *I report*
interficiō *I kill*

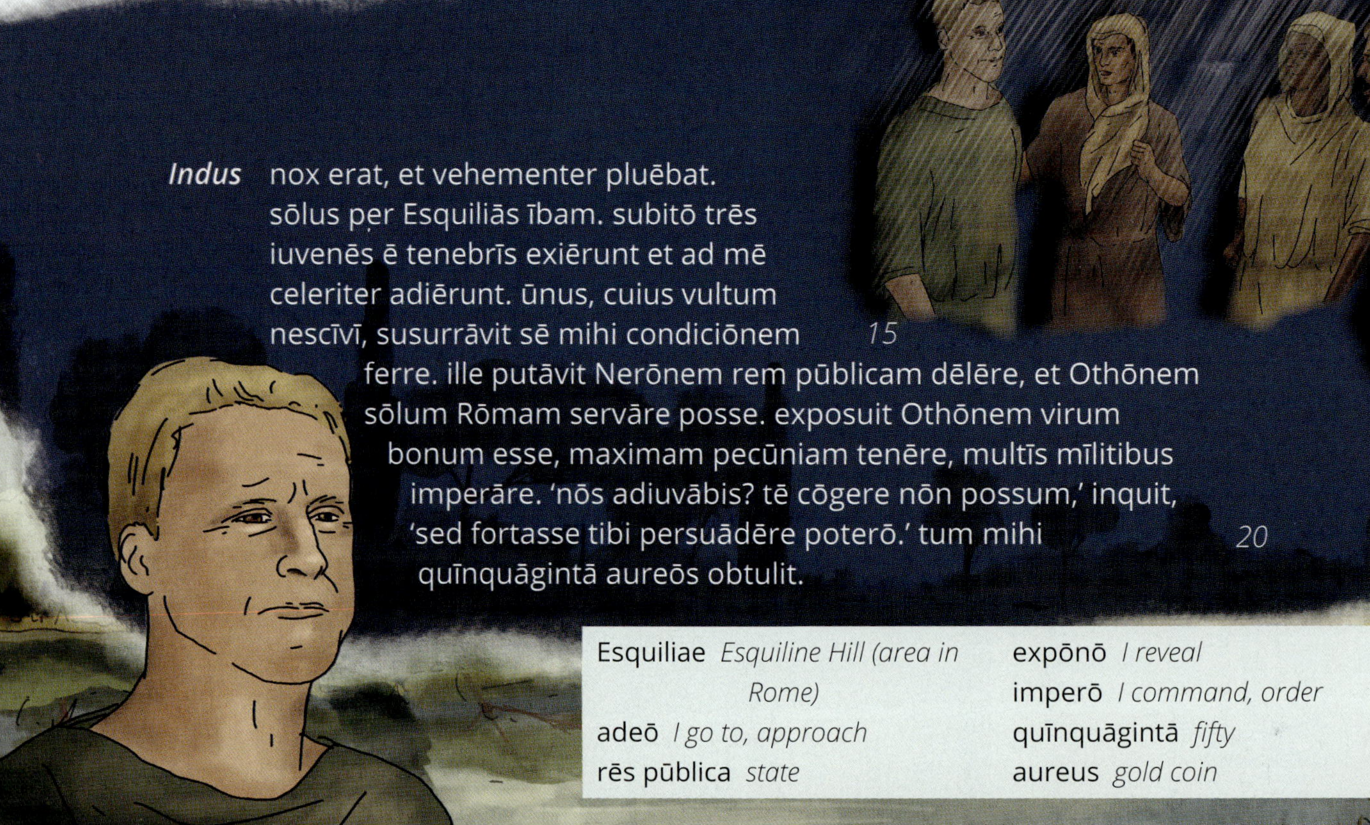

Indus nox erat, et vehementer pluēbat. sōlus per Esquiliās ībam. subitō trēs iuvenēs ē tenebrīs exiērunt et ad mē celeriter adiērunt. ūnus, cuius vultum nescīvī, susurrāvit sē mihi condiciōnem ferre. ille putāvit Nerōnem rem pūblicam dēlēre, et Othōnem sōlum Rōmam servāre posse. exposuit Othōnem virum bonum esse, maximam pecūniam tenēre, multīs mīlitibus imperāre. 'nōs adiuvābis? tē cōgere nōn possum,' inquit, 'sed fortasse tibi persuādēre poterō.' tum mihi quīnquāgintā aureōs obtulit.

Esquiliae *Esquiline Hill (area in Rome)*
adeō *I go to, approach*
rēs pūblica *state*
expōnō *I reveal*
imperō *I command, order*
quīnquāgintā *fifty*
aureus *gold coin*

LANGUAGE NOTE 3: EŌ, ĪRE, IĪ

1. Look at the following sentences:

ad templum Minervae eō.
I am going to the temple of Minerva.

ad amīcam Umbriciam ībō.
I shall go to my friend Umbricia.

sōlus per Esquiliās ībam.
I was going alone through the Esquiline.

quō īs?
Where are you going?

ī ad forum.
Go to the forum.

Quārtilla ad tabernam iit.
Quartilla went to the shop.

2. **eō** (*I go*) doesn't belong to one of the regular conjugations. It changes its form differently from other verbs and is therefore known as an **irregular** verb. There is a full chart of the forms of **eō** on page 285.

3. Now look at these sentences. What do you notice about the verbs in red?

ūnus malus perībit.
One evil person will die.

manēre aut abīre cōnstituistī?
Have you decided to stay or to leave?

ad plaustrum rediimus.
We returned to the wagon.

orbem terrārum trānsī!
Go across the world!

vōs ē fullōnicā exībātis.
You were leaving the fullonica.

ad mē celeriter adiērunt.
They came quickly towards me.

4. The verbs in red are all formed from a prefix (such as **per**-, **trāns**-, **ab**-) and the verb **eō**. They are known as **compounds** of **eō**. So far you have met the following compounds of **eō**:

abeō	*I go away, depart*
adeō	*I go to*
exeō	*I go out, leave*
pereō	*I die, perish*
redeō	*I go back, return*
trānseō	*I go across, cross*

Other compounds of **eō** include:

ineō	*I go in, enter*
obeō	*I go to meet, meet*
subeō	*I go underneath*

vīndēmia

Giscō cum Celere ad rādīcēs Vesuviī ambulāverat, ubi iam et verba Indī in animō volvēbat et vīneam suam īnspiciēbat. servī Ampliātī vīndēmiam colligēbant. quamquam sōl fervidus eōs fatīgābat, servī identidem ūvās dēcerpēbant. Giscō Nymphium, quī servīs praeerat, salūtāvit.

Giscō hae ūvae vīnum optimum facient?

Nymphius sine dubiō, domine. vīndēmia enim est ūberior quam exspectāverāmus.

Giscō optimē! haec verba audīre mihi placet. nunc ībō ad torculum, ubi mustum gustābō.

Giscō atque Celer dē monte redībant et urbī appropinquābant. prope moenia erat praedium Ampliātī, ubi torculum erat. aliī servī ūvās in lacibus calcābant, aliī eās in torculō premēbant, aliī mustum in dōlia fundēbant. servus quīdam pōculum Giscōnī obtulit. Giscō mustum gustāvit.

Giscō quam dulce est hoc mustum! vīnum erit optimum.

subitō Celer lātrāvit. Giscō sē vertit et Ampliātum, quī forte aderat, cōnspexit.

Ampliātus plūrimās amphorās huius vīnī vēndēmus, mī Giscō. tē dīvitem faciam, sīcut prōmīsī.

Celer iterum lātrāvit.

Giscō tacē, Celer!

Ampliātus canī nōn placet mē vidēre. itaque necesse est vōbīs discēdere. crās apud mē cēnābis ... sed sine cane venī!

vīndēmia *grape harvest*
rādīx *foothill*
Vesuvius *Vesuvius (mountain near Pompeii)*
vīnea *vines*
colligō *I collect, gather*
fervidus *boiling hot, fiery*
fatīgō *I tire out, tire*
identidem *repeatedly*
ūvae, f. pl. *grapes*
dēcerpō *I pull off*
praesum *I am in charge*
ūber *plentiful*
torculum *wine press*
mustum *must (unfermented grape juice)*
praedium *land, estate*
premō *I press*
dōlium *very large jar*
fundō *I pour out*
forte *by chance*

LANGUAGE PRACTICE

3. Complete each sentence with the correct form of the verb, then translate.

a. cōtīdiē ego ad portum urbis .... , ubi nāvēs spectābam. (ībās, ībant, ībam)

b. heri sōla in silvam iniistī. quō tū crās .... ? (ībis, ībō, ībit)

c. mīlitēs periērunt quod montem altissimum .... temptāvērunt. (trānseunt, trānsit, trānsīre)

d. Currāx sē vertit et ā fullōnicā .... (abiī, abiistis, abiit)

e. ad templum sacrum .... , quod deae dōna dare volumus. (adīmus, adiī, adeunt)

f. vōsne mox domum .... , aut apud rēgem manēbitis? (redībātis, redītis, redībitis)

Wine

Wine was the main agricultural product of Pompeii. It was a major export, producing great wealth for some Pompeians. Wine played a central part in Roman life, providing pleasure, nutrition, and profit. Other than water it was the main drink for all classes of people. There were different qualities of wine, catering for the dinner parties of the wealthy and the bars frequented by the ordinary people. Drinking wine wasn't just a pleasure. Wine was also an important source of energy and carbohydrates in the diet, and was often used as a medicine.

The Romans drank wine that had been diluted with hot or cold water, sometimes even ice. They often added flavorings, such as honey, herbs and spices, and even garum. At dinner parties slaves mixed the wine in a large vessel, then served it to the guests in jugs. An inferior wine, made from mixing the grape pulp with water, then pressing it again, was given to agricultural workers and enslaved people. Most wine was drunk within the year, but some good wines were kept for as long as twenty years. One of the most highly prized was Falernian, which was produced in Campania, not far from Pompeii.

Wine and religion

Bacchus (also known as Liber), the god of wine, was said to have discovered the vine. He was worshiped at an annual festival, the Liberaria, on March 17. There were also two wine festivals: the Vinalia Rustica, held on August 19 just before the grapes were picked, and the Vinalia Urbana on April 23, when Romans tasted the previous year's wine and prayed for a good harvest. Romans offered wine to the gods in both public and private religious ceremonies.

Dolia for fermenting wine, from a villa in the countryside near Pompeii.

1. Picking the grapes

The grape harvest (***vīndēmia***) was from late August until early October. Often the vines were grown on a trellis or pergola, or sometimes they were trained to grow around a tree.

2. Crushing the grapes

The grapes were taken in carts to the pressing room. Workers crushed the grapes by treading on them with their bare feet. This mosaic is from Mérida, in Spain.

3. Pressing

Next, the grape pulp was crushed by a mechanical press (***torculum***) to produce the must, a mixture of grape juice and solid matter such as skins and pips.

4. Fermentation

The must was drained into large stone jars (***dōlia***), which were half-buried in the ground. A dolium could hold 450 liters or more, the equivalent of twenty amphorae. At this stage, extra ingredients were sometimes added: boiled grape must to aid fermentation; flavorings such as honey or herbs; sea water or salt, which was thought to be a preservative. The dolia were then sealed, and lids were fixed on.

5. Transportation and storage

In the spring, when the wine was ready, it was poured into smaller vessels, such as amphorae, for transporting and storing. Ordinary wine was sometimes transported in ox skins.

Bacchus

In Greek and Roman mythology, Bacchus (known as Dionysos to the Greeks) was the god of wine. He was also associated with fruit and fertility, madness, and drama. Why might the Greeks and Romans have felt there was a connection between these apparently different areas?

SOURCE 1

A Roman statue of Silenus holding the infant Bacchus.

Bacchus and Silenus

Silenus was Bacchus' tutor and companion. In Source 1, what impression does the artist give of both Silenus and Bacchus? Are you surprised to see a god portrayed as a baby? Why do you have this reaction?

The Bacchae

Look at Source 2. In the play *Bacchae*, the Greek playwright Euripides told the story of King Pentheus, who tries to ban the worship of Bacchus. In response, Bacchus drives his followers temporarily insane, and they tear King Pentheus limb from limb.

Some interpret the story of the *Bacchae* as a warning against the dangers of alcohol, others as a warning against the dangers of prohibiting it. Is the consumption of alcohol problematic in society today? What are the arguments for and against controlling or prohibiting alcohol consumption?

The lid of a Greek bowl showing the Bacchae (followers of Bacchus).

SOURCE 2

SOURCE 3

Boy, server of the Falernian,
pour out for me stronger cups.
But you, water, the ruin of wine,
get away from here.

Catullus

in vīnō vēritās

Pliny the Elder

Attitudes to wine

Read the quotations in Source 3. For what different reasons might Catullus not want water added to his wine? What does the fact that water was often added to wine tell us about Roman attitudes to drinking wine?

What does the Latin phrase ***in vīnō vēritās*** mean? What does Pliny suggest happens when people drink wine? Do you think Pliny is praising the effects of wine or warning against them? Should we always tell the truth?

Bacchus and Ariadne

When Princess Ariadne fell in love with Theseus, she helped him to kill the Minotaur. But Theseus later abandoned Ariadne on the Greek island of Naxos. As Ariadne searched for Theseus, Bacchus saw her and fell in love. Bacchus asked Ariadne to marry him – he promised her the sky as a wedding gift – and she accepted. He placed her crown in the sky as a constellation of stars.

Look at Source 4. The Italian artist Titian painted the moment when Bacchus and Ariadne first met. What elements of the myth of their meeting can you see in his painting? What aspects of the worship of Bacchus can you find?

SOURCE 4

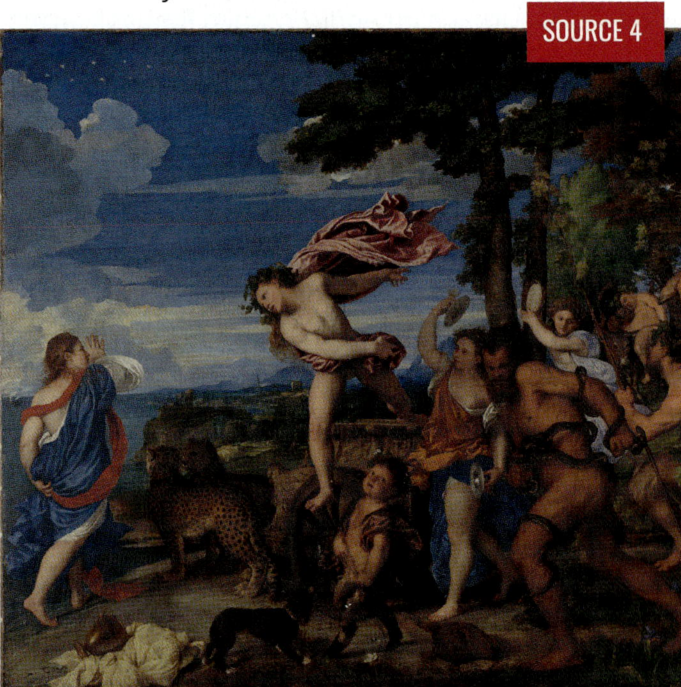

Chapter 19: lacrimae

mors fīliī

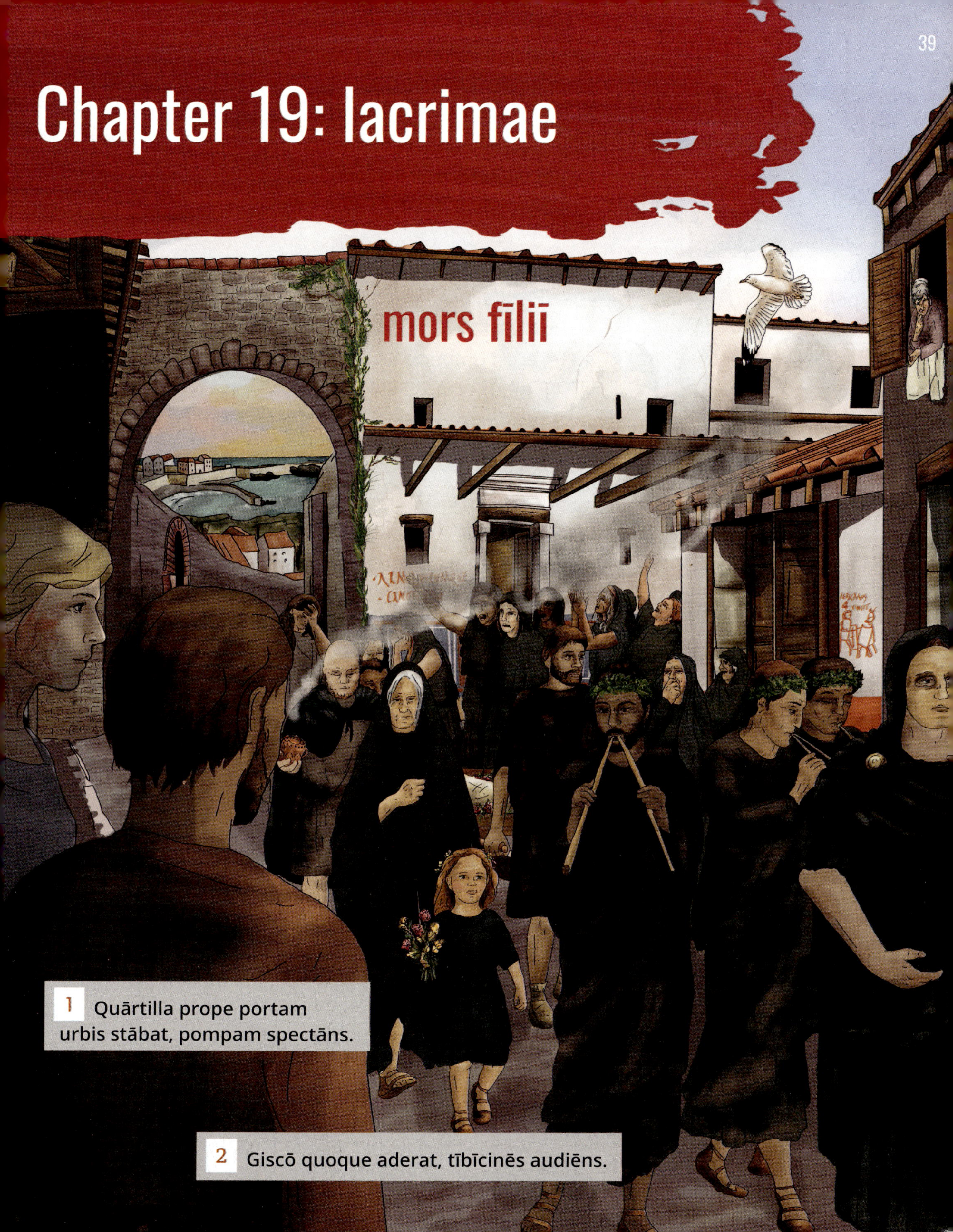

3 quis mortuus est?
4 ille, quī vehementer lacrimat clāmatque, est Umbricius Scaurus, patrōnus Umbriciae. miser Scaurus! fīlius eius mortuus est. fīlius trīgintā annōs vīxit. ille īnfantem uxōremque relīquit.
5 estne Umbricia in pompā?
6 certē. ecce! Umbricia adest, lacrimāns atque clāmāns.
trīgintā *thirty*
7 Giscō Umbriciam, lacrimantem atque clāmantem, prope plaustrum cōnspexit.
8 mox pompa ad forum pervēnit. plūrimī Pompēiānī tacitē stābant, ōrātiōnem intentē audientēs.
9 subitō Giscō Currācem, ad sē currentem, vīdit.
10 Currāx ad Giscōnem omnia dē pittaciō vīnōque rettulit, susurrāns. Giscō Currācem, quiētē susurrantem, audīvit.
Giscō tamen nihil dīxit, in animō rem cōgitāns.

11 deinde pompa ex urbe Pompēiīs exībat, lentē prōcēdēns. Quārtilla pompam, lentē prōcēdentem, spectābat.
12 in agrō, familiārēs Scaurī iuvenem in rogum imposuērunt, et corpus cremāvērunt.
13 familiārēs et lībertī et aliī clientēs Scaurī rogum multās hōrās spectābant, clāmantēs atque lacrimantēs.
rogus *funeral pyre*
impōnō *I place*
cremō *I cremate*
14 tandem familiārēs ad sepulcrum iērunt, cinerēs vōtaque ferentēs.
cinis *ash, ashes*
15 in sepulcrō recumbēbant, cēnam cōnsūmentēs vīnumque bibentēs.

Funerals and tombs

The funeral

Many Romans believed that if someone was not buried properly their spirit would haunt the living, so proper treatment of the dead was essential. When a person died, the body was laid out on a couch in the atrium for a period of mourning by family and friends. Men did not shave, as a sign of mourning. On the eighth day, the funeral couch was carried in a procession to the place of cremation or burial, which would be outside the town. Members of the family walked in the procession, wearing dark clothes. The size of the funeral procession was a way of displaying status, so, in order to increase the number of clients in the procession, sometimes a wealthy Roman freed his slaves in his will. There would also be hired musicians and mourners. Sometimes, if the deceased was a prominent citizen, there was a eulogy (***laudātiō fūnebris***) in the forum. Funerals were elaborate occasions, organized by professional undertakers.

In the funeral procession of elite families, male family members or hired actors wore masks representing the deceased and his ancestors. These lifelike reproductions of a man's face were made during his lifetime, and kept in a cupboard in the atrium. No masks have survived, as they were made of wax and they were fragile.

Whether the dead were buried or cremated changed over time and varied across the Empire. At the time of our stories, Romans usually cremated their dead on a funeral pyre. Then the ashes and bones were collected and put in an urn or chest, which was placed in the tomb. Sometimes a few of the dead person's possessions were burned as well or placed in the tomb, so that they could continue to enjoy them after death. The funeral ended with a sacrifice and a feast with family and friends.

Even a simple funeral could be expensive. Many people therefore belonged to funeral clubs (***collēgia fūnerātīcia***), which paid for their funeral and tomb when they died; often these clubs were associations of tradesmen, such as fullers. The clubs would not have benefited the very poor, who would not have been able to afford the membership fees and contributions. On the other hand, the town council often gave money to pay for the funerals of prominent citizens, as well as sometimes land for the tomb and a statue. Aulus Umbricius Scaurus, the son of the garum manufacturer of the same name, died before his father. His tomb outside the Herculaneum Gate had this inscription:

> To Aulus Umbricius Scaurus, son of Aulus, of the Menenian tribe, duumvir with judicial power. The town councilors voted the site for his monument, 2,000 sesterces for his funeral, and a statue on horseback to be put up in the forum. His father Scaurus set up this monument to his son.

Tombs

As you learned in Chapter 2, Romans placed their dead in tombs lining the roads outside the town. Several members of a family could be buried in a family tomb, and the family's slaves and freedmen were often buried there too when they died. Inside the tomb there were recesses in the walls for the urns containing the ashes. Some tombs were very large and grand. It was common for a tomb to have a statue or portrait bust of the deceased person, as well as an epitaph. Some tombs had gardens and were decorated with wall paintings. Often these grand tombs belonged to rich freedmen, who were proud of their success and wanted to show off their wealth and status. Some tombs were much smaller and simpler, and many poor people could not afford a tomb at all.

The fictional freedman Trimalchio says to Habbinas, whom he has nominated to build his tomb:

> I ask you particularly to paint my little dog at the foot of my statue, and wreaths, and perfume bottles, so that, thanks to you, I'll be able to live on after death. And another thing! See to it that it measures a hundred feet facing the road and two hundred into the field behind. I want every kind of fruit round my ashes and plenty of vines. After all, it's a mistake to have nicely decorated houses when you're alive and not take any trouble about the ones you have to live in for longer. I'll put one of my freedmen in charge of looking after my tomb. And, on my right, put up a statue of my wife Fortunata.

Petronius

The poor

Large tombs called ***columbāria***, which were often underground, provided a decent, relatively cheap means of burial for poorer people. Usually they held the remains of between fifty and one hundred people, although one found in Rome held 3,000. They had rows of recesses along the walls, with pots sunk into them to contain the ashes of the dead. Each pot had an inscription to identify the dead person. Some also had a more expensive memorial, for example a portrait bust. Funeral clubs often had columbaria for their members.

A columbarium at Ostia.

But what happened to the bodies of the many people who could not afford to join a funeral club? Some poor people cremated their dead and put the ashes in cheap or used jars which they then buried in the ground. Some corpses were thrown into mass graves. The poet Horace describes a burial ground on the Esquiline Hill in Rome, which was in his day being turned into gardens:

> A fellow-slave would have the corpses brought here when they had been thrown out of their narrow rooms, and would place them in a cheap box; here stood a common tomb for the poorest people.

Honoring the dead

It was important to honor the dead. People brought offerings of food and drink, for example wine, to the tombs of family members. Some tombs had a pipe that ran down into the urn containing the ashes, so that drink could be poured in. On the anniversary of the death there was a feast with family and friends, and some tombs even had a dining room attached. Every year between February 13 and 21 parents and family members who had died were honored at the festival of the Parentalia. Mourners went to the cemeteries on the outskirts of the town, carrying flowers and jugs of wine and milk. Here is Ovid's description of the Parentalia:

> Tombs must be honored.
> Appease the spirits of your ancestors,
> and bring small gifts to their ashes.
> The spirits of the dead ask for little;
> they prefer your dutifulness to an expensive gift.
> A garland of flowers is enough,
> and a scattering of meal, a few grains of salt,
> bread soaked in wine, and some loose violets.

*Stylized busts, called **columellae**, marked the site where urns containing the ashes of the dead were buried. These were found at Pompeii.*

One of the inscriptions found on a columella reads:

DAPHINE VIX(IT)
ANNIS XXII

LANGUAGE NOTE 1: PRESENT PARTICIPLES

1. In the sentences below, look at the words in red. What do you notice about them?

   Quārtilla in viā stābat, pompam spectāns.
   Quartilla was standing in the street, watching a procession.

   Giscō aderat, audiēns.
   Gisco was there, listening.

   Currāx Giscōnī rem nārrāvit, susurrāns.
   Currax, whispering, told the story to Gisco.

2. The words in red are known as **present participles**, and are formed from verbs. In the first sentence **spectāns** describes Quartilla, in the second sentence **audiēns** describes Gisco, and in the third sentence **susurrāns** describes Currax.

3. Now look at these sentences. Why do you think **lacrimāns** changes its form in the second and third sentences?

   Umbricia adest, lacrimāns.
   Umbricia is there, weeping.

   Giscō fēminam lacrimantem cōnspexit.
   Gisco noticed the weeping woman.

   familiārēs rogum multās hōrās spectābant, lacrimantēs.
   The relatives were watching the pyre for many hours, weeping.

4. Like adjectives, participles change their endings to agree (in case, number, and gender) with the nouns they describe.

5. Present participles denote actions taking place at the same time as the main verb. For example, in the first sentence in paragraph 1 above, Quartilla was watching the procession at the same time as she was standing in the street.

A mosaic from the House of the Faun, depicting a scene of the River Nile in Egypt.

in hortō Iūliae

Iūlia in hortō suō stābat, imāginem spectāns. in imāgine erant deī Aegyptiī. Iūlia deam Īsidem, quam artifex Graecus creāverat, adōrābat. subitō Giscōnem intrantem cōnspexit.

Giscō Iūlia? Iūlia! mihi auxilium dare dēbēs.

Iūlia quid accidit?

Giscō Currāx mihi pittacium, quod ē cellā Ampliātī rettulerat, ostendit. Ampliātus, amīcitiam simulāns, mē dēcipit. Ampliātus dīcit vīnum meum esse Falernum!

Iūlia nōn intellegō, mī Giscō.

Giscō Ampliātus vīnum meum vīlī pretiō emit, sed quasi Falernum magnō pretiō vēndit. sīc sē ipsum, nōn mē, dīvitem facit! putō mē dēbēre dē hāc rē Ampliātum rogāre!

Iūlia necesse est tibi cavēre, mī Giscō. Ampliātus enim vir dīvitissimus est; itaque potentissimus quoque est. Ampliātus nōn modo est amīcus ūtilis sed etiam erit inimīcus difficilis. nōlī bellum cum eō gerere.

Giscō vah! hodiē apud Ampliātum cēnābō. ibi, in lectō recumbentēs et vīnum bibentēs, colloquium habēre possumus ...

Iūlia sed quis alius tē adiuvābit? Pompēiānī illī maximās grātiās agunt, quod templum Īsidis reficit. neque erit facile Ampliātum vincere sine comitibus.

Giscō fortasse vēra dīcis, Iūlia. sed Ampliātus inīquē negōtium agit.

Giscō Iūliam in hortō stantem relīquit et ad proximam tabernam pedem rettulit. fēmina ibi manēbat, rem in animō volvēns. Īsidem iterum supplicāvit.

Aegyptius *Egyptian*
creō *I create, make*
simulō *I pretend*
dēcipiō *I cheat*
Falernum *Falernian (a very expensive wine)*
vīlis *low, cheap*
pretium *price*
quasi *as if*
ipse *himself*
potēns *powerful*
modo *only*
ūtilis *useful*
inimīcus *enemy*
colloquium *conversation*
facilis *easy*
neque *and not, nor*
inīquē *unjustly, unfairly*
supplicō *I pray to*

Isis

Isis was one of the most important deities worshiped in ancient Egypt. In one myth she retrieves the parts of the body of her husband Osiris, who was killed and dismembered by Seth. She then reforms his body and brings him back to life. For this reason she is often associated with childbirth and fertility, but also played a prominent role in funerary rites.

The ancient cult of the Egyptian goddess spread throughout the Mediterranean and reached Rome some time in the second century BC. The cult of Isis was not exclusive and worshipers could continue to practice the Roman state religion. By the time of our stories the worship of Isis was fully integrated into the Roman religious landscape. There was even a temple to Isis and Serapis, another Egyptian god, on the Campus Martius in Rome. Other temples to Isis have been found as far north as Londinium.

As the worship of Isis spread, her associations expanded too. In addition to her original roles of mother, wife, and healer, she was worshiped as a protector of the dead and a goddess of fortune and the sea. A festival held by sailors every spring at the start of the sailing season began to be associated with Isis and became known as the ***Nāvigium Īsidis***. Coastal towns relying on sea trade enthusiastically adopted the cult of Isis, the gentle guardian of sailors.

The cult of Isis was universal, and she was worshiped by men and women and at all levels of society. The deity had so many different aspects that she appealed to large numbers of people.

A marble statue of Isis which was found in the portico of the Temple of Isis in Pompeii. In her left hand she holds an ankh, the symbol of life. Her right hand would have held a sistrum, which is now missing. Many traces of color remain on the surface of the statue.

The mysteries of Isis

A bronze sistrum. It was shaken to make a jingling noise during ceremonies, to ward off evil. Statues of Isis often depict her holding a sistrum and many sistra have been found in Pompeii.

The mysteries of Isis were secret initiation rites for the most dedicated followers of her cult. People who had gone through the initiation were not supposed to discuss what they had experienced with anyone else, so we now have very little information about the ceremonies. One piece of evidence is *The Golden Ass*, a novel written by Apuleius in the second century AD. The main character, Lucius, becomes a follower of Isis and takes part in the initiation. Apuleius does not give many details about what exactly happened as part of the sacred rites, but he describes Lucius' experience of meeting the deity herself.

Straight from the Nile

In the southeast corner of the sanctuary of Isis at Pompeii there was an underground basin which contained water. In the temples of Isis in Egypt this water came from the River Nile. However, in temples outside Egypt the basin would be filled with rainwater. Like the River Nile's annual flood, which made the surrounding land fertile, the rainwater was valued for its life-giving power. This water was used in religious ceremonies and to purify initiates of the cult.

QUESTIONS

1. In what ways is Isis similar to other deities worshiped by the Romans and in what ways is she different?
2. Why do you think the cult of Isis was so popular?

Isis at Pompeii

The original Temple of Isis at Pompeii was built at the end of the first century BC. It was badly damaged in the earthquake of AD 62 and was rebuilt soon afterwards. At the time of Vesuvius' eruption in AD 79 it was the only temple in Pompeii that had been fully restored, a sign of its significance in the town.

The temple was a fusion of Egyptian, Greek, and Roman design. It had an outer courtyard surrounded by columns, and an inner sanctum which housed the statues of Isis and her husband Osiris. At the back there was another building, called the Ekklesiasterion, where members of the cult worshiped the goddess. Although painted in a Roman style, much of the imagery was Egyptian and there were also Egyptian statues.

Above right: a wall painting from the Ekklesiasterion, showing Isis welcoming the Greek princess Io in Egypt. Isis is shown holding a snake, with a crocodile at her feet, both symbolic of her Egyptian origins.

Below: the Temple of Isis at Pompeii as it looks today.

Rebuilding the temple

At the entrance to the sanctuary there was a dedicatory inscription (*below*). It tells us that the rebuilding of the temple after the earthquake was paid for by Numerius Popidius Ampliatus in the name of his son, Celsinus. In return for the funding, Celsinus was awarded the honor of a seat on the town council, even though he was only six years old.

Numerius Popidius Ampliatus had previously been an enslaved man. His status as a freedman meant that he himself was not eligible to hold any kind of public magistracy. By financing the restoration of the temple, Ampliatus secured a place for his freeborn son among the most important men in Pompeii.

N·POPIDIVS·N·F·CELSINVS
AEDEM·ISIDIS·TERRAE·MOTV·CONLAPSAM
A·FVNDAMENTO·P·S·RESTITVIT·HVNC·DECVRIONES·OB·LIBERALITATEM
CVM·ESSET·ANNORVM·SEXS·ORDINI·SVO·GRATIS·ADLEGERVNT

QUESTIONS

1. Why do you think it was so important to Ampliatus that his son should hold public office?
2. The rebuilding of the temple would have been a big expense and shows the wealth of the freedman Ampliatus. What does this inscription tell us about social mobility in Pompeii?

cēna Ampliātī

illā nocte in trīclīniō Ampliātī Giscō cum aliīs hospitibus cēnābat. vōx ancillae canentis eōs dēlectābat. servī vīnum hospitibus adferēbant.

Ampliātus amīcī, vōbīs offerō vērum Falernum. vīnum est vīta. gaudēte, amīcī: dum vīvimus, bibere possumus. nunc vōbīs rem mīrābilem ostendere volō.

servus minimam larvam argenteam in trīclīnium attulit. Ampliātus larvam tractābat, nōnnūllās figūrās fingēns. attonitī erant hospitēs.

Ampliātus sīc omnēs erimus, postquam mors nōs auferet. ergō vīvere dēbēmus, dum licet esse bene.

cēnantēs Ampliātum laudābant. sed Giscō, quī vīnum gustāverat, magnā vōce īrātissimē interpellāvit.

Giscō hoc vīnum est optimum, sed nōn est Falernum. Ampliātus nōs dēcipit. hoc vīnum est meum!

hospes 1 minimē, mī Giscō. Ampliātus vīnum emit. sī vult, potest dīcere vīnum esse Falernum.

Giscō sed multī hoc vīnum quasi Falernum ement.

hospes 2 stultus es, sī Ampliātum accūsās. Ampliātus tē dīvitem facit!

Giscō sed sē faciet multō dīvitiōrem!

hospes 3 melius est tibi habēre pecūniam parvam quam inimīcum.

Ampliātus grātiās vōbīs agō, mī amīcī. multōs amīcōs habeō et in trīclīniō et in hāc urbe, ut scītis. cavē, mī Giscō.

Corēlia satis negōtiī! minimē decet enim cēnantēs dē negōtiō dīcere. nōnne hī glīrēs sunt optimī?

cēterī cibum cōnsūmentēs et vīnum bibentēs iterum colloquia habēbant. Giscō tamen tacēbat, multa cōgitāns.

canō *I sing; play (an instrument)*
vērus *real, true*
dum *while*

larva *skeleton*
argenteus *silver, made of silver*
tractō *I handle, manipulate*
figūra *shape*
fingō *I form*
ergō *therefore*
interpellō *I interrupt*

accūsō *I accuse*
satis *enough*
minimē *not at all, very little*
decet *it is right for, proper for*

This silver cup was found at a villa at Boscoreale, just outside Pompeii. It is decorated with a ring of skeletons of famous Greek poets and philosophers, including Sophocles, Euripides, and Epicurus. Also engraved in Greek are Epicurean maxims including 'Enjoy life while you can, for tomorrow is uncertain', and 'The goal of life is pleasure'. The decoration and wording were not meant to be spooky or morbid, but instead reminded drinkers to enjoy life to the full.

The afterlife

Romans had many different ideas about the afterlife. State religion was not very much concerned with what happened after death. However, most people seem to have believed in some kind of survival after death, although it was generally not a happy existence. The dead joined the ***Mānēs*** (sometimes called the ***Dī Mānēs***), the spirits of the ancestors, who were thought of as a collective divinity, not a group of individuals. They lived outside the town in the tombs, and their survival depended on having someone, usually their descendants, to look after the tombs and bring offerings of food and drink. They had an existence in some ways similar to this life: they were hungry and thirsty, and they wanted to communicate with the living.

If the Manes weren't content, for example if they were hungry or lonely, they could harm the living. When someone had died but not been buried, their ghost haunted the house, and could be dangerous. There was a festival, the Lemuria, at which special rites were performed to exorcize the ghosts.

RESEARCH

1. Find out about the Lemuria.
2. Research other cultures and religions which practice veneration or worship of ancestors.

This stone grave marker would have lain on top of the tomb. It was dedicated to a woman called Tyrannia by her husband. The hole in the center allowed libations of milk, honey, wine, or oil to be poured into the tomb as offerings to the deceased.

Some new religions offered a more optimistic view of the afterlife. Christianity promised resurrection of the body and a glorious life in heaven as a reward for being good in this life. Followers of Isis also hoped for some kind of life after death; they would find Isis shining in the Underworld.

A few exceptional individuals were believed to become gods after they died. The first Roman to be deified was Julius Caesar. After that, the emperors, and some members of their families, became gods after death.

A few philosophers did not believe in any kind of survival after death. For example, followers of the Greek philosopher Epicurus thought that the human body was made of atoms, which eventually dispersed into the air. Stoics such as Seneca believed that there is no existence either before or after death, but every person possesses a spark from the divine fire which periodically destroys the universe.

A miniature bronze skeleton, about 2.5 inches tall. The arms and legs were movable.

Greek myths told stories about life after death and described a mythical Underworld. The Romans used these depictions of the Underworld in their art and literature, but it is hard to know whether many people took these ideas seriously.

> Not even children, unless they are tiny, believe in the existence of the Manes and the Underworld.
>
> *Juvenal*

QUESTIONS

1. What different beliefs do people today have about what happens after death?
2. Compare Roman funerals and the treatment of the dead with modern practices. What are the main similarities and differences?

Egypt

In the rest of the Empire, outside Italy, people had different customs and beliefs surrounding death. For example, in Egypt the custom of mummifying the dead continued after Egypt became a province of the Roman Empire. The portraits here were painted on thin panels of wood, probably around the time of a person's death, and they may have been carried in the funeral procession. After the body was mummified by the embalmers, the portrait panel was laid over the face of the mummy, and kept in place by parts of the mummy wrappings.

LANGUAGE NOTE 2: FERŌ, FERRE, TULĪ

1. Look at the following sentences:

   trīstem nūntium fers.
   You bring sad news.

   necesse est eīs dōna ferre.
   It's necessary for them to bring gifts.

   Poppillus pānem ad mēnsam tulit.
   Poppillus brought bread to the table.

   vīnum ad Āfricam ferēbāmus.
   We were carrying wine to Africa.

   fer aquam!
   Bring water!

   haec est nāvis quae līberōs tulerat.
   This is the ship which had carried the children.

2. **ferō** (*I carry, bring, bear*) is an irregular verb, like **eō** (which you met in the previous chapter). There is a full chart of the forms of **ferō** on page 286.

3. Note that **ferō** can also mean *I bear* as in *I endure, I put up with*. For example:

   Lūcriō dolōrem ferre vix poterat.
   Lucrio was hardly able to bear the pain.

4. Now look at these sentences. What do you notice about the verbs in red?

   hic puer vīnum attulit.
   This boy has brought wine.

   vītam novam nōbīs offerēbat.
   He was offering a new life to us.

   pecūniam, bona, statuās abstulērunt.
   They stole money, goods, and statues.

   Indus rettulit senātōrēs Nerōnem interficere velle.
   Indus reported that the senators wanted to kill Nero.

5. The verbs in red are all compounds of **ferō**. Their meanings are as follows:

   adferō, adferre, attulī *I bring*
   auferō, auferre, abstulī *I take away; carry off, steal*
   offerō, offerre, obtulī *I offer*
   referō, referre, rettulī *I bring back; report, tell*

   Other common compounds of **ferō** include:

   cōnferō, cōnferre, contulī *I collect; bring to*
   dēferō, dēferre, dētulī *I carry away; report*
   differō, differre, distulī *I scatter; publish; differ; defer*
   īnferō, īnferre, intulī *I bring upon, bring against*
   bellum īnferō *I make war on*
   sufferō, sufferre, sustulī *I offer; endure*

epistula ex Ephesō

Rūfīna Giscōnī s. d.

magnō gaudiō epistulam sub signō tuō nūper accēpī, mī Giscō. mihi placuit cognōscere tē nōn parvam pecūniam facere. sī fēlīx eris, Ampliātus patrōnus tuus erit.

hodiē turba ambulantium atque clāmantium viās iterum implet. in urbe Ephesō, sīcut Rōmae, cīvēs tempus agunt fābulās in theātrō spectantēs, templum deae Artemidis vīsitantēs, aut cum amīcīs in popīnīs pugnantēs. nocte sanguis eōrum in viīs effluit. māne ad mē veniunt, vulnera ostendentēs et medicāmenta quaerentēs. multa dē pōtiōnibus cognōvī, quārum nōnnūllae sānāre, paucae necāre possunt.

ego ac Lūcriō pauperibus aegrīsque auxilium offerimus. aliī cibum, aliī vestīmenta cupiunt. saepe pedibus etiam in montēs eō, ubi habitant senēs quī in urbem dēscendere nōn possunt. nōn est facile nōbīs eīs subvenīre. adveniet hiems. mors plūrimōs auferet.

quid agit Quārtilla? vēndere Currācem eī cōnstituistī? dē Sabīnā cōtīdiē cōgitō. spērō eam nōn sōlam esse. fortasse illa līberōs etiam peperit. saepe dē parvō Attōne atque Catiā, quae audācior fortiorque erat quam omnēs amīcae, cōgitō.

valē.

Giscō, postquam epistulam ā Rūfīnā in mēnsā posuit, vōta Dīs Mānibus dedit, multa dē Catiā in animō memorāns. lacrimae eius in terram tacitē cecidērunt. oculōs ad Attōnem vertit. eī dormientī in terrā, Giscō ōsculum dedit.

Ephesus *Ephesus (city in what is now Turkey)*
s. d. = salūtem dīcit *sends greeting*
signum *seal*
Artemis *Artemis (Greek goddess of hunting and the moon)*
medicāmentum *medicine, drug*
pōtiō *potion*
sānō *I heal*
spērō *I hope, expect*
pariō *I give birth*
audāx *bold, daring*
Dī Mānēs *Manes (spirits of the dead)*
memorō *I bring to mind, recall*

LANGUAGE NOTE 3: USE OF PRESENT PARTICIPLES

1. Look at how present participles are used in the following sentences:

cēnantēs Ampliātum laudāvērunt.	*The diners praised Ampliatus.* (literally, *People dining praised Ampliatus.*)
vōx canentis eōs dēlectat.	*The voice of the singer delights them.* (lit. *The voice of the person singing delights them.*)
dormientī Giscō ōsculum dedit.	*Gisco kissed him as he slept.* (lit. *To him sleeping, Gisco gave a kiss.*)
turba spectantium in forō convēnit.	*A crowd of spectators gathered in the forum.* (lit. *A crowd of people watching gathered in the forum.*)

2. Present participles can be used instead of nouns to represent a person or group of people doing something.

LANGUAGE PRACTICE

1. Translate these sentences into English. Each sentence contains a present participle.
   - **a.** ad incendium festīnō, aquam portāns.
   - **b.** vīdistisne canem vestrum, in hortō nostrō dormientem?
   - **c.** equī dē monte lentē dēscendēbant, plaustra gravia trahentēs.
   - **d.** avēs, in caelō volitantēs, dulce canunt.
   - **e.** līberī, nōlīte fortem ducem dormientem excitāre!
   - **f.** bibentēs in popīnā maximōs clāmōrēs sustulerant.
   - **g.** manus fugientium saevōrum mox in silvā conveniet.
   - **h.** comitī dē Iūliā rogantī, Giscō nihil dīxit.

2. Change the verb in italics from present tense to perfect tense by selecting the correct option. Then translate the new sentence. For example:

fūr librum *aufert.*	(abstulī, abstulistī, abstulit)
fūr librum abstulit.	*The thief stole the book.*

a. ego Quārtillae auxilium *offerō*.	(obtulī, obtulistī, obtulit)
b. tū magnam pecūniam ā bibentibus *aufers*.	(abstulī, abstulistī, abstulit)
c. ille cibum meliōrem amīcīs fēlīcibus quam uxōrī *offert*.	(obtulī, obtulistī, obtulit)
d. Rūfīna Lūcriōque miserīs cīvibus vestīmenta *adferunt*.	(attulimus, attulistis, attulērunt)
e. nōs gladiōs *ferimus*, quod hostēs in agrīs vīdimus.	(tulimus, tulistis, tulērunt)
f. vōs *refertis* Ampliātum malum hominem esse.	(rettulimus, rettulistis, rettulērunt)

Orpheus and Eurydice

Orpheus was the son of the god Apollo. He was famed for his beautiful singing and skill at playing the lyre. He fell in love with the nymph Eurydice and the two were soon married. But their happiness was short-lived. One day, running through the forest, Eurydice stepped on a poisonous snake and died. Orpheus, devastated by the death of his beloved wife, descended into the realm of the dead to try to bring her back.

- Read or listen to the myth of Orpheus and Eurydice.

The power of music

Look at Source 1. It was claimed that Orpheus was able to charm wild creatures with his music. In this story he even manages to charm the god of the Underworld, Hades, with his playing.

- How does music have the power to influence our moods?

A Roman mosaic from Sicily.

SOURCE 1

SOURCE 2

Orpheus and Eurydice by the French sculptor Rodin.

Grief and loss

After the death of Eurydice, Orpheus was heartbroken and found no joy on earth without her.

- Think about how people today grieve when they lose a loved one. What can help people come to terms with the loss?

After he had listened to Orpheus' music, Hades agreed to let Eurydice return to the world of the living, on the condition that Orpheus did not turn to look at her before he reached the sunlight.

- Look at Source 2. How has the artist portrayed Orpheus and Eurydice differently from one another? Why do you think Orpheus is covering his eyes?

Coming back alive

Stories about humans going to the Underworld are common in mythology. In the Greek and Roman myths often they must pass the three-headed dog, Cerberus, who guards the entrance, and cross the River Styx on the boat of the ferryman Charon.

RESEARCH

1. To what extent can these myths tell us something about what people believed would happen to them after death?
2. What lessons do you think the myth of Orpheus and Eurydice might be teaching us?
3. Find out about one of the following characters from mythology and their motivation for entering the realm of the dead: Hercules, Aeneas, Theseus, Alcestis.

Chapter 20: mūnera

Carthāgō

mūnus *gladiatorial show*
Carthāgō *Carthage (city in North Africa)*

1 Sabīna amīcam salūtat.

2 Sabīna ab amīcā salūtātur.

ā, ab *by*

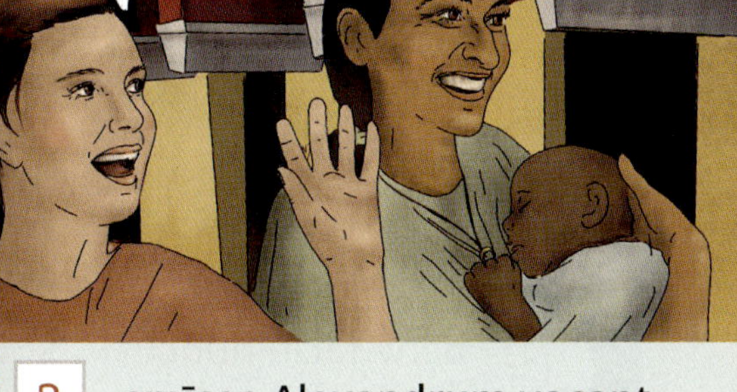

3 amīcae Alexandrum vocant.

4 amīcae ab Alexandrō vocantur.

5 Hermionē Hectorem tenet.

6 Hector ā mātre tenētur.

7 nunc Hector ā Sabīnā tenētur.

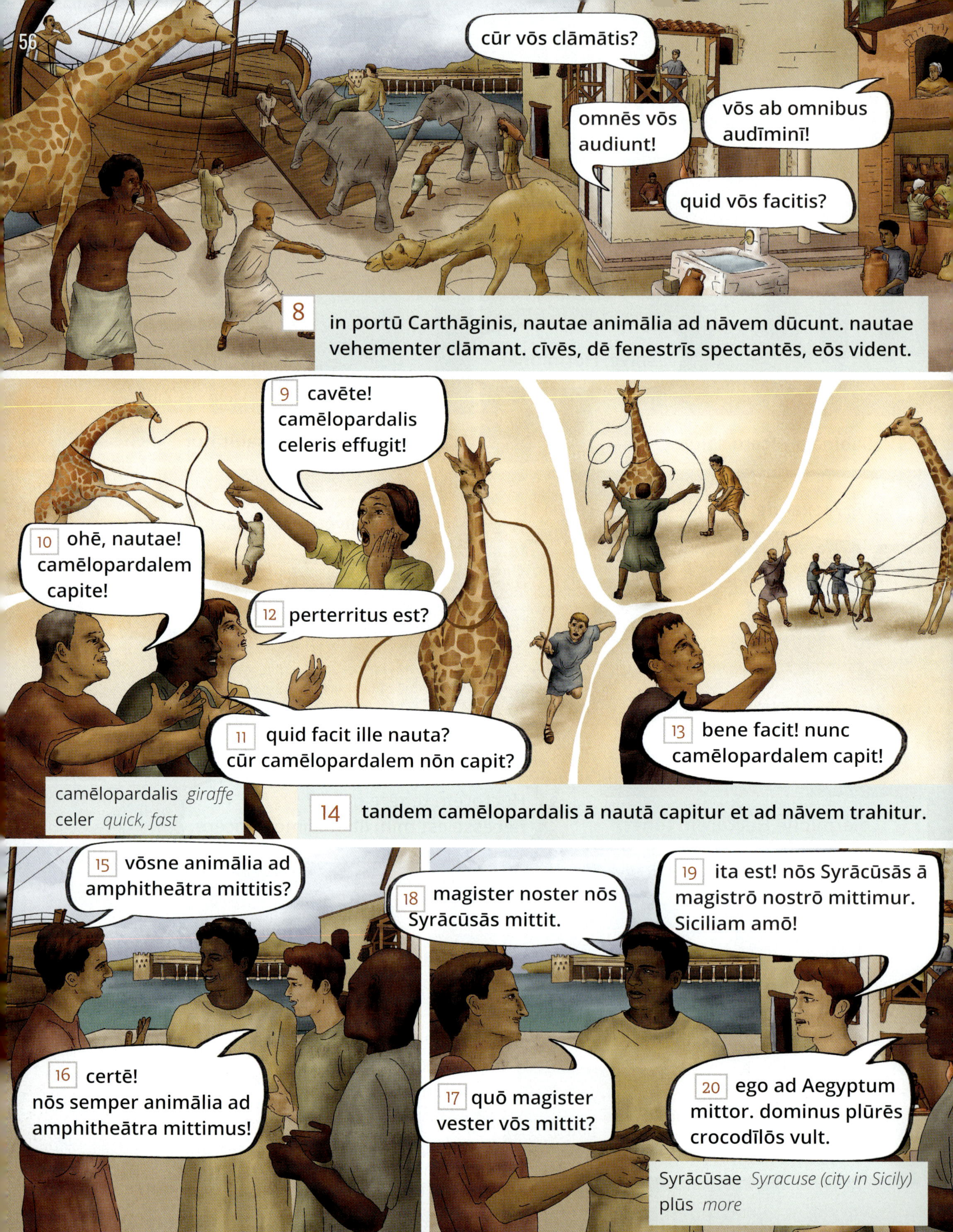
cūr vōs clāmātis?
omnēs vōs audiunt!
vōs ab omnibus audīminī!
quid vōs facitis?
8 in portū Carthāginis, nautae animālia ad nāvem dūcunt. nautae vehementer clāmant. cīvēs, dē fenestrīs spectantēs, eōs vident.
9 cavēte! camēlopardalis celeris effugit!
10 ohē, nautae! camēlopardalem capite!
11 quid facit ille nauta? cūr camēlopardalem nōn capit?
12 perterritus est?
13 bene facit! nunc camēlopardalem capit!
camēlopardalis *giraffe*
celer *quick, fast*
14 tandem camēlopardalis ā nautā capitur et ad nāvem trahitur.
15 vōsne animālia ad amphitheātra mittitis?
16 certē! nōs semper animālia ad amphitheātra mittimus!
17 quō magister vester vōs mittit?
18 magister noster nōs Syrācūsās mittit.
19 ita est! nōs Syrācūsās ā magistrō nostrō mittimur. Siciliam amō!
20 ego ad Aegyptum mittor. dominus plūrēs crocodīlōs vult.
Syrācūsae *Syracuse (city in Sicily)*
plūs *more*

Carthāgō

Carthage was founded in about the eighth century BC by merchants from the Phoenician city of Tyre, who wanted a trading base in the western Mediterranean. The advantages of the site were a good harbor and fertile land. The Carthaginians later came into conflict with the Romans in a dispute over Sicily, and the resulting Punic* Wars (246–146 BC) ended in the destruction of Carthage by the Romans.

In the late first century BC the city was rebuilt as a Roman colonia, and the Romans made it the capital of the province of Africa. By the first century AD it was the fourth largest city in the Empire, with a population of over 100,000 – only Rome, Alexandria, and Antioch were larger. It also became an outstanding center of education.

Very little trace of the Roman buildings has survived, because the stones were reused later by the local population. Archaeologists have recovered the original grid plan of the streets. On the western outskirts there are remains of the stone amphitheater, built in the first century AD.

*The Romans called the Carthaginians ***Poenī***, from the Greek word for Phoenician. ***Pūnicus*** is the adjective, 'Carthaginian'.

Amphitheaters

An amphitheater was an open-air oval arena surrounded by tiers of seating. Amphitheaters were specially built to hold various entertainments, including gladiatorial fights, wild animal hunts, and perhaps even naval battles. The first amphitheaters were made of wood, similar to the one erected by Nero on the Campus Martius in AD 57. The earliest stone amphitheater was at Pompeii, built in about 70 BC. The floor of the central arena where the displays took place was covered with sand (the word ***harēna*** means 'sand'). In some amphitheaters there were subterranean rooms and passages below the arena, where the gladiators and the animals waited before entering the arena.

More than 200 amphitheaters have been found across the Roman Empire. In cities such as Rome, Pompeii, Londinium, Arelate, and Carthage crowds gathered in these distinctively Roman structures to watch distinctively Roman entertainments. Amphitheaters were a symbol of Roman identity (***Rōmānitās***), a way of binding together a multicultural empire.

The most famous amphitheater that survives from the ancient world is the Colosseum in Rome, the construction of which began soon after the death of Nero. It was opened in AD 80, in the center of the city, replacing the lake of Nero's Domus Aurea. The Colosseum was the largest and grandest amphitheater in the Roman world, with a seating capacity of about 50,000, and its design became a model for amphitheaters throughout the Empire.

The amphitheater of El Djem in modern Tunisia. It was built in the third century AD and could hold 35,000 spectators.

In Greek ***amphi*** means 'both', and ***theatron*** means 'theater'. Roman theaters were semicircular, so an amphitheater was a double theater, i.e. two semicircular theaters.

LANGUAGE NOTE 1: ACTIVE AND PASSIVE

1. Look at the following sentences. What do you notice about them?

   Sabīna amīcam salūtat.
   Sabina greets her friend.

   Sabīna ab amīcā salūtātur.
   Sabina is greeted by her friend.

2. In the first sentence, Sabina is doing something: she is greeting her friend. The verb **salūtat** is therefore said to be **active**.

   In the second sentence, Sabina is being greeted, rather than doing the greeting. Therefore, the verb **salūtātur** is said to be **passive**.

3. Now look at these sentences:

   tū ā mātre tenēris.
   You are being held by your mother.

   nōs Syrācūsās mittimur.
   We are being sent to Syracuse.

   The endings of the verbs tell us who is being held, or who is being sent.

4. Compare the active and passive forms of the present tense of **vocō**:

Present active		Present passive	
vocō	*I call*	**vocor**	*I am called*
vocās	*you call*	**vocāris**	*you are called*
vocat	*he/she/it calls*	**vocātur**	*he/she/it is called*
vocāmus	*we call*	**vocāmur**	*we are called*
vocātis	*you call*	**vocāminī**	*you are called*
vocant	*they call*	**vocantur**	*they are called*

5. Just as **vocō** can mean *I call* or *I am calling*, so **vocor** can mean *I am called* or *I am being called*.

LANGUAGE PRACTICE

1. Complete each sentence with the correct form of the verb, then translate.

   a. nōnne tū ā leōne celerī .... ? (terrēris, terrētur, terrēmur)

   b. exercitus ab Othōne ferōciter .... (dūciminī, dūcor, dūcitur)

   c. nōs ā clāmantibus .... (monēris, monēmur, moneor)

   d. hī nautae ā turbā rīdentium .... (spectāmur, spectāris, spectantur)

   e. ego quoque ab amīcīs cārīs .... (vocāris, vocāminī, vocor)

   f. vōs mīlitēs tōtum diem prōcēdere .... (cōgiminī, cōgeris, cōgitur)

ad amphitheātrum

1 diēs fēstus est, et omnēs cīvēs Carthāginis maximē gaudent. mūnera in amphitheātrō ā prōcōnsule Aprōniānō dantur. pompa mox ad amphitheātrum adveniet.

prōcōnsul *governor*

2 Sabīna prope amphitheātrum marītum exspectat, et ex omnī parte ā turbā clāmantium opprimitur.

3 tandem, vultū laetō, Sabīna marītum ad sē adeuntem cōnspicit.

4

Sabīna	hīc sum, Alexander!
Alexander	salvē! Hermionē nōn adest?
Sabīna	minimē, hodiē labōre occupātur, et sanguinem vidēre eī nōn placet.
Alexander	hahae! sed tibi sanguis vulneraque placēbunt, mea Sabīna?
Sabīna	nōn labōrāre et tēcum in amphitheātrō sedēre certē mihi placēbit!

occupō *I occupy, keep busy*

5 Alexander ā sene muliere salūtātur.
6 domine! venī, venī! illae quae hoc philtrum emunt ab omnibus laudantur propter vultum pulcherrimum atque comās splendidās! nōnne uxōrī philtrum emēs, domine? sūdor gladiātōrum inest, quod ...
mulier *woman*
philtrum *potion*
propter *because of*
coma *hair*
sūdor *sweat*
gladiātor *gladiator*
inest *is inside*
7 vae! abī! pah, sūdor gladiātōrum! ubīque nōs dēcipimur ...
pah *pah! pff!*
8 ab illā nōn movēris, mī Alexander? nōn illī crēdis? dē sūdōre multum audiēbam ...
9 ecce! pompa ad nōs adit.

Sabīna ecce, vidēsne hās avēs ingentēs, Alexander? numquam anteā tālia animālia vīdī.
Alexander strūthocamēlī sunt. pedēs celerēs ac rōstra saeva habent.
Sabīna hahae! sīcut uxor tua, fortasse?
Alexander numquam id dīcam, mea columba!

bēstia *wild animal*	strūthocamēlus *ostrich*
agō *I drive, lead*	tālis *such*
pardus *leopard*	rōstrum *beak*

in lūdō

illō diē aliī gladiātōrēs in amphitheātrō pugnābant, aliī in lūdō manēbant. clāmōrēs spectantium audiēbantur ā gladiātōribus quī sedentēs in lūdō cōgitābant.

'māne nōs gladiātōrēs per viās urbis dūcēbāmur,' inquit Dāmōn. 'cīvēs nōs laudābant. sed nunc cīvēs mortem exspectant. nōn intellegō.'

'tālis est vīta gladiātōrum,' respondit gladiātor senior, nōmine Barca. 'aliī hodiē pugnant, aliī crās pugnābunt. aliī vīvent, aliī ... audīte! silentium est ...'

'aliquis aliquem vulnerāvit,' susurrāvit ūnus.

alius respondit, 'sed quid accidet? quōmodo ēditor pollicem vertet?'

mox turba iterum clāmābat. brevī tempore, duo servī lūdum intrāvērunt, gladiātōrem exanimātum portantēs. gladiātor, quī ā servīs portābātur, vulnus habuit. vulnus ā medicō īnspiciēbātur.

'amīcus noster vīvet?' rogāvit Dāmōn.

'saepe in amphitheātrō vulnerābar,' Barca inquit. 'nunc igitur amīcōs nōn habeō. in harēnā facilius est cum hostibus quam amīcīs pugnāre.'

'vulnerābāris quod pessimē pugnābās!' Dāmōn respondit.

'minimē, stulte!' Barca clāmāvit. 'is quī pessimē pugnat interficitur. adhūc supersum quod ā spectātōribus amābar.'

trēs gladiātōrēs Barcam intentē audiēbant. ūnus dīxit, 'numquam in harēnā pugnāvimus; crās prīmum pugnābimus. valdē timēmus. quid in harēnā facere dēbēmus?'

'heri ā lanistā laudābāminī; nunc audācēs esse dēbētis,' respondit Barca. 'gladiātor audāx enim spectātōrēs dēlectat. gladiātor cui spectātōrēs favent vīvet.'

'sed hic gladiātor,' inquit medicus, 'periit. servī, corpus auferte!'

omnēs in lūdō tacēbant, iterum cōgitantēs.

lūdus *gladiator training ground*

ēditor *sponsor (of gladiator shows)*
pollex *thumb*
exanimātus *unconscious*
medicus *doctor*

harēna *arena; sand*

pessimē *very badly*

adhūc *still, until now*
supersum *I survive, stay alive*

prīmum *for the first time*

lanista *trainer (of gladiators)*

LANGUAGE NOTE 2: IMPERFECT PASSIVE

1. Compare the following sentences:

   spectātor Barcam laudābat.
   The spectator was praising Barca.

   Barca ā spectātōre laudābātur.
   Barca was being praised by the spectator.

2. You have now met the passive of the imperfect tense. Notice that both the active and the passive of the imperfect tense are marked by **-ba-** in the ending.

3. Now look at these sentences:

   nōs per viās dūcēbāmur.
   We were being led through the streets.

   ā lanistā laudābāminī.
   You were being praised by the trainer.

   The endings of the verbs tell us who was being led, or who was being praised.

4. Compare the active and passive forms of the imperfect tense of **vocō**:

Imperfect active		Imperfect passive	
vocābam	*I was calling*	**vocābar**	*I was being called*
vocābās	*you were calling*	**vocābāris**	*you were being called*
vocābat	*he/she/it was calling*	**vocābātur**	*he/she/it was being called*
vocābāmus	*we were calling*	**vocābāmur**	*we were being called*
vocābātis	*you were calling*	**vocābāminī**	*you were being called*
vocābant	*they were calling*	**vocābantur**	*they were being called*

5. Just as **vocābam** can mean *I was calling* or *I used to call*, so **vocābar** can mean *I was being called* or *I used to be called*.

6. Note that in both the present and the imperfect passive, the personal endings of the verb are the same: **-r**, **-ris**, **-tur**, **-mur**, **-minī**, **-ntur**.

Part of a mosaic from a villa near Lepcis Magna, in what is now Libya.

Gladiators

The word gladiator means 'a man who fights with a sword (***gladius***)'. Gladiators were trained professional fighters, and they fought with a variety of weapons and equipment, not just swords. For the Romans, watching these men fight, sometimes to the death, was a form of entertainment. Gladiatorial fights may have begun as part of the celebrations at the funerals of prominent men. Over time, the connection with funerals disappeared. Presenting gladiatorial shows as gifts (***mūnera***) to the people became a way for rich men, especially emperors, to display their power and win popularity.

Who were the gladiators?

Becoming a gladiator was not usually a choice: most were slaves or condemned criminals. However, some free men chose to become gladiators. This could have been the only alternative to destitution. There is some evidence that women occasionally fought in the arena, but this was extremely rare.

Life as a gladiator

A troupe of gladiators lived together as a familia (household) in a ***lūdus***, a training camp. The ludus was run by a ***lanista***, who was sometimes a retired gladiator. Often gladiators from the same troupe fought each other in the arena. However, they spent most of their time training, and fought only a few days a year. It was expensive to buy and train a gladiator, and he had to be in peak condition if he was to fight well. Therefore gladiators had a nourishing, if basic diet, often a stew of beans and barley. The ludus would also have its own doctors.

Although fights often ended without a death, most gladiators did not survive long enough to gain their freedom. However, if a gladiator was skillful and lucky he was given a wooden sword, which was the sign of his freedom, and he could retire. Like charioteers, gladiators could gain fame, fortune, and popularity, and they were idolized as celebrities. This graffito was found on the wall of the gladiator barracks at Pompeii:

Celadus, suspīrium puellārum.
Celadus, the girls' crush.

The shows were free and in theory anyone could attend, but you had to have a ticket. These were wooden, bone, or lead tokens which sometimes showed the area where you would be sitting and your seat number. We don't know how these tokens were allocated. The entertainment began with a procession through the streets of the town, in which the sponsor of the show (***ēditor***), musicians, the gladiators, and some of the animals paraded before the crowd. The area around the amphitheater would be crowded with stalls selling food, drink, and souvenirs.

There were at least twenty different types of gladiator, each with his own specialist armor, weapons, and tactics, but only a few can be identified with certainty today. The gladiatorial fights were single combat between pairs of gladiators, and usually different types of gladiator fought each other. Trumpets sounded the start of the contest, and flutes signaled the first fight. The fight went on until one of the gladiators was wounded or submitted. The trumpet sounded and the referee restrained the victor. The wounded man appealed for mercy by making a gesture with his hand.

The spectators made their wishes felt by turning their thumbs up or down, then the sponsor for the show made the final decision. Probably turning the thumb up towards the chest meant death. Quite often, if the gladiator was popular or had fought well, he was granted mercy.

This stone relief from Halicarnassus (in modern Turkey) shows two female gladiators. The gladiators are named: Amazon and Achillea. They are armed with swords and shields, but no helmets. They are standing on a platform, and on each side of the platform is the head of a spectator.

The Symmachius mosaic

This mosaic from Rome tells a story, arranged in two frames. Look at the lower frame first.

4

From left to right along the top are the words:

'necō' 'haec vidēmus' 'Symmachī homō fēlīx'

- Who do you think is meant to be speaking each of these phrases?
- Symmachius was probably the sponsor of the games. Why is he described as **fēlīx**?

3

Now look at the upper frame. Describe what is happening here.

Upper Frame

Lower Frame

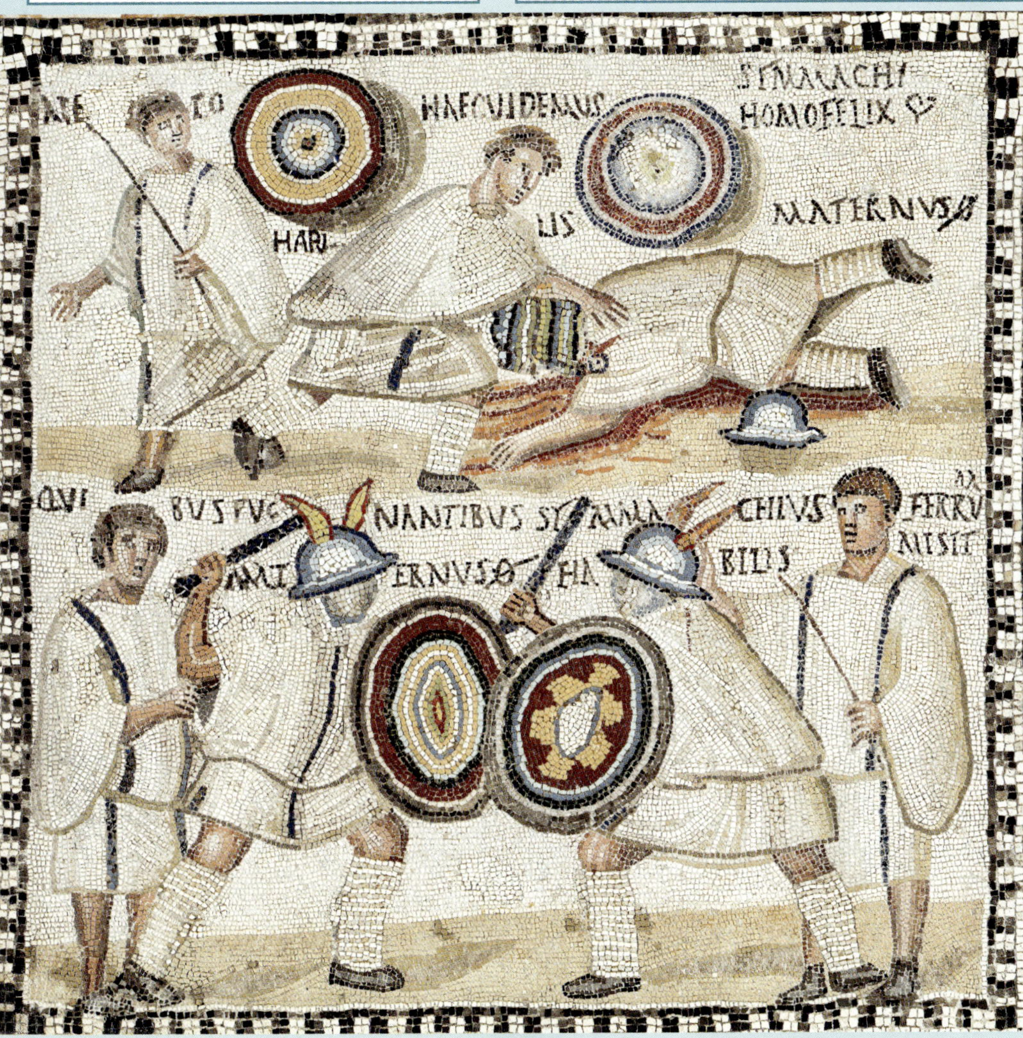

1

Two gladiators are facing each other. Their names, Maternus (*left*) and Habilis (*right*), are written beside their heads. Next to Maternus' name is the symbol Ø, which means 'death'.

- How would the spectators distinguish between these two gladiators?

2

Behind each gladiator is a man wearing a tunic.

- Who do you think these men are?

Barca

Barca sum. gladiātor sum. per septem annōs in harēnā pugnābam. prīmō nōn fortis, minimē audāx eram; in omnī proeliō timēbam. ā lanistā vituperābar, quod spectātōrēs mē perterritum putābant. saepe tēlīs vulnerābar. mē gladiātōrēs tamen nōn necāvērunt: semper ab ēditōre servābar. paulātim audāx fīēbam, et ā spectātōribus amābar. in plūrimīs proeliīs vincēbam, sed numquam rudis ab ēditōre mihi dabātur, numquam lībertās reddēbātur. fortasse lanista mē āmittere nōlēbat. fortasse īnfēlīx sum, aut deīs mē pūnīre placet. sed hodiē, in amphitheātrō Carthāginis, fortasse rudem accipiam. ferōciter pugnābō. vespere līber iterum erō?

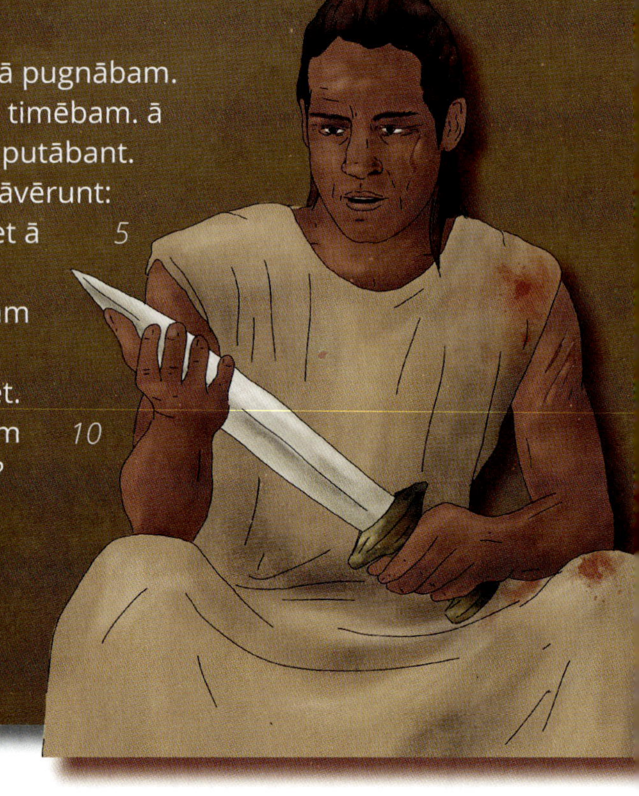

septem *seven*	rudis *wooden sword*
paulātim *gradually*	reddō *I give back, restore*
fīō *I become*	līber *free*

in plaustrō

sub vesperum plaustrum per viās urbis ā lanistā dūcitur. duo gladiātōrēs in plaustrō ad lūdum feruntur. ūnus, vultū sanguineō et bracchium vulnerātum tenēns, Barca est. alter, graviter spīrāns, in plaustrō iacēns, est Dāmōn.

vulnerātus *wounded*

Dāmōn eratne amīcus tuus?

Barca quis?

Dāmōn ille murmillō, quem in harēnā necāvistī, erat amīcus tuus?

murmillō *murmillo (type of gladiator)*

Barca amīcōs nōn habeō.

tacuērunt. plaustrum lentē prōcēdēbat. subitō Dāmōn gemitum terribilem dat, quasi strangulātus.

gemitus *groan*
strangulātus *strangled*

Barca heus, lanista! venī! ille exspīrat.

lanista hercle!

lanista claustrum plaustrī aperit. Dāmōnem nōn iam spīrantem in plaustrō videt. subitō in capite ā Barcā verberātur. lanista ad terram cadit. Barca per viās effugit.

claustrum *lock*

Watching the games

SOURCE 1

Martial describes a fight with an unusual outcome:

Priscus and Verus continued to fight,
and for a long time their courage was equal.
The crowd cried out repeatedly for mercy for both men,
but the emperor obeyed the rule
that the fight should continue until one gladiator raised his finger in submission.
However, an end was found for that equal contest.
They fought as equals, they submitted as equals.
The emperor awarded the wooden swords and the palms of victory to both.
Courage and talent won this prize.
Under no emperor except you, Titus, has this happened.
Although two fought, each was the victor.

Martial

SOURCE 2

Seneca describes how the spectators react to an animal fight:

We are sometimes delighted when a brave youth receives on his spear the wild animal that attacks him, or when he faces a charging lion without flinching.

Seneca

SOURCE 3

Pliny praises some games presented by Emperor Trajan:

The show inspired men to endure honorable wounds and have contempt for death, since a love of praise and desire for victory were seen even in the actions of slaves and criminals.

Pliny

SOURCE 5

Oil lamps like this were sold as souvenirs of the games.

SOURCE 4

Cicero argues that watching gladiators fight provides a role model for young Roman men:

What gladiator ever groaned or turned pale? Did one ever disgrace himself, not only when he stood fighting, but also when he fell? Did any gladiator, after he had fallen and been ordered to accept the sword, draw back his neck? So great is the power of training, practice, and habit.

Cicero

QUESTIONS

1. What information do these sources provide about fights in the arena?
2. What attitudes towards gladiators are shown in these sources?
3. Look at Sources 3 and 4. According to Pliny and Cicero, how might the spectators be affected by watching fights in the arena?
4. Think about these sources and what you have learned in your study of the rest of this chapter. Why do you think gladiatorial shows and animal fights were such popular forms of entertainment among the Romans?

LANGUAGE NOTE 3: THE ABLATIVE WITH PASSIVE VERBS

1. Look at the following sentences.

   Barca saepe ā gladiātōribus vulnerābātur.
   Barca was often wounded by gladiators.

   Barca saepe tēlīs vulnerābātur.
   Barca was often wounded by weapons.

2. In Latin, passive verbs are often accompanied by a word in the ablative case, explaining by whom or by what the action was carried out.

3. If the action was carried out by a living thing (for example, a person or an animal), Latin uses **ā** or **ab** with the ablative. However, if the action was caused by an object, Latin often uses the ablative without **ā** or **ab**.

LANGUAGE PRACTICE

2. Complete each sentence with the correct form of the verb, then translate.

   a. illī sunt gladiātōrēs, quī saepe in lūdō .... (pūniēbātur, pūniēbantur, pūniēbar)

   b. soror tua ā mīlite audācī .... (adiuvābātur, adiuvābāris, adiuvābāmur)

   c. nōs prope amphitheātrum ā patre nostrō .... (salūtābāris, salūtābātur, salūtābāmur)

   d. rēgnum ā fīliō rēgis malī diū .... (regēbantur, regēbar, regēbātur)

   e. prīmō vōs ab ūnō gladiātōre .... (vulnerābar, vulnerābāris, vulnerābāminī)

   f. ego ā tribus fēminīs benignīs .... (cūrābāmur, cūrābar, cūrābātur)

3. Complete each sentence with the correct form of the verb, then translate.

   a. dōnum cārum ad templum deae .... (adferēbāris, adferēbāmur, adferēbātur)

   b. nōs Icēnī ab exercitū Rōmānō .... (opprimor, opprimeris, opprimimur)

   c. manus gladiātōris .... (tollēbātur, tollēbāmur, tollēbāris)

   d. mūnera sonōre tubae .... (nūntiantur, nūntiātur, nūntiāris)

   e. vōs mūrīs atque tēctīs diū .... (dēfendiminī, dēfendor, dēfenduntur)

   f. ego iterum ad rēgem .... , quod scelus fēceram. (mittēbātur, mittēbantur, mittēbar)

Animals in the arena

> The whole region from Carthage to the Pillars of Hercules is fertile, although full of wild animals. The inhabitants are skilled in hunting, a pursuit that the Romans encourage because of their passion for wild beast fights. The local people are masters of both wild beasts and of farming.
>
> *Strabo*

It wasn't only men who fought and died in the arena. The Romans also staged fights between animals and between men and animals, and held animal hunts. Often the animals were those available locally. In Italy, they included goats, deer, bulls, wolves, wild boars, and hares. However, ancient writers put the emphasis on fierce and exotic animals. These prized animals were captured in distant parts of the Empire and beyond, then transported to Rome with enormous cost and difficulty: hippopotamuses came from Egypt, rhinoceroses from Ethiopia, and tigers from India.

However, most of the exotic animals for the arena came from North Africa, which was home to various wild cats (lions, leopards, and cheetahs), elephants, and ostriches. Once captured, many of these animals were taken to Carthage, from where they were transported by ship to Ostia, a journey which took only four days in good weather.

Capturing animals

The peoples of North Africa were skilled hunters, used to protecting their livestock from lions and leopards. It is likely that the Romans relied on these local hunters to capture the animals. One method was to dig a pit, then bait it with meat such as a lamb. The hunters then lay in wait at a safe distance until the lion or leopard approached the pit, attracted by the smell. When the animal fell into the pit, the hunters lowered a cage, baited with meat. Once the animal was trapped inside, they raised the cage up with straps. Hunting dogs were used to catch ostriches, by driving them towards a net or other enclosure. The captured animals were taken to local towns, such as Carthage, in cages on ox-drawn wagons. Some were then put on ships and exported to Rome, while others were destined for the arenas in the towns of North Africa.

Trained animals

Not all the shows put on in amphitheaters were violent. Some animals, especially elephants, were taught to perform tricks for the entertainment of the crowd:

> **elephantum minimus Aethiops iubet subsīdere in genua et ambulāre per fūnem.**
> A young Ethiopian boy commands an elephant to fall down on its knees and walk along a rope.
>
> *Seneca*

damnatio ad bestias

The Romans practiced capital punishment, often by the most brutal and painful methods, such as crucifixion. Another method was ***damnātiō ad bestiās***, 'condemnation to the wild beasts'. Condemned prisoners were executed publicly by being taken into the arena and left to be mauled and killed by savage animals. Christians sometimes suffered this cruel punishment.

Both the hunters and the animals in this mosaic have names. The mosaic is from a villa in Tunisia, which belonged to a man called Magerius.

Hannibal

A map of the Mediterranean in 218 BC.

In 218 BC Carthage was one of the greatest powers of the western Mediterranean. It controlled (either directly or through alliances) a large part of the North African coast and much of the Iberian Peninsula. It had a professional, multicultural army, with contingents from Africa, Spain, and Gaul. Each of these peoples had its own way of fighting: Carthage's Numidian allies were expert light cavalry, slingers came from the Balearic Islands, while Spain, Gaul, and Africa provided heavy cavalry and infantry. Led by Carthage's brilliant general, Hannibal, this army was almost invincible.

In this period Rome controlled Italy and, after its victory over Carthage in 241 BC, the island of Sicily. The regions of Italy had become allies of Rome (often after being defeated in war) and had to provide men for the Roman army. Rome at this time did not have a professional army: citizens and allies were called up when Rome was at war.

The Second Punic War started with Hannibal's decision to invade Italy. Roman sources tell us that he wanted to avenge the humiliation of Carthage and of his father, Hamilcar, in the First Punic War. However, most modern scholars think that he wanted to reduce Rome's power rather than to destroy her. To do this, he took the war to Roman territory, aiming to eliminate the basis of Rome's power by undermining her system of alliances.

Hannibal crosses the Alps

Rome's control of Sicily meant that the sea route was closed to Hannibal. He therefore chose a daring overland march from Carthaginian Spain, through southern Gaul, and into Italy. He left Spain with an army of about 50,000 infantry, 9,000 cavalry, and forty elephants. To reach Italy he had to overcome great difficulties, marching for hundreds of miles through potentially hostile territory in Gaul and crossing the River Rhône, but none was as daunting as crossing the Alps, which he did as winter was approaching. It took Hannibal's army fifteen days to cross the highest pass. They had to battle with harsh terrain, bad weather, and regular skirmishes with the local tribes. By the time Hannibal reached the plains of northern Italy, he had about 20,000 infantry and 6,000 cavalry, fewer than half the number of men who had set off from Spain.

Hannibal now started his invasion of Italy. He defeated Roman armies in two battles, both north of Rome (Trebia, December 218 BC and Lake Trasimene, June 217 BC). The Romans needed time to recover from the disasters and refused to meet Hannibal in battle until they had rebuilt their army. Hannibal continued destabilizing the Roman alliances by attacking Rome's allies in southern Italy. Finally, by the summer of 216 BC the Romans had put together two huge new armies and were ready to meet Hannibal.

Cannae

The battle took place in August 216 BC at Cannae. The Romans had about 80,000 infantry and 6,000 cavalry. Hannibal's troops, swelled in number by men from Gallic tribes, totaled about 40,000 infantry and 10,000 cavalry. Even so, Hannibal's troops managed to encircle the Roman army and attack it from the rear. The Romans were massacred: nearly 70,000 were killed. Hannibal surely expected Rome to start peace talks, but the Romans refused to negotiate and never considered themselves defeated. The war continued for fourteen more years. Despite his victories, Hannibal never managed to subdue the Romans nor persuade enough of Rome's allies to abandon her. Year after year in Italy his army diminished, and with it his chance of victory. Rome continued to put new men on the field.

Zama

Finally, a new Roman leader, Publius Cornelius Scipio, took the war to enemy territory, first in Spain and then in Africa. Scipio had learned lessons from Hannibal and had trained his army intensively. In 203 BC Hannibal was called back to Carthage to defend his own territory, and the two armies faced each other at Zama in 202 BC. The Romans destroyed their enemy and won the war.

Chapter 21: vīta

ad lītus

lītus *shore*

1 Alexander! Alexander! ubi es?

2 Sabīna Alexandrum vocābat.

3 Alexander, ā Sabīnā vocātus, dē cellā festīnāvit.

4 quid est, mea ursa?

5 ad portum adeō, quod animālia dēscrībere volō. mēcum venīs?

ursa *bear*
dēscrībō *I draw*

6 Sabīna marītum invītābat.

7 Alexander, ā Sabīnā invītātus, sacculum cēpit et domum relīquit.

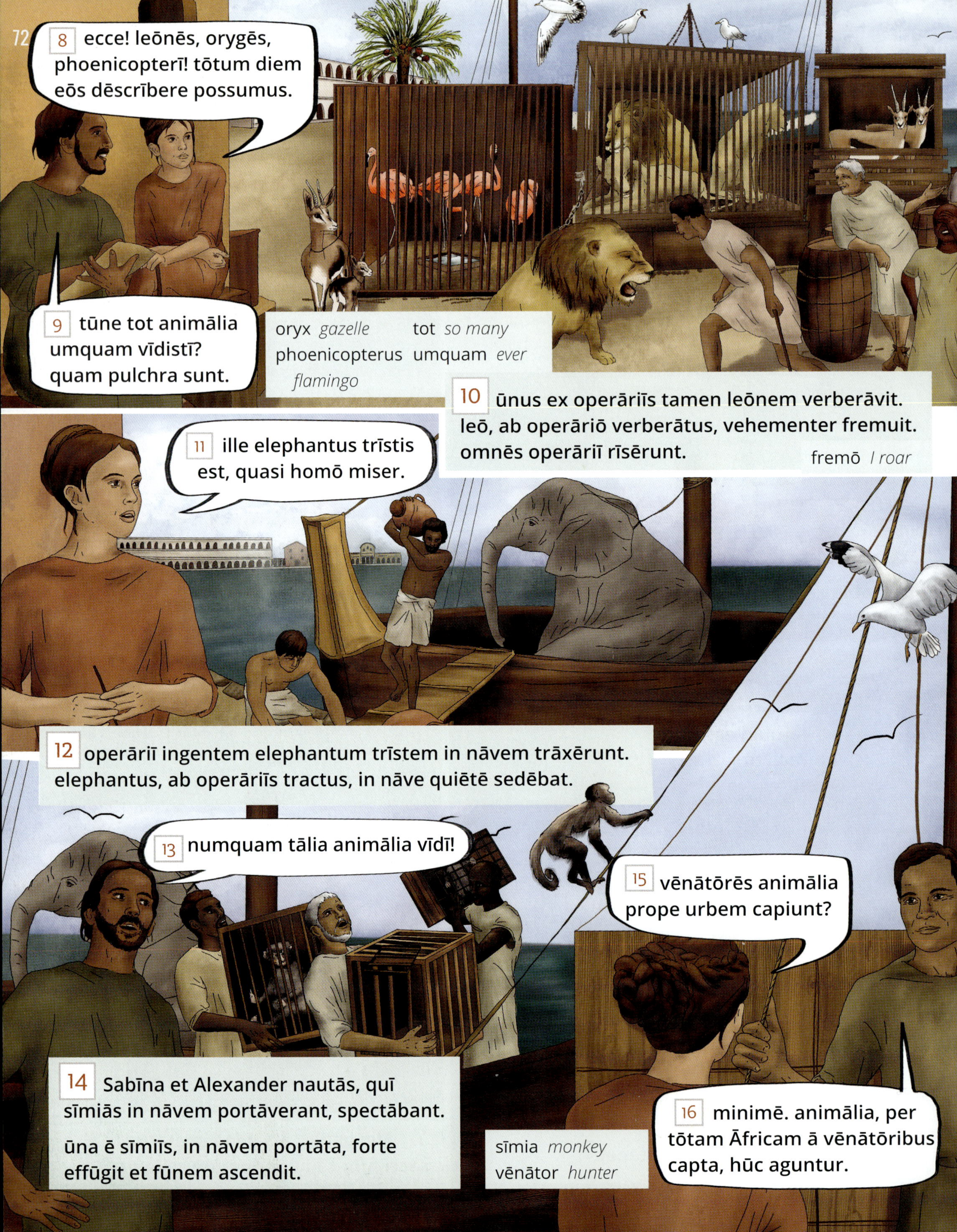
8 ecce! leōnēs, orygēs, phoenicopterī! tōtum diem eōs dēscrībere possumus.
9 tūne tot animālia umquam vīdistī? quam pulchra sunt.
oryx gazelle
phoenicopterus flamingo
tot so many
umquam ever
10 ūnus ex operāriīs tamen leōnem verberāvit. leō, ab operāriō verberātus, vehementer fremuit. omnēs operāriī rīsērunt.
fremō I roar
11 ille elephantus trīstis est, quasi homō miser.
12 operāriī ingentem elephantum trīstem in nāvem trāxērunt. elephantus, ab operāriīs tractus, in nāve quiētē sedēbat.
13 numquam tālia animālia vīdī!
15 vēnātōrēs animālia prope urbem capiunt?
14 Sabīna et Alexander nautās, quī sīmiās in nāvem portāverant, spectābant.
ūna ē sīmiīs, in nāvem portāta, forte effūgit et fūnem ascendit.
sīmia monkey
vēnātor hunter
16 minimē. animālia, per tōtam Āfricam ā vēnātōribus capta, hūc aguntur.

17 paucās post hōrās, Alexander atque uxor per lītus ambulābant. ibi virī piscēs capiēbant. piscēs, ā virīs captī, in harēnā iacēbant. fēlēs eōs intentē spectābat.
fēlēs *cat*

18 Sabīna fēminam cōnspexit. fēmina, ā Sabīnā cōnspecta, rīsit. Sabīna intellēxit fēminam cōnspectam Hermionēn esse.

frīgēscō *I get cold*
horreō *I shudder*
19 Sabīna atque Hermionē ad mare adiērunt pedēsque in mare imposuērunt. pedēs, in aquam impositī, frīgēscēbant. amīcae horruērunt. tum Sabīna cōnsilium cēpit.

20 aqua est calida, Alexander! hūc venī!

21 Alexander, ā mātrōnīs vocātus, in mare cucurrit.
22 ai! aqua est frīgidissima! vōs estis mendācēs!

Animals

WORK

In the Roman world animals did many of the jobs now done by machines. Transport by land relied on horses, mules, oxen, and donkeys for both long and short journeys. In some parts of the Empire people rode camels and used them as pack animals. Agriculture was another area dependent on animals. Oxen and mules pulled plows, and donkeys and horses worked mills. Dogs were used to guard livestock from wolves and other wild animals. In war, the cavalry had an important role in the Roman army, and occasionally elephants or camels were ridden in battle. In the home, there were guard dogs, while cats and weasels were kept for catching mice and rats.

HUNTING

Hunting was a popular sport among upper-class Romans, as well as a means of providing meat. Horses and special hunting dogs were involved in the chase. In some parts of the Empire, catching animals for shows was a lucrative business. Hunting scenes were a popular subject in art.

FOOD

How much meat and fish people ate varied, depending on where they lived and how rich they were. For most people meat was a rare luxury. The urban poor occasionally had a share of the meat from a sacrifice, some scraps in a stew, or a cheap sausage. Ordinary people living in the countryside had access to game such as small birds and rabbits, which they could catch themselves. Peasant farmers generally kept a range of animals such as pigs, goats, and chickens. Those living by the sea would eat a wide variety of fish and shellfish. Wealthy Romans feasted on exotic creatures such as flamingos and peacocks. Vegetarianism was rare, but a few people followed a vegetarian diet for philosophical or medical reasons. In his youth, Seneca was a vegetarian, on the grounds that eating meat was cruel, unhealthy, and extravagant.

RELIGION

Animals played an essential part in Roman religion, principally as victims in sacrifices. As you learned in Chapter 3, the entrails of a sacrificed animal were inspected by a soothsayer (***haruspex***), who interpreted them as a way of finding out the will of the gods. The observation of birds – their position in the sky, direction of flight, and calls – was another means of finding out whether the gods were well-disposed or not. Some gods were associated with particular animals: Jupiter with an eagle, Athena with an owl, Bacchus with a tiger or leopard. Followers of Isis believed that cats were the earthly form of the goddess, and in Egypt they were regarded as sacred. Snakes were thought to be the guardians of altars, tombs, and houses, and were also associated with Asclepius, the god of healing.

This mosaic from Tunisia shows a brightly-colored peacock.

A relief showing three seated camels from Palmyra, Syria.

ENTERTAINMENT AND PLEASURE

Romans were fascinated by unfamiliar and exotic animals and birds. Many animals were displayed and killed in the arena as entertainment. Some were trained to perform tricks: elephants were taught to dance and even walk a tightrope. Some wealthy individuals kept animals in private parks; for example, the grounds of Nero's Domus Aurea contained many kinds of wild and domesticated animal.

Part of the Lod mosaic in Israel. Which animals can you spot?

MEDICINE

Galen, who was a doctor in a gladiator training camp and in the army, treated wounds with honey, which has healing properties. A more unlikely-sounding treatment was spiders' webs, which were placed on wounds to stop bleeding. However, modern science has shown that cobwebs have antiseptic properties and contain vitamin K, which helps blood to clot. Sheep's wool was a remedy for swelling: wool contains lanolin, an ingredient in many skin treatments today. Other remedies, however, would have been less effective. A treatment for female infertility was to eat the eye of a hyena, mixed with licorice and dill.

PETS

> Regulus' son had many little ponies, he had dogs, large and small, he had nightingales, parrots, blackbirds. All of them Regulus slaughtered around the boy's funeral pyre. That wasn't grief; it was the display of grief.
>
> *Pliny*

However, there is evidence that many owners had a more affectionate attitude to their pets, especially dogs. Dogs were the animals most commonly kept as pets. Birds, especially those which could be taught to talk such as parrots, were also popular. The parrot was an exotic bird, introduced from India, but more readily available birds were also kept.

> Issa is naughtier than Catullus' sparrow.
> Issa is purer than a dove's kiss.
> Issa is more charming than any girl.
> Issa is more precious than Indian pearls.
> Issa is Publius' darling little dog.
>
> *Martial*

Some owners included dogs in their funeral statuary (like the tombstone for Anthus, *below*) or set up tombstones for their pet dogs.

CLOTHING

Almost all clothing was made from animal products: wool from sheep, leather from the hides of cattle and other animals, furs, silk from silkworms. The feathers of birds such as ostriches and peacocks decorated the helmets of some gladiators and the heads of racehorses, and peacock feathers were used for fans.

QUESTION

Think about Roman attitudes towards animals. How similar are they to ours today?

LANGUAGE NOTE 1: PERFECT PASSIVE PARTICIPLES

1. Look at the following sentences. What do you notice about the words in red?

   Alexander, ā Sabīnā vocātus, dē cellā festīnāvit.
   Alexander, having been called by Sabina, hurried from the room.

   sīmia, in nāvem portāta, fūnem ascendit.
   The monkey, having been carried onto the boat, climbed up a rope.

   piscēs, ā virīs captī, in harēnā iacēbant.
   The fish, having been caught by the men, were lying on the sand.

2. The words in red are a form of the verb known as the **perfect passive participle**. Like adjectives, perfect passive participles change their endings to agree (in case, number, and gender) with the nouns they describe.

3. Perfect passive participles denote actions which have taken place before the action of the main verb. For example, in the first Latin sentence above, Alexander was called by Sabina before he hurried from the room.

4. Notice some of the ways in which perfect passive participles may be translated into English:

   leō, ab operāriō verberātus, fremuit.
   The lion, (having been) beaten by the workman, roared.
   The lion, after/when it had been beaten by the workman, roared.
   The lion, which had been beaten by the workman, roared.
   The lion, because it had been beaten by the workman, roared.

5. When you look up a verb in the dictionary, you are usually given four parts. For example:

   vocō, vocāre, vocāvī, vocātus *call*
   mittō, mittere, mīsī, missus *send*

   The first part is the present tense (*I do something*), the second part is the infinitive (*to do something*), the third part is the perfect tense (*I did something*), and the fourth part is the perfect passive participle (*having been somethinged*).

LANGUAGE PRACTICE

1. Choose the correct participle to complete the sentence, then translate.

   a. Icēnī, ā mīlitibus Rōmānīs .... , eīs resistere cōnstituērunt. (cōnsūmptī, portātī, oppressī)
   b. plaustrum, ab equīs validīs .... , plēnum saxīs erat. (dictum, laudātum, tractum)
   c. tandem captīvus, multās hōrās labōrāre .... , periit. (cēlātus, coāctus, inventus)
   d. avēs, ā sorōre vestrā .... , canere nōlēbant. (captae, apertae, dēbitae)
   e. nōs canī, ā līberīs scelestīs .... , aquam dedimus. (cōnstitūtō, cōnsūmptō, vulnerātō)
   f. vōs cibum, ab ancillā in mēnsā .... , cōnsūmpsistis. (invītātum, positum, raptum)

in tēctō

Sabīna domī vestīmenta lavābat. tum in tēctum ascendit, corbem gravem portāns. in corbe vestīmenta lauta portābat, quae ūmida erant. sōl in caelō lūcēbat et ventus super tēctum susurrābat. in tēcta īnsulārum Rōmae ascendere perīculōsum erat, sed nōnnūlla tēcta Carthāginī erant aequa. hīc Sabīna herbās cūrābat, vestīmenta suspendēbat, sub vesperum cum Alexandrō vīnum bibēbat.

Sabīna vestīmenta in līneā suspendit. vestīmenta suspēnsa ventō siccābantur.

Sabīna autem nōn statim dēscendit, sed in tēctō paulisper iacēbat. sōl calidus atque ventus dulcis eam dēlectābant. Sabīna brevī tempore oculōs clausit. avēs marīnās in caelō volitantēs audiēbat.

subitō gemitum audīvit Sabīna. statim oculōs aperuit, surrēxit atque valdē timēns circumspectāvit.

sub vēlō prope herbās virum vulnerātum sē cēlantem cōnspexit. et simul vir eam cōnspexit.

domī *at home*
corbis *basket*
lautus *washed*
ūmidus *wet, damp*
Carthāginī *in Carthage*
aequus *level, flat*
herba *herb, plant*
suspendō *I hang, suspend*
līnea *line*
siccō *I dry*
autem *however*
paulisper *for a little while*
claudō *I close*
marīnus *of the sea, marine*
vēlum *cloth, sheet*

A cat hunts a bird in this mosaic from the House of the Faun, Pompeii.

fugitīvus

Barca nōlī timēre, domina. in perīculō nōn es.

Sabīna quis es? unde vēnistī et cūr in tēctō nostrō ades?

Barca Barca sum. gladiātor eram. multōs annōs poenās dabam propter scelus quod in adulēscentiā fēcī. sed poenās dedī. lībertātem meruī.

Sabīna (*susurrāns*) sed līberātus nōn es ... effūgistīne?

Barca rēctē dīcis. ē lūdō effūgī. sed vulnerātus sum, ut vidēs. necesse est mihi in urbe mē cēlāre dum aeger sum.

Sabīna hīc manēre nōn potes!

Barca adiuvā mē, domina. nōlī custōdēs vocāre, tē ōrō. nihil nisi vītam rogō.

fugitīvus *runaway*

scelus *crime*
adulēscentia *youth*
mereō *I earn, deserve*

rēctē dīcis *you are correct*

LANGUAGE NOTE 2: PERFECT PASSIVE PARTICIPLES WITH THE VERB 'TO BE'

1. Look at how this sentence is translated:

   virum vulnerātum cōnspexit. *She saw the wounded man.*

2. Now look at how these two sentences can be translated:

   vulnerātus sum. *I have been wounded.*
   lit. *I am (in a state of) having been wounded.*

   līberātus es. *You have been freed.*
   lit. *You are (in a state of) having been freed.*

3. Look out for perfect passive participles combined with **sum**, **es**, **est**, etc. in the following stories.

LANGUAGE PRACTICE

2. Translate the following short sentences.

   a. nōs gladiātōrem līberātum vidēmus.
   b. ego vīllam incēnsam intrāvī.
   c. custōs superātus in terrā iacēbat.
   d. puellae pecūniam inventam ferēbant.
   e. salūtātus sum.
   f. cōnspecta es.
   g. audītī sumus.
   h. vocātī sunt.

Adorning the body

Wealthy women wore jewelry made of gold and precious stones such as emeralds and amethysts. Pearls were also very desirable. Semi-precious stones were cheaper, and were often set into rings, worn by men and women. Habinnas, in Petronius' *Satyricon*, says that if he had a daughter he would cut off her ears to avoid the expense of earrings. Jewelry made of iron, bronze, and glass was more affordable for ordinary people; bronze was sometimes gilded to look like gold.

Bracelets and armbands in the shape of a snake, like this one from Egypt, were popular. One found in Pompeii was engraved with the words: ***dominus ancillae suae***.

Roman men often wore signet rings. A gemstone with an engraved image (an intaglio) was set into the ring. The ring was used to make a signature, and images of gods and animals were common. You pressed it into hot wax when signing or sealing a document such as a letter or a will.

Carnelian, a red semi-precious stone, was a favorite for signet rings because hot wax does not stick to it; it was also relatively cheap, and believed to have magical powers. Garamantian traders, who lived in the Sahara south of Carthage, brought carnelian to the Roman provinces in North Africa. Poorer people would have had intaglios made of glass paste. The ring above has a carnelian intaglio with a female portrait.

Image 1: This woman from Egypt has pearl earrings, a hairpin studded with pearls, and necklaces of gold, pearl, and emerald. This portrait was painted for her tomb.

Image 2: This girl, in a wall painting from Pompeii, has a gold hairnet and gold earrings. Many women had pierced ears.

- What image of themselves do you think these women wanted to present?

This pendant in the shape of a crescent was an amulet (good-luck charm) to protect the wearer from harm. Amulets were worn by both adults and children.

Brooches (*fībulae*) were essential for fastening cloaks, but could also be decorative. Brooches in the shapes of animals were a popular style all over the Empire in the second century AD. This one, from Gaul, is made of copper, with details picked out in enamel. To make enamel, colored glass was pulverized, heated, then melted directly onto the metal surface. The rooster may have been regarded as lucky.

DISCUSSION

1. Why did the Romans adorn their bodies? How similar is this to what we do today?
2. Do you think the desire for adornment is universal?

amīca

postrīdiē Sabīna cum amīcā domī suae aderat. amīca prope eam sedēbat, speculum tenēns vultumque suum īnspiciēns. gemmae dē auribus eius suspēnsae sunt et comae ā Sabīnā compositae sunt. cicātrīx pigmentō cēlāta est. Sabīna paulisper in cubiculum abierat et tum vestīmenta rettulit. amīca stolam atque pallam induit.

Barca vērō putās mē custōdēs dēcipere posse?

Sabīna fortasse ... necesse erit tibi tacēre propter vōcem raucam. quō effugiēs?

Barca cognōvī in montibus extrā urbem nōnnūllōs fugitīvōs habitāre. vīcus ab eīs clam aedificātus est.

sed extrā iānuam forte aderat vīcīnus. tōtus sermō ab eō audītus est. vīcīnus gladiātōrem, quem in amphitheātrō spectāverat, agnōvit. celerrimē discessit.

simulatque Barca domō in viam ā Sabīnā ductus est, custōdēs aderant.

Barca ā custōdibus agnitus est, et statim petītus est.

Barca statim pallam dēiēcit, in plaustrum saluit, deinde in mūrum ascendit et ad tēctum pervēnit. effugiēns super tēcta urbis ā nūllō captus est.

dē vītā eius nihil umquam posteā audītum est.

speculum *mirror*
gemma *jewel*
compōnō *I arrange*
pigmentum *makeup*
palla *robe*
induō *I put on*
clam *secretly*
vīcīnus *neighbor*
sermō *conversation*
dēiciō *I throw down*

LANGUAGE NOTE 3: PERFECT PASSIVE

1. You have now met sentences such as these:

   ego in amphitheātrō vulnerātus sum.
   I have been wounded in the amphitheater.

   puella in tabernam ā mercātōre ducta est.
   The girl was led into the shop by the merchant.

   fēminae statim ab Alexandrō vocātae sunt.
   The women were immediately called by Alexander.

2. The perfect passive participle combined with **sum**, **es**, **est**, **sumus**, **estis**, **sunt** forms the **perfect passive** tense. The perfect passive participle provides the perfect and passive elements of the meaning, and **sum**, **es**, **est**, etc. provides the person.

3. Look at the way the perfect passive of **vocō** is formed:

vocātus sum	*I have been called, I was called*
vocātus es	*you have been called, you were called*
vocātus est	*he has been called, he was called*
vocātī sumus	*we have been called, we were called*
vocātī estis	*you have been called, you were called*
vocātī sunt	*they have been called, they were called*

4. Note that the ending of the participle shows gender as well as number. For example:

missa est	*she has been sent* or *she was sent*
missae sunt	*they (female) have been sent* or *they were sent*
missum est	*it has been sent* or *it was sent*

The front and back of a silver hand mirror, from the first century AD. It would have been polished to give a clear reflection.

Fashion

The design of Roman clothes was simple and changed little over time. The tunic was the standard garment for men, women, and children, rich and poor. Upper-class men sometimes wore a toga. Clothing differed according to the weather: woolen cloaks and socks in cold conditions and lighter fabrics in the heat.

Clothes were time-consuming and expensive to make. Only the wealthiest individuals could afford new clothes regularly and for most people clothes were practical rather than fashionable. There was also a big market in secondhand clothing.

Hairstyles

There's not just one style: choose what suits you,
And check in the mirror beforehand.
A long face suits a plain parting,
Round faces call for a tight bun on top,
Leaving the forehead and ears uncovered.
One girl lets her hair fall on both shoulders,
Another ties it up in the style of the goddess Diana.
Loose, flowing locks suit this girl,
While that one braids her hair tightly.

Ovid

Women's clothing

A woman usually tied her tunic with a belt around the waist. The length of the tunic could display her class. Wealthy women wore long tunics that reached to the floor. Lower-class women wore shorter tunics, which were more practical for their daily activities and less expensive. Tunics could have long or short sleeves. At the shoulders and along the sleeves, the tunic was sewn with thread or fastened with brooches.

Wealthy women who were married wore a ***stola*** over their tunic. The stola was a sleeveless tunic, usually plain, undyed cloth, which symbolized the woman's married status and her modesty. This would also be belted.

Upper-class women wore a large shawl called a ***palla***. They wrapped this around their shoulders or used it to veil their heads in public, particularly at religious ceremonies. Often the palla was draped over the left shoulder as shown here.

Not much is known about what underwear women wore. They did have an equivalent of a bra: a band of fabric or leather tied around the chest.

This illustration, based on a statue of Livia the wife of Emperor Augustus, shows how an upper-class married woman would dress. Augustus and his family wanted to project an image of traditional values: modesty and frugality.

Although the style of the garments varied very little, wealthy people could display some flair in the colors, fabrics, and adornment of their clothes. Other than wool and leather, linen was a popular choice. There was some cotton, which came from India, southern Egypt, and the Kingdom of Kush. Cotton would have been very expensive and rare. At the time of our stories silk was extremely desirable, although often condemned for its extravagance and the immodesty of such a translucent fabric. Silk arrived already spun and woven, imported from China along the Silk Routes. The most ostentatious garments were decorated with patterns in bright, rich colors and even embroidered with gold and gemstones.

A bust of a wealthy woman from the late first century AD.

With regard to hair, wealthy Roman women did not opt for the natural look. Instead, they favored extremely elaborate styles. Trends changed frequently and were so distinct that archaeologists can sometimes date a statue or coin from the hairstyle alone.

Wealthy women had trained slaves, called ***ōrnātrīcēs***, to do their hair and makeup. These women styled extravagant creations with tools such as heated curling tongs, and sometimes even glued or sewed on separate hairpieces. It wasn't unusual for wealthy women to purchase hair extensions or wigs. The blonde hair of Germans and the dark hair of Indians were the most desirable.

Cosmetics

cūra dabit faciem; faciēs neglēcta perībit.
Care will give beauty; beauty, if neglected, will die.
Ovid

Women used a wide range of products to enhance their appearance. Some ingredients were expensive and rare, while others were readily available.

STEP 1

Face creams were essential for clear, smooth skin. There were products for different skin types. Women could use swan or goose fat to get rid of wrinkles, or honey mixed with lentils or irises to disguise scars and spots. Some of the more extravagant ingredients were crushed oyster shells, frankincense, and lanolin (the oil from sheep's wool, which would have smelled terrible). For a full-body treatment, wealthy women, such as Nero's wife Poppaea, bathed in asses' milk. To cover stubborn spots or blemishes, women could paste a small leather patch on the skin.

STEP 2

Once the skin was smooth, women applied face whitener. Pale skin was considered attractive for a woman, as it showed that she was privileged enough not to have to work outdoors. One variety of face whitener was made from white lead – even though the Romans knew it was poisonous! Safer alternatives included white chalk mixed with vinegar or egg.

A pink cheek was an attractive feature, displaying youth and health. Blush was made from ground-up minerals, such as ochre and red lead, or from rose or poppy petals. Poor women used wine dregs and mulberries as a cheaper alternative.

STEP 3

Roman women darkened their eyebrows and lined their eyes with soot. This was applied with a rounded stick that had been dipped in water or oil. For a more striking look, women could apply colored eyeshadow made from ground minerals such as azurite, which was a deep blue.

STEP 4

Women could redden their lips with henna or a juice from crushed beetles. This was a fashion that changed over time and by region. Romans prized healthy, white teeth and even had false teeth made from bone and ivory.

trīstia

Sabīna et Hermionē prope mare sedēbant. Hector, quī ab Hermionē portātus erat, ad pedēs eārum dormiēbat. illae Apiōnem, marītum Hermionēs, memorābant.

Hermionē Apiōn fātō ablātus nōbīs magnam pecūniam nōn relīquit. nunc sōlī relictī sumus, et cōtīdiē labōrāre cōgor. quot cūrae mihi sunt!

Sabīna vōs nōn estis sōlī, mea Hermionē! Alexander et ego amīcī vestrī sumus, ut scīs.

Hermionē Alexander est benignissimus. fēlīx es. sed familia mea longē abest. nam Apiōn nōs Carthāginem ex Aegyptō addūxit. ille, quī ā rhētoribus optimīs doctus erat, aliquōs hīc docēre coepit.

Sabīna dolōrem tuum intellegō. familia mea quoque longē abest.

Hermionē deī illōs, quī ā nōbīs amātī sunt, abstulērunt. Apiōn, quī vulnerātus erat, ante partum Hectoris periit. fīlium numquam vīdit.

Sabīna saltem tibi gaudium fert Hector.

Hermionē īnfantem amō, sed eum sine Apiōne cūrāre difficile est. īnfāns multa requīrit, et omnia nōn habeō. vīta est ... cūr lacrimās, mea Sabīna?

Sabīna Alexandrō īnfantem parere volō, sed adhūc gravida nōn sum. Alexander est minimē laetus, quod nōn est pater. fortasse māter nōn erō.

Hermionē paulisper tacēbat. verba, quae ā Sabīnā dicta erant, cōnsīderābat.

Hermionē nōbīs vīta inīqua est, mea Sabīna.

Sabīna tibi cōnsentiō.

fātum *fate, destiny; death*
cūra *care, worry*
addūcō *I lead to*
rhētor *teacher of oratory*
partus *birth*
saltem *at least*
requīrō *I need*
gravidus *pregnant*
cōnsīderō *I think about*
inīquus *unfair*

LANGUAGE NOTE 4: PLUPERFECT PASSIVE

1. Look at the way these sentences are translated:

   Hector ab Hermionē portātus erat.
   Hector had been carried by Hermione.

   puella ā rhētore optimō docta erat.
   The girl had been taught by an excellent teacher.

   verba ā Sabīnā dicta erant.
   The words had been spoken by Sabina.

2. The perfect passive participle combined with **eram**, **erās**, **erat**, **erāmus**, **erātis**, **erant** forms the **pluperfect passive** tense.

3. Look at the way the pluperfect passive of **vocō** is formed:

vocātus eram	*I had been called*
vocātus erās	*you had been called*
vocātus erat	*he had been called*
vocātī erāmus	*we had been called*
vocātī erātis	*you had been called*
vocātī erant	*they had been called*

4. You have now met the perfect passive participle used in the following ways:

vocāta	*having been called*
vocāta est	*she has been called* or *she was called*
vocāta erat	*she had been called*

LANGUAGE PRACTICE

3. Choose the correct verb to complete the sentence, then translate.

   missī sunt   facta erant   coācta eram   servātī erāmus   posita sunt   datus est

   a. vestīmenta fēminārum ā mātribus ....
   b. ānulus parvus iuvenī ....
   c. nūntiī ad lēgātum celeriter ....
   d. ego Rōmae eōs propter ignem relinquere ....
   e. dōna omnium gentium in templō ....
   f. ab amīcīs nostrīs et fortūnā bonā ....

Africa and Rome

Africa was home to a large number of societies and civilizations, many of which were thousands of years old. The Roman provinces in Africa were mainly situated north of the Sahara, looking to the Mediterranean. However, exploration and contact extended much further south.

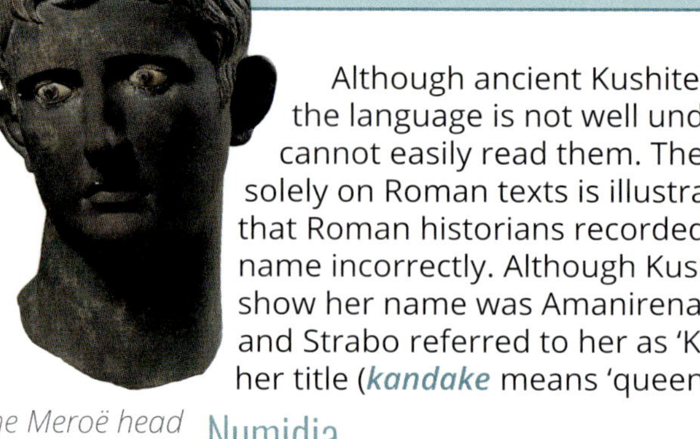
The Meroë head of Augustus.

The Kingdom of Kush

In 31 BC the Roman general Octavian ended a series of civil wars by defeating his rival, Mark Antony, who was allied with Cleopatra, queen of Egypt. As a result Egypt, and its great wealth, fell under Roman rule as the province of Aegyptus. The Romans soon moved further south, intent on gaining control of gold and other valuable resources in the area. This brought them into conflict with the Kingdom of Kush, which lay to the south of Egypt (in modern Sudan).

The Kushites were eager not only to defend their interests and maintain their independence, but also to conquer territory from the Romans. Under their leader Queen Amanirenas, they sent a force north into Egypt, taking advantage of the fact that the Roman governor of Egypt was away on an expedition to Arabia. The Romans hurried south to repel the attack, and although the Romans were initially successful, the Kushites launched a series of campaigns over the following years. They captured a number of Roman forts and towns, and carried off treasure. Eventually, in 20 BC, the two sides signed a peace treaty, and a neutral buffer zone, which both Romans and Kushites were able to enter, was established between them. Both sides benefited financially from an improved trade deal.

Among the trophies which the Kushites took from the Romans were statues of Emperor Augustus. The Kushites buried the head of one of these statues under the steps of the Temple of Victory in their capital, Meroë. Their message was clear: visitors to the temple would be trampling on the head of the Roman emperor.

A votive plaque from Meroë. The inscriptions are in Meroitic script.

Although ancient Kushite inscriptions exist, the language is not well understood, and we cannot easily read them. The danger of relying solely on Roman texts is illustrated by the fact that Roman historians recorded even the queen's name incorrectly. Although Kushite inscriptions show her name was Amanirenas, Pliny the Elder and Strabo referred to her as 'Kandake', mistaking her title (***kandake*** means 'queen') for her name.

Numidia

As far back as the ninth century BC, the Numidians lived in small proto-urban settlements, in what is now northern Algeria. When the neighboring civilization, the Carthaginians, went to war with the Romans, the Numidians provided some of the elite cavalry troops in Hannibal's army. At different times the Numidian kings used these troops to support either the Carthaginians or the Romans, in an attempt to maintain their own independence from both major powers.

After the defeat of Carthage, the Numidians remained independent for 100 years, until 46 BC, when much of the area became a Roman province. However, in AD 17 Tacfarinas, a Gaetulian who may have been an auxiliary in the Roman army, led a rebellion against Roman rule. He organized local men into a Roman-style army, and engaged the Romans in guerrilla warfare and open battle for the best part of seven years, before finally being defeated.

Coin of Masinissa, king of Numidia.

An African imperial dynasty

By the third century AD the African provinces were some of the most successful economically. Many rich Africans had secured membership in the Senate and the region provided a number of Roman emperors, most notably Septimius Severus, from Lepcis Magna in Africa Proconsularis. The Severan dynasty which he founded ruled the Roman Empire for over forty years, until AD 235.

RESEARCH

Find out more about:

- the female leaders Cleopatra and Amanirenas.
- an African civilization that the Romans came into contact with: for example, the Numidians, Garamantes, Gaetuli.
- Septimius Severus.

Chapter 22: līberī

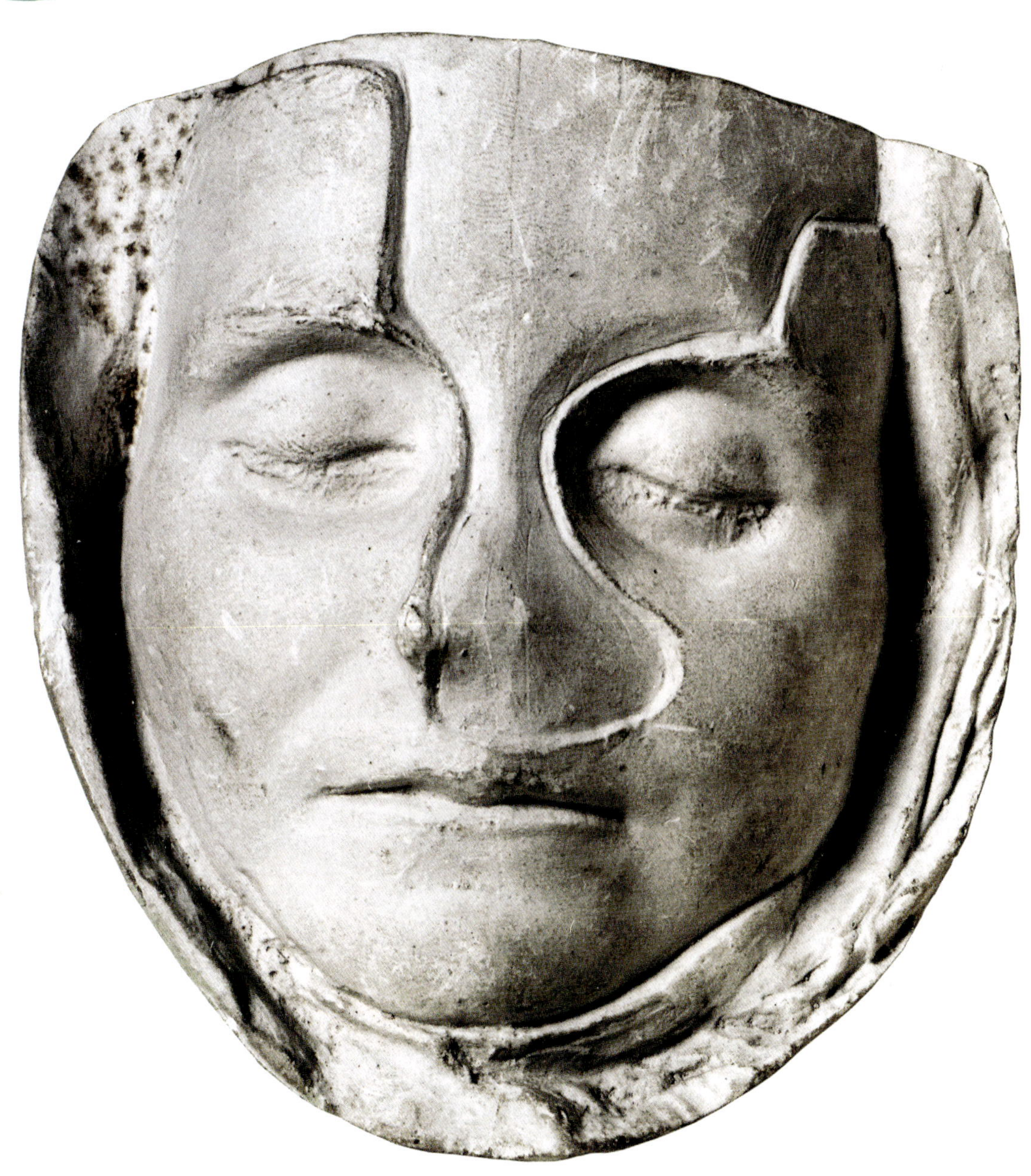

D(IS) M(ANIBUS) / ET MEMORIAE / CL(AUDIAE) VICTORIAE / QUAE VIXIT ANN(OS) X / MENS(EM) I DIES XI / CLAUDIA SEVERI/NA MATER FILIAE / DULCISSIMAE ET SIBI VIVA FECIT

partēs imāginis

1 in vīllā virī dīvitis, Hector ā Sabīnā magnā cum cūrā tenētur. nam in aliā parte urbis parva manus līberōrum ā mātre eius docētur. dum Hector forte dormit, Sabīna partēs imāginis lentē ac quiētē pōnit.

2 Alexander in trīclīnium ingreditur.

3 Sabīna ab Alexandrō salūtātur.

4 Alexander Sabīnam hortātur.

ingredior *I go into, enter*   peior *worse*   hortor *I encourage, urge*

loquor *I speak, talk*

Hermionē grammatica

1 intereā sub arbore prope lītus sedēbant līberī, grammaticam audientēs. Hermionē dē carminibus et mūsicā et astrīs diū loquēbātur.

2 līberī ab Hermionē multa docēbantur et saepe ab eā laudābantur.

grammatica *teacher* carmen *poem, song* mūsica *music* astrum *star*

Our character Hermione is based on a real person. This is a mummy portrait from Egypt with the name Hermione Grammatike written on it in Greek. Hermione is a **grammatica**, *a teacher of literature; a male teacher was a* **grammaticus**.

3 trēs līberī linguā Graecā loquēbantur.

4 Hermionē līberōs hortāta est.

5 ūnus puer carmen scrībere cōnābātur. frūstrā tamen scrībere cōnātus, putābat carmina esse molesta. nam arte poētārum Rōmānōrum nōn semper dēlectābātur. sōlārium proximum saepe spectābat. mox dormiēbat.

6 subitō alius puer advēnit. paedagōgus eum sequēbātur, librōs portāns.

7 Hermionē gemitum dedit.

lingua *language*
Graecus *Greek*
Vergilius *Vergil (Roman poet)*
cōnor *I try*
molestus *annoying*
ars *art, skill*
poēta *poet*
sōlārium *sundial*
paedagōgus *paedagogus (enslaved person who took a child to school)*
sequor *I follow*
mē paenitet *I am sorry*
magistra *teacher*

Education

The Romans had no public education system, and it was entirely up to the father whether his children should attend school. Children of wealthy families were usually taught at home by private tutors, who were often Greek slaves, while other children could attend a class run by a private teacher. The fees would have varied, but poor families would not have been able to afford them. Many fathers chose to send their children to school at least for a couple of years because literacy was a useful skill, and education offered the chance of a more prosperous life.

Lessons took place in the teacher's home, a rented room, or outdoors in a public place, such as a palaestra or the colonnade of a forum. A slave known as a ***paedagōgus*** (a Greek word which means 'someone who accompanies a child') went with the child to school and supervised behavior. Discipline was strict and corporal punishment was common.

The first stage of education, for children aged between about seven and eleven, was provided by the ***lūdī magister*** (literally, 'master of the school'). The pupils learned reading and writing and some simple math. Some children went on to study with a ***grammaticus***.

Hermione was a grammatica. Most of her students would have been boys, aged between about twelve and sixteen, from well-off families, although there may have been some students from poorer families. The grammaticus taught Latin and Greek poetry and language. The poetry was mainly Greek, such as the *Iliad* and *Odyssey* of Homer, and a few Latin authors such as Vergil and Horace. The students had to learn passages of poetry by heart, recite them aloud, and analyze them in detail. Other subjects, such as history and geography, were taught only insofar as they were needed for understanding the literature. When they left the school of the grammaticus, a few boys went on to study with a teacher called a ***rhētor***; this was the equivalent of modern higher education. You will find out about this stage of education in Chapter 24.

Some girls went to the school of the magister. However, it was more common for a girl to be educated at home, where she would learn practical skills: spinning and weaving and how to run a household. In upper-class families girls sometimes studied Greek and Latin literature with a private tutor, and ***docta puella*** was a term of praise.

Why Greek?

The Romans had conquered the Greeks, yet cultured Romans admired Greek literature, oratory, and philosophy. Greek language and literature played an important part in Roman education. The ability to speak and read Greek also had practical advantages, since Greek was used more than Latin in the eastern provinces of the Roman Empire. Children from wealthy families would probably have learned Greek from enslaved members of the household; others would have learned it at school. Teachers in Rome and other parts of the Empire were often Greek or Greek speakers.

This wooden tablet covered in black wax and engraved with Greek writing is one of a pair, which would have been tied together. The tablets belonged to a schoolchild in Egypt in the second century AD. The top two lines are a quotation from the Greek poet Menander, and were probably written by the teacher. The child has then copied the lines twice. Has the child made any mistakes?

LANGUAGE NOTE 1: DEPONENT VERBS

1. Look at the following sentences:

   trēs līberī linguā Graecā loquēbantur.
   Three boys were speaking in Greek.

   Hermionē eōs hortāta est.
   Hermione encouraged them.

   puer, carmen scrībere cōnātus, mox dormiēbat.
   The boy, having tried to write out the poem, was soon asleep.

2. The verbs **loquēbantur**, **hortāta est**, and **cōnātus** look passive but are translated as active. Verbs which look passive but have active meanings are known as **deponent** verbs.

3. It is useful to learn which verbs are deponent. So far you have met the following:

   cōnor *I try*
   hortor *I encourage, urge*
   ingredior *I go into, enter*
   loquor *I speak, talk*
   sequor *I follow*

   Other common deponent verbs are:

   mīror *I wonder at, admire*
   morior *I die*
   patior *I suffer, endure*
   proficīscor *I set out*
   precor *I pray, pray to*
   ēgredior *I go out*
   prōgredior *I go forward, advance*
   regredior *I go back, return*

Claudia Victoria

This plaster cast of the face of young Claudia Victoria was buried with her, along with her toys. It was found in Lugdunum (modern Lyon, France). The plaster cast was used to create a wax death mask, which the family would have kept. It is the only such cast of a Roman child's face that has been found. This inscription was on the tombstone:

D(IS) M(ANIBUS) / ET MEMORIAE / CL(AUDIAE) VICTORIAE / QUAE VIXIT ANN(OS) X / MENS(EM) I DIES XI / CLAUDIA SEVERI/NA MATER FILIAE / DULCISSIMAE ET SIBI VIVA FECIT

To the Manes and to the memory of Claudia Victoria, who lived for ten years, one month, and eleven days. Claudia Severina, her mother, made this tomb for her dearest daughter and for herself when she was still alive.

QUESTION

Look at the mask and the inscription. What can you deduce about how Claudia Victoria's mother felt about her daughter?

mātrimōnium

Alexander Sabīnaque ē vīllā virī dīvitis ēgressī sunt, et per urbem ambulābant. in forō homō in umbrīs sedēns ā Sabīnā cōnspectus est. homō coniector erat.

Sabīna	Alexander, fortasse ille coniector nōs adiuvāre poterit?
Alexander	mea columba, ā tālibus virīs saepe dēceptī sumus, ut bene scīs. melius est deōs auxilium rogāre.
Sabīna	cōtīdiē Iūnōnem precor, sed concipere multōs mēnsēs iam cōnātī sumus ...

Alexander Sabīnaque ā coniectōre salūtātī sunt. Alexander gemitum quiētum dedit, sed cum coniectōre locūtus est.

coniector	bonam fortūnam vōbīs videō! id quod cōnāminī mox ēveniet!
Alexander	vērum est? et quid cupimus?
coniector	dīvitēs esse certē vultis!
Alexander	vidēsne, Sabīna? nihil intellegit.

Sabīna Alexanderque ē forō ēgressī sunt et domum rediērunt. per iānuam ingrediēns, Sabīna subitō lacrimāre coepit. ab Alexandrō amanter tenēbātur. tandem marītum sīc adlocūta est: 'omnia iam cōnātī sumus, Alexander. quid aliud facere possumus? deōs precāmur, cum obstetrīcibus loquimur, tot dōna Laribus damus, ego māla Pūnica cōnsūmō.' paulisper tacēbat. tum, susurrāns, 'fortasse deī mātrimōniō nostrō nōn favent.'

ēgredior *I go out, leave*
coniector *fortune teller*
precor *I pray to, pray*
ēvenit *happens*
amanter *lovingly*
adloquor *I speak to, address*
obstetrīx *midwife*
mālum Pūnicum *pomegranate, Carthaginian apple*

Sabīna dēspērat

trēs post mēnsēs Sabīna ē templō, in quō Bonam Deam precāta erat, ēgrediēbātur. multās cūrās volvēbat in animō, in manū tenēns fībulam, quae ab amitā data erat. dē mātrimōniō dēspērābat quod scīvit Alexandrum līberōs maximē cupere. tum Hermionēn in viā cōnspexit, īnfantem portantem et cum Alexandrō loquentem. Alexander comās Hectoris trīste mulcēbat. dē vultū Sabīnae ad terram dēcidit lacrima.

Children

> We longed for children, but fate did not give them to us. You were heartbroken to see me without children. You wanted to put an end to my distress, so you suggested a divorce. You offered to let me replace you with another, more fertile wife.
>
> *In Praise of Turia (a funeral speech given by Turia's husband).*

Although Turia's husband did not accept her offer, infertility was regarded as reasonable grounds for a man to divorce his wife – it was generally the woman who was thought to be infertile.

There were practical reasons for having children. They were an investment for the future, as they were expected to look after their parents in their old age, and provide a proper burial and commemoration. For the upper classes, moreover, it was important to have a son, to carry on the family name and inherit the family property. It was also a citizen's duty to have children and bring them up, to provide the next generation of citizens. Emperor Augustus was concerned about the low birth rate in the upper classes and introduced laws that gave incentives to couples to have children.

Infertility

So, what could a couple do if their marriage was childless, apart from separating? First of all, they would appeal to the gods, especially the gods of childbirth and fertility, Juno and Isis, with prayers, sacrifices, and other offerings. Treatments for infertility were available; these included drinking pomegranate juice, wearing an amulet of mistletoe, and applying a mixture of crushed snails and saffron to a woman's body.

Adoption

Another solution was to adopt a child. Adoption was a common practice among the upper classes, if a couple could not produce a male heir naturally or if their children had died. It is difficult to know how common it was among the lower classes. Women could not adopt, and girls were rarely adopted. An upper-class man with several sons sometimes chose to have one or more of them adopted, if he could not afford to provide for all of them in a manner suitable to their class. In return, he would be making a connection with another powerful or wealthy family. It was fairly common for adult men in their twenties or thirties to be adopted, as long as the adoptive father was older than the man he adopted.

Adoption was regularly practiced in the imperial family, as a way of providing a male heir. Augustus, when he was eighteen, was adopted by his great-uncle, Julius Caesar. Augustus, in turn, adopted his stepson Tiberius, who became the next emperor. Nero was the adopted son of his great-uncle and stepfather, Emperor Claudius.

Exposure of infants

If a newborn baby was unwanted, perhaps because it was physically weak or illegitimate, the father could reject it by leaving it in a public place. We don't know how common the practice of infant exposure was. Babies who were exposed did not necessarily die; they might be brought up by someone else as a slave or a foundling. In Rome's foundation myth, the twins Romulus and Remus were exposed, and brought up by a wolf.

This terracotta figure shows a woman breastfeeding a child. The figure may have been dedicated as a votive offering in the hope of conceiving a child, or in thanks for the safe delivery of a baby.

Growing up

Childbirth was dangerous for both the mother and the baby. It is estimated that around a third of babies did not reach their first birthday, and half would have died before they reached ten. Without modern medicine babies were susceptible to disease and infection: a minor infection when teething could prove fatal. Growing up in the Roman Empire was marked by certain milestones. The symbolism of these rites of passage was heightened by awareness of the dangers.

First days

> In most cases the umbilical cord comes away on the seventh day; but until it falls away, the child is more like a plant than an animal.
>
> *Plutarch*

Babies were born at home, usually with a midwife in attendance. Being a midwife was a profession reserved for women, many of them freedwomen. The mother either breastfed the baby herself, or, if she was from a wealthy family, she might have a wet nurse. The wet nurse might be a slave in the household, or she could be hired. In Rome, wet nurses offered their services at the ***columna lactāria***.

diēs lūstricus

When a baby was eight (for girls) or nine (for boys) days old, there was a ceremony called the ***diēs lūstricus***. After surviving the dangerous first week of life, the baby was officially welcomed into the family. The baby was given a name and, if appropriate, registered as a citizen.

The bulla

The son of a Roman citizen was given a ***bulla***, which he wore until adulthood. The bulla was an important amulet, protecting him against evil spirits and disease, and proclaiming his status as a freeborn Roman citizen. A wealthy boy might have a bulla made of gold (see page 97); a poorer boy's bulla would have been made of a less expensive material such as other metals or leather.

A child's life was precarious, and children were in need of protection. Crescent-shaped amulets called ***lūnulae*** (like the one on page 79) were given to young girls.

Reaching adulthood

A boy's father or guardian decided when he came of age, based on physical changes to his body. Usually this was around fifteen or sixteen. When a boy became a man he put on the ***toga virīlis***. He also dedicated his bulla to the household gods, the Lares, although he might still wear it for special occasions in his adult life. A sacrifice was offered, then he was registered as an adult citizen and his new status was celebrated with a feast. The ceremony was traditionally held on March 17, the Liberalia, but this was not always the case. It's unclear how much these rites were practiced among the lower social classes.

There was no such coming of age ceremony for a girl. The end of childhood was marked by her betrothal and marriage, and she would dedicate her dolls to Venus or the Lares on the night before her wedding.

This large stone relief, either a votive offering or a funerary marker, comes from Carthage and shows a young man reaching adulthood.

QUESTIONS

1. Do you think that the high rate of infant and child mortality would have led to parents being less attached to their children?
2. Why do you think amulets like the bulla were considered so important?

aurum

Alexander, sub vesperum ex urbe ēgressus, per agrōs prope Carthāginem errābat. lūnam auream mīrābātur, multās cūrās in animō volvēns.

in silvam quandam ingrediēns, Alexander vōcēs nōnnūllōrum subitō audīvit. statim sē post arborem cēlāvit. ex hōc locō antrum obscūrum in silvā spectāre potuit. manus virōrum, quī facēs portābant, prō antrō conveniēbat.

dux eōrum, nōmine Ocar, crēdidit in antrō esse aurum, cēlātum ā Dīdōne, antīquā rēgīnā Pūnicā. comitēs sīc hortātus est: 'antrum inībimus, aurum Dīdōnis inveniēmus, et praemium ā Nerōne poscēmus!' tum comitēs facēs in antrum portāre iussit. omnēs antrum ingressī sunt praeter virum seniōrem, quī extrā antrum relictus est.

mox illī revēnērunt inter sē laetē loquentēs et arcam portantēs. arca erat gravis, sed ā duōbus comitibus portārī poterat. Ocar arcam statim aperīre voluit. Alexander ad eōs fūrtim prōgrediēbātur, sed ab Ocare nōn vidērī poterat. vir senior autem exclāmāvit: 'nōlī eam aperīre! aurum ā Dīdōne fortasse dēvōtum est. deōs precārī dēbēmus!'

Ocar tamen precārī nōluit, sed aurum quam prīmum mīrārī voluit. simulatque arcam aperuit, ingēns sonitus ex antrō resonāvit. perterritī omnēs quam celerrimē effūgērunt. ursa magna eōs per silvam secūta est.

tum Alexander arcam apertam īnspexit. inerant saxum ingēns et tabella, in quā haec verba scrīpta erant: 'dēceptus es.'

aureus *golden*
mīror *I wonder at, admire*
antrum *cave*
ineō *I go into, enter*
poscō *I ask for, demand*
praeter *except, apart from*
prōgredior *I advance*
quam prīmum *as soon as possible*
sonitus *noise*
tabella *writing tablet*

Dido's treasure

In the time of Nero, some people believed that there was a hidden treasure near Carthage, left by Queen Dido. According to the historian Tacitus, the Carthaginian Bassus had a dream that the treasure was hidden in a cave on his estate, and he traveled to Rome straight away to tell Nero about his vision. Nero promptly and publicly celebrated his good fortune, and sent a group of men to retrieve the gold. Sadly for both Nero and Bassus it was never found, and Bassus unsurprisingly met an unhappy end.

A Carthaginian coin from around 290 BC. On one side is the head of the Punic goddess Tanit, who was associated with fertility. On the other side is a horse, an animal that was linked to the founding myth of Carthage.

LANGUAGE NOTE 2: PRESENT PASSIVE INFINITIVES

1. Since Chapter 5 you have met the present active infinitive. For example:

   Ocar eōs facēs portāre iussit.
   Ocar ordered them to carry torches.

   Lūcīlius amīcōs vidēre potest.
   Lucilius is able to see his friends.

2. Now look at these sentences:

   Ocar arcam ā comitibus portārī voluit.
   Ocar wanted the chest to be carried by his companions.

   Alexander ab Ocare vidērī nōn poterat.
   Alexander was not able to be seen by Ocar.

3. **portārī** (*to be carried*) and **vidērī** (*to be seen*) are known as **present passive infinitives**. The present infinitives of the four conjugations are as follows:

	Active		*Passive*	
first conjugation	**vocāre**	*to call*	**vocārī**	*to be called*
second conjugation	**tenēre**	*to hold*	**tenērī**	*to be held*
third conjugation	**mittere**	*to send*	**mittī**	*to be sent*
fourth conjugation	**audīre**	*to hear*	**audīrī**	*to be heard*

4. Deponent infinitives appear passive but have active meanings. For example:

   Ocar precārī nōluit. *Ocar didn't want to pray.*

5. Note that when deponent verbs are listed in a dictionary, three forms (present tense, present infinitive, and perfect tense) are given as follows:

   hortor, hortārī, hortātus sum *urge, encourage*

This gold bulla is about 1 inch in length. It would have been worn as a pendant hanging around the neck from a cord or a leather strip. It is decorated with the head of a Gorgon. Why do you think this might be an appropriate image?

Childhood

What was it like to be a child in the Roman Empire? The lives of children varied depending on time, place, wealth, and social status – and we can't recover the voices of the children themselves. To form a picture of what children's lives might have been like, we have to put together scraps of evidence produced mostly by adults: writings, epitaphs, representations in art, and toys.

A child was considered old enough to work and begin training to be an adult from at least the age of seven, and even younger for enslaved children and those in poor families. They might have trained in a craft or skill, or helped in the household or on a farm, while children in more affluent families were starting their formal education.

SOURCE 1

An epitaph from Rome:

Piēris, ōrnātrīx, vīxit an(nōs) VIIII. Hilara māter posuit.

Pieris, a hairdresser, lived nine years. Hilara, her mother, set up (this tombstone).

SOURCE 2

An epitaph from Rome:

Vicentia, darling daughter, a worker in gold, who lived for nine years nine months.

SOURCE 3

An epitaph from Antipolis (modern Antibes) in Gallia Narbonensis:

To the spirits of the dead of the boy Septentrio, twelve years old, who danced and entertained in the theater at Antipolis for two days.

SOURCE 4

An epitaph from Carthage:

Thyas a dancer, belonging to Metilia Rufina, lived fourteen years.

QUESTIONS

Look at Sources 1–4:

1. What do they reveal about child labor in the Roman world?
2. Is it possible to know which of these children were enslaved or free?

SOURCE 5

This stone (below) marks the grave of a boy from a mining region in Spain. He is carrying a hammer and a basket. The inscription reads:

Quartulus, four* years. May the earth lie lightly on you.

**Or nine years. Scholars disagree about the correct reading of the inscription.*

- What sort of work might children have done in mines?
- Is this gravestone definitive evidence that young children worked in the mines?

Toys and dolls

SOURCE 6

This doll made of terracotta could have been a toy or an offering to a god. The body, head, and legs have been made in one piece, but the arms could move. She has a snake armband on her right arm. Dolls were made out of other materials too, including wood, bone, ivory, and linen.

- How similar is this doll to dolls that children play with today?
- Why do some children like playing with dolls?

SOURCE 7

Toy rattles in many different shapes have been found.

- What shape is this rattle?
- What do you think it is made of?
- What might have been inside to make the rattling noise?

Attitudes to children

Study Sources 8–10.

What can we learn from them about the attitude of adults to children?

SOURCE 8

Pliny writes to a friend:

> I am writing these words to you with great sadness, since the younger daughter of our friend Fundanus has died. She had not completed her fourteenth year, and already she possessed the good sense of an old woman and the seriousness of a married one, although she also had a girl's sweetness and a maiden's modesty. How she would cling to her father's neck! How much she loved her nurses, her attendants, and her teachers! How studiously and intelligently she applied herself to her studies! And how restrained and careful she was when she played! She was already engaged to an outstanding young man; the wedding day had already been chosen; we had already been invited.

SOURCE 9

Pliny's friend Helvidius had died several years earlier. In this letter Pliny describes another misfortune suffered by his family:

> What a sad and terrible thing has happened to the Helvidian sisters! Both have died in childbirth, each having given birth to a girl. Now only one of Helvidius' three children survives. The son is left alone to look after a household which until recently had several firm supports.

SOURCE 10

Wealthy Romans sometimes gave money to a town, to be used to feed poor children. This inscription records one such gift:

> Caelia Macrina, daughter of Gaius, in her will left 1,000,000 sesterces to the people of Tarracina, in memory of her son Macer. The income from the money is to be given to 100 boys and 100 girls: five denarii each month to each citizen boy up to the age of sixteen, and four denarii each month to each citizen girl up to the age of fourteen.

QUESTIONS

Consider all that you have studied in this chapter.

1. Compare the lives of children today with the lives of Roman children.
2. What difficulties are there in trying to find out about Roman children?

Fortūna

I

'curre, Sabīna! mox nāvis discēdet!' clāmābant fabrī.

in portū Carthāginis, paucī fabrī, impedīmenta portantēs, ad nāvem ruēbant. nam dominus vīllae magnificae, in quā multōs mēnsēs labōrāverant, vīllam alteram quoque in urbe Pompēiīs tenēbat. illius vīllae tamen magna pars tremōribus dēlēta erat. itaque parva manus fabrōrum trāns mare altum proficīscī parābat.

Sabīna Alexanderque eōs lentē sequēbantur. sub umbrā arboris mōrī cōnstitērunt. inter sē complexī sunt et ōsculum dedērunt postrēmum.

omnia temptāta erant, sed ā Fortūnā relictī erant miserī. haec illum tam trīstem cōtīdiē vidēre, ille vītam sine līberīs patī nōn poterat. itaque duo amantēs trīstēs dīvortium et fīnem dolōris facere cōnstituerant. multās inter lacrimās, ille in terrā mānsit, ascendit in nāvem haec. tum ē portū Carthāginis lentē ēlābēbātur nāvis. in puppe stetit Sabīna, Alexandrum, terram, vītam suam respiciēns.

II

octo post diēs longōs, nāvis, fabrī, Sabīna in portum Pompēiōrum advēnērunt. illa plūrimōs mercātōrēs, quī per portum garum Umbriciae ac Quārtillae ubīque vēndēbant, cōnspexit. ē nāve ēgressa, canem lātrantem audīvit, et versa vīdit fabrōs ā puerō vocārī. 'salvē! ego sum Currāx. tū cellam quaeris?'

impedīmenta n. pl. *baggage*
tremor *earthquake*
proficīscor *I set out*
mōrus *mulberry tree*
cōnsistō *I stop*
complector *I hug, embrace*
postrēmus *final*
patior *I suffer, endure*
dīvortium *divorce*
ēlābor *I slip out*
puppis *stern*
respiciō *I look back at*
octo *eight*
versus *having turned*

III

eā nocte, Sabīna, Giscō, Quārtilla, et Currāx in popīnā sedēbant. 'hīc mihi,' inquit Giscō, 'negōtium difficile est. crās Rōmam proficīscēmur, Sabīna. nōbīscum veniēs?'

intereā minor nāvis Pompēiōs quam celerrimē petēbat. sed magnae erant undae et ventus erat validus. tempestās appropinquābat. in nāve parvā Neptūnum precātus est Alexander.

minor *smaller*

LANGUAGE PRACTICE

1. Choose the appropriate verb to complete each sentence.

regressa sum   cōnāris   hortāta est   loquēbāmur   sequēbāminī   prōgressī sunt

- **a.** grammatica puerōs frūstrā ....
- **b.** vōs eās .... , quod viam invēnerant.
- **c.** postquam gladium in forō vēndidī, domum ....
- **d.** cūr tū equum ad aquam dūcere .... ?
- **e.** prīmā lūce .... , quod iter longum facere volēbant.
- **f.** prope flūmen convēnimus et multās hōrās ....

2. Choose the correct form of the verb to complete the sentence, then translate.

- **a.** mūrus vīllae proximae tempestāte .... (dēlētī erant, dēlētus erat, dēlēta eram)
- **b.** aliquis in popīnam .... et senī aliquid dīcit. (ingredior, ingrediuntur, ingreditur)
- **c.** nōs multās cūrās propter amōrem .... , sed nunc laetī sumus. (passī sumus, passus es, passae sunt)
- **d.** aurum rēgīnae in antrō nōn .... (positus eram, positum erat, posita erās)
- **e.** animālia ex agrīs ā mīlitibus crūdēlibus .... (trahēbar, trahēbāris, trahēbantur)
- **f.** quamquam Claudia .... , etiam nunc vultum eius vidēre possumus. (mortua est, mortua sum, mortuae sumus)

3. Choose the most appropriate infinitive to complete the sentence, then translate.

- **a.** tū quattuor līberōs .... temptās. (proficīscī, hortārī, cōnspicī)
- **b.** ego ā fīliō imperātōris .... nōlō, quod eum timeō. (aedificārī, sequī, salūtārī)
- **c.** iānuam statim aperīte! in vīllam .... cōnor. (ingredī, patī, dīcī)
- **d.** aliī .... volēbant, aliī redīre. (pōnī, prōgredī, vēndī)
- **e.** vōs, ad summum montem prōgressī, ... nunc potestis. (aperīrī, iubērī, vidērī)
- **f.** puerum vulnerātum ad parentēs eius .... voluerāmus. (portārī, cōnārī, amārī)

Dido and Aeneas

The Trojan hero Aeneas, son of the goddess Venus, appeared in Homer's epic poem the *Iliad*. However, it was the poet Vergil who developed Aeneas' story in a Roman setting. Aeneas, along with his son Iulus and a group of Trojans, escaped from Troy after the city had been captured by the Greeks. He had been told by the gods that his destiny was to go to Italy and found the Roman race, but on the way his ship was wrecked in a storm near Carthage. Queen Dido welcomed Aeneas and his followers, and Aeneas and Dido fell in love. However, Jupiter sent Mercury to remind Aeneas that it was his duty to go to Italy. He left Dido, and, in her despair, she killed herself.

SOURCE 1

Then Dido answered:
'Don't be afraid, Trojans. Forget your troubles.
If you choose to go to Italy or to Sicily,
I shall provide a protective escort and give you supplies.
Or do you want to settle here with me as equals?
The city I am building is yours. Draw up your ships.
I shall treat Trojans and Tyrians the same.'

Vergil

Dido meets the Trojans

Look at Source 1. The Trojans have landed in Carthage, unsure of the reception they will get. Dido herself had previously had to flee from her native land and find a new home.

- What is your reaction to the way in which Dido responds to the Trojans here?
- In what different ways today do individuals and rulers react to refugees who may have been forced to leave their own countries because of war? To what extent do you think the world has a collective responsibility to help such people?

Divine connections

The family of Julius Caesar claimed to be descended from Aeneas' son, Iulus. Do you think they really believed this to be true? For what reasons might they make such a claim?

Many people today try to trace their own family tree. Why do you think this is? How important do you think it is to know about your own family's past?

SOURCE 2

This mosaic from Somerset, UK, shows Aeneas, Iulus, Venus, and Dido.

Interfering goddesses

Look at Source 2. Dido and Aeneas fell in love because of the meddling of Venus and Juno – with disastrous results. Why do you think so many Greek and Roman myths depict gods and goddesses as indifferent to the suffering of mortals? Would you expect the gods to be better than humans? How do you think the Romans regarded their gods?

This mosaic dates from around AD 350, more than three hundred years after Vergil wrote his poem.

- Why do you think the story about Dido and Aeneas has continued to be told by artists, storytellers, and composers?
- Can you think of other love stories that have been repeatedly retold?

The final showdown

Look at Source 3. Dido accused Aeneas of being a heartless traitor. How far do you think this was true?

- How well does the artist depict the emotions of Dido and Aeneas in this picture?
- Do you feel sorry for Dido? For Aeneas? For neither? Is this story still relevant now?

SOURCE 3

Dido accuses Aeneas in this drawing by Jean-Michel Moreau le Jeune.

Chapter 23: honor

Lōcusta

1 in parvā cellā, intrā Domum Auream, dīligenter labōrābat fēmina.

studeō *I study, concentrate on*
cum *when, since*
conterō *I grind, crush*

2 fēmina, nōmine Lōcusta, herbīs studēbat, animālia īnspiciēbat, librōs legēbat.

3 cum Lōcusta librōs lēgisset, herbam quandam cēpit et lentē contrīvit.

4 tum herbam contrītam in pāne posuit cellamque circumspectāvit.

5 mūrem in urnā invēnit. cum mūrem invēnisset, pānem eī dedit.

mūs *mouse*

venēnum *poison*
morior *I die*

haedus *goat*

paulum *a little bit*

12 deinde, ad hortum ductus, nōnnūllās hōrās frūmentum cōnsūmēbat et contentus lūdēbat.
contentus *happy, contented*
13 in cellā tamen Lōcusta nūntium exspectābat.
14 quīntā hōrā febris haedum tenēbat. ille subitō oculōs clausit, conlāpsus est, mortuus est.
conlābor *I collapse, fall down*
15 cum nūntius mortis ad Lōcustam pervēnisset, illa rīsit.
16 parāta sum. fer mihi mendīcum!

spēs et metus

pater Lūcīliī, cum ex Siciliā redīsset, ab imperātōre laudātus erat. Nerō eī maximās grātiās ēgerat, quod prōvinciam optimē administrāverat. Lūcīlius, quī ipse iam Rōmam regressus erat, apud patrem habitābat.

pater, cum imperātor eum laudāvisset, fīliō multōs honōrēs spērābat. eī dīxit: 'fortasse nunc Nerō tē quaestōrem faciet. dum equitēs sumus, multī honōrēs nōbīs darī nōn possunt. sed sī quaestor fīēs, in senātum veniēs. senātōrēs fierī possunt aedīlēs, praetōrēs, etiam cōnsulēs. sī eris senātor, maximam glōriam familiae nostrae dabis!'

māter Lūcīliī, cum haec audīvisset, respondit: 'fortasse melius est fīliō uxōrem quaerere. sī erit marītus, maximam laetitiam mātrī dabit!'

Lūcīlius, cum parentēs haec dīxissent, rīdēbat, et 'mea māter,' inquit, 'sine dubiō uxōrem dūcere volō! sed, mī pater, num putās imperātōrem mē quaestōrem facere velle? sum amīcus Othōnis, quī est inimīcus Nerōnī.'

'ānxius sum dē tuā amīcitiā cum Othōne,' pater susurrāvit, 'sed prōcūrātor optimus eram, et tū tribūnus mīlitum erās. quamquam tempora incerta sunt, necesse est nōbīs spērāre.'

'certē quaestor esse volō,' Lūcīlius respondit. 'mihi facilius erit Othōnem adiuvāre, sī senātor erō. sed sollicitus sum, quod tot senātōrēs mortuī sunt. aliquid malum Rōmae accidit.'

subitō Tīrō intrāvit. 'domine, nūntius adest.'

cum nūntius advēnisset, Lūcīlius et parentēs tacēbant. tum nūntius 'Tiberius Claudius Epaphrodītus, lībertus Augustī,' inquit, 'ad montem Palātīnum statim īre tē iussit.'

metus *fear*

regredior *I go back, return*
honor *honor*
quaestor *quaestor*
eques *member of equestrian class*
senātus *Senate*
aedīlis *aedile*
praetor *praetor*
glōria *glory, fame*
laetitia *joy, happiness*

sollicitus *worried, anxious*

Palātīnus *Palatine (hill in Rome)*

LANGUAGE NOTE 1: CUM + PLUPERFECT SUBJUNCTIVE

1. Since Chapter 17 you have met the pluperfect tense. For example:

   nāvis, quae ex Aegyptō nāvigāverat, nunc ad portum perveniēbat.
   The ship, which had sailed from Egypt, was now arriving at the harbor.

   amīcus meus epistulam scrīpserat.
   My friend had written a letter.

   These forms are known as the **pluperfect indicative**.

2. Now look at the following sentences and notice how the verbs in red are translated:

   cum Lōcusta librōs lēgisset, herbam cēpit.
   When Locusta had read the books, she took a herb.

   cum māter haec audīvisset, respondit.
   When his mother had heard these things, she replied.
   or *Since his mother had heard these things, she replied.*

3. The -**isse**- in the ending of the Latin verb indicates a different form of the pluperfect tense, known as the **pluperfect subjunctive**. The pluperfect subjunctive is used after **cum** (meaning *when*, *since*, or *because*).

4. The pluperfect subjunctive of **vocō** (*I call*) is as follows:

vocāvissem	*I had called*
vocāvissēs	*you had called*
vocāvisset	*he/she/it had called*
vocāvissēmus	*we had called*
vocāvissētis	*you had called*
vocāvissent	*they had called*

LANGUAGE PRACTICE

1. Choose the correct form of the verb to complete the sentence, then translate.

   a. Lōcusta, cum mūrī pānem .... , eum intentē spectābat.
   (dedissem, dedissēs, dedisset)

   b. cum Sabīna ad urbem Pompēiōs .... , Currācem in portū audīvit.
   (pervēnissēmus, pervēnisset, pervēnissent)

   c. nōs, cum arcam .... , nūllum aurum invēnimus.
   (mōvissētis, mōvissēmus, mōvissent)

   d. cum tū iter longum .... , diū dormiēbās.
   (fēcissēs, fēcissētis, fēcissem)

   e. vōs, cum gladiōs .... , ad castra hostium profectī estis.
   (rapuissēmus, rapuissētis, rapuissent)

   f. Rōmānī, cum ducēs captīvōrum .... , oppidum incendere coepērunt.
   (occīdissem, occīdissēs, occīdissent)

The Senate

The Senate at the time of our story was a group of about 600 men. They met regularly in Rome to decide issues relating to the law and to the government of Rome and the Empire, often with the emperor in attendance. The Senate also elected some magistrates and acted as a law court in some important cases. Although the senators debated the issues of the day, by the time of Nero the Senate no longer had the same power and independence it used to have during the Republic. Augustus presented himself as 'first among equals' (***prīmus inter parēs***), governing with the advice of the Senate. However, as time went on, the emperors turned more and more to a small group of trusted advisers, known as the emperor's council (***cōnsilium***) or 'the friends of the emperor' (***amīcī prīncipis***). Ultimately, the emperor had supreme power.

Senatorial, equestrian, and plebeian

The members of the Senate were Roman citizens who came almost exclusively from the two highest social classes: the senatorial families and the equestrians (***equitēs***). There were strict qualifications for membership of this elite.

Senatorial – Membership in the senatorial class was hereditary. If you were in the senatorial class, you had the automatic right to compete for a place in the Senate. Members of the senatorial class had to have wealth worth at least one million sesterces.

Equestrian – The equites (literally, cavalrymen) got their name because they had originally formed the cavalry in the Roman army. They had to be of citizen birth and have a fortune of at least 400,000 sesterces.

Plebeian – Senators and equestrians were only a tiny proportion of the population of Rome and the Empire. Most citizens belonged to the class known as the ***plēbs***, the ordinary people.

Sons of senators were expected to pursue a political career. Most new senators were from the senatorial class and were elected by the Senate. However, by the time of our stories the patronage of the emperor played a role: the emperor could raise a man to the senatorial class or admit someone directly to the Senate. Some men from the equestrian class, including a few from the provinces, succeeded in this way in becoming senators. As the first in their families to become senators, they were known as 'new men' (***novī hominēs***). Members of the Senate (senators) did not receive a salary and were not allowed to make money from trade.

Friends in high places

In order to succeed in public life, a young man needed the patronage of someone with power and influence. Lucilius in our story is from a very wealthy equestrian family. His father had connections with influential senators and had been given an important official position in Sicily by Nero.

A senatorial career

Young men of the senatorial class expected to follow a career path in government and the army known as the ***cursus honōrum*** (series of offices). A few young men from equestrian families also followed this path. The training started with several years of higher education, which included the study of public speaking, law, and philosophy. The men then competed for a series of annual offices in a fixed order, culminating in the governorship of a province, which was a well-paid position, and possibly the consulship.

Other privileges of senators

- they were eligible for some priesthoods
- they had special seats at religious ceremonies, in the theater, and at the games
- a broad purple stripe on their tunics was a sign of status

QUESTIONS

1. Why would a young man aspire to a career as a senator?
2. Look at the diagram of the cursus honorum on the facing page.
   a. What qualifications would a man need to start on the cursus honorum?
   b. How did a man's progress through the steps of the cursus honorum prepare him for the task of governing a province?

cursus honōrum

6. cōnsul The consuls were the chief magistrates and presided at meetings of the Senate. They were chosen by the emperor, and sometimes the emperor himself held the consulship. Two consuls took office on 1 January each year and the years were named after these men. The consuls could change several times during the year.

5. praetor The praetors presided over the law courts and were in charge of the games. They were usually at least thirty years old, but some ambitious men reached this step on the ladder earlier. After serving as praetor, a man could go on to govern a province or command a legion stationed in one of the provinces.

4. aedīlis or tribūnus plēbis The six aediles had charge of the infrastructure of the city of Rome, looking after public buildings and roads. During the time of the Republic the ten tribunes of the plebs protected the rights and interests of the ordinary Roman people, the plebs, but their role was reduced during the Empire. It was possible to bypass this step and go straight from the quaestorship to the praetorship.

3. quaestor The quaestorship was an important post, because it qualified a man to be a member of the Senate. There were twenty quaestors each year, with a minimum age of twenty-five. They served for one year, carrying out general financial duties, either in Rome or in one of the provinces. The quaestors were elected by the Senate. However, the emperor had the right to recommend some of the candidates, and these men were always elected.

2. tribūnus mīlitum Soon after becoming a vigintivir, often in the next year, the ambitious young man went abroad to serve in the army as an officer in a legion, a military tribune.

1. vigintivir The first step on the ladder of a political career was to become a vigintivir. Each year twenty young men, aged about twenty, were chosen to serve as junior officials in Rome. They helped to manage the law courts, the prisons, and the mint. Most of them were from the senatorial class.

not members of the Senate

Vespasian

AD 9	born
27	military tribune
c.27–29	served in the army
30	vigintivir
c.35	quaestor in Crete
38	aedile
40	praetor
41–47	commander of legio II Augusta; took part in the invasion of Britannia
51	consul November–December
c.62	governor of Africa
66	in Greece with Nero
66–68	in charge of the army suppressing the revolt in Judaea
69–79	emperor

Vespasian was a ***novus homō*** and the first emperor to come from an equestrian family. His grandfather was a centurion, his father a tax collector in the province of Asia, then a moneylender.

Gold coin with the head of Emperor Vespasian. The inscription reads:

IMP CAESAR VESPASIANVS AVG
Imperator Caesar Vespasianus Augustus

Emperors after Augustus took his names (Augustus Caesar) and the title imperator (general).

QUESTION

In what ways is Vespasian's career standard and in what ways is it exceptional?

Epaphrodītus

Lūcīlius atque Tīrō per viās urbis ad Domum Augustī prōgressī sunt. cum urbs clāmōsa esset, in lectīcā Lūcīlius ferēbātur.

fabrī, architectī, servī, lībertī viās implēbant, īnsulās, templa, domōs aedificantēs. multī pauperēs in viīs sedēbant. cum pauperēs Tīrōnem cibum atque pecūniam rogārent, ille paucōs assēs ad eōs iēcit. simulac Lūcīlius Tīrōque ad Domum Augustī in monte Palātīnō advēnērunt, ā duōbus servīs salūtātī sunt, et in ātrium ductī sunt. Lūcīlius, cum in ātriō ingentī stāret, multōs hominēs occupātōs vīdit. aliī chartās, in mēnsīs positās, legēbant, aliī nūntiōs in tabellīs scrībēbant, aliī signum imperātōris in epistulīs imprimēbant, aliī vōcibus gravibus inter sē loquēbantur.

- architectus *architect*
- simulac *as soon as*
- charta *sheet of papyrus*
- imprimō *I press onto, press into*

tum Lūcīlius Tīrōque ad lībertum quendam ductī sunt. Tīrō, cum lībertum agnōvisset, susurrāvit eum esse Epaphrodītum, lībertum fidēlissimum Nerōnis. Epaphrodītus, cum ipse Lūcīlium cōnspexisset, eum salūtāvit et cōnsīdere iussit. Epaphrodītō servus quīdam epistulam sub signō imperātōris trādidit, quam lībertus quiētē lēgit. frontem contrāxit Epaphrodītus, Lūcīlium paulisper īnspiciēns. cum Lūcīlium īnspexisset, eum sīc adlocūtus est:

'quaestor in prōvinciā Achaeā mortuus est. nunc Nerō quaestōrem novum, fidēliōrem imperātōrī, quaerit. ille tē nōmināvit. iuvenēs audācēs sīcut tē requīrimus, quī dīligenter labōrant et quī prīncipī magis quam senātōribus fidēlēs erunt. pater tuus, cum prōvinciam Siciliam administrāret, fidēlis imperātōrī erat. tibi quoque crēdere possumus, Lūcīlī?'

Lūcīlius, haec verba maximē mīrātus, ardenter respondit. 'rem intellegō. multum tibi dēbeō.'

cōnsīdō *I sit down*
frontem contrahō *I frown, scowl*
nōminō *I nominate*
magis *rather, more*

Imperial freedmen

Epaphroditus was a freedman in the household of Nero and worked as one of the Emperor's secretaries. In AD 65 Epaphroditus found out that a group of senators was plotting to assassinate Nero. He reported the conspiracy to the Emperor and the conspirators were executed. Nero rewarded Epaphroditus' loyalty by giving him large gardens on the Esquiline Hill.

Epaphroditus was not the only freedman to become a wealthy and influential member of the emperor's court. Claudius and Nero gave some of their freedmen important roles in the government of the Empire. These freedmen reported directly to the emperor, and he trusted them and relied on their loyalty because they owed their position entirely to him. When Nero made his visit to Greece in AD 66–67 he left one of his freedmen, Helius, in charge of his affairs in Rome.

Slaves and freedmen in the household of the emperor (***familia Caesāris***) were often highly educated and skilled. They worked as secretaries, accountants, and administrators, both in Rome and on the staff of the governors in the provinces. Those based in the provinces reported directly to the emperor and kept him informed about what was happening there.

The senators resented the influence that these freedmen had over the emperor, as it reduced the power of the Senate. They also looked down on the emperor's freedmen as social inferiors, because they had once been enslaved.

DISCUSSION

Discuss the relationship between the Senate and emperor. What tensions would there be?

Management of the Empire

The Roman Empire was vast. It covered some 1.35 million square miles, an area now divided into more than thirty countries. The estimated population of the Empire was between 40 and 70 million. Such a huge area was governed by only a small number of officials who were chosen in Rome.

In 27 BC Augustus, the first Roman emperor, divided the provinces into two types: imperial and senatorial. Imperial provinces were typically those on the frontier of the Empire which might require the presence of a large army. Senatorial provinces had been part of the Empire for longer and were more stable. This division was not absolute, and the emperor could change provinces from senatorial to imperial and vice versa.

For most people living in a province of the Roman Empire, the emperor and the events in Rome were unimportant. It was the governors, legionary commanders, magistrates, and officials who held power in the provinces. The Roman authority in a province had three main tasks: protecting against external attacks and suppressing large scale revolts; ensuring all tax was paid to Rome; and administering justice in cases that involved Roman citizens or local dignitaries. In almost all other matters the cities were usually left to manage themselves by a council of the local elite, who were either chosen or approved by the Roman representative in the province. These local elites, therefore, were very powerful and it was in their interest to ensure that their cities were loyal and fulfilled their duties to Rome. Roman rule was thus a collaboration between the local elite and the Roman government.

SOURCE 1

Augustus himself took control of the more important provinces and those which could not easily or safely be governed by annual officials. He distributed the rest by lot among the eligible senators; but sometimes he changed the status of the provinces, and he often visited them himself.

Suetonius

A map showing the Roman Empire in the time of Nero.

SENATORIAL PROVINCES

The governor of a senatorial province was known as a ***prōcōnsul***. Proconsuls were chosen by the Senate, although the emperor had the right to intervene. These men would hold the position for only one year. Asia and Africa were the most desirable of the senatorial provinces – rich and peaceful. Appointment to the office of governor in one of these was the height of a senatorial career.

Senatorial provinces were more stable and generally did not have a large military presence. Since the governors of senatorial provinces did not command large armies, the chance that the Senate might use military force to try to seize power from the emperor was reduced.

SOURCE 2

Augustus' real purpose was that the senators should be unarmed and peaceful, while he alone had arms and maintained soldiers.

Cassius Dio

IMPERIAL PROVINCES

Most of the imperial provinces were governed by senators as deputies of the emperor (***lēgātī Augustī***). A few, such as Aegyptus and Iudaea, were governed by equestrians. Both types of governor were appointed by the emperor and, unlike the governors of senatorial provinces, they held the office in the province until the emperor recalled them. The ability to choose the governors of imperial provinces gave the emperor control of almost all the military power. It also meant that the emperor retained the loyalty of the most powerful officials in the provinces.

Administration

A governor, whether senatorial or imperial, was accompanied to his province by advisers and administrative staff. Many of these were imperial freedmen. They worked closely with the local councils, who took care of the daily running of the towns: the collection of taxes, public building works, and maintenance of the water supply and sewer system. Since the local councils continued to manage their own affairs, each province retained its own identity, and there was considerable variation between the provinces of the Empire.

Aegyptus

The governor of Aegyptus (***praefectus Aegyptī***) was a man of equestrian rank appointed by the emperor. Aegyptus became a province after Queen Cleopatra and her Roman ally, Mark Antony, were defeated at the Battle of Actium in 31 BC by Octavian. Octavian later took the name Augustus when he became the first emperor. Aegyptus was strategically extremely important because it was the main source of grain to feed the growing population of Rome and was often referred to as the 'breadbasket of the Empire'. It was considered the personal property of the emperor. Two or three legions, along with auxiliary soldiers, were stationed there to guard the province.

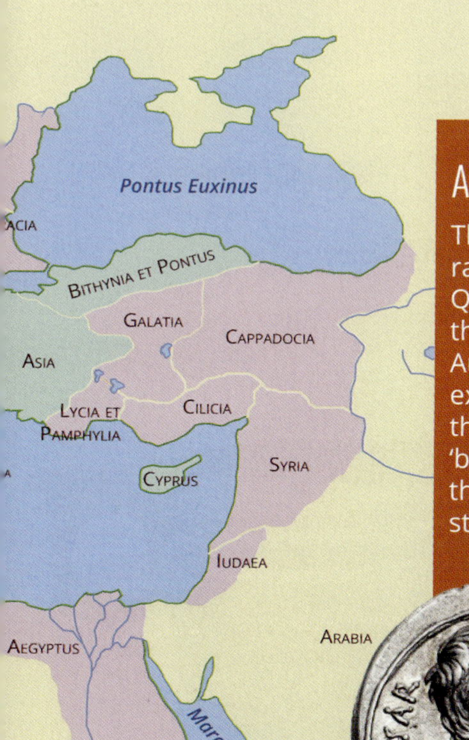

Caesar was one of the names of Emperor Augustus and became one of the titles of the Roman emperors.

venēnum

in Caeliō monte, quattuor senātōrēs in trīclīniō domūs splendidae recumbēbant. Clōdius, vir magnae auctōritātis, trēs fīliōs atque lībertum fidēlissimum ad cēnam invītāverat.

cum ancillae cibum in mēnsās pōnerent, fīliī inter sē loquēbantur. tum Clōdius fīliōs ita adlocūtus est:

'heri, cārissimī fīliī, cum dē vītā meā cōgitārem, vōs ad cēnam invītāre cōnstituī. nam scītis mē esse veterem atque labōre cōnfectum et nōn diūtius ad cūriam īre. mox mors mē auferet. vōs invītāvī quod hērēdem legere dēbeō. sed difficile est. putō ūnum ex vōbīs ...'

subitō, Clōdius iugulum suum manibus prehendit. spūma ex ōre ērūpit. tum conlāpsus est. lībertus ad eum festīnāvit et, cum patrōnum īnspexisset, 'mortuus est!' exclāmāvit.

statim duo frātrēs īrātissimē inter sē clāmābant: 'tū eum necāvistī!' 'ego hērēs iūstus sum!' 'ego ā patre plūrimum amātus sum!' 'tūne venēnum eī dedistī?!' tertius tamen, cum ad patrem ruisset, eum complexus est et precārī coepit: 'nōlī mē relinquere, pater! dī immortālēs, eum nōbīs reddite!'

tum Clōdius oculōs aperuit, et surrēxit. cum fīliī attonitī tacērent, pater vīvus lībertum adloquī coepit:

'certē nōndum mortuus sum. ingenia vēra tamen fīliōrum meōrum intellēxī, et hērēdem iūstum nunc lēgī. cum duo inter sē clāmārent, ūnus mē servāre cōnābātur. cum illī sē ipsōs cūrārent, hic mē cūrābat.'

Caelius *Caelian (hill in Rome)*
auctōritās *power, importance*
hērēs *heir*
iugulum *throat*
prehendō *I grab*
spūma *foam, froth*
ōs *mouth*
ērumpō *I burst out, shoot out*
plūrimum *very much, most of all*
ingenium *nature, character*

A terracotta drinking cup, decorated with a pattern of vines.

LANGUAGE NOTE 2: CUM + IMPERFECT SUBJUNCTIVE

1. Since Chapter 7 you have met the imperfect tense. For example:

   nōs gladiōs portābāmus et aquam bibēbāmus.
   We were carrying swords and drinking water.

   ego dē verbīs eius cōgitābam.
   I was thinking about her words.

   These forms are known as the **imperfect indicative**.

2. Now look at the following sentences and notice how the verbs in red are translated:

   cum dē vītā meā cōgitārem, vōs ad cēnam invītāre cōnstituī.
   When I was thinking about my life, I decided to invite you to dinner.
   or *Since I was thinking about my life, I decided to invite you to dinner.*

   cum fīliī tacērent, pater lībertum adlocūtus est.
   When his sons were silent, their father addressed his freedman.

3. **cōgitārem** and **tacērent** are forms of the verb known as the **imperfect subjunctive**. Like the pluperfect subjunctive, the imperfect subjunctive is used after **cum** (meaning *when* or *since*).

4. Notice that the imperfect subjunctive is formed by adding personal endings (**-m**, **-s**, **-t**, **-mus**, **-tis**, **-nt**) to the present active infinitive (e.g. **cōgitāre** or **tacēre**). The imperfect of **vocō** (*I call*) is therefore as follows:

vocārem	*I was calling*
vocārēs	*you were calling*
vocāret	*he/she/it was calling*
vocārēmus	*we were calling*
vocārētis	*you were calling*
vocārent	*they were calling*

5. Now compare the following sentences:

   urbs clāmōsa erat.
   The city was rowdy.

   cum urbs clāmōsa esset, Lūcīlius in lectīcā ferēbātur.
   Since the city was rowdy, Lucilius was being carried in a litter.

6. The infinitive of **sum** (*I am*) is **esse** (*to be*). Therefore, the imperfect subjunctive of **sum** is as follows:

essem	*I was*
essēs	*you were*
esset	*he/she/it was*
essēmus	*we were*
essētis	*you were*
essent	*they were*

Poison

Poisoning – or at least the accusation of poisoning – was common in the Roman world. The historians Tacitus and Suetonius record that Nero and his mother, Agrippina, were accused of using poison to get rid of their rivals and enemies. However, some of the deaths could have been from natural causes and the accusations of poisoning false.

Locusta

Locusta was a notorious poisoner, employed by both Nero and Agrippina. According to some Roman historians, Agrippina wanted to murder her husband, Emperor Claudius. Locusta therefore provided a poison which could be sprinkled on a mushroom. Claudius was alert to the possibility of poison in his food and drink, so Halotus, a slave or freedman of the emperor, tasted it first. Somehow Agrippina got round this precaution, perhaps by involving Halotus in the plot. Agrippina had also secured the help of one of Claudius' doctors, Xenophon. When it seemed that the poison wasn't working quickly enough, Xenophon rushed up to Claudius when he was trying to vomit and thrust down his throat a feather smeared with a faster-acting poison.

Nero had been adopted by his stepfather Claudius, and after Claudius' death Nero succeeded him as emperor. However, Claudius had another son, Britannicus. Nero regarded Britannicus as a threat, so he is said to have murdered him with poison he had obtained from Locusta. Suetonius, in his biography of Nero, reported that the first poison did not work, because Locusta had provided only a small amount so that it would not be detected. Nero made her concoct a stronger dose, which he experimented with, trying it first on a young goat, then, in an even stronger dose, on a pig. The poison was given to Britannicus at dinner in his drink. An unpoisoned drink was first tasted by the slave or freedman whose job it was to test any food or drink beforehand. The drink was very hot, so Britannicus refused it. It was then diluted with some cold water, to which the poison had been added.

Nero rewarded Locusta by giving her a large estate. Suetonius says that he even sent students to her, to learn from her expertise in concocting poisons. Later, when Nero feared he might need to take his own life, he obtained some poison from Locusta, which he kept hidden in a golden box. After Nero's death, Locusta was executed for her crimes by his successor, Emperor Galba.

Antidotes

Making a slave or freedman taste the food and drink first was one way to avoid being poisoned. Another precaution was to take a regular antidote. Tacitus claims that when Nero was planning the murder of his mother, one of the reasons he rejected poison was because Agrippina was in the habit of taking antidotes.

In the first century BC, Mithridates, king of Pontus, created an antidote containing fifty-four ingredients, which was known as mithridatum. Mithridates took a tiny dose every day. The story goes that it was so effective that when, after being defeated by the Romans, he tried to kill himself by taking poison, he was immune and had to ask a soldier to kill him with a sword. After Mithridates' death, the Roman general Pompey took the recipe for mithridatum and had it translated into Latin by his freedman Lenaeus. Later, Nero's doctor Andromachus improved on the recipe.

Poisons

Most of the poisons used by the Romans came from plants. Examples are opium (made from the juice of the poppy), aconite (also known as monkshood), and belladonna (deadly nightshade).

Snake venom was less common, but when Octavian (later Emperor Augustus) defeated Queen Cleopatra of Egypt, she chose to kill herself rather than be captured and taken to Rome as a prisoner. The popular belief was that she deliberately let a poisonous snake – an asp or a cobra – bite her. However, some Roman historians suggested that she introduced the poison by scratching or injecting her skin with a sharp implement such as a needle.

QUESTION

How easy would it have been for the Romans to prove or disprove accusations of poisoning?

LANGUAGE PRACTICE

2. Translate each sentence into Latin by choosing the correct word or phrase from each pair.

a. *When the old man was eating dinner, he suddenly fell to the ground.*

cum senis | cēnam | cōnsūmeret, | semper | dē terrā | cecidit.
cum senex | cibum | cōnsūmēbat, | subitō | ad terram | cadit.

b. *Since the girl was going to the temple, her father was relating many things about it.*

cum puella | ad templa | adīret, | pater multōs | sine eō | nārrābat.
cum puellae | ad templum | adībat, | pater multa | dē eō | nārrāverat.

c. *Since I was finishing the sword, the children were preparing to sell it in the city.*

cum gladium | cōnficiēbam, | librī | eōs | in urbe | vēndere | parāre.
cum gladiōs | cōnficerem, | līberī | eum | in urbem | vēndēbat | parābant.

d. *When you looked around the house, you noticed a very old painting.*

imāginem | veterem | cōnspeximus, | cum domus | circumspectārēs.
imāginis | veterrimam | cōnspexistī, | cum domum | circumspectābās.

e. *Since the loyal cavalry obeyed their commander, we were quickly overpowered.*

ferōciter | superāvimus, | cum eques fidēlis | lēgātīs | pārēbant.
celeriter | superātī sumus, | cum equitēs fidēlēs | lēgātō | pārērent.

f. *When we were walking here, we felt more tremors.*

cum hunc | prōcēderēmus, | minōrēs tremōrēs | sēnsimus.
cum hūc | prōcēdēbāmus, | plūrēs tremōrēs | sentīmus.

3. Complete the sentences by translating the verbs in bold into Latin. You will need to use the subjunctive form of the verb. Use the chart on p. 282 for help.

a. Since **we had called** our parents, they ran as quickly as possible.
cum parentēs .... , quam celerrimē cucurrērunt.

b. I was walking along the shore, as **I was holding** the baby.
per lītus ambulābam, cum īnfantem ....

c. Since **you had sent** the messenger, the cavalry arrived before dawn.
cum tū nūntium .... , equitēs ante lūcem pervēnērunt.

d. When **they had heard** the woman's voice, they recognized it at once.
cum vōcem fēminae .... , eam statim agnōvērunt.

e. When **you were sending** gifts, they were sending their legions.
cum vōs dōna .... , illī legiōnēs mittēbant.

f. Since my enemy **was listening to** the conversation, I said nothing.
cum inimīcus sermōnem .... , nihil dīxī.

Establishing the Principate

The Republic ended with a series of civil wars between Rome's most powerful generals, backed by their armies. When one of these wars, between Julius Caesar and Pompey, ended with success for Caesar, instead of returning power to the Senate and the People, he became 'dictator' for life. Other senators, worried that Caesar would go a step further and make himself king, organized a plot to kill him in 44 BC.

Caesar's assassination did not bring peace. Two men rose to avenge it, Mark Antony, one of Caesar's most trusted lieutenants, and a surprise newcomer: Caesar's nineteen-year-old great-nephew, Octavian. Caesar had adopted him and made him his heir, so Octavian inherited Caesar's money and command of his armies, as well as his ambitions. Antony and Octavian first took revenge for the death of Caesar by killing his assassins. Then they divided the Empire into two areas of influence. Antony took the rich East and Octavian the poorer West.

Antony divorced his wife and married instead the queen of Egypt, Cleopatra. The Senate, alarmed at what they saw as the ultimate horror – that Antony and Cleopatra would become king and queen of Rome – allowed Octavian to command an army against them. In a naval battle near Actium in 31 BC Antony and Cleopatra were defeated, and Octavian became the unchallenged ruler of Rome.

Octavian

As Octavian had been adopted by Caesar, he had acquired Caesar's name and had become a member of the Julian family, which traced its ancestry back to Aeneas and therefore to the goddess Venus. He had Caesar's wealth and the allegiance of his armies. All this, and the victory at Actium, gave Octavian an outstanding place in Roman politics.

In 31 BC Octavian was in a similar position to Caesar after his victory over Pompey. Rome, however, had changed: after so many years of civil war in which many aristocrats had died, the Senate was willing to accept a solution which would bring peace. Cleverly, Octavian did not repeat Caesar's error of openly becoming a sole ruler. Instead, he surrendered the powers given to him by the Senate to defeat Antony and claimed he wanted to become a private citizen. The Senate, thinking that the gap left by Octavian would lead to a new civil war between ambitious senators, begged him to stay. In this way, Octavian was seen not to be seizing power, as Caesar had done, but to be obeying the Senate. In 27 BC the Senate granted Octavian the titles ***Augustus*** (The Revered One) and ***Prīnceps*** (Leader).

Augustus

Between 31 BC and his death in AD 14 Augustus created a new system for ruling Rome. He claimed that he had restored the Republic. Every year there were elections to choose the magistrates of the state (for example, consuls and praetors) and the Senate continued to meet to make the laws of Rome. But something had changed: one of the senators, Augustus, had more power than any of the others and made all the important decisions.

He achieved this because he had ***auctōritās***: the respect that a Roman politician gained from outstanding victories and achievements, and ancestry, which in the case of Augustus linked him to Caesar, to Aeneas, and to Venus. Over the years he also took some key roles: he was ***imperātor*** (Commander-in-Chief of the army), and the legions swore allegiance directly to him, not to Rome or the Senate. He was ***pontifex maximus*** (Chief Priest), and he had ***tribūnicia potestās*** for life, which gave him the power to intervene in or veto any decision of the Senate, without having to be elected as a magistrate. Finally, despite having all these powers, he did not give himself a title that would single him out as a ruler. Instead, he claimed he was equal to the other senators, while at the same time being the first of them: ***prīmus inter parēs, prīnceps***. This was clearly contradictory, but it sounded good, and the Romans were prepared to accept it. After years of war, Augustus guaranteed peace, and with it the prosperity of the whole Empire.

Succession

This new political system, with its contradictions, was based on the overwhelming personality of Augustus. Had he died young, perhaps it would not have survived, but he remained in power for forty-five years. During this time, as the historian Tacitus says, the Romans forgot their earlier freedoms and were prepared to accept this in exchange for peace and prosperity. As Augustus grew old, the continuation of the system depended on succession. There was no way of appointing an heir for a title (emperor) that did not legally exist, so the next princeps needed some of Augustus' auctoritas. As he had no sons, and his grandsons had died young, he adopted his wife's son, Tiberius, who became the next emperor.

Chapter 24: Achaea

Athēnae

Athēnae *Athens*

Parthenōn *Parthenon (temple of Athena)*
Athēnīs *in Athens*
discō *I learn*

4 Tīrō tot librōs lēgerat ut ipse quoque multa dē Athēnīs scīret. nam māter eius, quae Graeca erat, tot fābulās dē urbe nārrāverat ut Tīrō Athēnās amāret.
ut *that, so that, in order that*
5 Lūcīlius ac Tīrō per Viam Sacram prōgressī sunt. Tīrō, Propylaea mīrātus, dominum ad Parthenōnem secūtus est.
Propylaea n. pl. *Propylaea (gateway to the Acropolis)*
6 Parthenōnem aedificāre erat difficillimum.
7 certē. tanta erat difficultās ut artificibus fabrīsque multōs annōs labōrāre necesse esset.
8 et servīs, domine.
9 quid? āh, certē, Tīrō, et servīs.

Athēna *Athena (Greek goddess)*
adeō *so much, so greatly, to such an extent*
olea *olive tree*

lapicīdīnae *stone quarries*
Caryātides *Caryatids (female statues)*

Roman Athens

Graecia capta ferum victōrem cēpit.
Captive Greece captured her uncivilized conqueror.
Horace

The history of Athens stretches far back in time: the first settlements were established in the fourth millennium BC. A legend tells that the goddess Athena (whom the Romans associated with Minerva) won the role of patron of the city by giving the Athenians an olive tree, a symbol of peace and wealth. By the fifth century BC Athens had become one of the most powerful cities of the Mediterranean.

When the Romans conquered Greece, Athens had been a thriving independent city state for almost a thousand years. In 86 BC the Roman general Sulla destroyed a large part of the city and surrounding fortifications but preserved many public buildings, monuments, and temples.

The Acropolis of Athens (from the Greek words ***akron*** meaning 'highest point' and ***polis*** meaning 'city') was a rocky hill in the center of the city and was the site of the first settlement. It was on the Acropolis that, in the fifth century BC, the Athenian politician Pericles organized the construction of the Parthenon, the Propylaea, the Erectheum, and the temple of Athena Nike (Victory). All of these buildings were still standing at the time of the Roman conquest, and, although damaged, they survive today.

Temple of Rome and Augustus

The Athenians built this small circular temple on the Acropolis some time after 19 BC. It was dedicated to Rome and Emperor Augustus and there was probably a statue of Augustus inside.

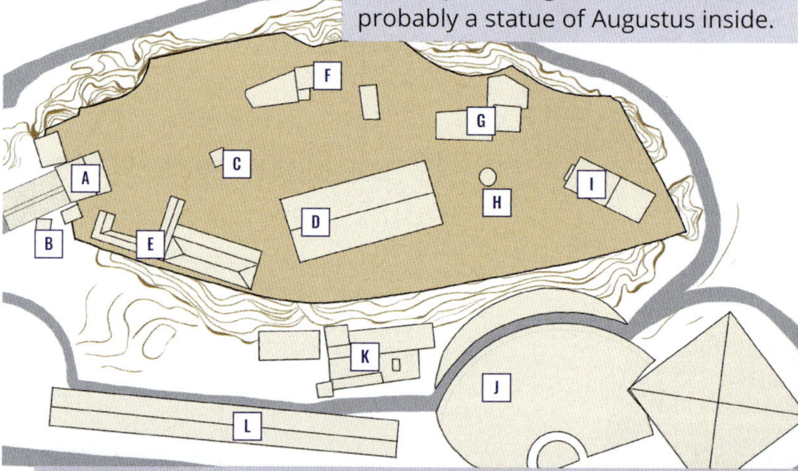

Plan of the Acropolis in the time of Nero.

A Propylaea
B Temple of Athena Nike
C Statue of Athena Promachus
D Parthenon
E Sanctuary of Artemis Brauronia
F Erechtheum
G Sanctuary of Zeus
H Temple of Rome and Augustus
I Sanctuary of Pandion
J Theater of Dionysus
K Sanctuary of Asclepius
L Stoa of Eumenes

The Athenian Acropolis as it looks today.

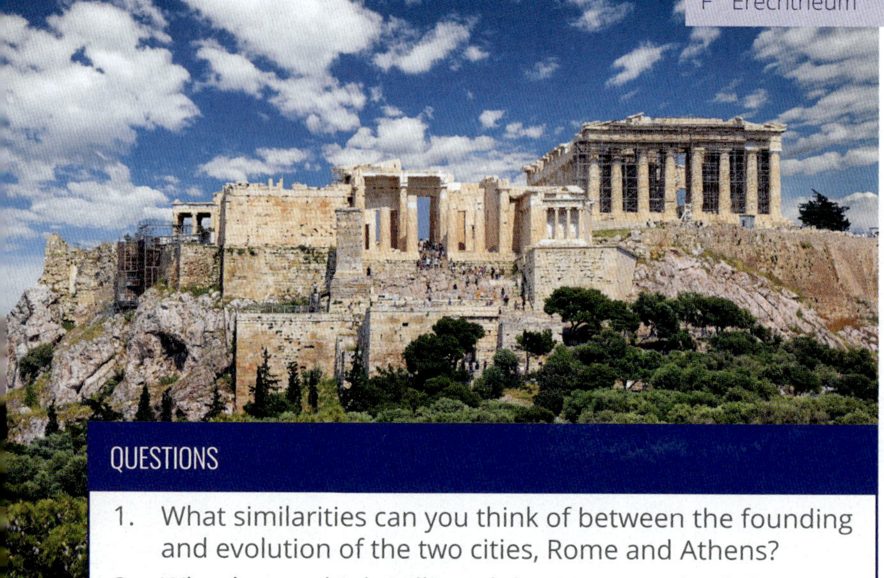

QUESTIONS

1. What similarities can you think of between the founding and evolution of the two cities, Rome and Athens?
2. Why do you think Sulla and the Romans who followed him preserved many public buildings in Athens?

The agora

Below the Acropolis lay the ***agora***, a flat open square space, which was the center of the town. Much like a Roman forum, the agora was used for various civic, commercial, and social activities. Around the sides were long covered colonnades (which the Greeks called stoas). These provided shade and a meeting place for friends to discuss business, politics, and philosophy.

In the center of the agora the Roman general Agrippa commissioned the construction of a new performance hall, the Odeum of Agrippa. It was completed in 15 BC and was built with the same plan as the Odeum in Pompeii.

Collection or theft?

The Romans copied Greek styles of architecture. They modeled their public buildings, such as temples and colonnades, on those of the Greeks. When the Romans invaded and formed the province of Achaea, successful Roman generals brought spoils of war back to Rome. Greek works of art were paraded through the streets and exhibited publicly. Wealthy Romans were captivated and soon began amassing vast collections of Greek art and sculpture, which they displayed in their houses.

Artists were commissioned to make copies of Greek sculptures, either exact replicas or variants adapted to the taste of the buyer. Often they made marble copies of bronze originals because marble was cheaper and easier to work with. It is often the Roman copies that have survived to this day, rather than the Greek originals.

Augustus ordered the repair of the Erechtheum. His architects and craftsmen also made plaster casts of the columns, which were in the shape of young women. These were brought back to Rome, where they were used to make replicas which stood in the Forum of Augustus, in the heart of Rome.

A reconstruction of the porch of the Erechtheum.

The Parthenon sculptures

The Parthenon was decorated with carved marble sculptures designed by the famous artist Pheidias. These were painted in bright colors, but only a few traces of paint remain today.

The Parthenon has a long history. It was built in the fifth century BC, and then preserved by the Romans for centuries. Around AD 500 it was converted to a Christian church and part of the decoration was removed and destroyed. Later, the Ottoman Empire conquered Greece, and in the 1460s the Parthenon became a mosque. When the Venetians attacked in the late 1600s, the Parthenon was used to store gunpowder. A huge explosion destroyed most of the roof and some of the surviving sculptures.

In 1801 Lord Elgin, the British ambassador to the Ottoman Empire, removed about half the remaining sculptures and transported them to Britain. They are now on display in the British Museum in London. The Greek government has demanded the return of these sculptures and has left spaces for them in a specially-built museum in Athens.

DISCUSSION

Should the sculptures be returned and displayed in Athens? Think of arguments on both sides.

A section of the Parthenon frieze showing men on horses as part of an Athenian procession.

LANGUAGE NOTE 1: RESULT CLAUSES

1. Look at the following sentences. What do the clauses in red have in common?

   Tīrō tot librōs lēgerat ut multa dē Athēnīs scīret.
   Tiro had read so many books that he knew many things about Athens.

   Athēna eōs adeō amābat ut eīs oleam daret.
   Athena loved them so much that she gave the olive tree to them.

   templum tam altum erat ut Lūcīlius imāginēs vidēre vix posset.
   The temple was so tall that Lucilius was hardly able to see the images.

2. The clauses in red are known as **result clauses** because they tell us the result of an action. For example, in the first sentence, the result of Tiro reading many books was that he knew a lot about Athens.
3. Result clauses are introduced by **ut** (meaning *that*) and are followed by a verb in the subjunctive (e.g. **scīret**, **daret**, **posset**).
4. Look out for the following words, which are often followed by result clauses:

adeō	*to such an extent, so much*	**tam**	*so*
ita	*in such a way*	**tālis**	*such, of such a kind*
tot	*so many*	**tantus**	*so great, so much, so big*

LANGUAGE PRACTICE

1. Complete each sentence with the most appropriate result clause, then translate.

ut illī vulneribus multīs perīrent.	ut eōs effugere nōn possem.	ut nōs omnēs eum amārēmus.
ut nautae nāvem vix servārent.	ut tōtum diem rīdēret.	ut semper dē aliīs cōgitārent.

   a. puella tam laeta erat ...
   b. tot hostēs appāruerant ...
   c. līberī ita doctī erant ...
   d. tālis erat vīta gladiātōrum ...
   e. dux adeō labōrāverat ...
   f. tanta tempestās erat ...

memorantēs iuventūtem

'Lūcīlī! heus, Lūcīlī!' Lūcīlius sē ad vōcem vertit, et amīcum nōmine Philōnem ad sē dē Arēopagō festīnantem cōnspexit. Philō tam celeriter cucurrit ut ad Lūcīlium anhēlus advenīret. amīcī inter sē laetī complexī sunt. Lūcīlius vultum Philōnis diū spectābat, Philō umerum Lūcīliī tenēbat. Lūcīlius adeō attonitus erat ut nūlla verba loquī posset. tandem 'quam īnsignis nunc es!' Philō amanter dīxit.

♦ ♦ ♦

Philō Lūcīliusque prope porticum Attalicam ambulābant, memorantēs iuventūtem suam, cum philosophōs audīrent.

Philō tam callidus erās ut tē saepe laudārem.

Lūcīlius vah! tam blandus erās ut tibi minimē crēderem.

Philō tandem tibi persuāsī.

Lūcīlius ūnum prō certō habeō. tot contrōversiās dē virtūte et iūstitiā et rērum nātūrā post cēnam habēbāmus ut saepe nōn dormīrēmus.

Philō etiam nunc fortasse nōn cōnsentīmus!

Lūcīlius et quid nunc agis? fēlīx es?

Philō cum discessissēs, tam trīstis eram ut diū dēspērārem. sed tandem Fortūna mihi fāvit, et nunc fēlīx sum. vīta mea est plēna bonōrum. amīcōs fidēlēs habeō. puellam sapientem atque benignam in mātrimōnium dūxī. et amātor quoque optimus mihi est, similis ingeniō atque animō.

Lūcīlius tibi invideō, Philō. omnia bona merēs. sed mihi tālis vīta nōn erit.

Philō intellegō, Lūcīlī. tū quoque bonam fortūnam merēs, mī amīce.

Lūcīlius mihi vīta alia est, sed multa bona quoque habeō, et multa gaudia.

Philō bene! et nunc ad popīnam – Graecō mōre bibēmus!

iuventūs *youth*
Arēopagus *Areopagus (hill in Athens)*
anhēlus *breathless*
umerus *shoulder*
īnsignis *distinguished*
porticus Attalica *the Stoa of Attalus*
philosophus *philosopher*
prō certō habeō *I am sure*
iūstitia *justice*
nātūra *nature*
amātor *lover*
similis *similar, alike*
invideō *I envy*
mōs *custom*

Rhetoric

The ability to make speeches in public was an essential skill for any upper-class Roman who wanted a career in politics, the law, or the army – the professions to which an ambitious man aspired. He would have to speak persuasively in the Senate, argue a case in the law courts, address the people in local elections, encourage his troops before battle, or give speeches on special occasions in praise of the emperor or distinguished men. A young man like Lucilius would have acquired the art of persuasion, known as rhetoric, at the school of the rhetor, which he would have attended from the age of about fifteen or sixteen.

Rhetoric became an important part of Roman education in the first century BC, influenced by Greek culture. The study of rhetoric had been developed by the Greeks, and teachers of rhetoric in Rome and elsewhere in the Roman world were often Greek.

At the school of the rhetor students learned the rules and techniques for making speeches and continued to study literature – Cicero's speeches and Livy's history were particularly recommended. Students practiced by composing and delivering speeches, varying their tone of voice and using appropriate gestures. They presented arguments in imaginary legal cases, gave advice to historical or mythical figures, and argued for or against a point of view. Seneca the Elder recorded some examples:

- The 300 Spartans sent against the Persian king Xerxes debate whether they should retreat.
- Which is preferable, town or country life?
- Is marriage desirable?
- Who deserves the greater praise, the lawyer or the soldier?

Some legal cases were very far-fetched. For example:

> A man captured by pirates wrote to his father asking for a ransom. He was not ransomed. The daughter of the pirate chief forced him to promise that he would marry her if he was released. He promised. She left her father and followed the young man. He returned to his father and married the girl. By chance, there was an orphaned girl. The father ordered his son to divorce the daughter of the pirate chief and marry the orphan. He refused, so his father disinherited him.

Students debated whether the father had the right to disinherit his son in this situation.

QUESTIONS

1. Do you think that public speaking is still a valuable skill?
2. In what different ways is the art of persuasion used today?

Rhetoric today: a case study

Barack Obama delivered his final public speech as US president in 2017. In this extract, he considers the power of citizens working together to bring about change in society:

> For 240 years, **our nation**'s call to citizenship has given **work and purpose** to each new generation. **It's what** led **p**atriots to choose republic over tyranny, **p**ioneers to trek west, slaves to brave that makeshift railroad to freedom. **It's what p**ulled immigrants and refugees across oceans and the Rio Grande. **It's what p**ushed women to reach for the ballot. **It's what** powered workers to organize. It's why GIs gave their lives at Omaha Beach and Iwo Jima, Iraq, and Afghanistan. And why men and women from Selma to Stonewall were prepared to give theirs, as well.
>
> *Barack Obama, Farewell Address*

Obama's speech uses many of the traditional techniques of rhetoric:

anaphora: a series of sentences beginning with the same word or phrase.

word pairs: two words used where one would be sufficient; often the words have the same or similar meanings.

alliteration: words beginning with the same letter.

emotive language: words which provoke an emotional response in the listener or reader.

tricolon: a group of three phrases or clauses of similar grammatical structure.

1. Find other examples of these techniques in the extract.
2. a. Which emotions is this speech designed to evoke in the audience?
   b. How do rhetorical techniques contribute to this?

LANGUAGE NOTE 2: COMPOUND VERBS

1. In Chapters 18 and 19 you saw how compounds of the verbs **eō** (*I go*) and **ferō** (*I bear, bring*) are formed using prefixes, such as **ex**- (*out, away*) and **re**- (*back*). For example, **exeō** means *I go out* and **referō** means *I bring back*.

2. Many other verbs use prefixes to form compounds. For example, **adveniō** (*I come to, arrive*) is a compound of **ad** + **veniō**, and **dēspērō** (*I despair*) is a compound of **dē** + **spērō**.

3. Some common prefixes are:

ā-, **ab**-	*away*	**inter**-	*among, between*
ad-	*to, towards, at*	**per**-	*through, along*
circum-	*around*	**prō**-	*forwards*
cum-	*together*	**re**-	*back*
dē-	*down, out of*	**sub**-	*under, up to*
ē-, **ex**-	*out, away*	**trāns**-	*across*
in-	*in, on, into, onto*		

4. Sometimes the form of the prefix changes when it is combined with a verb:

auferō (*I steal, take away*)	=	**ab** + **ferō**
compōnō (*I arrange*)	=	**cum** + **pōnō**

5. Some verbs change slightly when a prefix is added:

recipiō (*I take back*)	=	**re** + **capiō**
retineō (*I hold back, restrain*)	=	**re** + **teneō**

LANGUAGE PRACTICE

2. Separate these compound verbs into a prefix and a verb, giving the meaning of each. For example:

adferō (*I bring to*): **ad** = *to* **ferō** = *I bring*

a. absum (*I am absent*)
b. addūcō (*I lead to*)
c. āmittō (*I lose*)
d. conveniō (*I meet*)
e. exclāmō (*I exclaim*)
f. intellegō (*I understand*)
g. inveniō (*I find*)
h. pereō (*I die*)
i. prōmittō (*I promise*)
j. reddō (*I give back*)
k. reficiō (*I repair*)
l. subveniō (*I help*)

vīta beāta

in forō Athēniēnsī plūrima bona ā multīs mercātōribus vēndēbantur. tot mercātōrēs magnīs vōcibus exclāmābant ut verba eōrum intellegere difficile esset. duo puerī in mediō forō fīcōs vēndere temptābant, exclāmantēs: 'hūc venīte! hīc fīcōs optimās inveniētis!' et 'vītam beātam quaeritis, Athēniēnsēs? sī hās fīcōs cōnsūmētis, vītam beātam sine dubiō obtinēbitis!' cum haec audīrent, Athēniēnsēs rīdēbant. senex quīdam, cum fīcōs ēmisset, puerōs interrogāre coepit. 'quīdam cibum bonum cōnsūmit. putātisne eum ergō vītam beātam dūcere? audīte, omnēs!' sīc puerōs adlocūtus, ad turbam sē vertit: 'quālis vīta vērō est beāta?' plūrimī Athēniēnsēs adeō contrōversiās amābant ut circum senem cōnsisterent et sententiās magnīs vōcibus dīcerent:

beātus *happy, blessed*
Athēniēnsis *Athenian*
fīcus *fig*
obtineō *I gain, obtain*
interrogō *I question*
circum *around*
sententia *opinion*

pietās *sense of duty, piety*
sapientia *wisdom*

senex, cum haec verba audīvisset, respondit: 'hercle! tot sententiās audīvimus ut nihil dēcernere possēmus.'

puer exclāmāvit: 'quot hominēs, tot sententiae! sed dē hāc rē cōnsentiunt omnēs: fīcōs nostrās esse optimās!' omnēs maximē rīdēbant, et nōnnūllī fīcōs ēmērunt.

dēcernō *I decide, settle*

ACTIVITY

'quālis vīta vērō est beāta?' (line 9)

Choose two of the characters shown on page 128 and imagine a backstory for them that explains their responses. Who are they? What might their lives be like now, and how might they have been different in the past? Do your characters already live a **vīta beāta** or do they hope to achieve it?

The reconstructed Stoa of Attalus.

Philosophy

What is philosophy?

Philosophia is a Greek word which means 'love of knowledge'. Ancient Greek philosophers investigated questions such as the origin of the universe, the meaning of life, and the nature of the gods. Philosophy included what today we would call science or religion. Philosophers asked questions such as: What is the universe made of? What is knowledge? What is a good life? What is the best kind of government? They tried to answer these questions in a systematic way, with discussion and logical argument. Some Roman intellectuals were influenced by the ideas of Greek philosophers. Young men, for example the orator and politician Cicero and the poets Horace and Lucan, went to Athens to study philosophy.

> The unexamined life is not worth living for a human being.
>
> *Plato (quoting Socrates)*

Socrates and Plato

Socrates lived in Athens in the fifth century BC. He is famous for engaging his fellow Athenians in conversations which forced them to try to analyze and defend their ideas about such matters as 'What is courage?' or 'What is justice?' Socrates did not write anything down, but his pupil Plato later composed several works reporting these conversations. It is difficult to know whether Plato is faithfully recording the ideas of Socrates; at times he may be putting his own ideas into Socrates' mouth. Later Greek and Roman philosophers were greatly influenced by Socrates and Plato, and Plato's works are still studied today. His most famous is the *Republic*, in which he describes how an ideal state should be governed.

An engraved carnelian gemstone with a portrait of Socrates. It is just half an inch high.

Mosaic from Pompeii, showing philosophers in discussion.

EPICUREANS

The Greek philosopher Epicurus (*right*) lived in the fourth to third centuries BC. He thought that the aim of life was pleasure. However, by pleasure he did not mean indulging physical desires and living a life of luxury; he believed that pleasure is freedom from pain and anxiety, and the pleasures of the mind are greater than those of the body. He started a philosophical community of friends in Athens, which he called The Garden. Its members, who included women and slaves, lived a simple life.

According to Epicurus, the two things that cause most mental pain are fear of death and fear of the gods. He argued that death isn't to be feared, because there is no life after death. He developed a theory of the physical structure of the universe, known as the atomic theory. According to this theory, everything in the universe, including our minds and our souls, is made up of tiny, invisible, indivisible particles. He called these particles atoms (the Greek word is ***atomata***, which means 'things that can't be cut up'). When we die, the atoms which make up our bodies and souls disperse, and so there is no survival after death. This atomic theory also explains the physical universe without the need for gods: the universe was created by accident, and phenomena such as thunder and lightning are caused by the random movement of atoms, not by the gods. Epicurus believed that the gods exist, but did not create the world, and take no interest in human life. Therefore, he argued, there is no reason to fear them.

Epicureanism was popular among some intellectuals in Rome and Italy in the first century BC. The most well-known Roman follower of Epicurus is Lucretius, who wrote a long poem explaining Epicurean philosophy, *On the Nature of the Universe* (*De Rerum Natura*). Often people misunderstood Epicurean philosophy or criticized Epicureans for living a selfish life devoted to luxury and physical pleasure. In fact, the opposite was the case. The aim of the true Epicurean was to live a simple life free from pain, anxiety, and fear. This meant that Epicureans preferred not to take part in public life and avoided careers in politics and the law.

The poet Horace summed up the Epicurean attitude to life in the phrase ***carpe diem***, which means 'enjoy the day', 'live in the moment'.

STOICS

Zeno (*below*), who lived in Athens in the third century BC, was the first Stoic philosopher. The Stoics were named after the colonnade (***stoa***) in Athens where Zeno taught. Like the Epicureans, the Stoics were mainly interested in questions of how one should behave (moral philosophy). They believed that the aim of life is virtue (goodness). A good man does not need anything else to be happy, so things usually regarded as desirable, such as health, wealth, power, pleasure, even liberty, don't matter. What is important is to face hardship and misfortune with endurance and dignity, controlling emotions such as anger, sadness, and fear. On the other hand, it is natural to want what are normally considered the good things in life, so someone could be a Stoic while pursuing wealth and taking part in political life.

Stoics believed that the world is controlled by reason, which they identified with divine power. Everything that happens is the result of this divine reason. Therefore, you should be content with your fate. For example, if you fall seriously ill or lose all of your possessions, you should accept this as part of the divine plan.

Stoicism became the most popular branch of philosophy among the Romans. Two famous Roman Stoics, Seneca and Epictetus, lived at the time of our stories. Although their beliefs were similar, their lives were very different. Epictetus was a slave, then freedman, of Epaphroditus. Seneca was an extremely wealthy man; he was a senator, and the tutor and adviser of Nero. He believed that by playing an active part in politics he could do good for his fellow men.

DISCUSSION

1. What do you think Socrates meant when he said: 'The unexamined life is not worth living'? Do you agree?
2. Which philosophical system do you find more appealing, the Stoic or the Epicurean?
3. What do you think is the best way to live?

in Isthmō

prope urbem Corinthum, Nerō, rastellum aureum in manibus tenēns, ā magnā turbā spectābātur. prīnceps, mīlitēs et captīvōs adlocūtus, Isthmum perfodere parābat, quod ibi eurīpum creāre cōnstituerat. Nerō, cum mīles tubā signum dedisset, effodere coepit.

'nunc omnia vīdī,' inquit senex quīdam quī prope Lūcīlium adstābat. 'nam hodiē videō hominem quī putat sē posse terram mūtāre.'

Lūcīlius, quī haec verba audīverat, 'tacē, senex!' inquit. 'mox in hōc locō nāvēs nāvigāre poterunt, et dūcēs rēmōs illīc, ubi nūper arābās. haec erit nāvibus via brevior et tūtior. nōnne prīnceps optima facit?'

'ōlim,' respondit senex, 'alius tyrannus, Xerxēs nōmine, duo maria iūnxit et magnum exercitum in Graeciam dūxit. Xerxēs tam superbus erat ut deī eum pūnīrent. exercitus eius victus est et plūrimī mīlitēs mortuī sunt. Xerxēs ipse domum rediit sed post paucōs annōs necātus est. Nerō Xerxēn in animō habēre dēbet. hominem nōn decet opera mūtāre deōrum.'

'cavē, senex,' inquit Lūcīlius. 'verba tua sunt perīculōsa.' sed, quod putābat senem vēra loquī, eum pūnīre nōlēbat.

subitō mīlitēs Nerōnī plausērunt, quī corbulam plēnam humī in manibus portābat. deinde, ā mīlitibus iussa, multa mīlia captīvōrum Iūdaeōrum quoque effodere coepērunt.

Isthmus *Isthmus (land between two seas)*
Corinthus *Corinth*
rastellus *mattock*
perfodiō *I dig through*
eurīpus *canal*
effodiō *I dig*
adstō *I stand near*

dūcō rēmōs *I row*
illīc *there*
arō *I plow*
tyrannus *ruler*
Xerxēs *Xerxes*
iungō *I join*
Graecia *Greece*
superbus *arrogant*

corbula *little basket*
humus *earth*
mille, pl. mīlia *thousand*
Iūdaeus *Jewish*

The Corinth canal was finally completed in 1893. It follows the same route as Nero's attempt.

LANGUAGE NOTE 3: 4TH DECLENSION NOUNS

1. You have already met many nouns of the first, second, and third declensions. For example:

1st declension:	puella, puellae, *f.* (*girl*)	
2nd declension:	amīcus, amīcī, *m.* (*friend*)	dōnum, dōnī, *n.* (*gift*)
3rd declension:	nox, noctis, *f.* (*night*)	caput, capitis, *n.* (*head*)

2. Now look at the following sentences. What do you notice about the endings of **manus** and **exercitus**?

   fībulam in manū tenēbat.
   She was holding a brooch in her hand.

   Xerxēs magnōs exercitūs in Graeciam dūxit.
   Xerxes led great armies into Greece.

   manus and **exercitus** belong to the **fourth declension** of Latin nouns, so their endings are different from those you have met so far.

3. The endings of **manus**, *f.* (*hand; group*) are as follows:

	singular	*plural*
nominative	**manus**	**manūs**
genitive	**manūs**	**manuum**
dative	**manuī**	**manibus**
accusative	**manum**	**manūs**
ablative	**manū**	**manibus**

4. Notice that the genitive singular of fourth declension nouns ends **-ūs**. This can be used to distinguish them from second declension nouns when looking them up in a dictionary. For example:

second declension:	hortus, hortī, *m.* (*garden*)
fourth declension:	exercitus, exercitūs, *m.* (*army*)

5. Other common fourth declension nouns include **cāsus** (*accident*), **cursus** (*race*), **metus** (*fear*), **senātus** (*Senate*), and **vultus** (*face; expression*).

LANGUAGE PRACTICE

3. Choose the correct form of the noun to complete each sentence, then translate.

   a. cum leō mē peteret, ... perterrita eram. (metūs, metum, metū)

   b. dux .... mīlitēs gravibus verbīs adlocūtus est. (exercitūs, exercituī, exercitū)

   c. ille duās .... ad caelum subitō sustulit. (manūs, manū, manibus)

   d. .... hōrum līberōrum plēnī gaudiō mox erunt. (vultuum, vultus, vultūs)

Greece and Rome

A map showing the areas where Greek poleis were established (800–480 BC).

In ancient times, Greece was not a country in itself but made up of a number of city states called ***poleis*** (singular ***polis***), each of which had a powerful city at its center. The Greek philosopher Aristotle wrote that a polis should be large enough to be self-sufficient but small enough for 'the citizens to know one another's characters.' The first poleis, such as Athens, Corinth, and Sparta, were in what is now known as mainland Greece. The inhabitants of these city states all spoke Greek (although different dialects emerged) and shared a common culture and religion. They may have shared a feeling of 'Greekness' but would identify themselves as Athenian or Spartan, much more than simply as Greek.

Expansion

Because of the increasing size of the city states and the resulting shortage of good farming land, Greek people and therefore Greek ideas spread all over the Mediterranean. The influence of the Greeks became so strong that Sicily and southern Italy became known as Magna Graecia (Great Greece). Similar expansion eastwards led to the founding of poleis as far as the area around the Black Sea (***Pontus Euxīnus***). By 600 BC there were about 1,500 poleis around the Mediterranean.

The rise of Athens

By the fifth century BC, Athens had grown to be the most powerful of the city states. There were sometimes conflicts between the different poleis, but when the Greek cities in Anatolia (modern Turkey) were being oppressed by the Persians, Athens retaliated and was joined by other poleis in the ensuing conflict. Although this showed that the Greeks could be unified against an external threat, Athens continued to grow in power and influence over the other cities, which led to resentment, and ultimately to war. The Peloponnesian War (431–404 BC) against Sparta ended in complete disaster for Athens, while Sparta, in time, was defeated by Thebes. By the mid-fourth century BC, all the poleis were in a weakened and disorganized state. At this time, Philip, the king of Macedonia, began to bring virtually the whole of Greece under his control, and his son Alexander would extend this empire even further.

Alexander the Great

A marble head of Alexander. For another depiction of Alexander, see page 21.

Alexander was born in Macedonia in 356 BC. From the age of sixteen he acted as ruler in Macedonia when his father was away, and when Philip was assassinated Alexander succeeded him without opposition. His ruthlessness was shown from the start when he immediately executed those alleged to be behind Philip's murder, along with all possible rivals and those opposed to him, and quickly assembled an army to secure his control over mainland Greece.

Alexander then proceeded to head a Greek invasion of Asia. He defeated the Persian king Darius at the Battle of Issos, then continued east as far as what are now Russia, Afghanistan, and north-west India. He also conquered Egypt and founded the city of Alexandria. His conquests spread the Greek language and Greek customs far and wide.

Greece and Rome

After Alexander's sudden death in 323 BC there was a power struggle, and his empire was split into three areas controlled by different successors. At this time the power of Rome was growing. Over the next 200 years Rome gained control of the Greek cities in southern Italy, mainland Greece, Egypt, and parts of Asia. The Greek world was now part of the Roman Empire, and Greek ideas, culture, and literature continued to spread westwards through the Roman territories.

Chapter 25: Olympia

Nerō omnia vincit

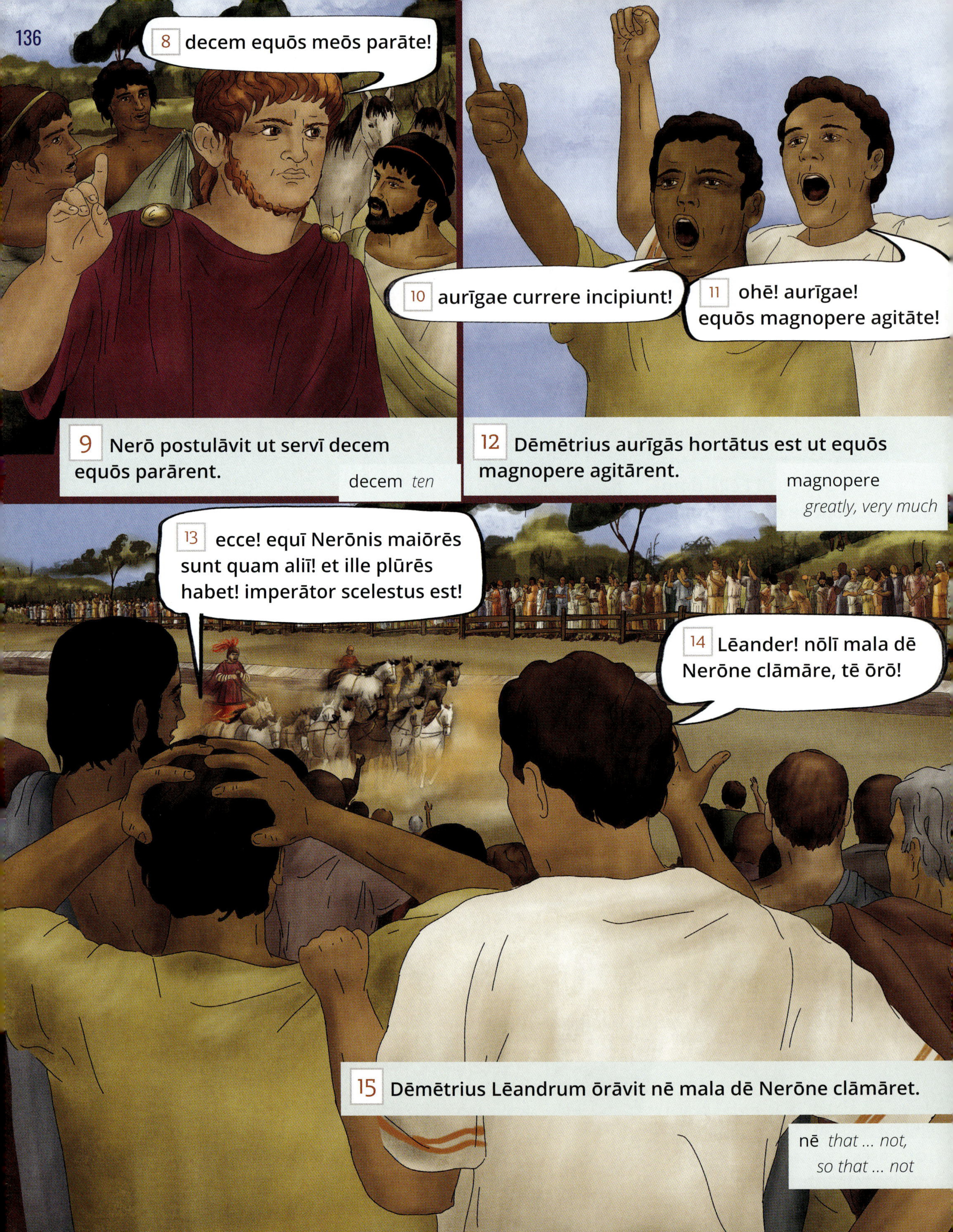
8 decem equōs meōs parāte!
9 Nerō postulāvit ut servī decem equōs parārent.
decem *ten*
10 aurīgae currere incipiunt!
11 ohē! aurīgae! equōs magnopere agitāte!
12 Dēmētrius aurīgās hortātus est ut equōs magnopere agitārent.
magnopere *greatly, very much*
13 ecce! equī Nerōnis maiōrēs sunt quam aliī! et ille plūrēs habet! imperātor scelestus est!
14 Lēander! nōlī mala dē Nerōne clāmāre, tē ōrō!
15 Dēmētrius Lēandrum ōrāvit nē mala dē Nerōne clāmāret.
nē *that ... not, so that ... not*

16 āhhh! servī, mē adiuvāte! ad terram cecidī!
17 Nerō servīs imperāvit ut sē adiuvārent.
18 mē in currum repōnite!
currus chariot
repōnō I put back
19 Nerō servīs imperāvit ut sē in currum repōnerent. servī statim pāruērunt et eum in currum sustulērunt.
20 ēheu! rota frācta est! prōgredī nōn possum!
21 hercle! ē quadrīgā cecidī!
22 ō mē miserum! equī pessimī sunt. currere minimē volunt!
23 equī meī sunt peiōrēs. etiam sē vertunt!
24 eugē! nunc vincam! optimus aurīga sum!
rota wheel
pessimus very bad, worst
eugē hurray!

The Olympic Games

Every four years from 776 BC until at least AD 393, a festival in honor of Zeus (the Greek equivalent of Jupiter) took place at Olympia in southwestern Greece. The festival attracted visitors from all over the Greek world, and the site was at its largest in the second century AD, when Olympia was part of the Roman province of Achaea.

Like the Romans, the Greeks honored their gods with competitive events. For the Greeks, these included chariot-racing, athletics, combat sports, and competitions in drama, music, and singing. At Olympia there were no musical or dramatic competitions.

The word 'athletics' comes from the Greek ***athlos*** (contest), and several athletic events were a feature of the ancient Olympics. These events were originally intended to be part of military training: a citizen of an ancient Greek city state was expected to be prepared to fight in war.

The athletic and combat events took place outdoors in a rectangular area, where the earth was leveled and topped with a thin layer of sand. A straight running track (not an oval) took up most of this space. The track was wide enough for twenty runners and 630 feet long (this distance was called a ***stadion*** in Greek). All the athletic and combat events took place on this track. There was room for about 45,000 spectators on the surrounding slopes – there were no seats. The athletes, except the charioteers and horse riders, competed in the nude.

This amphora was given as a prize for an athletic competition in around 500 BC. It shows two fighters in the pankration, and a referee.

Events

RUNNING

There were races of varying distances. The most prestigious was the stadion, a race in which athletes ran one length of the track. The longest race was twenty-four lengths.

COMBAT EVENTS

There were three combat events: wrestling, boxing, and the ***pankration*** ('all force'). The pankration allowed any kind of fighting except biting and gouging (stabbing fingers into an opponent's eyes, mouth, or nose).

PENTATHLON

The pentathlon consisted of five events: long jump, discus, javelin, running, and wrestling.

HORSE RACES

There were races for chariots and for riders on horseback, held on a separate track near the stadium. Since the charioteers and riders were usually employed by the owners of the horses, the owners received the prize.

The competitors

Originally, contestants had to be free Greek males, but by the first century AD there was some relaxation of this rule, allowing non-Greeks to enter. Athletics played an important part in the education of Greek boys, and the Greeks admired men who performed and competed in public. Women were not allowed to participate. There was a race for girls at a separate women's festival, the Heraea, and women could compete at some of the many other Greek festivals.

Some festivals offered generous cash prizes. Winning at Olympia brought huge glory, but no financial reward. Although the prize was just a crown of olive leaves, the victor could put up a statue of himself at Olympia, and when he returned to his home city he often received gifts and money. It was possible to have a professional career as an athlete, going from festival to festival.

Nero at the Olympics

In AD 66–67 Nero visited Greece and toured the athletic and musical festivals. He arranged for the usual dates of the major festivals to be rescheduled so that they all took place in one year and he could compete. He also added musical competitions to the Olympics. He entered competitions for chariot-racing and playing the cithara (a stringed musical instrument) and won all the events he entered.

LANGUAGE NOTE 1: INDIRECT COMMANDS

1. Since Chapter 12 you have met sentences like these:

   servī, mē adiuvāte!
   Help me, slaves!

   nōlī clāmāre verba mala!
   Don't shout out rude words!

   These are known as **direct commands**: someone is giving a command directly to someone else.

2. Now look at these sentences:

   Nerō servīs imperāvit ut sē adiuvārent.
   Nero ordered the slaves to help him.
   (lit. *Nero ordered the slaves that they help him.*)

   Dēmētrius Lēandrum ōrābat nē verba mala clāmāret.
   Demetrius was begging Leander not to shout out rude words.
   (lit. *Demetrius was begging Leander that he not shout out rude words.*)

   The clauses in red are known as **indirect commands**, as the direct command is being reported.

3. Indirect commands are introduced by **ut** (or **nē** when someone is told not to do something) and are followed by a verb in the subjunctive (e.g. **adiuvārent**, **clāmāret**).

4. Although **ut** often means *that*, indirect commands are usually represented in English by an infinitive (e.g. *He ordered the slaves* ***to help*** *him*).

5. You may find indirect commands after verbs such as **imperō** (*order*), **ōrō** (*beg*), **petō** (*beg, ask*), **moneō** (*advise, warn*), **persuādeō** (*persuade*), and **hortor** (*encourage, urge*).

LANGUAGE PRACTICE

1. Choose the correct verb to complete the sentence, then translate.

   a. ille lēgātus equitibus imperāvit ut hostibus ferōcibus ....
   (prōmitterent, dēspērārent, resisterent)

   b. rēgem scelestum petīverāmus ut cibum līberīs pauperibus ....
   (terrēret, praebēret, appārēret)

   c. ducem vestrum monuistis nē pecūniam senum ....
   (raperet, sentīret, occīderet)

   d. soror nōs hortāta est ut sibi semper ....
   (addūcerēmus, acciderēmus, pārērēmus)

   e. heri illa tē saepe ōrābat ut librum ....
   (regerēs, redderēs, gererēs)

   f. hic vir mihi persuāserat nē maiōrem cēnam ....
   (fugerem, cōgerem, cōnsūmerem)

somnium

Nerō, ē somnō subitō excitātus, exclāmāvit. adeō perterritus erat imperātor ut custōdēs Batāvōs fidēlēs statim ad sē vocāret. 'rēs dīrās somniō vīdī! ōmen est!

'in silvā dēnsā eram. super mē novem vulturēs volitābant in caelō. prōgressus per silvam, leōnem aegrum cōnspexī. cum animal adiuvāre vellem, eī appropinquābam. sed leō, morbō tandem cōnfectus, conlāpsus est. leōnem hortātus sum ut surgeret, sed iam perierat. trīstis eum adlocūtus sum: "ubi est coniūnx tua? quō comitēs fidēlēs abiērunt? cūr in hōc locō sōlus mortuus es? quam crūdēle est fātum!" tum vōx procul audīta est: "cavē, Nerō! tāle fātum tibi mox aderit!" et faciēs appāruit. Lōcusta erat.

'intellegitisne? Lōcusta mē necāre vult,' susurrāvit Nerō. Batāvī, cum dē somniō audīvissent, prīncipem graviter monēbant nē cibum cōnsūmeret, nisi ā servō gustātum.

somnium *dream*
novem *nine*
vultur *vulture*
coniūnx *partner, wife*
faciēs *face*

The stadium at Olympia as it looks now.

Pherenīcē et Cynisca

in fundō, quī prope Olympiam erat, māter et duae fīliae sedentēs labōrābant. clāmōrēs virōrum audīre poterant. fīlia minor Pherenīcē, quīnque annōs nāta, 'māter,' inquit, 'cūr clāmōrem maximum audīmus?' eī respondit Eirēnē māter, 'hodiē plūrimī lūdōs spectant. imperātor ipse adest.'

fīlia maior, Cynisca nōmine, mātrem rogāvit cūr lūdōs nōn spectāret. 'nōn licet mātrōnīs lūdōs spectāre,' inquit Eirēnē. 'ergō domī maneō.' Pherenīcē cognōscere volēbat num mātrōnae lūdōs umquam spectāvissent. māter dīxit, 'ex lēge, mātrōna quae lūdōs spectāns invenītur morte pūnītur.'

'quot mātrōnae inventae sunt?' rogāvit Cynisca. 'ūna,' respondit māter. 'illa fīlium in lūdīs pugnantem spectābat. quamquam vestīmenta virī gerēbat, victōriam celebrāns agnita est. sed, quod pater et frātrēs et fīlius corōnās Olympiacās accēperant, nōn necāta est.' Pherenīcē quaesīvit quod nōmen huic fēminae fuisset. Eirēnē rīdēns 'eius nōmen tibi dedī!' inquit. Pherenīcē quoque rīdēbat.

tum soror rogāvit cūr nōmen suum esset Cynisca. Eirēnē fābulam nārrāvit. 'ut trāditum est, ōlim erat fīlia rēgis, Cynisca nōmine. aurīgās et equōs habēbat, et eīs imperāverat ut in lūdīs currerent. equī Cyniscae tam celerēs erant ut omnēs aliōs vincerent. quamquam Cynisca nōn aderat, corōnam Olympiacam accēpit.'

Cynisca laetissima clāmāvit, 'ego quoque corōnam accipere cupiō!' 'sunt lūdī in quibus puellae contendunt,' inquit māter. 'fortasse vōs exercēre dēbētis!' statim Cynisca et Pherenīcē per agrōs currere coepērunt.

quīnque *five*
nascor *I am born*
num *whether*
ex lēge *according to law*
corōna *garland, crown*
Olympiacus *Olympic*
trādō *I hand down*
contendō *I compete*
exerceō *I exercise, train*

An inscription recording athletic prizes from various Greek games, from the second century AD.

Sport and exercise

The most popular sports in ancient Rome were those in which respectable Roman citizens were spectators rather than participants: the gladiators, charioteers, and animal fighters in the arena were almost always enslaved people or convicted criminals. Originally, the sports and exercise enjoyed by upper-class Roman men were those which were a kind of military training. Cato the Elder (234–149 BC) saw to the physical education of his son:

> He taught his son not only to throw a javelin, to fight in armor, and to ride a horse, but also to box, to endure both heat and cold, and to be a strong swimmer in the river's rough currents.
>
> *Plutarch*

HUNTING

Hunting was a favorite leisure activity of upper-class Roman men. They often owned country estates where they would go to relax, away from city life. Pliny, for example, went hunting when he stayed at his country villa. In one of his letters he says this about being on his country estate:

> **ibi animō, ibi corpore maximē valeō. nam studiīs animum, vēnātū corpus exerceō.**
>
> There, I am extremely healthy in both mind and body, as I exercise my mind by studying and my body by hunting.

Sometimes he combined physical and intellectual activity. In another letter, this is how he describes catching three wild boars:

> **ad rētia sedēbam; erat in proximō nōn vēnābulum aut lancea, sed stilus et pugillārēs.**
>
> I was sitting by the nets; next to me there was no hunting spear or javelin, but a pen and writing tablets.

The prey and the hunting methods employed varied across the Empire. In Italy, hunters went on foot or on horseback, using trained hunting dogs, and the prey included deer, wild boar, and hare.

ATHLETICS

In Achaea and the eastern part of the Empire, Greek-style sports continued to be popular under Roman rule. Moreover, the influence of Greek sport began to be felt in Rome. Athletic and combat sports – running, discus, javelin, wrestling, boxing, and the pankration – started to play a part in the culture and entertainment of the city.

Some emperors promoted Greek-style sporting exhibitions and competitions, often with athletes who came from Greece for the occasion. Nero introduced a festival, the Neronia, which was modeled on Greek festivals and included competitions in athletics. Tacitus records that this innovation had a mixed reception. Most people were pleased, but some thought that athletics had a bad influence on Roman youth – this hostility was based partly on their disapproval of the Greek practice of exercising naked.

Emperor Domitian built the first Greek-style stadium in Rome on the Campus Martius, specifically for athletic training and competitions. It was opened in AD 86 as the venue for the first Capitoline Games in honor of Jupiter.

BOXING AND WRESTLING

Young Roman men boxed and wrestled as a form of exercise in the palaestra at the baths. Boxing and wrestling were also spectator sports, and matches were included in some of the games. Roman boxing was a brutal and dangerous sport. The fighters wrapped leather thongs, sometimes reinforced with pieces of metal, round their hands. They were designed to cause injury to one's opponent, not for protection. This poem about a boxer called Olympikos gives an idea of the injuries a boxer could suffer:

A pair of terracotta figurines.

> Olympikos, who now looks like this, once had a nose, a chin, eyebrows, ears, and eyes. Then he entered a boxing contest and lost them all. As a result, he did not even receive his share of his father's estate. His brother had a picture of him, which he showed to the judge. The judge decided that the picture was of another man, who bore no resemblance to Olympikos.
>
> *Lucillius*

SWIMMING

Men and women enjoyed swimming, both in pools at some bath complexes, and in rivers, lakes, and the sea. Some luxurious private houses also had their own pools. In Rome, men swam in the River Tiber. Cicero said to Clodia:

> You have gardens next to the river, at the spot where all the young men go to swim.

Baiae, on the Bay of Naples near Pompeii, was a fashionable seaside resort where wealthy Romans went for holidays. The poet Propertius described his girlfriend Cynthia swimming at Baiae.

FENCING

Romans practiced fencing with wooden swords, with the tips covered to avoid injuries.

BALL GAMES

The medical writer Galen recommended playing ball games as a cheap and safe way of keeping fit, and various ball games were popular forms of exercise. A special court for playing ball games was attached to some baths, and private villas sometimes had their own court. A favorite game was ***trigōn*** (triangle): three players stood in the form of a triangle and threw balls to each other.

HORSE RIDING

Horses were expensive, so only the rich were able to afford to ride for pleasure. Riding was one of the forms of exercise which was enjoyed on the Campus Martius in Rome. Boys and young men from elite families displayed their skill in the Troy Game (***lūsus Troiae***), a horse parade and paramilitary drill performed regularly in the Circus Maximus. Nero took part when he was nine years old.

SOURCE 1

Look at Source 1.

This section of a mosaic from a villa in Sicily dates from the fourth century AD.

- What are the women wearing?
- What are they doing?
- Focus on the three figures in the bottom panel on the left. What do you think is happening here?
- How useful do you think this mosaic is as evidence for the life of women in Rome in the time of our stories?

SOURCE 2

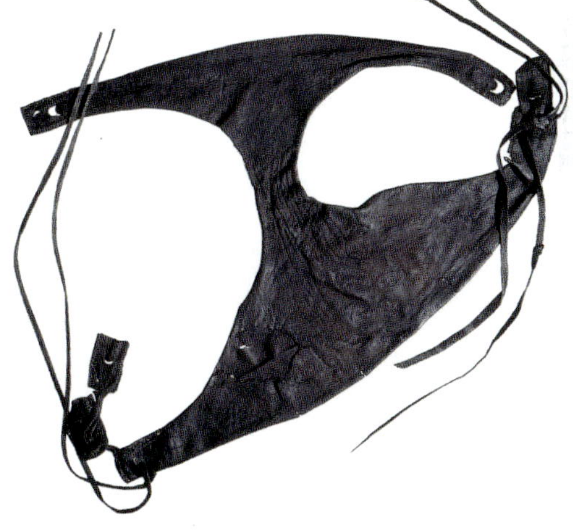

Look at Source 2.

This object is from Roman London.

- What do you think this object might be?
  (Hint: it is something you can see in Source 1.)
- What do you think it is made of?
- To whom might it have belonged?

LANGUAGE NOTE 2: INDIRECT QUESTIONS

1. You have so far met many direct questions. For example:

   cūr clāmōrem audīmus?
   Why are we hearing shouting?

   ubi est Hermionē?
   Where is Hermione?

2. Now look at the following sentences:

   mātrem rogāvit cūr clāmōrem audīrent.
   She asked her mother why they were hearing shouting.

   Sabīna quaesīvit ubi esset Hermionē.
   Sabina asked where Hermione was.

   The clauses in red are known as **indirect questions**, as the direct question is reported.

3. Indirect questions are introduced by question words (such as **cūr**, **ubi**) and are followed by a verb in the subjunctive (e.g. **audīrent**, **esset**).

4. You may find indirect questions after verbs such as **rogō** (*ask*), **petō** (*seek, ask*), **quaerō** (*inquire, ask*), **intellegō** (*understand*), **cognōscō** (*find out*), and phrases such as **incertus sum** (*I am uncertain*) and **dubium est** (*it is doubtful*).

5. When **num** introduces an indirect question, it means *whether* or *if*. For example:

   nesciēbam num ille cibum cōnsūmpsisset.
   I did not know whether he had eaten the food.

LANGUAGE PRACTICE

2. Choose the correct form of the verb to complete the sentence, then translate.

   a. nesciēbāmus num vōs opus ante lūcem .... (cōnfēcissētis, cōnfēcissem, cōnfēcissent)

   b. quaesīvī quot diēs tū sōlus domī .... (mānsissem, mānsissēs, mānsisset)

   c. tandem ille intellēxit quālēs cīvēs in eō locō .... (habitārent, habitārēmus, habitārētis)

   d. cognōscere volēbātis quōmodo captīvī portās .... (frēgissem, frēgissent, frēgissēs)

   e. imperātor incertus erat quantae hostium cōpiae .... (esset, essem, essent)

   f. eōs rogāvistī cūr illī tam longum iter .... (facerēs, facerētis, facerent)

statua nova prīncipis

prope templum Iovis magna turba spectātōrum stābat. Nerō, corōnam gerēns, laetissimus prōcēdēbat. prō templō erat statua nova vēlō cēlāta. omnēs scīre volēbant quae faciēs statuae esset. artifex, quī statuam fēcerat, prope opus suum imperātōrem ānxiē exspectābat. aderat quoque Crītō, ūnus ex iūdicibus lūdōrum. Crītō Nerōnem adlocūtus est:

'optime prīnceps, cōtīdiē ostendis tē esse benignum sapientemque. heri dēmōnstrāvistī tē esse quoque aurīgam meliōrem quam omnēs aliōs. nunc es victor Olympiae et statua victōriam tuam dēmōnstrāre dēbet. optime prīnceps, iam statuam tibi fēcimus.'

Nerō, cum haec verba audīvisset, statim clāmāvit, 'mihi maximē placet hanc statuam accipere, quae inter āthlētās optimōs semper stābit.' nōnnūllī spectantium rem rīdiculam esse putābant. statua enim ante victōriam Nerōnis facta erat. omnēs tamen tacēbant.

imperātor Crītōnem rogāvit quis statuam fēcisset. 'artificem perītissimum statuam tuam facere iussimus, optime prīnceps. omnēs artem eius adeō mīrātī sunt ut eī nōmen "Promētheum" darent. centum diēs hanc statuam faciēbat. eam vidēre vīs?'

Promētheus vēlum dē statuā lentē dētrahēbat. statua aēnea in sōle fulgēbat. omnēs obstupefactī statuam īnspiciēbant. subitō vōx minima audīta est: 'statua nōn est similis prīncipī!' omnēs putābant haec verba vēra esse, quod statua erat multō pulchrior maiorque quam imperātor. Crītō ērubēscēbat. Promētheus perterritus erat.

Nerō statuam iterum īnspiciēbat. 'haec statua pulchra mihi valdē placet,' clāmāvit. omnēs statim prīncipī plaudere coepērunt.

iūdex *judge*
victor *winner*
Olympiae *at Olympia*
āthlēta *athlete*
rīdiculus *laughable*
perītus *skillful*
Promētheus *Prometheus (mythical sculptor, created mankind)*
centum *hundred*
dētrahō *I pull down*
aēneus *bronze*
obstupefaciō *I astonish, amaze*
minimus *very small, tiny*

The body

Many Romans considered that, for a man, the care of one's body was an important duty and a demonstration of self-control, virtue, and discipline. A man's body not only displayed physical qualities but also indicated what sort of man he was and what sort of life he lived. Health experts were available, ranging from doctors to personal trainers. There was also a flourishing business in manuals, which gave advice on how to maintain a healthy body, what to eat and drink, how often to bathe, what type of exercise to do, and how long to sleep. In general, the Romans conceived of a healthy body in terms of balance and moderation: one should not get too hot, nor too cold, one should exercise regularly but not too strenuously, one should be neither too fat nor too thin.

It is important to remember that only those with the luxury of time and money could afford to choose their diet or spend hours in the palaestra. The majority of the population was engaged in work that was physically demanding.

Keeping fit

Roman doctors prescribed moderate daily exercise to keep healthy. Suggested exercises included reading aloud, ball games, running, and walking (walking uphill or downhill was encouraged in order to vary the movement of the body more). Although regular exercise was advised, Celsus, a medical writer from the first century AD, says that, unlike an athlete, one should not exercise to the point of exhaustion and should take a short rest after.

Physical disabilities

It is difficult to estimate how common physical disabilities were in the Roman Empire, but it is likely that the proportion of the population who had a disability would have been considerably higher than it is today. There are many reasons for this, including malnutrition, disease, hard labor, and injuries caused by sports, warfare, and dangerous jobs. Generally, the Romans were not sympathetic towards people with disabilities and some physical deformities were mocked. Attitudes towards different disabilities varied, and the law made allowances for certain disabilities. For example, people who were deaf were given a representative in court if necessary.

The biggest factor determining an individual's quality of life was undoubtedly wealth. In a society without a welfare state, people with disabilities did not receive public money and support, and if they were unable to work would have to rely on their families or resort to begging.

SOURCE 1

Celsus prescribes a healthy lifestyle:

> A man should sail, hunt, rest sometimes, but more often he should exercise; for while laziness weakens the body, work strengthens it; the former brings on old age, the latter prolongs youth. It is good sometimes to go to the hot bath and sometimes to wash with cold water. A man ought not to avoid any kind of food that is commonly eaten. Sometimes he should eat more than he needs, and another time he should hold back.

SOURCE 2

> **mēns sāna in corpore sānō**.
> A healthy mind in a healthy body.

Juvenal

SOURCE 3

Plutarch describes a dinner party where some guests refuse the luxurious meal, saying that plain foods are healthier and easier to digest. In response, another guest defends the feast:

> For what kind of pain, what deprivation, what sort of drug can cure a disease as easily and simply as taking a bath at just the right time or a glass of wine when you need it? And food too, when enjoyed, can immediately cure all ailments and restore the body to its natural balance.

SOURCE 4

A character in one of Plutarch's dialogues repeats the common idea that it is best to practice healthy habits when the body is fit and well, not just when one is sick:

> Choose the life that is best, and habit will make it pleasant.

DISCUSSION

How similar are Roman ideas about maintaining a healthy body to modern ideas?

The idealized body in art

Polykleitos was a Greek sculptor who lived in the fifth century BC. He created a formula to depict the ideal male body, based on a mathematical ratio. It centers on the idea of balance and symmetry. Instead of being particularly lifelike, the proportions of his sculptures are in fact exaggerated and idealized, creating an unattainable standard of the perfect physique. None of Polykleitos' original bronze sculptures has survived. However, the Romans made many marble copies – more than twenty-five full-size copies of Polykleitos' *Diadoumenos* exist today. These would originally have been painted in bright colors, but almost no trace of the paint remains.

To make sculptures seem more lifelike, ancient artists developed the technique of depicting the body at the point of movement. In this statue (*right*) the figure's weight is resting on one leg and his torso is slightly turned, as if he is just about to walk away.

Right: a Roman marble copy of Polykleitos' 'Diadoumenos' (Youth tying a ribbon). The ribbon is a symbol of winning an athletic competition.

Brains vs brawn

Some Romans cautioned against too much exercise. Seneca wrote to Lucilius Senior, comparing intellectual and physical training:

> For it is foolish, my dear Lucilius, and improper for an educated man to be straining his muscles and broadening his shoulders and strengthening his chest. Although feasting will bring gains for you and your muscles will swell, you will never equal a prime bull in either strength or weight. And what's more, by over-feeding your body your soul is strangled and is less lively. And so, as much as you can, keep your body in check and let your mind be free.

Weight-training was practiced by athletes as a means of building strength, as well as increasing muscle size and definition. Exercises included biceps curls and lunges. Female weightlifters are also mentioned by Juvenal.

QUESTION

Do you think that physical and intellectual achievements are equally valued nowadays?

Left: a Roman statue of Hercules. As a hero famous for his superhuman strength, he was the perfect patron of athletics, and statues such as this one were popular in Roman palaestrae where athletes and citizens trained.

necāre nec necārī

'hōc tempore sine difficultāte eum necāre possum, propter propinquitātem nostram. necāre tamen nec necārī – id est multō difficilius,' Indus sibi putābat.

ille pōculum exhaustum dēposuit et tabernam circumspectāvit. plēna erat iuvenibus dīvitibus puellās petentibus, āthlētīs victōriā gaudentibus, comitibus inter sē multa loquentibus āleamque lūdentibus. in angulō sedēbat parva manus hominum, quī circum minimam mēnsam tacitē bibēbant. Indus faciēs eōrum nōn agnōvit. incertus erat num sē spectārent. sub vestīmentīs pugiōnem tam lentē quaesīvit ut nēmō sentīret. undique perīcula, aut speciem perīculōrum, vīdit, sed proelium committere hodiē minimē volēbat.

ille gemitum dedit. Lūcīlius eī imperāverat ut cōnsilium, quō Nerōnem necāre possent, paucīs diēbus caperet. Indus tamen cōnsilia pessima modo habēre adhūc potuerat. intereā legiōnēs Othōnis nōndum parātae erant. etiam īnsuper lēgātī imperiō aliārum legiōnum iam cōgitābant num ipsī ad bellum proficīscī dēbērent, et incertī erant cui favērent. Indus nesciēbat quōmodo Othō pācem inter lēgātōs servāret. praetereā Giscō, cui sōlī ille crēdere poterat, ab urbe Pompēiīs profectus, Rōmam iam advēnerat; Nerō tamen etiam nunc Olympiae erat. sine dubiō rēs nōn facilis erat.

Lūcīlius, eō tempore tabernam ingressus, tam subitō apud eum sēdit ut Indus suam manum pugiōne vulnerāret. ille ab Indō statim petīvit num cōnsilium cēpisset. hic prīmō rīsit, deinde respondit sē optimum cōnsilium habēre.

'Lūcīlī, necesse est Nerōnī suā manū perīre.'

propinquitās *closeness, proximity*

exhauriō *I finish, empty*
ālea *game of dice, a die*
angulus *corner*
undique *everywhere*
speciēs *appearance*

īnsuper *moreover*
lēgātus *commander*
imperium *command*
praetereā *besides, furthermore*

LANGUAGE NOTE 3: 5TH DECLENSION NOUNS

1. Look at the following sentences. What do you notice about the endings of **diēs** and **rēs**?

    paucīs diēbus nāvigābunt.
    They will sail in a few days.

    contrōversiās dē rērum nātūrā habēbāmus.
    We used to have discussions about the nature of things.

    There are five declensions of Latin nouns, and **diēs** and **rēs** belong to the **fifth declension**.

2. The endings of **rēs** *f.* (*thing, matter*) are as follows:

	singular	*plural*
nominative	**rēs**	**rēs**
genitive	**reī**	**rērum**
dative	**reī**	**rēbus**
accusative	**rem**	**rēs**
ablative	**rē**	**rēbus**

3. When looking up words in a dictionary, fifth declension nouns can be identified by their nominative singular ending -**ēs** and genitive singular ending -**eī** (or -**ēī**). For example:

    diēs, diēī, *m.* — *day*
    spēs, speī, *f.* — *hope*

4. Other common fifth declension nouns include **aciēs** (*edge; battle line*), **faciēs** (*face, appearance*), **fidēs** (*faith, loyalty*), and **speciēs** (*view; appearance*). Other than **diēs** and its compound **merīdiēs** (*midday*), all fifth declension nouns are feminine.

LANGUAGE PRACTICE

3. Choose the correct form of the noun to complete the sentence, then translate.

    a. duōs .... proelium dīrum patī cōgēbāmur. (diēs, diērum, diēī)
    b. in .... salūtis, ad silvam proximam fūgerant. (spēs, speī, spē)
    c. .... nostrās ad sōlem tollēmus atque gaudēbimus. (faciērum, faciēbus, faciēs)
    d. amor atque spēs sunt omnium .... parentēs. (rēs, rērum, reī)
    e. sanguinis .... ferre nōn possunt. (speciē, speciēī, speciem)

Echo and Narcissus

Echo was a nymph, a semi-divine spirit. She fell in love with Narcissus, an exceptionally beautiful young man, but he rejected her.

- Now read or listen to the story of Echo and Narcissus.

Changing shape

Both Echo and Narcissus were changed into something else. A common theme in myth is the metamorphosis (transformation) of a human or semi-divine being into another creature or something from nature such as an echo, a flower, or a tree. The Roman poet Ovid wrote a long poem, *Metamorphoses*, which connects many stories featuring metamorphosis into a single narrative. Some other myths featuring a metamorphosis are:

- Hyacinthus, a young man changed into a flower.
- Baucis and Philemon, a husband and wife changed into trees.

Look at Sources 1 and 2. What part of the myth did the painter choose to depict? What hints of the metamorphosis are within the paintings?

Narcissus and narcissism

You may have come across people being described as 'narcissists' or 'narcissistic'. What kind of behavior does this describe? How does narcissism relate to the story of Narcissus?

SOURCE 1

A painting of Echo and Narcissus by John William Waterhouse, from 1903.

SOURCE 2

'The Metamorphosis of Narcissus' by Salvador Dalí, painted in 1937.

Impossible love

Narcissus had already rejected many admirers – both male and female – before seeing his own reflection in the pool. His instant infatuation with his own beauty leads ultimately to his downfall, as he wastes away and is in the end transformed into a flower.

- Look at Source 3. How does Ovid reflect the impossible nature of Narcissus' love in his words? Do you think the story of Narcissus is a warning?

SOURCE 3

It is himself he desires, though he does not know it, and the admirer is himself admired. While he desires, he is desired; at the same time, he inflames and he burns. Often he gave worthless kisses to the deceitful stream. Often, trying to embrace the neck he could see, he plunged his arms into the water and did not catch himself in it.

Ovid

RESEARCH

1. Find out about the story of Hyacinthus and the story of Baucis and Philemon.
2. Why do you think people have found the idea of metamorphosis so fascinating? Do you know any modern stories which feature a transformation?

Chapter 26: Delphī

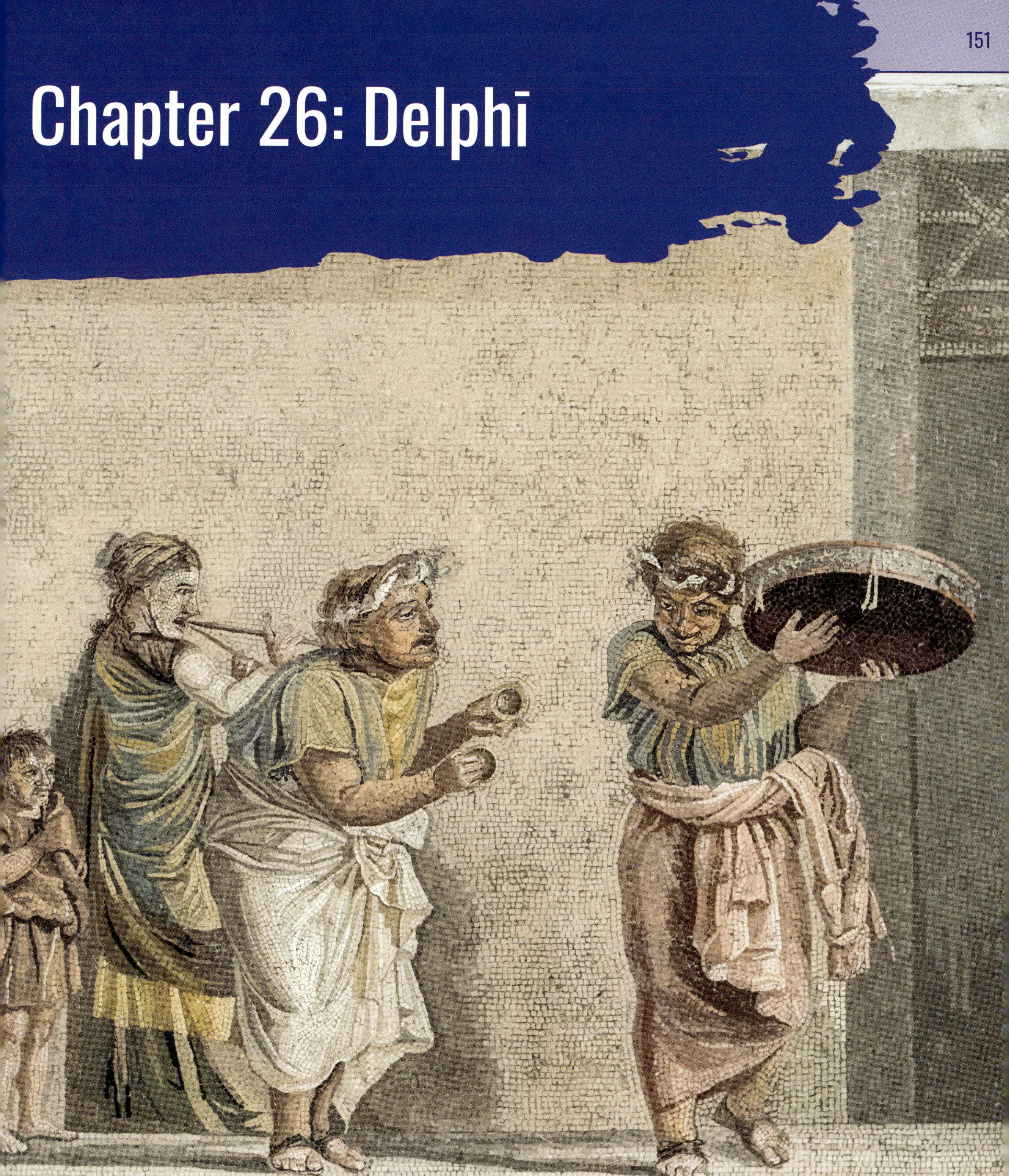

A mosaic from Pompeii showing a group of musicians.

mūsicus (īn)fēlīx
1 prō templō Apollinis Delphicī, quīnque mūsicī canēbant et saltābant, terram pedibus pulsantēs.
mūsicus *musician*
Delphicus *Delphic, of Delphi*
saltō *I dance*
2 cūr vōs ad templum deī vēnistis?
3 abhinc octo diēbus nōs ad templum profectī sumus ut dōna deō Apollinī offerrēmus.
abhinc *ago*
4 alius mūsicus tamen nōn saltābat.
5 cūr tū hūc vēnistī?

6 ego quoque longē prōgressus sum ut dōnum deō darem. auxilium ā deō petō.
7 abhinc diēbus decem, canis meus mortuus est.
8 multum vīnum igitur bibēbam. nam trīstis eram.
9 cum essem ēbrius, īrāta erat amīca mea. postrīdiē illa mē relīquit ut alium peteret.
ēbrius *drunk*
10 trīstior eram. itaque per tōtam noctem plūs vīnī bibēbam et tībiīs lyrāque canēbam, nē dē trīstibus cōgitārem.
11 circum mē silva erat, unde multa animālia cautē appropinquābant, ut carmina dulcia audīrent.
tībiae *pipes*
lyra *lyre*
cautē *cautiously*

12 lyram in terrā mox dēposuī, ut tībiīs canerem et saltārem.
13 propius propiusque animālia convēnērunt, ut tībiās audīrent et mē saltantem spectārent.
propius *nearer*
14 sed haedus appropinquāvit et lyram, in terrā dēpositam, calcāvit. eam frēgit.
15 itaque ad tabernam adiī ut lyram novam emerem. nunc tamen pecūniam nūllam habeō.
16 tum ad summum theātrum prōcessērunt ut lātum prōspectum peterent.
17 fēlīx es! sine dubiō Apollō tibi favet.
18 certē! sī nūllum canem, nūllam puellam, nūllam pecūniam habēs, mūsicus optimus eris!
lātus *wide, broad*
prōspectus *view*

LANGUAGE NOTE 1: PURPOSE CLAUSES

1. Look at the following sentences:

   longē prōgressus sum ut dōnum deō darem.
   I traveled a long way to give a gift to the god.
   (lit. *I traveled a long way in order that I might give a gift to the god.*)

   illa mē relīquit ut alium peteret.
   She left me to look for another man.
   (lit. *She left me in order that she might look for another man.*)

   lyrā canēbam nē dē trīstibus cōgitārem.
   I was playing the lyre so that I wouldn't think about sad things.
   (lit. *I was playing the lyre in order that I might not think about sad things.*)

   The clauses in red tell us what the purpose, or aim, of an action was and are therefore called **purpose clauses**.

2. Purpose clauses can answer the question '*Why?*' For example, '*Why did you travel a long way?*' or '*Why did your girlfriend leave you?*'

3. Purpose clauses are introduced by **ut** (meaning *in order that, so that*) or **nē** (meaning *in order that ... not, so that ... not*) and are followed by a verb in the subjunctive (e.g. **darem**, **peteret**, **cōgitārem**).

A terracotta tile showing three musicians.

Music

Music played an important part in Roman life. On the streets of the towns and cities performers offered musical entertainment, and in private homes musicians and singers accompanied dinner parties. The Romans enjoyed concerts and other forms of musical entertainment. Dramatic performances (tragedies and comedies) and pantomimes, which were quite similar to modern operas, also involved music and singing. Spectacles in the arena, such as gladiator fights, were accompanied by musicians. In the army, various instruments were used in battle to signal attack and retreat, and to proclaim victory.

Almost all religious ceremonies required music. Certain instruments were thought to ward off bad spirits; for example, the sistrum was used in the worship of Isis and the tibia was played at sacrifices. Songs were performed on some public occasions. For instance, during the Ludi Saeculares in 17 BC, a choir of young boys and girls sang the *Carmen Saeculare*, a hymn which had been composed for the occasion by the poet Horace.

Who played music?

Ordinary people in towns and in the countryside made music on simple instruments. Writers, such as Vergil, wrote poetry set in the idyllic countryside. These poems refer to the pipes and songs of shepherds. Although these poems are idealized descriptions, scholars believe some forms of modern Italian folk music probably descend from ancient Roman folk music played on the pipe and drum.

In Rome, professional musicians were usually people of low status, often foreign immigrants. Some enslaved people were skilled musicians or singers, and they provided entertainment at dinner parties. Although some young men and women from upper-class families played an instrument, it was thought improper to be too skilled a performer or a professional musician. Some Romans wrote about their disapproval of how much Greek culture and music were infiltrating Roman society, and they associated this with decadence and loose morals:

> Romans, I cannot bear that our city is now Greek; and yet, how few of these dregs are even Greek! For Syrian Orontes* has long since flowed into the Tiber, bringing its language, customs, harps, pipes, and even its traditional tambourines.
>
> *A river that flows through Syria. *Juvenal*

Musical competitions

As we saw in Chapter 25, musical contests were common at festivals in Greece and the eastern provinces of the Empire. Traditional competitions had five main categories: singing with the cithara, reciting poetry to music, solo pipe playing, solo cithara playing, and singing accompanied by the pipe. Musical competitions were not common in Rome until Nero introduced one as part of the Neronia, a new Greek-style festival. There were also musical competitions at the Capitoline Games, first celebrated in AD 86.

Musical performances were physically demanding and required a great deal of stamina. Musicians trained in the manner of athletes to get themselves in peak condition. Suetonius wrote that Nero used to lie on his back and place a lead weight on his chest to strengthen his breathing. The panel of judges took into account not only the technical skill of the musicians, but also their showmanship and performance. The audience's response was also considered when awarding prizes.

Written music

There are no surviving examples of music written in a Latin notation. However, some musical texts in Greek notation have been found. The oldest example of a complete piece of music is the Seikilos song:

C Z Z K I Z I K I Ż I K O C O Φ
Ὅ σον ζῇς, φαί νου, μη δὲν ὅλ ως σὺ λυ ποῦ·
C K Z İ K İ K C O Φ C K O İ Ż K̇ C C C X I
πρὸς ὀλ ί γον ἐ στὶ τὸ ζῆν, τὸ τέ λος ὁ χρόνος ἀπαι τεῖ.

The lyrics are written in Greek, which was the most widely spoken language in the eastern provinces. The letters above the lyrics indicate the tone, and the signs above them indicate the duration of the note. Although we can interpret the notation, scholars debate exactly how the song would have sounded.

The Seikilos song was inscribed on a funerary monument (*right*). It was found near Ephesus, a city in modern-day Turkey which was part of the Roman Empire. The monument has been dated to the first or second century AD.

WIND INSTRUMENTS

Tuba

A tuba was a long, straight tube made of bronze, with a flared end. It could produce only a limited range of notes. It was used to give signals, especially in the army, and it accompanied games in the arena and parades.

Cornu

A cornu was a curved, metal horn which circled around the arm of the musician. Like the tuba, it was used in the army and as an accompaniment for parades and spectacles. Examples can be seen in the relief below and on page 63.

Tibia

A tibia was a pipe, similar to a modern oboe. Double pipes were common; although the two pipes were not usually joined, both were held between the musician's lips and played simultaneously (see pages 151 and 155). Openings along the pipe could be covered by the player's fingers; this enabled a wide range of notes to be produced. A player sometimes wore a leather head strap to hold the pipe or pipes in place and lessen the strain on the cheeks. Different versions of the pipe included one held horizontally like a modern flute, and one similar to bagpipes.

STRING INSTRUMENTS

Lyre

Originally a lyre was a tortoise shell with strings stretched across. Later, lyres were made of wood. A musician held the lyre in one hand and plucked the strings with the other, using a plectrum. The number of strings varied, although seven was common. The various notes were produced by the differing thickness of the strings.

Cithara

Similar to the lyre, but larger, the cithara could have up to twelve strings and produced a louder sound. It was held upright and the musician sometimes plucked it with both hands, like a modern harp.

Above: in this wall painting from the dining room of a villa at Boscoreale, near Pompeii, a woman is playing a cithara.

PERCUSSION

To keep time and rhythm, musicians would clap their hands and stamp their feet and play percussion instruments. Drums and tambourines were common, as well as rattles and bells. Roman musicians also used ***cymbala*** (cymbals), small metal discs with concave centers, which were clashed together to produce a bright, ringing sound.

A small metal cymbal. It would originally have been one of a pair.

WATER ORGAN

The water organ is the earliest example of a keyboard instrument. Water, supplied in a continuous flow, drove air through pipes of varying sizes along the organ and produced different notes. An example of the water organ being played to accompany a gladiatorial fight can be seen on page 63.

Nerō canēns

in theātrō Nerō lyram digitīs increpāns magnā vōce canēbat. dum prīnceps canēbat, multī spectātōrēs eum audiēbant. omnēs crēdēbant spectāculum esse rīdiculum. aliī putābant vōcem prīncipis esse pessimam; aliī carminibus ipsīs nōn dēlectābantur. spectātōrēs cōnfectī sunt, cum iam septem sedērent hōrās. nēmō tamen ē theātrō exīre audēbat nē imperātōrem offenderet.

subitō, dum prīnceps canit, senex, quī prope scaenam sedēbat, cum gemitū conlāpsus est. statim duo sacerdōtēs ad senem exanimātum cucurrērunt ut eum ē theātrō quam celerrimē portārent. dum senex portābātur, Nerō carmen canere persevērābat.

digitus *finger*
increpō *I play, pluck*
spectāculum *sight, spectacle*
offendō *I offend*
persevērō *I carry on*

sacerdōtēs senem ad fontem portāvērunt ut eī aquam darent. sacerdōs senior alterī imperāvit ut pōculum ferret. 'nōnne senex īnfēlīx mortuus est?' respondit ille lacrimāns, 'eī aqua est inūtilis!'

simulatque haec verba audīvit, senex ūnum oculum aperuit. 'nōlīte timēre, amīcī,' susurrāvit. 'vīvus sum! mihi ignōscite. mortem simulāvī ut ē theātrō exīrem. carmina prīncipis audīre patī nōn poteram plūra.'

sacerdōtēs paulisper tacēbant, sed mox rīdēbant. 'grātiās tibi agimus,' inquit sacerdōs iūnior, 'quod nōs quoque servāvistī!'

'cōnsentiō,' susurrāvit alter. 'vōx prīncipis est peior quam omnēs aliae. Nerō certē Apollinem offendit.'

'minimē decet imperātōrem in scaenā canere,' senex respondit. 'Nerō redīre Rōmam, rem pūblicam cūrāre dēbet.'

in theātrō intereā spectātōrēs similia cōgitantēs etiam nunc prīncipem audiēbant.

A coin from AD 64. On one side is the head of Emperor Nero, on the other Apollo playing the lyre.

Poetry

From epic to epigram

Along with art, athletics, and music, poetry was an area in which the Romans were influenced by the Greeks. Greek poets had developed several kinds (genres) of poetry, such as epic, and almost all Roman poetry was in one of these genres. Subject matter, vocabulary, and meter (rhythm) varied according to the genre.

epic: a long poem which tells a story from myth, legend, or history. Vergil modeled his epic poem the *Aeneid* on the *Iliad* and *Odyssey* of the Greek poet Homer. Like Homer's poems, the *Aeneid* is the story of one of the heroes of the Trojan War. Ovid's *Metamorphoses*, a collection of myths linked by the idea of transformation, is a different kind of epic poem.

didactic: a long poem which sets out to teach the reader about a particular topic. For example, *De Rerum Natura* (*On the Nature of Things*) by Lucretius, explains the main principles of Epicurean philosophy. Vergil's *Georgics* gives instruction on farming.

lyric: originally, in Greek, a poem sung along to the lyre. However, in Roman times the poem was recited or read without a musical accompaniment. Popular subjects of lyric poetry were love and drinking.

satire: a poem in which the poet comments on some aspect of his society, such as social life, morality, or literature. The tone varies: some are gently humorous, some are moralizing, others are harshly critical. Juvenal's *Satires* are a savage attack on the vices of his times. Satire was not modeled on Greek poetry. Quintilian wrote:

satura quidem tōta nostra est.
Satire, at least, is all our own.

epigram: short poems on various themes. Catullus wrote epigrams expressing his personal feelings of love and hate. Martial's epigrams are often witty and have a surprising twist at the end.

nōn amo tē, Sabidī, nec possum dīcere quārē.
hoc tantum possum dīcere – nōn amo tē.
I do not like you, Sabidius, and I can't say why.
Only this can I say – I don't like you.

Poetry and music

The Latin word for poem is ***carmen***, which means 'song'. The Romans took from the Greeks the idea that music and poetry are closely connected. Although there were competitions and performances involving words sung to music, most Roman poetry was not sung or accompanied by music. However, Roman poets sometimes refer to their poems as if they are songs. The *Aeneid* of Vergil was recited, not sung, yet its opening words are:

arma virumque canō ...
I sing of war and a man ...

Roman poetry was intended for reciting aloud, as well as for private reading. This means that the sound of the words and the meter are particularly important.

These lines from the *Aeneid* describe Aeneas' descent into the Underworld:

ībant obscūrī sōlā sub nocte per umbram
perque domōs Dītis vacuās et inānia rēgna:
quāle per incertam lūnam sub lūce malignā
est iter in silvīs, ubi caelum condidit umbrā
Iuppiter, et rēbus nox abstulit atra colōrem.

They went, unseen, in the lonely night through shadow
And through the vacant homes of Dis and the empty kingdoms:
It is just like a journey under the malignant light [given] by an uncertain moon
In the woods, when Jupiter has buried the sky in shadow
And black night has taken color away from things.

The poets

Some poets, such as Ovid, were from wealthy families and didn't need to earn a living from writing. Others relied on a patron to support them. Both Horace and Vergil benefited early in their careers from the patronage of Maecenas, a friend of Emperor Augustus; later, Augustus himself became their patron. Writing poetry was a favorite leisure activity of educated Romans. Amateur poets, such as Pliny, would entertain their friends at private recitals and dinner parties. Some women wrote poetry too, but we know very little about them. Sulpicia, an upper-class Roman woman who lived in the late first century BC, wrote love elegies, a few of which have survived.

triumphus

Calvia Crīspinilla vīllam intrāvit, in quā imperātor, dum Delphīs manēbat, habitābat. celeriter prōgrediēbātur, epistulās portāns. nōnnūllōs Batāvōs extrā cellam invēnit, quibus imperāvit ut iānuam aperīrent. 'imperātōrem requīrō, Inde,' inquit Crīspinilla. 'nūntiōs habeō.' Indus 'ignōsce mihi, domina, imperātor nunc carmina recitat, ille …' respondēre coepit, sed interpellāvit illa: 'nūntiōs magnī mōmentī ferō, Inde.' ille minimum gemitum dedit, et iānuam aperuit ut intrāre possent.

imperātor, vestīmenta splendida et corōnam auream modō deī Apollinis gerēns, in lectō recumbēbat. Crīspinilla, simulatque intrāvit, imperātōrem adlocūta est: 'prīnceps, epistula ā Vespasiānō scrīpta hodiē advēnit. rebelliō in Iūdaeā nōndum ab eō cui imperium dedistī repressa est. lēgātus plūrēs mīlitēs requīsīvit ut hostēs opprimeret. sed rēs Rōmae peior est. lībertīs ibi imperāvī ut fāmās ex Urbe referrent. apud senātōrēs sermōnēs turbulentī habentur, imperātōrem ad Urbem revocantēs. rēs est perīculōsa, prīnceps.'

tum Crīspinilla Nerōnem magnopere hortāta est ut Rōmam redīret, senātuī placēret, rebelliōnēs in prōvinciīs quam celerrimē reprimeret. Indus hanc ōrātiōnem intentē audiēbat.

Nerō tamen Graeciam relinquere nōlēbat, nē ā lūdīs et recitātiōnibus abesset. tum Indus Crīspinillae signum oculīs dedit et imperātōrī appropinquābat. sīc prīncipem adlocūtus est: 'fortasse tē decet Rōmae triumphum agere, prīnceps. ita omnēs artem et virtūtem tuam spectābunt.' hōc modō Indus Nerōnī persuāsit. imperātor Rōmam redīre cōnstituit, ut senātus populusque Rōmānus victōriās eius agnōscerent.

triumphus *military parade, triumph*
Calvia Crīspinilla *Calvia Crispinilla (adviser to Nero)*
Delphīs *in Delphi*
recitō *I recite*

modus *manner, style, way*

rebelliō *rebellion*
Iūdaea *Judea*
reprimō *I suppress*
fāma *rumor*
Urbs *Rome*
turbulentus *troublesome*
revocō *I call back*

recitātiō *recitation, public reading*

LANGUAGE NOTE 2: DUM (WHILE)

1. Look at the following sentences. In the clauses in red, what do you notice about the tenses of the verbs?

    dum prīnceps canēbat, spectātōrēs eum audiēbant.
    While the emperor was singing, many spectators were listening to him.

    dum prīnceps canit, senex conlāpsus est.
    While the emperor was singing, an old man collapsed.

2. **dum** (meaning *while*) can be followed by a present tense in Latin, even if the action was taking place in the past. The present tense is used when the action in the **dum** clause lasts longer than the action in the main clause.

Divine inspiration: the Muses

The nine Muses were Greek goddesses of literature, music, and dance (and some other intellectual pursuits). Ancient Greek writers, especially poets, claimed to draw inspiration for their work from the Muses. Asking the Muses for inspiration was a convention in Roman poetry.

Calliope	epic poetry
Clio	history
Euterpe	lyric poetry
Melpomene	tragedy
Terpsichore	dance
Erato	love poetry
Polyhymnia	hymns to the gods
Thalia	comedy
Urania	astronomy

The nine Muses are depicted in the lower frame of this Roman sarcophagus (*below*). Look at the Muses and what they are holding. Can you identify any of them?

SOURCE 1

Near the start of the *Aeneid*, Vergil writes:

> Muse, explain to me. Why was Juno offended?
> What suffering caused the queen of the gods to force
> A man, outstanding in his sense of duty, to experience so many disasters,
> And to suffer so much? Are the hearts of the gods so full of anger?

SOURCE 2

At the beginning of the *Metamorphoses*, Ovid calls on the gods:

> Gods, inspire my attempts and spin a thread into one continuous poem.

DISCUSSION

Look at Sources 1 and 2.

1. In what ways are the requests of Vergil and Ovid similar, and in what ways are they different?
2. What do you think inspires poets and musicians today?
3. Have you ever composed a song or a poem? Where did the idea come from?

LANGUAGE PRACTICE

1. Complete each sentence with the most appropriate purpose clause, then translate.

a. ad tabernam regressa eram ...
b. templum oppugnāvistis ...
c. illae minimīs vōcibus loquēbantur ...
d. ad alium locum praemia movēbās ...
e. ōlim tōtam noctem in silvā agēbat ...
f. hanc epistulam ad sorōrem mīsī ...

i. nē inimīcus tuus ea invenīret.
ii. nē līberōs excitārent.
iii. ut eam ad cēnam invītārem.
iv. ut cīvēs Rōmānōs occīderētis.
v. ut caelum et lūnam spectāret.
vi. ut pecūniam ablātam redderem.

2. Translate each sentence into Latin by choosing the correct word or phrase from each pair.

a. *Yesterday, while I was doing these things, something else worse happened.*

heri,	simulatque	haec	ēgeram,	aliud peius	accēpit.
hodiē,	dum	hic	agō,	aliud melius	accidit.

b. *Since the legions had obeyed their leader, he gave better rewards to them.*

dum	legiōnis	ducī	pārērent,	ille	praemia optima	eī	dedit.
cum	legiōnēs	ducibus	pāruissent,	illa	praemia meliōra	eīs	daret.

c. *As soon as we reached the sea, our ship was overcome by the wind and waves.*

postquam	ad mūrum	pervēnimus,	nāvis	ventum undāsque	superāvit.
simulatque	ad mare	pervēnērunt,	nāvem	ventō undīsque	superāta est.

d. *After the animals had gathered near the wide river, they drank and ate happily.*

postquam	animālia	prō	flūmina lāta	conveniunt,	laetē	bibēbant cēnābantque.
tandem	animal	prope	flūmen lātum	convēnērunt,	lentē	bibunt cēnantque.

e. *While you were fleeing to the mountains, you suddenly caught sight of a lion.*

tum	ad montēs	fugitis,	leōnem	semper	cōnspicitis.
dum	ad montem	fūgerātis,	leōnēs	subitō	cōnspexistis.

3. Translate each sentence and state whether it contains a result clause, a purpose clause, an indirect command, or an indirect question.

a. fīlius nūllō modō mātrem cōgere poterat ut vestīmenta nova emeret.

b. tibi imperium ā nōbīs datum est ut nōs servārēs.

c. verba eius in tantam īram nōs mōverant ut bellum mox gererēmus.

d. eum rogāvistī cūr nēmō hunc hominem umquam anteā vīdisset.

e. equitēs tam celeriter prōgressī sunt ut multās fēminās vīvās caperent.

f. cīvēs eōs ōrābant nē equōs terrērent.

Recitations

In a world before the invention of the printing press, reading aloud to an audience was a cheap and easy way for a writer to publicize his work. Some writers hoped to find an audience in public places, such as the forum, the colonnades, or the baths. In this poem Martial describes how Ligurinus follows people around Rome, making a nuisance of himself by reciting his poetry:

> **in thermās fugiō: sonās ad aurem.**
> **piscīnam petō: nōn licet natāre.**
> **ad cēnam properō: tenēs euntem.**
> **ad cēnam veniō: fugās ēdentem.**
> **lassus dormiō: suscitās iacentem.**

> I flee into the baths: you make a noise in my ear.
> I head for the pool: I'm not allowed to swim.
> I hurry to dinner: you keep me back as I go.
> I arrive at dinner: you chase me out as I eat.
> Worn out, I sleep: you wake me up as I lie.

Often an author read his work aloud to an invited audience at a formal event called a ***recitātiō***. Poetry readings were the most common form of recitation, but there were also readings of prose works, such as speeches and history. The author or his patron sometimes hired a hall (***auditōrium***) for the occasion. Some houses had a private auditorium, which the owner would make available for the use of friends or rent out. Other writers recited their work in their own homes. This could be an informal occasion. Pliny, for example, sometimes recited his work (he wrote poetry and speeches as well as letters) to friends after dinner in his triclinium, bringing extra chairs into the room.

Recitations played an important part in the cultural and social life of educated Romans, as this extract from a letter of Pliny shows:

> In the whole month of April there has hardly been a day when someone was not giving a recitation. I am delighted that literature is in a healthy state, that people's talents are flourishing and revealing themselves, even if audiences are slow in attending.

Pliny goes on to describe the inattentiveness and rudeness of some audience members, a point made more strongly by Juvenal:

> Must I always be only in the audience? Shall I never pay back Codrus? He has annoyed me so often with the ranting speeches of his *Theseid*. One poet has recited his dramas to me, another his elegies. Shall they go unpunished? Lengthy versions of *Telephus* have wasted a whole day of mine. Should that be unpunished?

Usually the author read his own work, but if he lacked confidence he might get one of his slaves or freedmen to read for him.

DISCUSSION

1. How do authors publicize their work today?
2. What part does literature, in particular poetry, play in modern life?

A small terracotta statue of Apollo playing the cithara. Some colored paint still survives.

ōrāculum ultimum

priusquam Rōmam rediit, Nerō ōrāculum adīre cōnstituit, ut tempus mortis suae cognōsceret. Crīspinillae igitur imperāvit ut omnia statim parāret.

itaque postrīdiē, dum aliī dormiunt, Pȳthia vātēs prīmō in fonte Castaliō lauta est ut sē parāret, deinde montem Parnāsum ascendere coepit. cum duōbus sacerdōtibus templum lātum deī Apollinis ingressa, dēscendit sub terram in adytum obscūrum sōla.

intereā Nerō, laurōs in manibus tenēns, per Viam Sacram prōcēdēbat. eum sequēbātur Indus, perterritum agnum et manum mīlitum dūcēns. tandem tremēns ad templum pervēnit imperātor, tum in tenebrās ēvānuit ut ōrāculum cōnsuleret.

ex adytō Pȳthia terribilēs canēbat ambāgēs, obscūrīs vēra volvēns, et ingentī clāmōre resonābat adytum. cum illa tacuisset, tum incēpit Nerō:

'dīc, ō vātēs sacra, quae Apollinī cāra es. quot annī mihi nunc manent?'

tālibus ōrābat verbīs. sīc loquī coepit vātēs:

'poscere fāta tempus est,' inquit illa. 'deus ecce deus! mors tibi, ō prīnceps, numerō LXXIII scrībitur. sed tū, Caesar, quī mātrem occīdistī, īram deī valdē excitās. abī hinc, tū male! pedem Rōmam refer!'

tālia locūta tacuit. Nerō tamen nōn tacēbat. īrā incēnsus iussit vātem in adytō claudī et duōs sacerdōtēs dē rūpe statim dēicī.

dum mīlitēs sacerdōtēs exclāmantēs atque lacrimantēs ē templō trahēbant, Indus putābat scelus esse deum in īram movēre. sibi dīxit 'fortasse deus opus meum cōnficiet.'

ōrāculum *oracle*
ultimus *final*
priusquam *before*
Pȳthia *Pythia (priestess of Apollo)*
vātēs *priestess*
Castalius *Castalian*
Parnāsus *Parnassus (mountain at Delphi)*
adytum *innermost chamber*
laurus *laurel, bay*
agnus *lamb*
cōnsulō *I consult*
ambāgēs *riddle*
numerus *number*
Caesar *Caesar (title of emperor)*
hinc *from here*
rūpēs *cliff*

The remains of the Temple of Apollo at Delphi.

Oracles

Delphi

The ancient Greeks believed that Delphi, on the slopes of Mount Parnassus just north of the Gulf of Corinth, was the center of the world. A sacred stone, called the ***omphalos*** (navel), marked the spot. Delphi was a sanctuary of Apollo, and the Pythian Games were celebrated there in his honor. The Games included contests in singing along to the cithara, cithara-playing, and pipe-playing, as well as athletics and chariot-racing.

The Delphic oracle

The Greeks believed that humans could communicate with the gods by consulting an oracle, and the oracle of Apollo at Delphi was the most important in Greece. At Delphi a priestess known as the Pythia, sitting on a tripod, became possessed by Apollo. In a trance-like state, she communicated messages from the god. Her utterances were mysterious and had to be interpreted by specialist attendants. The answers were given as riddles, which were hard to decipher and could often be understood in more than one way. People traveled to Delphi to consult the oracle, and asked questions such as: Will my wife and I conceive a child? Is my proposed marriage a good idea? Should I go on a voyage?

Romans and oracles

When they visited Greece, Romans sometimes consulted the Delphic oracle, as Nero did, and near Rome there were oracles of the goddess Fortuna at Praeneste and Antium. The oracle at Antium warned Emperor Caligula: 'Beware of Cassius!' Caligula, therefore, ordered the murder of Cassius Longinus, the governor of Asia. However, this was the wrong Cassius, and Caligula was assassinated by Cassius Chaerea.

Although Romans did sometimes consult oracles, they were not an important feature of Roman religion. As the geographer Strabo explained:

> In ancient times oracles were held in greater honor, but now they are neglected, since the Romans are satisfied with the oracles of the Sibyl and with prophecies obtained from the entrails of animals, the flight of birds, and other omens.

The Sibylline Books

According to legend, the last king of Rome, Tarquinius Superbus, bought a collection of prophecies from a female prophet, the Sibyl of Cumae (Cumae was an ancient oracular shrine near Pompeii). They were known as the Sibylline Books. Originally, they were stored in the Temple of Jupiter on the Capitoline Hill; Augustus had them moved to his new temple of Apollo on the Palatine. In times of crisis the Senate consulted the Sibylline Books for guidance.

Brutus and the Delphic oracle

The Delphic oracle played a part in the overthrow of Tarquinius Superbus and the establishment of the Republic by Brutus. A snake slid out of a wooden pillar in Tarquinius' palace, and he took this as a bad omen. He was so terrified that he sent his sons to Delphi to consult the oracle. Brutus accompanied them. The two princes asked the oracle which one of Tarquinius' sons would be king. The answer was: 'Whichever of you will be first to kiss his mother, will have the supreme power at Rome.' The sons decided by lot which of them should be first to kiss their mother when they returned to Rome. But Brutus interpreted the oracle differently. He pretended to stumble, and as he fell he touched his lips to the ground, because he regarded the Earth as the common mother of all humans. On his return to Rome, he overthrew Tarquinius.

A Roman cave complex at Cumae which may have been the site of the ancient oracle.

Marsyas

Stories about musical competitions, often involving the gods, are common in Greek and Roman mythology. Marsyas, who was a satyr, challenged the god Apollo to a musical contest with a devastating result.

- Read or listen to the story of Marsyas and Apollo.

SOURCE 1

SOURCE 2

'Apollo and Marsyas' by Dirck van Baburen.

God vs mortal

Look at Source 1. This Greek vase painting is sometimes interpreted as showing the contest between Apollo and Marsyas.

- Why do you think the scene has been interpreted in this way? Who might the other characters in the painting be?
- In what ways does this picture suggest the superiority of Apollo?
- Does knowing the ending of the story change the way you view this scene?

A fair contest?

In some versions of the myth Apollo wins by playing his lyre upside down or singing in accompaniment. Marsyas could not do this with the pipes.

- Would you consider this to be cheating?
- Are you surprised that the Greeks and Romans believed their gods might behave in this way?

Apollo's revenge

Look at Sources 2 and 3. How appropriate do you think Apollo's actions were?

SOURCE 3

'Don't tear me apart from myself!' Marsyas begged. 'Forgive me!' he shouted amid his screams. 'Don't skin me alive for playing my pipes!'

Ovid

- What does the punishment of Marsyas suggest about how the Greeks and Romans regarded the gods? Do you think their views are similar to views about gods today?

Dangerous behavior?

Look at Source 4. Misenus also challenged the gods to a music contest. Why do you think he did this?

- What music competitions can you think of today that involve contestants and judges? Why do you think people enter these contests? How are they treated by the judges?

SOURCE 4

One day Misenus was making music by blowing into a seashell, sending the notes resounding over the deep and, in his foolishness, challenged the gods to play as well as he did. And if the story is to be believed, his rival, the god Triton, took hold of him and drowned him in the waves.

Vergil

RESEARCH

Find out about:

- the Pierides and their fate.
- the musician Arion.

Chapter 27: Ephesus

trēs avēs parvae

1 prō casā parvā, duo tōnsōrēs labōrābant. in arboribus trēs avēs parvae dulce canēbant.

placetne tibi mē adiuvāre, Menander?

mihi placet, Phoebē.

ārea *square, courtyard*

2 avibus canentibus, Phoebē et marītus mēnsam in āream portābant.

5 virō salūtātō, Menander barbam tondēre coepit. multa dē fēstīs diēbus rogābat.

tondeō *I cut, shave*

6 tōnsōre barbam tondente, mātrōna litterās in tabellā quiētē scrībēbat.

7 mātrōnā scrībente, servus senex ē tabernā proximā ēvēnit.

ēveniō *I come out*

loquāx *talkative, chatty*

8 verbīs dictīs, Lūcriō in casam lentē ingressus est.

9 intereā vir, barbā tōnsā, pecūniam trādidit.

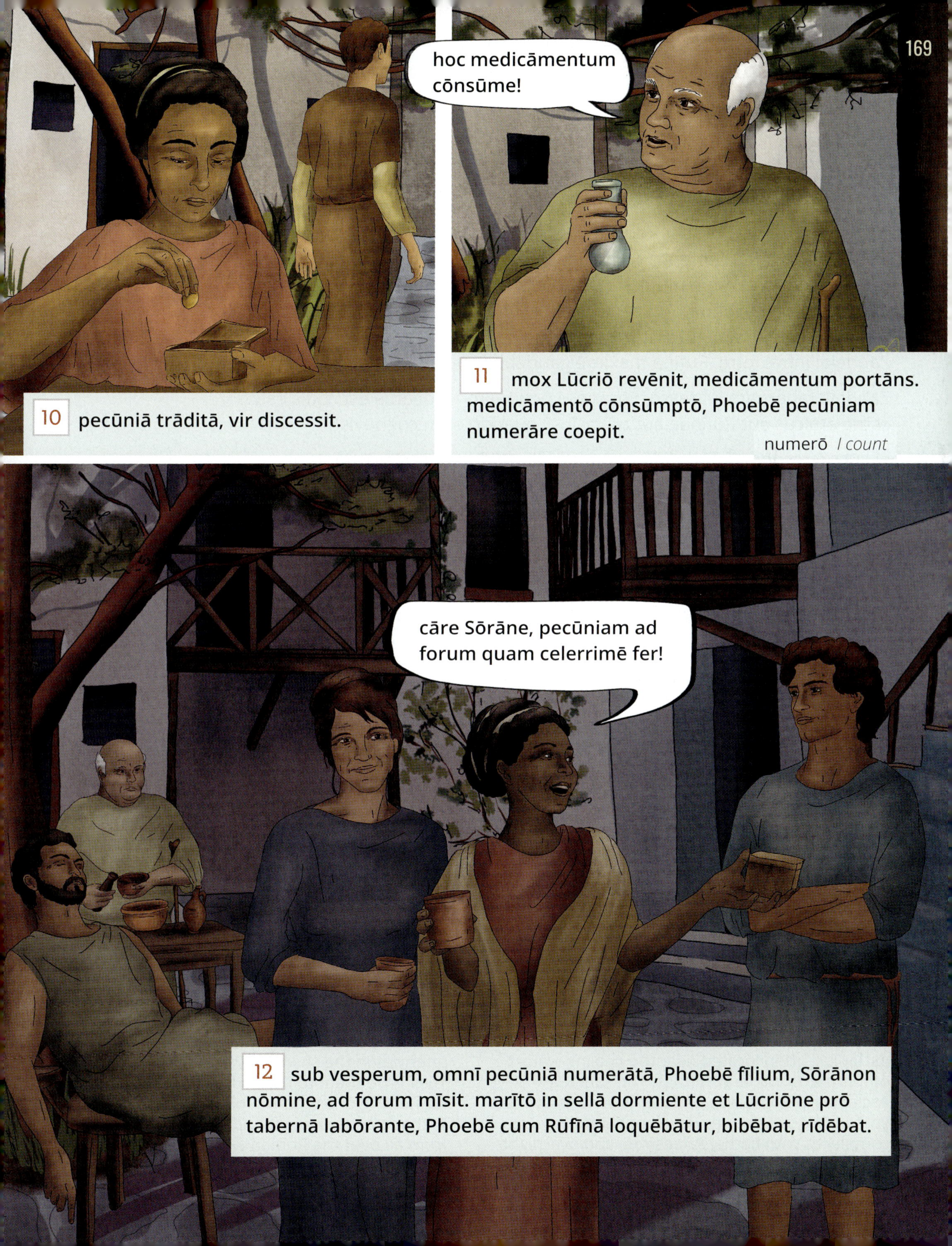

10 pecūniā trāditā, vir discessit.

11 mox Lūcriō revēnit, medicāmentum portāns. medicāmentō cōnsūmptō, Phoebē pecūniam numerāre coepit.

numerō *I count*

12 sub vesperum, omnī pecūniā numerātā, Phoebē fīlium, Sōrānon nōmine, ad forum mīsit. marītō in sellā dormiente et Lūcriōne prō tabernā labōrante, Phoebē cum Rūfīnā loquēbātur, bibēbat, rīdēbat.

mercātor revenit

Lūcriō cum Sōrānō prō tabernā Rūfīnae herbās parābat. puer herbās conterēbat. servus herbās contrītās commiscēbat ut medicāmenta compōneret. medicāmentīs compositīs, Lūcriō puerum rogāvit ut ea in corbulās pōneret. hominibus sīc labōrantibus, mercātor quīdam āream ingressus est. Lūcriōne cōnspectō, mercātor exclāmāvit, 'salvē, mī Lūcriō!' hīs verbīs audītīs, Lūcriō statim surrēxit et eum laetē salūtāvit: 'salvē, Zabdela! intrā, intrā, Rūfīna maximē gaudēbit!'

Zabdelā tabernam ingressō, Sōrānos Lūcriōnem adlocūtus est: 'quis est? estne amīcus aut Rūfīnae aut tuī ipsīus? quandō eum cognōvistis?'

eī Lūcriō respondit, 'Zabdela amīcus fidēlis Rūfīnae est. Christiānīs ab imperātōre damnātīs, popīnā incendiīs dēlētā, Rōmā discēdere necesse erat nōbīs. Zabdela nōbīs eō tempore magnum auxilium obtulit. nam trāns mare īre parābat cum negōtium Ephesī agere solēret. quamquam et perīculōsum sibi ipsī erat et ego pedem vulnerātus eram, ille in nāve nōs ferēbat. nōn modo nōs ut ex Urbe effugerēmus adiūvit Zabdela, sed etiam vītam meam servāvit. ille medicus in legiōnibus fuerat, priusquam mercātor factus est. ipse, meō vulnere suppūrante, ūnā cum Rūfīnā mē cūrābat et simul artem medicīnam Rūfīnam docuit. sīc nōs duōs servāvit Zabdela.'

hīs dictīs, Lūcriō corbulās ā Sōrānō parātās īnspexit. 'et tū nunc discipulus dīligēns es, et artem medicīnam bene discēs.' Lūcriō, Sōrānon sīc hortātus, puerum rogāvit ut corbulās ad aegrōs per urbem portāret.

commisceō *I mix together*

damnō *I condemn*

Ephesī *at Ephesus*

suppūrō *I am infected, suppurate*

medicīnus *of medicine*

discipulus *student*

dīligēns *hard-working, careful*

Asclepius

Many gods were believed to have healing powers, among them Apollo and his son Asclepius. The cult of Asclepius came to Rome from Greece in 293 BC at the time of an outbreak of the plague in the city, and then spread to the rest of the Empire. Rome and many other cities had sanctuaries of Asclepius, often located near the healing waters of thermal or mineral springs. The sanctuary of Asclepius in Rome was on Tiber Island. As the cult spread, the sanctuaries developed into large spa complexes with baths, palaestrae, and overnight accommodation for visitors. The interpretation of dreams was an important part of the healing process. Visitors often slept in cubicles or dormitories overnight, and their dreams were thought to contain advice from the god on how to cure their diseases. There were doctors at the sanctuaries, as well as interpreters of dreams.

Visitors to sanctuaries often brought votive offerings in the shape of their afflicted body part. They gave them to the god either as a request for healing or as thanks for a successful cure. Archaeologists have found thousands of these from all over the Roman world, made of clay, wood, stone, or bronze.

LANGUAGE NOTE 1: ABLATIVE ABSOLUTE

1. Look at the following sentences. What do you notice about the words in red?

   mātrōnā scrībente, Lūcriō ē tabernā ēvēnit.
   While the woman was writing, Lucrio came out of the shop.
   (lit. *With the woman writing, Lucrio came out of the shop.*)

   pecūniā trāditā, vir discessit.
   After he had handed over the money, the man left.
   (lit. *With the money having been handed over, the man left.*)

   Both sentences contain a noun and a participle in the ablative case. This combination of words is known as the **ablative absolute**. An ablative absolute is often used in Latin to give the time or circumstances of an action.

2. When the participle is in the present tense, the events of the ablative absolute happen *at the same time* as the main verb:

   marītō dormiente, Phoebē cum Rūfīnā loquēbātur.
   While her husband was sleeping, Phoebe was talking with Rufina.
   (lit. *With her husband sleeping, Phoebe was talking with Rufina.*)

   hominibus labōrantibus, mercātor āream intrāvit.
   When the men were working, a merchant entered the square.
   (lit. *With the men working, a merchant entered the square.*)

3. When the participle is in the perfect tense, the events of the ablative absolute happened *before* those of the main verb:

   hīs verbīs dictīs, Lūcriō casam ingressus est.
   Once he had said this, Lucrio entered the house.
   (lit. *With the words having been said, Lucrio entered the house.*)

   virō tabernam ingressō, Sōrānos Lūcriōnem multa rogāvit.
   After the man had entered the shop, Soranos asked Lucrio many things.
   (lit. *With the man having entered the shop, Soranos asked Lucrio many things.*)

Doctors

In the Roman world there was no publicly-funded health care and there were no hospitals, other than in the army. Doctors were not required to have official training or qualifications; anyone could offer their services as a doctor. Some doctors, particularly from the eastern provinces of the Empire, went to study in Alexandria, Ephesus, or Pergamum. Doctors could also learn their trade from lectures and public demonstrations of surgery, along with practical experience and guidance from medical handbooks. There was no standard practice, and the differences in approach led to competition between doctors and distrust. Celsus, who wrote about medicine (although he may not have been a practicing doctor), disapproved of doctors who learned from books:

> A man of few words, who has learned well by experience, will be a far better doctor than a man who, with no experience, talks a lot.

Attitudes to doctors

In the fifth and fourth centuries BC, Hippocrates and his followers made a collection of medical writings which formed the basis of the Greek medical tradition. Later, as the Roman Empire grew, Greek doctors came to Rome, bringing with them their systems and practices. Pliny the Elder described the reception of Archagathus, the first Greek doctor to come to Rome, in 219 BC:

> At first his arrival was praised and welcomed, but soon he got the name 'The Butcher', from his cruelty in cutting and searing, and brought the practice of medicine and all doctors into disrepute.

The ideas of Greek doctors were at odds with traditional Roman practices, which prescribed a simple diet, hard work, and personal hygiene as the key to good health. It was the role of the head of the household to look after those in his care. Cato the Elder (234–149 BC), a Roman senator famous for his conservative views, was distrustful of Greek doctors:

> Cato warned his son to be suspicious of all Greek doctors. He had written a guidebook which he consulted when he cared for and treated any who were sick in his household. He never got his patients to fast, but fed them cabbage and bits of duck, pigeon, and hare. This sort of diet was light and good for people who were sick. And, by following this treatment and diet he kept himself, and all those in his household, healthy.
>
> *Plutarch*

However, Greek doctors later gained respect for their knowledge, and their services were sought after. Julius Caesar, in the first century BC, granted citizenship to all who practiced medicine at Rome in order to entice others to move to the city.

Tombstone of an Athenian doctor called Jason, from the second century AD.

Pliny the Younger writes to Emperor Trajan:

> Last year, sir, when I was so seriously ill that my life was in danger, I consulted a doctor. I can thank him for his care and attentiveness only if you are kind enough to help me. And so, I ask you to give him Roman citizenship. For he is a foreigner, and was manumitted by a foreign woman. His name is Arpocras, and his patron was Thermuthis.

This epigram from Martial attacks the doctor Diaulus:

> **nūper erat medicus, nunc est vespillo Diaulus;**
> **quod vespillo facit, fēcerat et medicus.**
>
> Recently Diaulus was a doctor, now he is an undertaker;
> What he does as an undertaker, he had also done as a doctor.

QUESTION

What different attitudes to doctors and other medical practitioners do people have today?

Female doctors and midwives

We know that some women practiced as doctors because their profession is recorded on their tombstones. However, most of the evidence about female medical practitioners refers to midwives. The care of women in childbirth was primarily the responsibility of women, so midwives and female doctors were extremely important and played a key role in the community. Among the lower classes, women could gain knowledge through observing the work of others. In wealthier families, female slaves were often trained as midwives and doctors.

Soranos of Ephesus was a doctor who wrote extensively on female anatomy and midwifery. He was born in Ephesus, but studied and practiced in Alexandria and Rome. At the start of his book, *Gynaecology*, he describes what sort of woman makes the best midwife:

> A suitable woman must be literate, so that she can understand the theory. She must be clever, so that she can easily follow what is said and what is happening. She must have a good memory, to remember instructions. The most qualified midwife should be trained in all areas of care. She should be able to prescribe health plans and be reassuring to her patients. In order to deliver another woman's baby, it is not necessary for her to have had a child herself.

QUESTIONS

1. Why do you think Soranos feels that it is important for a midwife to be literate?
2. Are the qualities described by Soranos desirable for a modern midwife too?

A cupping vessel made of bronze.

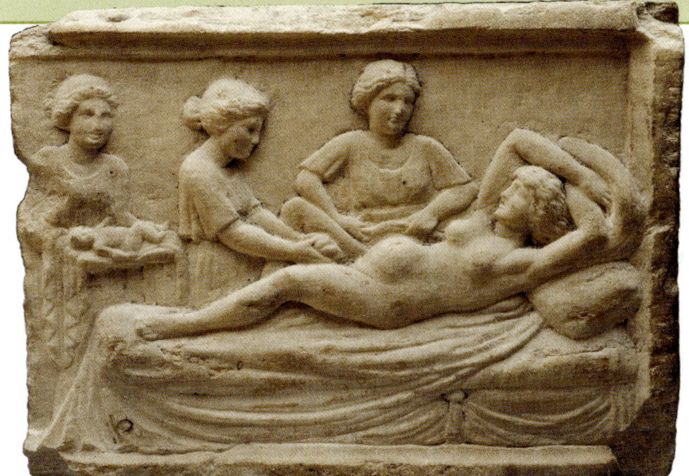

This relief shows a birthing scene. Three women attend the mother; one is holding the newborn.

Diagnosis and treatment

There were different schools of thought among Roman doctors about how best to diagnose and treat patients. Some doctors believed that all disease was caused by specific imbalances within the body: for example, being too hot or too cold. In order to understand the sickness, they tried to find the cause of the imbalance, which they then treated. In general, they prescribed a change of diet to stabilize the body.

Other doctors believed that the treatment should be dictated by the symptoms. These doctors had a reputation for prescribing pleasurable treatments, such as naps, wine, and hot baths. However, some people accused such doctors of dishonesty because they enticed patients with appealing cures and charged high prices for the pleasure. In modern times, however, medical research has shown that pleasurable activities and positive emotions may indeed reduce pain and speed up the healing process. This approach was certainly preferable to some other treatments offered by Roman doctors, such as eating boiled mice or smearing animal manure on inflamed skin.

Cupping

Cupping was a popular treatment. It was used to treat many afflictions, such as joint pain and headaches. In fact, Celsus said that almost all ailments could be treated with cupping. Special cups were heated and placed on the skin to create a vacuum which brought blood to the surface. Sometimes a small incision was made in the skin, then a cup was placed on top, and the blood or infected matter was drawn out.

Sōrānos

postrīdiē tempestās oriēbātur. super mare nūbēs ātrae vidēbantur. trāns tēcta vīs ventī tēgulās movēbat. per imbrem Sōrānos currēbat.

ille tamen nōn sōlus erat. parvum enim puerum quendam, quī eum ōrāverat ut sorōrem adiuvāret, sequēbātur. Sōrānos ipse incertus erat num puella etiam nunc vīveret. nam frāter, perterritus metū, paene nihil dīcere potuerat, cum ad tabernam advēnisset. Rūfīnā in montēs anteā profectā, Sōrānos puerum sōlus adiuvāre temptāre cōnstituerat.

itaque hī duo quam celerrimē currēbant. tum subitō cōnstitērunt. viam angustam ingressus, Sōrānos sorōrem puerī in terrā iacentem invēnit. circum eam turba convēnerat. Sōrānos mātrōnam quandam rogāvit quid accidisset. cui illa respondit, 'fēlēs eius in tēctō erat. puella ipsa, cum eam capere temptāret, per fenestram ēgressa, in tēctum ascendit. propter imbrem tamen lāpsa ad terram cecidit. vīvetne?'

cum in saccōs frūmentī forte cecidisset, puella vīva esse vidēbātur. multa vulnera tamen corporī erant: sanguis ē capite effluēbat, vultus vulnerātus est, ossa manuum pedumque frācta sunt. Sōrānos summā cum cūrā puellam sublātam in casam intulit.

eā in lectō lēniter positā, Sōrānos puerum rogāvit ut aquam atque acētum ferret. puerō regressō et vulneribus acētō lautīs, mel in caput ac vultum dīligenter imposuit. deinde stercore equī manūs pedēsque ūnxit. tōtum diem ad lectum puellae exspectābat, eam hortāns ut paulum vīnī biberet, dum parentēs eius sub vesperum redīrent.

orior *I arise, rise*
nūbēs *cloud*
āter *dark*
imber *rain*
lābor *I slip*
videor *I seem, appear*
os *bone*
īnferō *I carry into, carry in*
acētum *vinegar*
mel *honey*
ungō *I smear, rub*
dum + subjunctive *until*

LANGUAGE NOTE 2: DUM + SUBJUNCTIVE

1. Study the following sentences. What do you notice about the verbs in the clauses in red?

   Sōrānos ad lectum puellae exspectābat, dum parentēs eius redīrent.
   Soranos waited beside the girl's bed, until her parents returned.

   Menander et Phoebē in āreā loquēbantur dum vir advenīret.
   Menander and Phoebe were talking in the courtyard until the man arrived.

2. When **dum** is followed by a verb in the subjunctive, it can be translated *until*.

Ephesus

> The city of Ephesus, because of its advantageous situation, grows daily and is the largest commercial center in Asia west of the Taurus Mountains.
>
> *Strabo*

In the first century AD Ephesus, in the eastern Mediterranean, on the coast of what is now Turkey, was one of the leading cities of the Roman province of Asia. The Roman governor (proconsul) was based there, and it was also an important commercial and religious center. Ephesus was a very old city, built originally in the tenth century BC by Greek settlers. Before the region came under Roman rule in 133 BC, Ephesus already had large civic buildings in the Greek style, including a temple of Artemis (whom the Romans called Diana) and a theater. The theater was enlarged in the time of Emperor Claudius (AD 41–54), and a two-story stage building was constructed during the reign of Nero.

In the early second century AD Gaius Julius Aquila, who had served as a consul in Rome, commissioned the building of a library as a funerary monument for his father, Tiberius Julius Celsus Polemaeanus. Celsus had been born in Asia, possibly in Ephesus, and was one of the first men of Greek origin to become a consul in Rome. He finished his career as proconsul of Asia. The Library of Celsus was one of the largest libraries in the Roman world.

The native population of Ephesus was Greek, and Greek was the main language spoken. A few members of the leading families, like Tiberius Julius Celsus Polemaeanus, had become Roman citizens and moved into the Roman elite. There was a mix of religions. Most people worshiped the traditional Greek and Roman gods, but there was also a Jewish community and, in the first century AD, a significant number of Christians. The apostle Paul visited the city in about AD 53. He preached and tried to convert people to Christianity.

Part of the site of Ephesus as it looks now.

Surgery

Anatomy

Before the invention of the X-ray, knowledge of anatomy came mainly from the dissection of human corpses. However, among the Romans and Greeks there was a widespread feeling that it was wrong to tamper with a dead body. As a result, doctors rarely performed human dissections. This was a major obstacle to their study of the inside of the human body and its workings. In the third century BC, some Greek doctors in Alexandria, in Egypt, had performed human dissections. Herophilus, for example, was able to describe the brain in detail, explain the difference between arteries and veins, and describe the optic nerve and retina.

Knowledge of anatomy relied mainly on two procedures: close observation of the wounds suffered by victims of accidents and violence, and the dissection of animals. Galen, a Greek doctor who practiced in Rome in the second to early third century AD, had worked as a doctor in a gladiatorial school in his native Pergamum. He used his experience of treating wounded gladiators to expand his knowledge of the inside of the human body. He also dissected animals, especially monkeys, and experimented on live animals. For example, he cut nerves so that he could study their function; he observed that cutting a nerve in the larynx caused loss of voice and cutting nerves in the neck caused paralysis of the shoulder muscles. Although his findings were sometimes incorrect because he assumed that animals and humans were the same, they were not challenged until the sixteenth century.

Surgeons

> A surgeon should be a young man, or at least quite young. His hand must be strong and firm, and must never shake; and he should use his left hand as well as his right. He has to be keen-sighted and courageous. He must have compassion – but only enough to want to heal his patient. He must not allow a patient's shrieks to persuade him to operate too quickly or cut less than is needed. No howls of agony should stop him doing what has to be done.
>
> *Celsus*

This relief from Herculaneum shows a man treating a wounded soldier. Both men are nude, which indicates that the scene is from mythology.

Soranos wrote a book called *On the Art of Surgery*. Although this has not survived, other medical authors, such as Galen, describe surgical procedures. Their writings show that doctors regularly undertook minor surgery, although they performed invasive procedures and amputations only as a last resort.

Fractures and wounds could be difficult to treat. Roman doctors were able to set fractured bones with splints, stitch wounds, make incisions, and tie veins and arteries. Minor surgery included treating abscesses and cysts, and the removal of polyps, warts, and other blemishes. Cutting out bladder stones and removing cataracts from the eyes were some of the more serious operations performed by Roman surgeons. Drilling or cutting a hole in the skull, a procedure known as trepanation, relieved pain and pressure, and was a treatment for a fractured skull, when a piece of bone had been broken off and was pressing on the brain. Antyllus, a Greek surgeon who lived in Rome in the second century AD, removed aneurysms (swelling in an artery) by tying two threads around the swelling and cutting down between them.

Internal surgery was rare; it could be used to remove objects such as arrows and to close abdominal wounds. Galen performed some very advanced surgery: the removal of an infected breastbone, and sewing back the omentum (the fatty membrane that covers the intestines) of a patient who had suffered a sword wound. The knowledge and skill of Roman surgeons was impressive given that they did not have access to modern equipment and discoveries.

Amputation

Injured limbs were amputated if there was no other way of saving them, and amputation was used as a last resort to prevent the spread of infection and treat gangrene. Celsus advised that in cases of gangrene 'it does not matter whether amputation is safe, since it is the only remedy'. After he operated, the surgeon cauterized the wound to stop the bleeding and control infection: he heated a metal instrument over a fire and applied it to the site of the amputation. Fingers, toes, hands, and feet could be amputated successfully. Amputation of an entire arm or leg was dangerous, but was sometimes attempted. Part of an adult thigh bone found in a cemetery near Rome provides evidence of a successful amputation.

There is evidence for the use of artificial limbs, made of metal or wood. After Marcus Sergius Silus, a Roman general in the Punic wars, lost his right hand in battle, he had an artificial hand made of iron attached to the stump.

Pain relief

Some pain relief was available, but it was not very powerful. Surgery and the cauterizing of wounds would have caused severe shock and pain for the patient, and the lack of effective anesthetics meant that surgery deep inside the body was rarely attempted. Opium, which was extracted from poppy seeds, was the strongest painkiller; sometimes it was mixed with wine. A paste made from ground-up henbane seeds was smeared on areas of the body about to undergo surgery, to act as a local anesthetic.

Hygiene and care of wounds

The level of hygiene would have depended on the individual doctor. Some surgeons, at least, were aware of the importance of cleanliness. Before an operation, the surgical instruments, bandages, dressings, and any other materials were sterilized by boiling them in water, and the surgeon made sure his hands were clean. Wine and vinegar were used as antiseptics to clean wounds and to reduce the risk of infection. Honey, which has antibacterial qualities, was smeared on wounds, and turmeric and rosemary controlled inflammation. Turmeric was preferred, but it was expensive as it had to be imported from India or China along the Silk Routes.

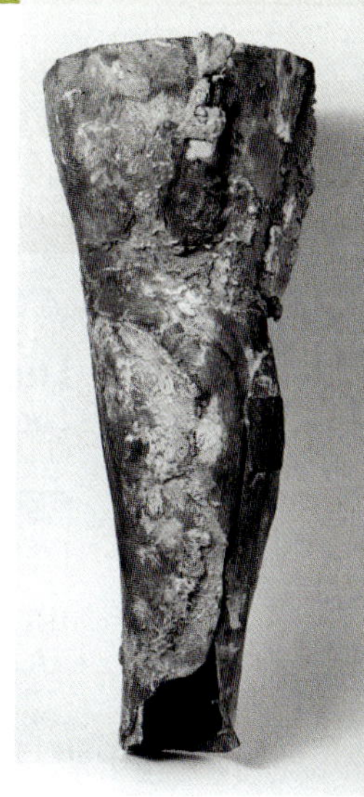

This artificial leg is made of bronze. Originally it was fitted to a wooden core.

Instruments

A large number of specialized surgical instruments has survived. This shows that some types of minor surgery were regularly performed by Roman doctors. The instruments include forceps, scalpels, knives, tweezers, hooks, probes, saws, arrow extractors, and tools for moving bones and cauterizing wounds. Most were made of bronze, though some silver tools have been found.

A collection of surgical instruments, including forceps for crushing the uvula (bottom left). The doctor crushed the uvula with forceps before cutting it off, in order to prevent hemorrhaging. The jaws of the forceps have fine teeth.

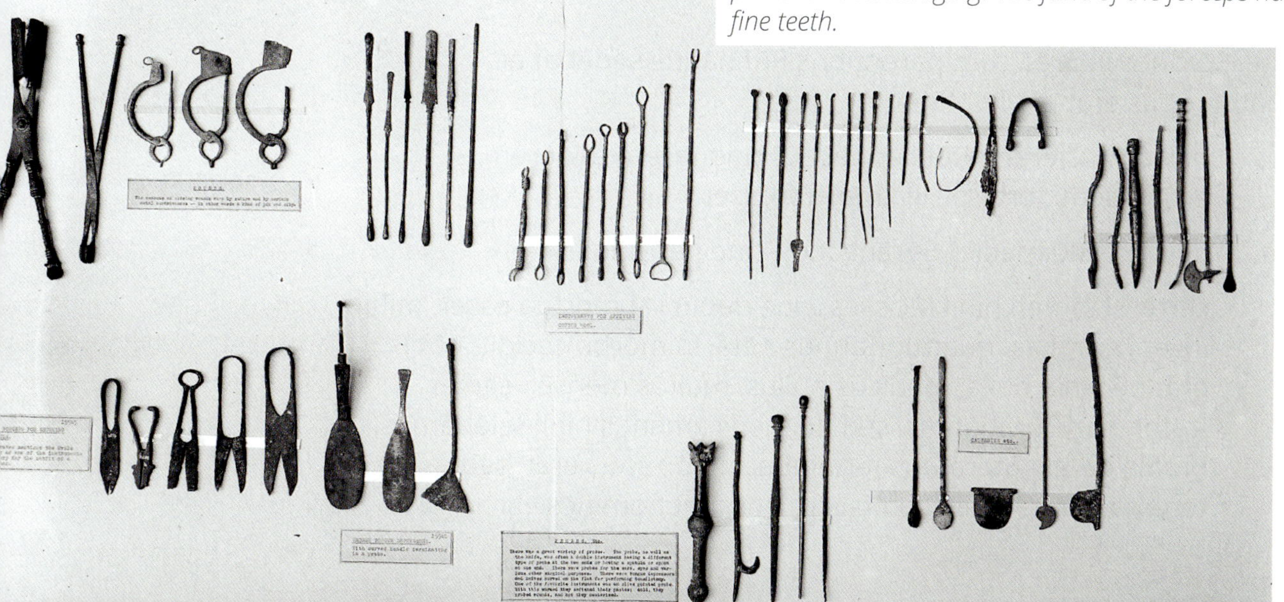

LANGUAGE NOTE 3: IPSE

1. Since Chapter 19 you have met forms of **ipse** (*self*). For example:

   Lūcīlius ipse apud patrem habitābat.
   Lucilius himself was living with his father.

   Ampliātus sē ipsum dīvitem facit.
   Ampliatus is making himself rich.

   ego multa dē mē ipsō didicī.
   I learned many things about myself.

   estne amīcus tuī ipsīus?
   Is he a friend of you yourself?

   illī sē ipsōs cūrābant.
   They were looking after themselves.

   aliī carminibus ipsīs nōn dēlectābantur.
   Others were not pleased by the poems themselves.

2. **ipse** is known as an **intensive pronoun**, because it intensifies, or emphasizes, a noun or pronoun.
3. There is a chart of all the forms of **ipse** on page 276.

LANGUAGE PRACTICE

1. Choose the correct form of **ipse** to complete the sentence, then translate.
   - **a.** .... frāter adest. (ipsum, ipsa, ipse)
   - **b.** tū rēgīnae .... grātiās ēgistī. (ipsam, ipsī, ipsō)
   - **c.** nōnnūllī captīvī mūrum .... ascendērunt. (ipsōs, ipsum, ipsīs)
   - **d.** nōs vultum deae .... vīdimus. (ipsīus, ipse, ipsa)
   - **e.** vōs puellās .... audīvistis. (ipsōs, ipsās, ipsōrum)

sermō cum Rūfīnā

eā nocte, Sōrānos in āreā cum parentibus Rūfīnāque sedēbat ac loquēbātur. opus erat eī societāte.

Sōrānos perterritus eram, Rūfīna. nescīvī quid facere dēbērem. sī errāvissem, fortasse illa mortua esset.

Phoebē tālis est vīta medicī, Sōrāne. nōn sine perīculō est.

Rūfīna certē. sī tamen nihil fēcissēs, sine dubiō illa mortua esset. mihi iuvenī erat fīlia. quattuor annōs nāta, in morbō cecidit. nōbīs erat pecūnia nūlla, medicus nūllus. multōs mēnsēs ego et frāter eam cūrābāmus. sed dē medicāmentīs nihil sciēbāmus. omnia quae poterāmus faciēbāmus. nōn satis erat, sed temptāvimus. nihil aliud facere possunt hominēs.

opus est mihi *I need*
societās *company*

medica mīrābilis

in tabernā Rūfīnae, Sōrānos ex librō dē morbīs medicāmentīsque recitābat. Rūfīna, dum puerum audiēbat, īnstrūmenta, herbās, fasciāsque compōnēbat. subitō in tabernam Rūfīnae duo hominēs ingentī cum clāmōre ingressī sunt. ūnus, iuvenis nōmine Castor, bracchium dextrum ad pectus tenēbat, dolōre vehementer gemēns. alter, nōmine Marus, Rūfīnā salūtātā, rem ānxius explicāvit: 'ēheu! medica, adiuvā eum, tē ōrō. inter nōs luctābāmur in palaestrā, et umerum eius vulnerāvī!' Rūfīna Castorem cōnsidere, Marum tacēre iussit. umerum bracchiumque paulisper īnspexit medica. 'nōlī timēre, Castor. bracchium tuum movēbō. breviter dolēbis.' Rūfīna prīmō bracchium lentē mōvit, deinde repente magnā vī id in umerum addūxit. ululāvit ille. Sōrānos, herbīs in umerum ūnctīs, bracchium ad pectus fasciīs ligāvit. postrēmō medica iuvenem monuit nē bracchium per decem diēs movēret dum ipsa fasciās solveret.

♦ ♦ ♦

palaestram postrīdiē ingressus, Marus magnopere mīrātus est cum Castorem ibi cōnspiceret. nūllō modō vulnerātus esse vidēbātur Castor. facile et discum et pilam manū dextrā mīsit, et comitem quendam fortiter amplexus est. 'mehercle!' sibi dīxit Marus, 'illa Rūfīna est medica mīrābilis!'

ē palaestrā ēgressus, Marus omnibus amīcīs rem nārrāvit, et mox per urbem Rūfīna medica mīrābilis laudābātur. sed Phoebē, ut rem audīvit, rīdēbat. Menandrō dīxit: 'Marus nescit Castorem habēre frātrem geminum!'

medica *female doctor*
fascia *bandage*
gemō *I moan, groan*
explicō *I explain*
luctor *I wrestle*
doleō *I feel pain, suffer*
ululō *I howl, yell*
ligō *I tie, bind*
solvō *I undo, let go*
mīror *I am amazed*
facile *easily*
discus *discus*
amplector *I embrace*
mehercle! *good heavens! by Hercules!*
ut *when, as soon as*
geminus *twin*

A grave marker for a female doctor, from Gaul.

Drugs and medicines

ēripit interdum, modo dat medicīna salūtem,
quaeque iuvet, mōnstrat, quaeque sit herba nocēns.

The art of healing sometimes destroys health, sometimes brings it, and it shows which plant helps, and which is harmful.

Ovid

The Romans made use of a wide variety of herbs and natural ingredients as remedies for ailments and illnesses. Their use was not reserved for doctors and medical practitioners, and it is likely that ordinary people had a basic knowledge of plants and their medicinal uses. In early Rome some natural ingredients, such as cucumbers, onions, and garlic, were used as treatments. Imperial expansion brought new ingredients to Rome from the Empire and beyond.

Most of our knowledge of Roman drugs comes from literature. A few writers wrote extensively on the medicinal uses of plants and herbs, as well as substances derived from animals and minerals. The fullest account of Roman pharmacology is Dioscorides' *De Materia Medica*, written in about AD 65. Dioscorides had traveled widely; the places he had visited included Greece, Crete, and Egypt. His catalogue of medicinal remedies, originally written in Greek, included about 600 plants, sometimes recording their Dacian, Thracian, Roman, Egyptian, and Carthaginian names as well. It was translated into Latin and later into Arabic, and influenced Arabic and European medicine for centuries.

Other evidence about Roman drugs comes from archaeological discoveries. A wooden box containing cumin and coriander seeds was found in a shipwreck near Rome. Five pills, stored in a tin container, have been found at the site of another shipwreck. The pills contain zinc, which is an anti-inflammatory.

This sheet from a thirteenth-century manuscript has an Arabic translation of Dioscorides' 'De Materia Medica'.

FRANKINCENSE AND MYRRH

Both frankincense and myrrh are derived from the resin that oozes from trees when their bark is cut; frankincense from the Boswellia and myrrh from the Commiphora. The sap is left to harden and is then collected from the trunk. It can be eaten in its dry form, chewed like gum, or steamed with oil to produce a fragrant liquid. Roman writers documented the anti-inflammatory and pain-relieving properties of the resins and prescribed them for a wide range of ailments, from indigestion to a bad cough.

The trees that produce these resins are native to Arabia and some regions of north-east Africa. The Romans imported the resins in huge quantities. Pliny the Elder wrote that the valuable dried resins had made the Arabians the richest people on earth.

CABBAGE

Cabbage was widely praised for its medicinal qualities. Cato recommended it as a cure for anything from sores and boils to dislocations and headaches. He even prescribed it as a treatment for deafness. Pliny the Elder recorded that Cato was not alone in praising the cabbage for its healing properties – a Greek called Chrysippus had also written a whole book on the benefits of cabbage.

ALOE

Dioscorides wrote that the aloe plant is beneficial for skin irritations, constipation, and healing boils and wounds. Aloe is also mentioned as a medicine in the works of Soranos and Galen and several other medical writers of the first and second centuries AD. The aloe leaves were cut and left while the juice slowly leaked out. This liquid was boiled, leaving a sticky, black residue, which was formed into lozenges. These could be melted down and combined with other drugs.

LANGUAGE PRACTICE

2. Choose the most appropriate participle to complete the sentence, then translate.

a. Menandrō cibum in mēnsā .... , Phoebē aquam fert. (impōnente, audente, regente)

b. līberīs .... , parentēs in āreā loquī solēbant. (cōgentibus, dormientibus, parcentibus)

c. fēle .... , mūrēs laetē lūdēbant canēbantque. (movente, absente, mūtante)

d. Sōrānō medicāmenta .... , Lūcriō herbās lēgit. (audiente, pūniente, compōnente)

e. vōbīs .... , ego ad urbem vēnī ut cibum emerem. (aperientibus, labōrantibus, pōnentibus)

f. puerō nūmen .... , soror vōtum facit. (precante, errante, cōnsūmente)

3. Choose the most appropriate participle to complete the sentence, then translate.

raptā	occīsō	oppugnātā	praebitō	missīs	cōnfectō

a. opere .... , virginēs domum nōndum regressae erant.

b. pecūniā .... , fūrēs in tenebrās fūgērunt.

c. rege ipsō .... , cōnsul exercituī hostium parcere cōnstituit.

d. nūntiīs ad ducem nostrum .... , in templō nōs cēlāvimus.

e. urbe ā rēgīnae cōpiīs .... , templum vestrum incēnsum est.

f. cōnsiliō eīs petentibus .... , nihil mē decuit aliud dīcere.

4. Translate each sentence into Latin by choosing the correct word or phrase from each pair.

a. *When we had seen our friends, we ran happily into the street.*

amīcīs videntibus,	in viā	laetē	cucurrimus.
amīcīs vīsīs,	in viam	celeriter	cucurristis.

b. *While the citizens were watching the race, the enslaved men were working in the mine.*

cursū ā cīvibus spectātō,	servī	in metallīs	labōrāverant.
cīvibus cursum spectantibus,	servōs	in metallō	labōrābant.

c. *After you had found your dog, your parents praised you very much.*

cane inveniente,	parentēs	tē	maximē	laudāvit.
cane inventō,	parentibus	tibi	pessimē	laudāvērunt.

d. *When I had encouraged my brother, I decided to return home.*

frātre hortante,	domum	regredior	cōnstituistī.
frātrem hortāta,	domōs	regredī	cōnstituī.

e. *While the queen was setting fire to the city, you were searching without success for your sister.*

rēgīnā urbem incendente,	sorōris	forte	quaerēbātis.
urbe ā rēgīnā incēnsā,	sorōrem	frūstrā	quaerēbāmus.

East and West

By the middle of the third century AD the Principate was in crisis. The northern borders of the Empire were under pressure from migration and invasion by the peoples of northern Europe and Eurasia. At the same time, because the Principate did not provide clear rules for succession (hereditary or otherwise), several military leaders fought for the throne. However, none had the ability or authority to hold onto power and create a stable dynasty.

Diocletian and the Tetrarchy

The situation changed in AD 284 when Diocletian, a powerful general born in Dalmatia, was proclaimed emperor. Diocletian was a strong statesman who set out to reform the Empire and create a more efficient system of administration. To avoid the threat of regular civil wars caused by usurpers, he made his friend Maximian, another successful general, co-ruler with responsibility for the western provinces, while Diocletian himself kept control of the eastern provinces. To address the problem of succession, each co-ruler took a junior partner. Diocletian and Maximian were known as ***Augustī***, and the junior partners were known as ***Caesarēs***. This system is known as the Tetrarchy ('the rule of four').

In AD 305 Diocletian abdicated and persuaded Maximian to do the same. The intention was that the two Caesares would take the title of Augusti and would choose two new Caesares from the most capable men available. As neither man was expected to choose his son as a Caesar, the risk of creating powerful family dynasties should have been avoided. Yet the plan did not succeed. Before long there were a number of competitors for the throne, and new civil wars broke out.

Constantine

The civil wars ended in AD 324 with one general, Constantine, taking control of the entire Empire. Constantine implemented a set of reforms which were crucial for the final centuries of the Empire. He solved the problem of succession by making it explicitly hereditary. As a result, powerful generals, supported by their troops, were not a direct threat to the imperial house. Constantine also created a new capital for the eastern section of the Empire by enlarging the old Greek city of Byzantium (on the north shore of the Bosporus) and renaming it Constantinople. This moved the center of power away from Rome and towards the wealthier Eastern Empire. It would later have significant consequences for the ultimate separation of the eastern and western provinces of the Empire. Finally, Constantine converted to Christianity and recognized the religion officially, ending centuries of persecution and paving the way for Christianity to become the Empire's official religion.

A marble portrait of Emperor Constantine.

The Byzantine Empire

After the death of Constantine, the principle of hereditary succession remained in place, but the idea that a single son would rule the whole Empire did not. Tensions often developed between co-rulers and led to a greater separation between the two halves of the Empire. When Theodosius I, the last sole ruler of the whole Roman Empire, died in AD 395, he bequeathed the throne to his two sons: Arcadius ruled the East, and Honorius the West. From then on, each half of the Empire acted independently. The West, unable to stop the continuous waves of invasions and the migrations of Germanic peoples, disintegrated into the separate kingdoms which would later develop into modern Europe. The Eastern Empire, however, lasted for another thousand years, through the Middle Ages, as the Byzantine Empire, a Greek-speaking kingdom with its capital in Constantinople.

The Byzantine emperor Justinian (AD 527–565) and his court.

Chapter 28: itinera

The remains of a Roman road in Petra, Jordan.

This story is based on events described in the Bible (*Acts 19: 23-41*). It uses some of the language of the Vulgate, a Latin translation of the Bible made in the late fourth century AD.

tumultus Ephesī

Lūcriōnī rogantī ā quibus tantus clāmor prīdiē factus esset, Sōrānos sīc respondit:

'nōn minimus tumultus dē Christiānīs factus est. argentārius enim quīdam, Dēmētrius nōmine, parvās statuās templaque minima Artemidis faciēns, lucrum nōn parvum facit, sīcut plūrimī aliī artificēs.

'cum hī artificēs convocātī essent et sēdārentur, Dēmētrius dīxit, "amīcī, scītis magnam pecūniam nōbīs esse dē artificiō nostrō. Christiānī autem dīcunt: 'eī nōn sunt deī quī manibus hominum factī sunt.' nunc et vidētis et audītis hōs Christiānōs ingentī turbae Ephesiōrum persuādēre. itaque artificium nostrum in redargūtiōnem veniet, templum magnae deae Artemidis in nihil reputābitur, et maiestās eius, quam tōta Asia et orbis colit, dēstruī incipiet."

'hīs audītīs, artificēs īrā implētī sunt et exclāmāvērunt, "magna est Artemis Ephesiōrum!" cum tōta urbs tumultū implērētur, duōbus Christiānīs raptīs, turba in theātrum impetum fēcit. aliī autem alia clāmābant. plūrimī nesciēbant quā ex causā convocātī essent!

'scrība tamen, cum multitūdō sēdāta esset, "virī Ephesiī," inquit, "quis nescit urbem Ephesiōrum magnam Artemidem colere? ergō vōs oportet sēdātōs esse et nihil temere agere. hūc enim addūxistis hōs Christiānōs quī nūllum scelus commīsērunt. sī Dēmētrius, et eī quī cum eō sunt, aliquem accūsāre volunt, illum in iūdicium vocāre dēbent. nam ea quae hodiē fēcistis explicāre vix possumus, et paene sunt sēditiōsa."

'et, cum haec verba dicta essent, multitūdinem dīmīsit.'

tumultus *riot*

prīdiē *on the previous day*

argentārius *silversmith*

lucrum *money, profit*

convocō *I call together*
artificium *business*

in redargūtiōnem veniō *I am held in contempt*
in nihil reputō *I consider worthless*
maiestās *majesty, authority*
colō *I worship*
dēstruō *I destroy*
impetum faciō *I charge*
causa *reason*
scrība *local official*
vōs oportet *you ought*
temere *rashly*
committō *I commit*
iūdicium *court, trial, judgment*
sēditiōsus *treasonous*

A coin from about AD 42. On one side is a portrait of Emperor Claudius. On the other side is the Temple of Artemis at Ephesus with the statue of the goddess inside. Note that she is referred to by her Roman name, Diana.

Temple of Artemis

The Temple of Artemis was located about two miles from the city of Ephesus. It had been destroyed and rebuilt twice. The third and final structure was built in around 323 BC and lasted almost six centuries. The temple was enormous. According to Pliny the Elder, it had 127 columns, each sixty feet high – significantly taller than the Parthenon at Athens. The temple was a tourist attraction and visitors came to worship, offer sacrifices and votives to the goddess, and admire the incredible structure of the temple itself, along with the collection of art it housed.

Wonder of the world

Ancient writers compiled lists of ***theamata***, 'things to be seen', usually numbering seven. These were awe-inspiring architectural and sculptural masterpieces located around the Mediterranean and Middle East. The lists of seven wonders varied between writers. The poet Antipater of Sidon, writing around 140 BC, gives this list:

> I gazed upon the wall of lofty Babylon on which chariots race, and the statue of Zeus by the River Alpheus, and the hanging gardens, and the Colossus of the Sun at Rhodes, and the great labor of the high pyramids and the mighty tomb of Mausolus at Halicarnassus, but when I saw the shining temple of Artemis rising up to the clouds, these other sites paled and I said, apart from Mount Olympus the sun has never shone upon anything so great.

RESEARCH

1. Find out about the structures that were included on the ancient lists of seven wonders.
2. If you were compiling a list of the seven man-made wonders of the modern world, what would you include?

Ephesian Artemis

The goddess Artemis (whom the Romans associated with the goddess Diana) was usually regarded as the goddess of the hunt, the moon, and chastity. She was also the protector of animals and unmarried girls. Ephesian Artemis was very different, perhaps because she had been assimilated with a local Anatolian earth goddess. In Ephesus she was worshiped as a goddess of fertility. Inside her temple was a statue of the goddess. Although the original statue does not survive, numerous copies have been found across the Roman Empire, attesting to her widespread popularity. Some features of Ephesian Artemis are similar to depictions of Persian and Egyptian deities, such as her stiff posture. The round balls hanging from her body are thought to represent fertility, and have been identified as breasts, eggs, beehives, gourds, or bulls' testicles.

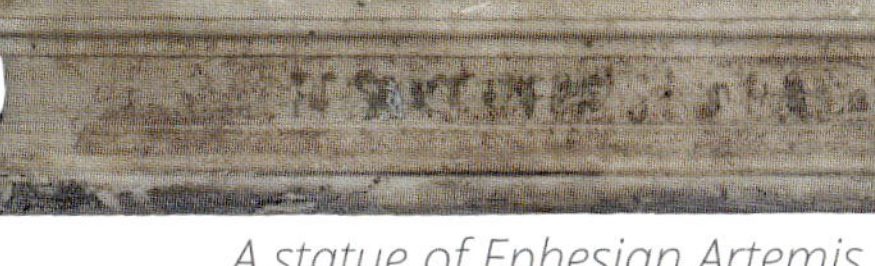

A statue of Ephesian Artemis.

The temple treasury

The Temple of Artemis also functioned as a kind of bank. The historian Dio Chrysostom described how wealthy citizens and foreigners deposited their money in the building, trusting in the safety of the religious sanctuary. Beyond safekeeping the deposits, the temple also offered loans on which it collected interest. This was not unlike other treasuries at religious sanctuaries elsewhere. In addition, the Temple of Artemis owned agricultural estates and quarries outside the city, from which it profited, and it received funds from civic fines and taxes. These sources of income generated enormous wealth.

LANGUAGE NOTE 1: IMPERFECT AND PLUPERFECT PASSIVE SUBJUNCTIVES

1. Since Chapter 23, you have seen verbs in the imperfect and pluperfect subjunctive. For example:

   cum in ātriō stāret, multōs hominēs vīdit.
   When he was standing in the atrium, he saw many men.

   cum parentēs haec audīvissent, respondērunt.
   When his parents had heard these things, they replied.

2. You have now met sentences like these:

   cum illī sēdārentur, Dēmētrius eōs adlocūtus est.
   When they were being calmed down, Demetrius addressed them.

   cum haec verba dicta essent, multitūdinem dīmīsit.
   When these words had been said, he sent the crowd away.

   The verbs in red are passive and subjunctive. **sēdārentur** is **imperfect passive subjunctive** and **dicta essent** is **pluperfect passive subjunctive**.

3. Compare the active and passive forms of the imperfect subjunctive of **vocō**:

Active	*Passive*
vocārem	**vocārer**
vocārēs	**vocārēris**
vocāret	**vocārētur**
vocārēmus	**vocārēmur**
vocārētis	**vocārēminī**
vocārent	**vocārentur**

4. Compare the active and passive forms of the pluperfect subjunctive of **vocō**:

Active	*Passive*
vocāvissem	**vocātus essem**
vocāvissēs	**vocātus essēs**
vocāvisset	**vocātus esset**
vocāvissēmus	**vocātī essēmus**
vocāvissētis	**vocātī essētis**
vocāvissent	**vocātī essent**

5. You can find the forms of the imperfect and pluperfect on pages 280–283.

The Palmyrenes buried their dead, instead of cremating them – cremation was the usual practice in the western parts of the Empire. Wealthy families built tombs in the form of towers outside the city walls, generally lining a road. The remains of the dead were placed in niches in the walls inside the tower, and each niche was sealed with a carved and painted portrait of the dead person.

This tomb tower is called the Tower of Elahbel. It was reconstructed in the early twentieth century.

camēlī

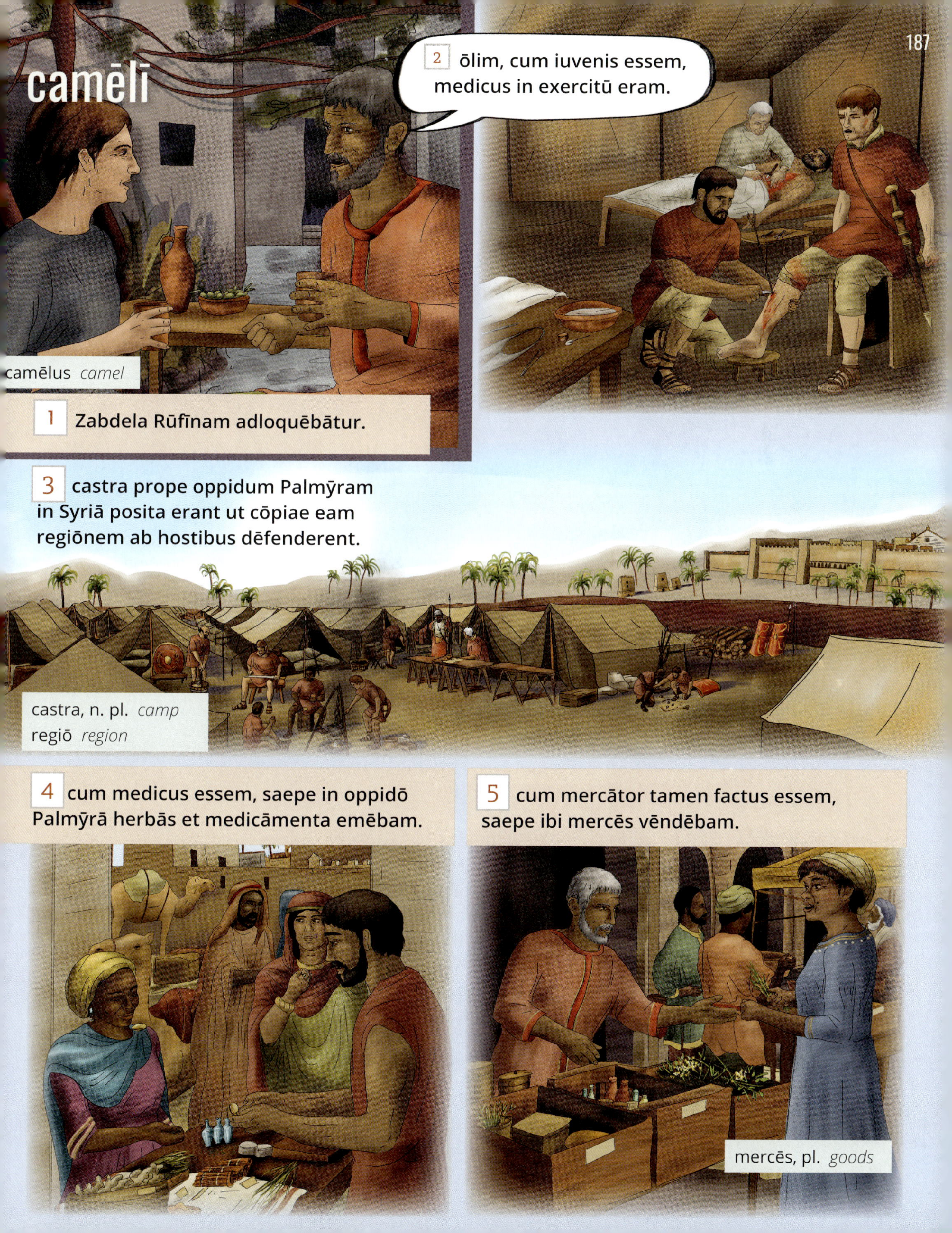

1 Zabdela Rūfīnam adloquēbātur.

camēlus *camel*

2 ōlim, cum iuvenis essem, medicus in exercitū eram.

3 castra prope oppidum Palmȳram in Syriā posita erant ut cōpiae eam regiōnem ab hostibus dēfenderent.

castra, n. pl. *camp*
regiō *region*

4 cum medicus essem, saepe in oppidō Palmȳrā herbās et medicāmenta emēbam.

5 cum mercātor tamen factus essem, saepe ibi mercēs vēndēbam.

mercēs, pl. *goods*

6 sed mercēs per sōlitūdinēs ferre perīculōsum est ...
7 ōlim cum manū mercātōrum iter faciēbam. nōs, mercēs ab Arabiā ferentēs, multōs diēs camēlōs agēbāmus.
8 camēlōsne umquam vīdistī, Rūfīna? animālia mīrābilia sunt, quae multōs diēs sine aquā prōgredī, aestum frīgusque patī possunt. fortiōrēs quam asinī sunt camēlī, sapientiōrēsque quam equī.
sōlitūdinēs, pl. desert
frīgus cold
9 ūnā nocte, cum stāgnum parvum inventum esset, tentōria posuimus.
stāgnum pool
tentōrium tent
10 quibus positīs, circum ignem cibum cōnsūmēbāmus, fābulās nārrantēs.

11 sed camēlī subitō vehementer grundīre incēpērunt. quōs, cum grundientēs atque exspuentēs audīrem, adiī. capita eōrum mulcēbam, verba dulcia susurrāns.
exspuō I spit
12 dum camēlōs cūrō, subitō ingentem clāmōrem audīvī. ex umbrīs fūrēs appāruerant. quī, pugiōnēs portantēs, comitēs meōs statim necāvērunt. scelere commissō, pecūniam mercēsque rapuērunt. quod cum intellēxissem, mē inter camēlōs cēlāvī nē fūrēs mē cōnspicerent.
13 mē diū cēlābam dum fūrēs, vīnō cōnsūmptō, obdormīrent. quod cum vīdissem, in camēlum fūrtim ascendī, et ad oppidum Palmȳram effūgī.
obdormiō I fall asleep
14 per sōlitūdinēs iter faciunt plūrimī mercātōrēs, nōnnūllī fūrēs.

Palmyra

Palmyra was an oasis in the Syrian desert, about 900 miles southeast of Ephesus. The journey between Palmyra and Ephesus by land and sea took three weeks, or seven weeks overland. There had been a settlement at the oasis, called Tadmor, since at least 2,000 BC. Although Tadmor was located in the desert, there were springs, and the soil was rich, which made agriculture and animal herding possible in the surrounding area. In pre-Roman times Tadmor was already an important commercial and religious center, and an administrative hub for the surrounding area. However, it began to expand rapidly in the first century AD, after it became part of the province of Syria and was renamed Palmyra by the Romans.

Between two empires

Palmyra, the easternmost settlement of the Roman Empire, lay on the border between two powerful empires: Rome and Parthia. At the time of our stories, relations between Parthia and Rome were stable. Nevertheless, Palmyra was of strategic, as well as economic, importance to Rome. The prosperity of Palmyra depended on peaceful relations between Rome and Parthia, and Roman troops were present there from AD 19.

People and culture

> The Palmyrenes are merchants and bring the products of India and Arabia from Parthia and dispose of them in Roman territory.
>
> *Appian*

Palmyra was a meeting point of cultures. The influence of both the Roman and the Parthian empires could be seen in religion, architecture, and art. As well as the local population, which included Arameans, Arabs, and other speakers of Semitic languages, many people were attracted by the opportunities for trade; some settled permanently and others were just temporary visitors. The merchants of Palmyra grew rich from trade between the Roman Empire and peoples to its east, and traces of Chinese silk have been found in tombs there. The culture of the pre-Roman population remained strong, even after Palmyra became a Roman city. It wasn't until the second century AD that some inhabitants began to attach Roman names to their own Semitic names.

As in other parts of the eastern Roman Empire, Greek language and culture were influential. The local language was Palmyrene, a dialect of Aramaic that is related to Hebrew. Greek was used for diplomatic and commercial purposes, and the official inscriptions that have been found are bilingual in Greek and Palmyrene. A few Latin inscriptions have been found from the later years of the city.

Archaeology provides evidence that after Palmyra came under Roman rule some people continued to wear traditional Parthian-style clothing. Men wore baggy pants, which were narrow at the ankle and tucked into short boots. Over their trousers, they had a knee-length tunic with long, fitted sleeves. Some men carried a knife in the belt of the tunic. Women had a headband and turban, with a veil covering the head, shoulders, and arms. Both men and women wore a cloak fastened at the shoulder with a large, circular brooch.

Buildings

In the first and second centuries AD Palmyra began to look like a Roman city, with the construction of many grand public buildings. The earliest we know of was the Temple of Bel, a local god, dedicated in AD 32. A forum was built in the second half of the first century AD, and, in the second century, a stone theater.

The Temple of Bel was built in a mixture of Roman and Middle Eastern styles. This photograph shows the remains of the temple before much of it was destroyed by ISIL in 2015.

The trade routes used by merchants for centuries to exchange goods between China and the Mediterranean are often known nowadays as the 'Silk Road'. However, 'Silk Routes' is a more accurate term, as there was a network of routes by land and sea. Luxury goods, including silk, were brought to the Roman Empire from as far away as China (the Roman name for the Chinese was **Sērēs**, from **sēricum**, the Latin word for 'silk'). In the first century BC, under Emperor Wu, the Han Dynasty in China began to open up the silk routes from China to Parthia. The Chinese exported silk in exchange for goods such as horses, gold, glass, and pottery, some of which came from the Roman Empire. In addition, pearls, cotton, and spices such as ginger, cinnamon, and pepper came to the Roman Empire from India, and frankincense and myrrh from Arabia. People usually did not travel the full length of these routes. Instead, there was a chain of traders; at each stopping place goods were sold or exchanged, and another merchant carried them to the next town.

The Silk Routes

The map shows the main trade routes in the first century AD, and indicates the territories of some of the empires.
China to Palmyra: about 4,000 miles.
Palmyra to Rome: about 2,000 miles.

Palmyra and the Silk Routes

Palmyra's location between the River Euphrates and the Mediterranean made it an important stopover for trading expeditions crossing the Syrian desert. The city provided essential supplies and facilities: water, salt, horses and camels, pasture for animals, and places to store goods. It was also a center for the exchange of goods.

Merchants based in Palmyra financed and organized caravans to carry goods to and from the River Euphrates, connecting with the silk routes overland through the Parthian Empire, and by sea from the Persian Gulf. On reaching the Euphrates, the merchandise was often loaded onto rafts made of inflated animal skins.

A caravan was a group of people traveling together over the desert. Traveling in a group offered protection from bandits and was more economical. The caravans were guarded by archers mounted on camels or horses. A caravan required financial backing, careful organization, and equipment. Before setting out, the travelers had to source camels and horses and the people to look after them, guides who knew the routes through the desert, guards to provide protection, and supplies of food and water.

This relief from Palmyra may depict a caravan or two soldiers with a war camel. Camels are well-adapted to arid conditions and can carry loads of 400 lbs. The camels used by the Palmyrenes were dromedaries (one-humped).

LANGUAGE NOTE 2: CONNECTING RELATIVES

1. Since Chapter 13, you have seen the relative pronoun used in relative clauses like this:

   Poppillus, quī erat pistor, pānem parābat.
   Poppillus, who was a baker, was preparing bread.

2. The relative pronoun can also be used to refer to people or ideas in a previous sentence. For example:

   subitō hominēs appāruērunt. quī comitēs meōs statim necāvērunt.
   Suddenly men appeared. They immediately killed my companions.
   (lit. *Suddenly men appeared. Who immediately killed my companions.*)

   camēlī grundīre incipiēbant. quōs, cum exspuentēs audīrem, adiī.
   The camels were beginning to grunt. I approached them, when I heard them spitting.
   (lit. *The camels were beginning to grunt. Which, when I heard them spitting, I approached.*)

   Giscō Luccum occīdit. quod cum pater Luccī intellēxisset, Giscōnem dēvōvit.
   Gisco killed Luccus. When Luccus' father had realised that, he cursed Gisco.
   (lit. *Gisco killed Luccus. Which thing, when Luccus' father had realised it, he cursed Gisco.*)

3. When a relative pronoun is used in this way it is known as a **connecting relative**.

LANGUAGE PRACTICE

1. Look back at Language Note 1 on page 186 and the charts on pages 282 to 283. Then fill in the gaps below. Questions **a.** and **f.** are done for you.

	Imperfect active subjunctive		*Imperfect passive subjunctive*	
a.	mitteret	s/he was sending	mitterētur	s/he was being sent
b.	tenērēmus	....	tenērēmur	....
c.	audīrem	....	....	I was being heard
d.	....	....	mūtārentur	....
e.	....	you (s.) were calling	....	....

	Pluperfect active subjunctive		*Pluperfect passive subjunctive**	
f.	mīsisset	s/he had sent	missa esset	she had been sent
g.	tenuissēmus	....	tentī essēmus	....
h.	audīvissem	....	....	I had been heard
i.	....	....	mūtātae essent	....
j.	....	you (s.) had called	....	....

* Choose whichever gender you wish for **h.** and **j.**

Aponia

magna turba erat in forō Ephesiō. aliī mercēs vēndēbant, aliī emēbant. inter quōs erat mercātor, quī nūper ad urbem advēnerat. zingiberī et alia arōmata vēndēbat. Rūfīna, cum medicāmenta facere vellet, hunc adloquēbātur.

in aliā forī parte pompa ad templum prōcēdēbat. nōnnūllī puerī puellaeque virginem dēdūcēbant. haec virgō erat Aponia, sacerdōs Artemidis et fīlia prōcōnsulis prōvinciae. puerīs puellīsque comitantibus, Aponia ad templum lentē prōcēdēbat ut sacrificium deae faceret. Aponia iuvenem quendam pompam spectantem cōnspexit et ērubuit. quī, vultū Aponiae vīsō, sē vertit et in turbam ēvānuit.

nunc Aponia, quae aegra erat, lentius prōcēdere coepit. cum Aponia ab omnibus spectārētur, fūr quīdam eīs obrēpēbat ut pecūniam auferret. quem, cum pompam mīrārentur, nōnnūllī ignōrābant. hic sacculum fēminae dīvitis rapere temptābat. subitō fēmina eum animadvertit et 'fūr! fūr!' clāmābat. fūr quam celerrimē fugiēns pompam perrūpit. Aponia, quae nunc aegerrima vidēbātur, attonita cōnstitit. paulisper immōta ibi stābat; deinde, oculīs clausīs, ad terram conlāpsa est.

ad sacerdōtem festīnāvit soror, quae quoque in pompā aderat, 'Aponia! Aponia!' clāmāns. 'aegra sum,' Aponia susurrāns respondit. 'dea īrāta est.'

'et māne aegra vidēbāris,' inquit soror ānxiē. 'heri vīdī tē medicāmenta cōnsūmere.'

tum ad turbam versa clāmāvit, 'necesse est nōbīs eī subvenīre. quaerite patrem nostrum! medicum addūcite!'

zingiberī, acc. s. *ginger*

dēdūcō *I escort, lead*

comitor *I accompany*

lentius *more slowly*
obrēpō *I creep up on*
ignōrō *I am unaware of*
animadvertō *I notice*
perrumpō *I break through*

The 'Beauty of Palmyra', a digital recreation of an ancient statue of a woman, found in Palmyra.

Travel and communication

A replica Roman milestone from the province of Raetia.

Transport and connectivity became increasingly important as the Roman Empire grew. The Romans had a network made up of more than 250,000 miles of road crisscrossing Europe, parts of North Africa, and the Middle East. About 50,000 miles of these roads were paved with stone. In some places the Romans constructed entirely new roads, connecting newly-acquired territories, while elsewhere they improved the existing roads. The road system facilitated the fast and reliable movement of people, goods, and messages. The roads were often built by the military, and their primary purpose was to allow troops to move quickly and efficiently around the Empire. However, the same infrastructure also opened up trade. By the first century AD, the extensive road network and the security of Roman rule, along with a single currency across the provinces, ensured the easy movement of people around the Empire.

Roads

Roman roads were engineered to be long-lasting and cost-effective. They are notable for their straightness, which reduced the length of the road. They were built on solid foundations and had cambered surfaces and drainage on either side. They were usually wide enough to permit two standard carts to pass, along with pedestrians. Although Roman engineers normally used locally-sourced materials, the same basic design was employed in constructing roads across the Empire. In the provinces the construction of the roads was generally funded by Rome, but their maintenance was left to the local government. Funds came from taxes or from private patronage. Tolls were also often imposed on Roman roads, particularly at bridges or at the gates of cities.

Milestones

The Roman mile (***mīlle passuum***) was 1,000 paces, which is about 1,620 yards, slightly less than a modern mile. Roads were marked at regular intervals with milestones (***mīliāria***), which recorded the distance from the start of the road and also the name of the official who was in charge of its construction. In this way, the road was located within the wider network, and travelers were reminded that they were on a Roman road.

The Golden Milestone (***mīliārium aureum***), which we saw in Chapter 2, was set up by Augustus in the Roman Forum in 20 BC. It symbolized the starting point of the network of roads that radiated out from Rome to all parts of Italy and the Empire. The names of important cities in the Empire and their distances from Rome were inscribed on it.

Via Appia

The Via Appia was one of the most important roads in Italy. It connected Rome with the port of Brundisium in the south. The poet Statius called it ***longārum rēgīna viārum*** ('queen of the long roads'). Procopius, a sixth-century AD historian, wrote about it hundreds of years after its construction, and praised its engineering:

> It is the most remarkable of achievements because the stone, which is very hard, did not exist in this part of the country and had to be brought from far away. The stones were smoothed and leveled, then cut into angular shapes and fitted next to each other, without being joined with cement or anything else. They are so well fitted and put together that they seem to give the appearance of a single piece of stone. Although many years have passed, and despite the continuous passage of so many carriages and pack animals, no stone has come loose from its original position, nor has any been worn, or even lost its shine.

On the road

When transporting heavy goods or traveling long distances, it was often quicker and cheaper to go by boat. However, traveling by road had the advantages that it was not so dependent on the seasons and was less dangerous. How people traveled on the road was determined by their means. Merchants used carts, often drawn by oxen. Wealthy people had carriages drawn by horses for longer distances. These provided some comfort and privacy, although without springs or suspension it was still a bumpy ride. Over shorter distances, a poorer traveler might simply walk. Other modes of transport included an open cart drawn by a mule, or a camel caravan. The fastest way to travel was on horseback, but this was generally only used for shorter distances.

Where to stay

About every twenty miles along a road (equivalent to one day's travel) there were official establishments called ***mānsiōnēs***. They provided somewhere to rest oxen or horses, or exchange horses for the next leg of the journey. The mansiones were operated by the state and could be used only by military or government officials, but soon commercial hostels and restaurants developed around them. These were generally arranged around a central courtyard and had stables on the ground floor for the animals. There were also rooms for guests and a place to eat. Some even had baths where travelers could refresh themselves and wash off the dust.

Dangers on the road

Travelers were often accompanied by guards; even so, they risked being ambushed and attacked by bandits. Juvenal desribed how someone traveling with precious belongings was a target:

pauca licet portēs argentī vāscula pūrī
nocte iter ingressus, gladium contumque timēbis
et mōtae ad lūnam trepidāns harundinis umbram
cantābit vacuus cōram latrōne viātor.

Though you might only be carrying a few vessels of plain silver,
Setting out on a journey at night, you'll fear the sword and spear,
And flinch at the shadow of a reed moving in the moonlight;
While an empty-handed traveler will sing in the robber's presence.

Travelers also had to beware of natural dangers. Some roads were susceptible to flooding, and tracks through mountain ranges were only passable in the spring and summer. On top of this, wild animals threatened unprotected travelers. In Apuleius' novel *The Golden Ass*, the main character is advised by locals not to travel on the nearby road at night because it is infested with packs of wolves:

> We must travel on this road with utmost care, keeping watch all around and alert to ambushes on all sides. We should travel only in daylight, in the middle of the day when the bright sun is high in the sky, since the dreadful beasts are less aggressive in daylight. And we must travel not spread out in small groups, but closely packed together. If we do this we might make it through.

cursus pūblicus

The ***cursus pūblicus*** was the imperial courier service that operated across the Empire. It allowed Rome to keep in contact with governors and officials stationed in distant provinces, and to send information and goods quickly and reliably. There were staging posts at intervals along the roads, where the message could be passed to the next courier. Only the emperor and people authorized by him could use the cursus publicus, and a permit was required. In a letter to Emperor Trajan, Pliny asked him to confirm what action he should take on out-of-date permits. Trajan replied:

> The permits whose date has expired should not be used. I shall make it a priority to send new permits to all the provinces before they are required.

Nevertheless the system could be abused, and sometimes certificates were forged or stolen. In general, however, anyone else who wanted to send a letter had to find someone traveling to its destination, and possibly pay them.

This relief, from Augsburg in modern Germany, shows an ox-drawn cart transporting barrels of wine.

Bastiza

senex quīdam in popīnā cum amīcā sedēbat, rem dē familiā suā nārrāns.

'ōlim in prōvinciā Moesiā habitābam. dē Moesiā umquam audīvistī, Perilla? terra pulcherrima est. sunt montēs magnificī, lacūs lātī, flūmina ferōcia. in altīs agrīs parentēs meī fundum tenēbant. cum nātus essem, parentēs mihi nōmen Bastizam dedērunt. in illō fundō adolēvī. adultus tamen in proximō vīcō habitāre māluī. ibi faber labōrābam, puellam dulcem in mātrimōnium dūxī. multōs annōs beātī vīvēbāmus. mihi peperit uxor duās fīliās. quae, cum parentēs in fundō vīsitārem, mē semper comitārī cupiēbant.

'ūnō diē, dum fundō parentum appropinquāmus, manum latrōnum cōnspeximus. aliī vaccās placidās agēbant, aliī pullōs in saccōs difficilius pōnēbant. ē fundō celeriter discēdēbant. fīliābus prope flūmen manēre iussīs, ad latrōnēs celerius ruī. quibus persuādēre voluī ut animālia līberārent. sed simulac mē animadvertērunt, duo mē statim rapuērunt, verberāvērunt, in vincula et coniēcērunt. mē atque animālibus sīc captīs, latrōnēs dē montibus dēscendēbant.

'nōn iterum parentēs, uxōrem, fīliās vīdī. nōn iterum nōmen Bastizam audīvī. nam cum ā latrōnibus vēnderer, vēnālicius mihi nōmen mūtāvit. vīvitne etiam nunc uxor? habentne līberōs fīliae? adhūc stat fundus parentum? nesciō. numquam in Moesiam regredī poterō. mihi enim est nūlla spēs lībertātis, nūlla pecūnia, artus inūtilis.'

hīs verbīs audītīs, Perilla Lūcriōnī dulce respondit: 'familia tua abest, sed sōlus nōn es.' tum dulcius addidit: 'Bastiza.'

adolēscō *I grow up*
adultus *grown up*
mālō *I prefer*
vacca *cow*
placidus *gentle, peaceful*
pullus *chicken*
difficilius *with more difficulty*
celerius *more quickly*
vinculum *chain*
coniciō *I throw*
vēnālicius *slave dealer*
artus *limb*
dulcius *more sweetly*
addō *I add*

A view of the Balkan mountains in Bulgaria, which used to be part of the Roman province of Moesia.

LANGUAGE NOTE 3: COMPARATIVE ADVERBS

1. Look at the following sentences. What do you notice about the words in red?

   Aponia lentius prōcēdere coepit.
   Aponia began to walk more slowly.

   ego ad latrōnēs celerius ruī.
   I rushed more quickly to the robbers.

2. **lentius** (*more slowly*) is the comparative form of the adverb **lentē** (*slowly*). **celerius** (*more quickly*) is the comparative form of **celeriter** (*quickly*). **lentius** and **celerius** are therefore known as **comparative adverbs**.

3. Look at the positive, comparative, and superlative forms of the adverb **facile** (*easily*):

   nōs piscem facile cēpimus.
   We caught the fish easily.

   nōs piscem facilius cēpimus.
   We caught the fish more easily.

   nōs piscem facillimē cēpimus.
   We caught the fish very easily.

LANGUAGE PRACTICE

2. Use the story **Bastiza** on page 196 to answer the following questions.

   a. From line 1, write down and translate a present participle.

   b. Explain why **prōvinciā** in line 2 needs to be in the ablative case.

   c. In line 3, is the word **ferōcia** an adjective or a noun?

   d. What tense is the verb **tenēbant** (line 4)?

   e. In lines 12–13, which of the following is **ut animālia līberārent**: a result clause, an indirect command, or a purpose clause?

   f. From lines 16–20, write down an example of an imperfect passive subjunctive verb.

   Look at the whole story to answer the following questions.

   g. Write down and translate a sentence which begins with a connecting relative.

   h. Write down and translate the comparative forms of the adverbs **dulce** and **difficile**.

   i. Write down and translate an ablative absolute.

   j. Write down the infinitive of a deponent verb.

The Parthians

We call them Parthians, because under their king Arshak they ousted the Seleucids from Parthia in 247 BC, but we have no idea what they called themselves. Nothing written by them survives, and our knowledge comes from Greeks and Romans (who were their enemies), from Chinese visitors, and from their coins. They were Iranian by culture and language – and probably part of the great group of Iranian peoples called 'Scythians' by the Greeks. Their empire lasted 500 years.

By 109 BC, Mehrdad II (in Greek, Mithradates) had eliminated Macedonian rule over the old Persian Empire. Greek influence gradually faded, as the old Zoroastrian religion was revived, and an alternative history slowly erased memories of the ancient Persians. The Parthian center moved westwards, into Mesopotamia (the territory between the Rivers Tigris and Euphrates), and a new capital city was built on the Tigris.

Mehrdad welcomed Zhang Qian, ambassador from the Chinese emperor Wu, who opened up the trade route between China and the west, now known as the Silk Routes. Around the same time the Parthians encountered the expanding Roman interests in Asia. It was agreed that the Euphrates would be their frontier. The Parthian Empire, having contact with both Rome and China, was now a force to be reckoned with.

Soon though, through no desire of their own, the Parthians found themselves in a confrontation with Rome. The Roman general Pompey agreed to a deal with the Parthian King, then cheated on it. As a result, Rome and Parthia became enemies, and ambitious Romans saw opportunities to imitate what Alexander had done. Roman generals were tempted to seek personal glory and wealth to help build or revive their political ambitions in Rome. Parthia was never really a threat to Rome, but Rome became a real threat to Parthia.

In 55 BC Orod was the new Parthian king, helped by Suren, a young Parthian aristocrat with his own private army. Suren was training this army to become invincible. His personal cavalry of 10,000 archers on horseback developed into a formidable force as a result of a simple innovation: he kept 1,000 camels in the rear with a fresh supply of arrows – the horsemen fired off their quiverful of arrows, and went back to the camels to reload. They would gallop at speed at the enemy, then turn their horses round, and fire their arrows as they appeared to retreat.

In Rome, meanwhile, the general and politician Crassus was permitted to raise an army to invade Parthia. For Crassus, it was a catastrophic failure. At the battle of Carrhae, in 53 BC, Crassus and half his army were killed. The standards of three Roman legions – the precious eagles – were captured. The Parthians had been outnumbered four to one – for them, it was a tremendous victory.

During the next 250 years many Romans attempted to copy the actions of Alexander by invading Parthia. Julius Caesar was assassinated before he could do so, but there were three more unsuccessful invasions (including a disastrous one by Mark Antony) before Augustus humbled himself to make peace, and the captured eagles were finally returned to Rome. When the Parthians did invade Roman territory, they themselves were defeated, but saved from conquest by an outbreak of the plague. Emperor Severus' final invasion in AD 198 ended in utter failure.

However, by now the Parthian Empire was falling apart. Civil war, the independence of great families like the Suren, and reliance on these nobles to provide the army, all undermined the authority of the Parthian kings. Busy confronting Rome, and based in Iraq, they didn't notice the rise of a new power in Persis, a self-governing region within the Parthian Empire. The two rival Parthian kings were each soon soundly defeated by Ardashir, king of Persis and founder of the Sasanian dynasty.

This stone carving of two lion griffins comes from Hatra, a town on the western border of the Parthian Empire.

Chapter 29: lēx

Rūfīna quaesīta

1 Aponia, ad domum patris prōcōnsulis portāta, morbō cōnfecta in lectō iacēbat.

2 quid accidit?

3 incerta sum, domine. fīlia tua vidētur esse aegerrima.

4 Aponia vidētur medicāmentum ignōtum cōnsūmpsisse.

5 Rūfīnam quandam quaesīvimus. illa esse medica optima dīcitur.

6 Rūfīna multōs aegrōs sānāvisse dīcitur, et plūrimōs pauperēs cūrāvisse.

7 certē, domine. illa multōs Ephesiōs adiūvisse dīcitur.

vidētur *seems*
dīcitur *is said*

LANGUAGE NOTE 1: PERFECT ACTIVE INFINITIVES

1. Look at the following sentences. What do you notice about the verbs in red?

   Aponia vidētur medicāmentum ignōtum cōnsūmpsisse.
   Aponia seems to have consumed an unknown drug.

   Rūfīna multōs aegrōs sānāvisse dīcitur.
   Rufina is said to have healed many sick people.

2. **cōnsūmpsisse** (*to have consumed*) and **sānāvisse** (*to have healed*) are both perfect tense, active, and infinitive. They are therefore known as **perfect active infinitives**.

3. The perfect active infinitive is formed from the perfect stem + -**isse**. The perfect active infinitives of the four conjugations are therefore as follows:

first conjugation	**vocāvisse**	*to have called*
second conjugation	**tenuisse**	*to have held*
third conjugation	**mīsisse**	*to have sent*
fourth conjugation	**audīvisse**	*to have heard*

4. Note the perfect active infinitives of the following irregular verbs:

sum	**fuisse**	*to have been*
possum	**potuisse**	*to have been able*
volō	**voluisse**	*to have wanted*

Rūfīna accūsāta

Rūfīna, ut ad domum prōcōnsulis pervēnit, rem esse dīram sēnsit, quod ancillae ad eam statim cucurrērunt.

ancilla crēdimus Aponiam medicāmenta ignōta cōnsūmpsisse.

Rūfīna cūr Aponia ea cōnsūmpsit?

ancilla nēmō scit, domina. soror eius dīcit Aponiam paucōs diēs aegram esse.

hīs audītīs, prīmō Rūfīna ōs ac pectus Aponiae celeriter īnspexit, deinde ventrem sacerdōtis summā cum cūrā tetigit. quō factō, eī paulum vīnī tūre herbīsque mixtum dedit. tōtam noctem medica iuxtā sacerdōtem sedēbat, eī aquam praebēns. sed Aponia oculōs nōn iterum aperuit. sōle ortō, Aponia mortua est.

venter *stomach*
tangō *I touch*
iuxtā *near, close to*

ancilla scīvit Rūfīnam omnia prō Aponiā fēcisse. prōcōnsul tamen, ut prīmum quae accidissent intellēxit, tam īrātus erat ut in magnum furōrem movērētur. īrātē dīxit Rūfīnam plūrimōs aegrōs aliōs sānāvisse. īrātius

ut prīmum *as soon as*
furor *rage, fury*

exclāmāvit Rūfīnam fīliam suam dē industriā interfēcisse. crēdidit enim Rūfīnam, quae Christiāna esset, maiestātem deōrum Rōmānōrum dēlēre cupīvisse.

prōcōnsul tū māvīs pauperēs senēsque quam iuvenēs dīvitēsque. tū fīliam meam adeō ōderās ut eam interficere vellēs.

Rūfīna tū magnopere dolēs. medica semper māvult cūrāre quam nocēre. sed fīlia tam aegra erat ut nēmō eam sānāre posset.

prōcōnsul medica? nōn es medica, sed sāga. et nunc poenās tū dabis.

dē industriā *on purpose*

māvīs ... quam *you prefer ... to/ rather than*

ōdī *I hate*

sāga *witch*

LANGUAGE NOTE 2: INDIRECT STATEMENTS WITH PERFECT ACTIVE INFINITIVES

1. Compare the way these sentences can be translated:

   dīcit Rūfīnam multōs aegrōs sānāvisse.
   He says Rufina was healing many sick people.
   He says Rufina (has) healed many sick people.
   He says Rufina had healed many sick people.
   (lit. *He says Rufina to have healed many sick people.*)

   dīxit Rūfīnam multōs aegrōs sānāvisse.
   He said Rufina had healed many sick people.
   He said Rufina had been healing many sick people.
   (lit. *He said Rufina to have healed many sick people.*)

2. In Latin, direct speech in any past tense is represented by a perfect infinitive when it is reported.
3. As **sānāvisse** is a perfect infinitive, the verb in the original statement was in a past tense. Therefore the original statement may have been *Rufina was healing many sick people* or *Rufina (has/had) healed many sick people*.

LANGUAGE PRACTICE

1. Translate the following sentences.
   - **a.** pater Aponiae putat Rūfīnam fīliam interfēcisse.
   - **b.** pater Aponiae putāvit Rūfīnam fīliam interfēcisse.
   - **c.** ancilla exclāmat sacerdōtem medicāmentum ēmisse.
   - **d.** ancilla exclāmāvit sacerdōtem medicāmentum ēmisse.
   - **e.** nēmō sēnsit canem cēnam cōnsūmpsisse et aquam bibisse.
   - **f.** comes fortis rettulit sē celerius quam mē opus cōnfēcisse.

Aphrodīsias

longō itinere factō, parentēs cum līberīs Sebastēīō iam appropinquābant.

1 vōsne urbem anteā vīsitāvistis, māter?

2 minimē, sed in hāc urbe templa pulcherrima ā fabrīs optimīs aedificāta esse dīcuntur.

3 imāginem auream Cupīdinis mox vidēbimus, quae ā Iūliō Caesare data esse dīcitur.

4 dōnum ā deā laetā acceptum esse vidētur, quod nunc Caesarēs orbem terrārum regunt!

Sebastēion *Sebasteion (temple dedicated to Augustus)*

Cupīdō *Cupid*

Emperor worship

The practice of dedicating temples to the emperor began with Augustus and has continued under other emperors, not only among the Greeks, but also among other nations subject to the Romans. In Rome itself and the rest of Italy no emperor, however deserving of renown, has dared to do this. Yet, even there various divine honors are given after their death to emperors who have ruled justly, and shrines are built to them.

Cassius Dio

The Sebasteion

The city of Aphrodisias, about eighty miles from Ephesus, was named after the goddess Aphrodite, whom the Romans associated with Venus. It had a grand temple complex, built between AD 20 and AD 60, dedicated to Aphrodite and to the Roman emperors from Augustus to Nero. The temple was known as the Sebasteion: ***Sebastos*** (revered one) was the Greek name for Augustus. Two prominent local families paid for its construction.

A processional avenue led up to the temple, flanked on either side by three-story buildings with colonnades whose upper stories were decorated with marble sculptures. The subjects included Roman emperors and Greek Olympian gods, and an inscription calls the emperors 'Olympian Emperor Gods' (***Theoi Sebastoi Olympioi***). The sculptures are a visual catalogue of the imperial conquests of the emperors, with the emphasis on peoples on the edges of the Empire. It is likely that the inhabitants of Aphrodisias had never even heard of some of these peoples.

Deification

When the dictator Julius Caesar died, he was deified (made a god). Augustus, Caesar's adopted son, dedicated a temple to him in the Forum Romanum. Augustus himself was deified by the Senate soon after his death. From then on emperors, and some members of their families, were regularly deified after death.

Augustus presented himself as 'first among equals' (***prīmus inter parēs***) and was cautious about being given extraordinary honors during his lifetime. Therefore, he discouraged emperor worship in Rome itself, and the emperors who followed him, with a few exceptions, did likewise. However, in some of the eastern provinces there was a tradition of worshiping rulers as gods while they were still alive, so it was natural for people there to honor the Roman emperor in the same way. Augustus gave permission to some towns in the province of Asia to establish the worship of the emperor along with Roma (the personification of Rome). The practice of emperor worship then spread gradually to other parts of the Empire. Often temples dedicated to the emperor were built in the provinces, and emperors were honored in similar ways to other gods, with prayers, processions, sacrifices, and games.

Encouraging emperor worship in the provinces had political advantages for Rome. It was a unifying factor across the Empire and was also a way of forming a bond between the elite provincial families and Rome. The wealthiest and most distinguished members of the local aristocracy often paid for the construction of temples and regarded it as a great honor to serve as a high priest.

Divine ancestry

Augustus was the adopted son and great-nephew of the deified Julius Caesar, and called himself ***dīvī fīlius*** (son of a god). Both Augustus and Caesar belonged to the Julian family, which traced its ancestry back to Iulus, the son of Aeneas, himself the son of the goddess Venus. This close association with a goddess made it easier for the Romans to see Julius Caesar and Augustus as gods themselves, at least after their deaths. Moreover, Augustus had brought peace to the Roman world after many years of civil wars. The poet Propertius called him ***mundī servātor*** (savior of the world). Perhaps it isn't hard to understand why Augustus was regarded by many as a god.

This relief from the Sebasteion shows Aeneas fleeing Troy carrying his elderly father on his shoulders and leading his young son, Iulus, by the hand. Behind them stands Venus.

LANGUAGE NOTE 3: PERFECT PASSIVE INFINITIVES

1. Study the following sentences. What do you notice about the verbs in red?

   templa pulcherrima in hāc urbe aedificāta esse dīcuntur.
   Very beautiful temples are said to have been built in this city.
   (lit. *Very beautiful temples are said to be (in a state of) having been built in this city.*)

   dōnum ā deā laetā acceptum esse vidētur.
   The gift seems to have been received by a pleased goddess.
   (lit. *The gift seems to be (in a state of) having been received by a pleased goddess.*)

2. **aedificāta esse** (*to have been built*) and **acceptum esse** (*to have been received*) are perfect tense, passive, and infinitive. Therefore they are known as **perfect passive infinitives**.
3. Perfect passive infinitives are formed from perfect passive participles with **esse**. The perfect passive infinitives of the four conjugations are therefore as follows:

first conjugation	**vocātus esse**	*to have been called*
second conjugation	**tentus esse**	*to have been held*
third conjugation	**missus esse**	*to have been sent*
fourth conjugation	**audītus esse**	*to have been heard*

Sebastēion

parentēs et līberī per viam lentē prōcēdēbant ut Sebastēion dīligentius īnspicerent. duās porticūs, ante templum aedificātās, mīrātī sunt. dum parentēs imāginēs īnspiciunt, senex īnfirmus eīs appropinquāvit.

'salvēte, amīcī,' inquit senex. 'habētisne pecūniam quam pauperī dare potestis?' cum senis miserērētur, māter nōnnūllōs assēs trādidit.

'grātiās tibi agō,' inquit senex. 'abhinc multīs annīs ad hanc urbem vēnī ut hās imāginēs facerem. dum tamen labōrō, rēs dīra accidit: dē scālīs cecidī et bracchium cōnfrēgī. nunc labōrāre nōn possum.'

pater senem rogāvit quās imāginēs fēcisset. duās imāginēs ostendēns, 'hīc dīvum Claudium, illīc Aenēān ē patriā effugientem sculpsī,' respondit.

māter vīdit figūram fēminae sub Claudiō sculptam esse. 'agnōscō hanc fēminam esse Britanniam,' inquit. 'haec imāgō nārrat prōvinciam ultimam ā Claudiō victam esse.'

īnfirmus *weak*
misereor *I pity, feel sorry for*
scālae *ladder*
cōnfringō *I break, smash*
dīvus *divine*
Aenēās *Aeneas*
patria *homeland*
sculpō *I carve, sculpt*
ultimus *furthest*

'rēctē dīcis, domina,' inquit senex. 'prīncipēs Rōmānī et hērōēs clārī et deī immortālēs hīc sculptī sunt. Claudius prōvinciam vīcit et Aenēās gentem Rōmānam condidit. Nerō autem tōtum orbem terrārum regit. nōs decet Nerōnī sīcut deō honōrem dare.'

quibus dictīs, senex lentē discēdēbat. līberī, templum pulcherrimum mīrātī, putābant haec verba in illō locō bene dicta esse.

clārus *famous, distinguished*
condō *I establish, found*

LANGUAGE NOTE 4: INDIRECT STATEMENTS WITH PERFECT PASSIVE INFINITIVES

1. Compare the way these sentences can be translated:

    dīcit templum ab optimīs fabrīs aedificātum esse.
    He says the temple was (being) built by the best craftsmen.
    He says the temple has/had been built by the best craftsmen.
    (lit. *He says the temple to have been built by the best craftsmen.*)

    dīxit templum ab optimīs fabrīs aedificātum esse.
    He said the temple had been built by the best craftsmen.
    (lit. *He said the temple to have been built by the best craftsmen.*)

    Note that the tense of the Latin infinitive reflects the tense of the original direct statement.

2. Now look at the following sentence:

    dīxit puellās ā mātre vocātās esse.
    She said the girls had been called by their mother.

    Note how the perfect passive infinitive has changed its form to agree with **puellās**.

A sculpture from the Sebasteion showing Agrippina crowning her son Nero with a laurel wreath.

Imperial propaganda

The emperors used propaganda to create a positive image of their rule. Rome represented peace, stable government, and civilization, an idea which was encapsulated in the term ***pāx Rōmāna***. Societies outside Roman rule were characterized as barbaric and uncivilized. These messages were spread through literature, art, buildings and monuments, performance, and coinage. Roman achievements were publicized, while negative stories were often suppressed or edited.

Unlike today, there were no media outlets to investigate or contest a story. Since another record of the facts was rarely available, the official version of events was sometimes the only one. Moreover, as the emperor was believed to be favored by the gods, or even a god himself, it was difficult to question him.

Literature

The *Res Gestae Divi Augusti* is a record of the accomplishments and deeds of Emperor Augustus, written in the first person. After his death it was inscribed on monuments and temples in Rome and throughout the Empire. An almost complete version, written in both Latin and Greek, survives on a temple to Augustus in Ankara, in modern Turkey. Here are two extracts:

> I rebuilt, at great expense, both the Temple of Jupiter and the Theater of Pompey, without an inscription of my name.
>
> I extended the frontiers of all the provinces of the Roman people which were bordered by nations not yet subject to our Empire.

Vergil's *Aeneid*, written during the reign of Emperor Augustus, narrates the founding of Rome by Aeneas. In the Underworld, Aeneas' father foretells the glory of Rome. He shows Aeneas Rome's future heroes, including Romulus, Julius Caesar, and Augustus. He then addresses a fictitious future Roman (the intended audience of Vergil's poem):

> 'You, Roman, remember to rule the nations with your authority, for these are your skills: to impose your customs onto peace, to spare those who submit, and to crush the proud.'

Statues

The emperor was the face of Roman power and his presence was felt everywhere. Few people living in the Empire would ever see the emperor in real life, but statues of him were displayed publicly, serving as physical reminders of Roman rule. He was depicted in various roles: military commander, priest, and statesman.

A marble statue of Augustus was found at the house in Rome of his wife, Livia. It is called the Augustus of Prima Porta, and was probably copied from a bronze statue made for public display. A copy of the marble statue is shown below, painted to reconstruct how it may have looked originally.

Image

Augustus wears armor and stretches out his right arm like a commander addressing his troops. His posture resembles a classical Greek statue (such as Polykleitos' *Diadoumenos* on page 147) – he is a perfect example of strength and youth. His legs and feet are bare, in the manner of an athlete or god. Portraits of Augustus made throughout his life depict him as young and handsome.

Breastplate

In the center are two figures: the one on the left represents Rome; on the right there is a Parthian, identifiable by his beard and loose pants. The Parthian is returning the Roman military standards (symbols that the Romans carried into battle), which had been captured in war thirty years before. Their recovery was considered a great achievement. All around, gods and personifications of countries conquered by Augustus allude to his military success and assert that his actions are blessed by the gods.

Cupid

Beside Augustus is a small Cupid, riding a dolphin. Cupid, the son of Venus, reminds the viewer of Augustus' divine lineage.

Buildings and monuments

In every land they conquered the Romans constructed buildings in the Roman style, such as baths and circuses. Triumphal arches, like those in Camulodunum and Rome commemorating Claudius' victory over the Britons, were more overt demonstrations of Roman might and superiority.

One example of architectural propaganda on a grand scale was Hadrian's Wall (*left*), which crossed northern Britannia, marking the boundary of Roman rule. It had a practical function as a border where tolls and taxes were collected. However, it was primarily a symbolic statement of Roman power at the furthest limit of the Empire. An ancient biography of Emperor Hadrian tells us:

Britanniam petīvit, in quā multa corrēxit mūrumque per octōgintā mīlia passuum prīmus dūxit, quī barbarōs Rōmānōsque dīvideret.

He set out for Britain and there he put right many things and was the first to build a wall eighty miles long, which would separate the barbarians and the Romans.

Performance

A Roman triumph was a victory parade in Rome which processed slowly from the Campus Martius to the Temple of Jupiter. During the Republic a victorious general returning to Rome would be awarded a triumph. However, once the Principate had been established only the emperor, in his role as Commander-in-Chief of the army, and members of his family could be granted a triumph.

Some parades lasted for as long as two or three days. At the front walked the conquered enemies, in chains and wearing their traditional dress. Next, captured weapons, precious treasures, and works of art were heaped on wagons. Behind these walked Rome's senators, and finally the general himself, drawn in a chariot and wearing the ***toga picta***, a purple toga with gold embroidery. Some generals even brought living trees and animals back from conquered lands and paraded them through Rome.

As a form of mass entertainment the Romans staged re-enactments of famous sea-battles. These were usually held in man-made lakes with seating for spectators, although on some occasions amphitheaters were flooded. Thousands of prisoners of war or convicts who had been condemned to die were dressed to mimic two opposing armies. But these spectacles were not simulations – they would have been violent and bloody. They were a manifestation of Roman power and they celebrated Roman victories.

Coinage

Julius Caesar was the first Roman to put his own portrait on coins during his lifetime. Before that, only gods or men who were no longer alive were depicted. Coins were an effective means of propaganda because they were part of everyday life and were dispersed all over the Empire. The simple images on them could communicate information, for example the accession of a new emperor. The imagery was particularly important because the majority of the population was illiterate.

Some emperors who ruled for only a short time still made sure that there was a coin with their portrait. For example, this coin depicts Emperor Galba, who was emperor for less than two months before being assassinated in AD 69. On the other side, the goddess Fortuna stands with her foot on a globe, making a sacrifice over an altar.

QUESTIONS

Consider the different methods of propaganda.

1. Who were they aimed at?
2. What messages were they communicating?
3. How effective do you think they were?

Iūdaea

praecō in forō Ephesiō in mediā turbā rēs Iūdaeās nūntiābat. nōnnūllī cīvēs praecōnem audiēbant. in forō Zabdela et Sōrānos forte aderant. sīc turbam adlocūtus est praecō:

'audīte, omnēs! rem novam dē exercitū nostrō cognōscite! dux clārus Vespasiānus, ab imperātōre ipsō ad prōvinciam Iūdaeam missus, ibi rebelliōnem reprimit. barbarī in illā prōvinciā adeō cupiditāte atque superstitiōne īnsānā agitātī sunt, ut auctōritātem prīncipis negāre, pācem rumpere, sine lēgibus vīvere māllent quam vītās tūtās agere.

'Vespasiānus nunc omnēs urbēs Iūdaeae iam vīcit, praeter Hierosolyma ipsa. dīcitur Iūdaeōs hostēs complūrēs fuisse et ferōciter pugnāvisse; cōpiās Vespasiānī tamen perītius pugnāvisse, hostēs superāvisse, urbēs Iūdaeās occupāvisse. eī quī caedem vītāvērunt ad urbem Hierosolyma effūgērunt. quam Vespasiānus, legiōnibus per hiemem parātīs, mox vincet. audīte, omnēs!'

Zabdela, hīs audītīs, Sōrānon gravī vōce adlocūtus est: 'vah! nōlī omnia crēdere, Sōrāne. multī Iūdaeī in urbem Hierosolyma convēnērunt ut Rōmānōs ibi oppugnārent. quōs superāre facile nōn erit Vespasiānō. Iūdaeī Rōmānīs resistunt nōn ob cupiditātem aut īnsāniam, sed quod vītās līberās agere volunt. certē potentēs sunt legiōnēs Rōmānae, sed populus Iūdaeōrum audāx est, prō deō suō atque lībertāte pugnāns. nōn semper bellō vincunt Rōmānī ...'

praecō *town crier, herald*
barbarus *foreigner; barbarian*
cupiditās *greed*
superstitiō *superstition*
negō *I deny; say that ... not*
rumpō *I break*
māllent: **mālō**
Hierosolyma *Jerusalem*
complūrēs *many, very many*
ob *because of*
īnsānia *madness*

This coin is from Gamla, a city in the Roman province of Judaea, which was besieged by the Romans during the Jewish Revolt in AD 66. Coins, such as this one, were minted within the besieged city. Scholars have interpreted the inscription to read: 'For the redemption of Holy Jerusalem'.

accūsātiō

multī Ephesiī in basilicam convēnerant, ut iūdicium medicae spectārent. Sōrānos in turbā aderat, et vidēbat Rūfīnam, prō tribūnālī stantem, ā duōbus hominibus custōdīrī. aderat quoque Aponius prōcōnsul cum amīcō, quī erat iūdex.

prīmō Aponius dīcēbat Rūfīnam fīliam suam interfēcisse et herbīs magicīs ūsam esse. tum ab Aponiō vocātus est Marus quīdam, quī dīxit et amīcum Castorem artibus magicīs ā Rūfīnā sānātum esse, et sē crēdere Rūfīnam sāgam esse. nōnnūllī in turbā magnīs vōcibus cōnsēnsērunt.

Rūfīna respondit sē nūllum scelus fēcisse, puellam aegram adiūvisse, illī medicāmenta dedisse. dīxit sē medicam dīligentem esse. multī Ephesiī, quōs Rūfīna iūverat, medicam dēfendere volēbant. sed ā prōcōnsule dissentīre nōn ausī sunt.

accūsātiō *accusation*

tribūnal *platform (for judge or magistrate)*

magicus *magic*
ūtor *I use, employ*

dissentiō *I disagree, dissent*
ausī sunt *they dared*

LANGUAGE PRACTICE

2. Complete each sentence with the correct form of the infinitive, then translate.

a. nōs audīvimus Britannōs ab imperātōre Claudiō ....
(victam esse, victōs esse, victum esse)

b. scīvistis Caesarem ōlim ā pīrātīs ....
(captum esse, captam esse, captī esse)

c. nūntius dīxit multās victōriās ā Vespasiānō clārō ....
(relātam esse, relātās esse, relātōs esse)

d. Zabdela igitur putāvit populum ā nūntiō ....
(dēceptus esse, dēceptī esse, dēceptum esse)

e. ducēs cognōvērunt hostēs ē castrīs ....
(profectī esse, profectōs esse, profectās esse)

f. mātrōna intellēxit fūrēs marītum dīvitem ad urbem ....
(secūtam esse, secūtum esse, secūtōs esse)

The law

Rome's legal system is one of its most enduring achievements and forms the basis of many countries' legal systems today. In 449 BC, Rome's laws were first written down on the Twelve Tables, wooden tablets which were displayed publicly. This formalization of the laws and their public display ensured that they were known to all, and that everyone was subject to the same laws. Over time the legal system was adapted and reformed. From the beginning of the Principate the highest legal authority was the emperor. He was also the source of all new legislation and he employed legal specialists to refine and interpret the law. Law and order was a fundamental part of the Pax Romana. As the Empire expanded, the Romans imposed their legal system on the territories that they conquered, and this was a way of maintaining peace.

In the provinces

Although inhabitants of Roman provinces were not automatically Roman citizens, they were subject to Roman laws. The governor had jurisdiction over the legal affairs within the province, and cases involving Roman citizens would be judged by him or another imperial representative. Non-citizens were usually allowed to be tried in accordance with their local legal system, although if the crime was serious the case could be brought to the governor. Serving as a judge was one of the governor's most time-consuming duties and each year he would travel around his province to hear and judge cases.

Access to the law

The law applied to all, but an individual wanting to bring someone to court had to be able to afford to take time off work, travel to where the trial would be held, and, in some cases, pay for a lawyer. A patron might be able to offer support or the service of a lawyer, but even so it was often preferable to settle disputes out of court, as Martial advises:

> **et iūdex petit et petit patrōnus.**
> **solvās cēnseō, Sexte, crēditōrī.**
> Both the judge and your patron ask for money.
> Sextus, I advise you just to pay your creditor.

In Petronius' *Satyricon* two characters have their cloaks stolen. When they see that the cloaks are being sold by the thief, one suggests that they take him to court. The other replies that in a city where they know nobody they have no chance of winning:

> **quid faciant lēgēs, ubi sōla pecūnia rēgnat,**
> **aut ubi paupertās vincere nūlla potest?**
> What can the laws do, when money alone rules,
> or when the poor man can win nothing?

Furthermore, the law gave no protection to those who were enslaved, who could be punished by their owners without trial.

Courts and trials

There was no equivalent of a modern police force. Within Rome military units maintained order, and the army kept the peace in the provinces. Their duty was to protect the state; they did not investigate crimes against individuals. There was no state prosecution, and private citizens had to bring cases to court. The court then summoned the defendant to trial, and witnesses and evidence were produced by both sides. Women could bring cases against people, be brought to trial, and could appear as witnesses in trials. In court they could either speak for themselves, or be represented by their legal guardian if they had one, usually their father or husband. Slaves could be

This is one of nine bronze tablets on which the municipal laws of the Roman colony Julia Genetiva, in southern Spain, were inscribed. The colony was founded by Julius Caesar, but these tablets are a later copy of the laws, from the late first century AD. The tablets would have been fixed to a building where they could have been read easily. Each one is over 3 feet wide.

witnesses, but their evidence was only admissible if it had been given under torture. The torture would be conducted either in the courtroom or another room, in the presence of witnesses. It was generally only used in serious cases and as a last resort. The judge (***iūdex***) was a private male citizen and since he might not have any special legal knowledge, he could consult an expert on specific issues of the law. Trials were held publicly. In Rome, cases were usually heard at the Basilica Iulia. Pliny the Younger wrote to a friend telling him about a speech he had made there in defense of a woman called Attia, who had been disinherited by her elderly father in favor of her new stepmother:

> There was a crowd of lawyers on both sides, and a dense ring of spectators around the wide court. There were even men and women hanging from the upper galleries eager to hear (which was difficult) and to see (which was easy). Fathers, daughters, and stepmothers waited with great anticipation.

Punishment

Punishments were intended as deterrents and so were usually carried out publicly in order to discourage others. Imprisonment was not a sentence – prisons were used to hold convicted criminals until they were punished, or accused persons while awaiting trial. Fines and whipping were common penalties. For a more serious crime a person might be condemned to labor, sent into exile, or executed. The punishment depended on whether or not the offender was a Roman citizen. Generally citizens were executed only if they were convicted of treason, and they could not be crucified. The punishment also depended on the individual's status: members of the senatorial and equestrian classes were punished less harshly than ordinary citizens.

This mosaic shows a method of execution: damnātiō ad bestiās.

dēfēnsiō

testibus ut Rūfīnam dēfenderent adductīs, Menander et Zabdela prō Rūfīnā loquēbantur. dīcēbant illam vītās multōrum servāvisse et artem atque ingenium eius ab omnibus laudārī. et Lūcriō in iūdicium vocātus est ut dominam dēfenderet. iūdex tamen nūntiāvit sē servō nōn crēdere nisi cruciātō.

Sōrānos itaque vīdit Lūcriōnem ā custōdibus dēdūcī. cīvibus inter sē murmurantibus, duās post hōrās illī regressī sunt. Lūcriō, vī dolōris paene conlāpsus et ā custōdibus adiūtus, prope tribūnal cōnstitit.

iūdex servum rogāverat num dominam suam herbās magicās, dēvōtiōnēs, incantātiōnēs facientem umquam cōnspexisset. scrība respondit Lūcriōnem negāvisse sē haec umquam vīdisse. hīs dictīs, cīvēs in turbā inter sē loquī coepērunt. iūdex, ā loquentibus vexātus, maiōre vōce iūdicium dare incēpit.

dēfēnsiō *defense*
testis *witness*
cruciō *I torture*
dēvōtiō *curse*
incantātiō *enchantment, spell*
vexō *I annoy*

prōvocātiō

sed iuvenis quīdam in turbā prope Sōrānon verba iūdicis subitō interrūpit: 'prōvocātiōnem ad Caesarem posce, Rūfīna! lībera es! cīvis es!'

fronte contractā Rūfīna breviter dubitābat, tum ad iūdicem sē vertēns, clārā vōce exclāmāvit: 'prōvocātiōnem ad Caesarem poscō. cīvis Rōmāna sum, et Rōmae in iūdicium vocārī mālō.' quibus verbīs maximē vexātus, iūdex 'sit!' exclāmāvit, omnēs dīmīsit et imperāvit ut Rūfīna Rōmam veherētur. Aponius, īrā incēnsus, ē forō exiit. tum Rūfīna, quae in plaustrō per forum vehēbātur, Sōrānon Menandrumque in turbā cōnspexit, et clāmāvit, 'audīte, Sōrāne, Menander! Rōmae certē perībō. nunc Lūcriōnem līberō. valēte, amīcī.'

prōvocātiō *challenge, appeal*
interrumpō *I interrupt*
clārus *clear*
sit *let it be so, okay*
vehō *I carry*

cīvis Rōmānus sum

A Roman citizen had certain privileges. These included being protected by law from unjust treatment and the right to appeal to have his or her case transferred to Rome.

SOURCE 1

Gavius was a Roman citizen living in Sicily. He was accused of being a spy for the escaped slave Spartacus. In the hope of avoiding being beaten and executed in Sicily, he asserted his rights as a Roman citizen. But Verres, the corrupt governor of Sicily, ignored his plea and had him stripped, beaten, and crucified.

Cicero prosecuted Verres for his actions. He was appalled at the unjust treatment of Gavius and addressed Verres in court:

> You confess that he shouted out, 'I am a Roman citizen,' but the name of citizenship did not cause you any doubt or even the slightest hesitation in your most cruel and shameful punishment.

SOURCE 2

Christians were sometimes persecuted for their beliefs. When the apostle Paul was charged with causing unrest and was about to be whipped, he asked:

> 'Is it legal for you to whip a Roman citizen who hasn't been found guilty?'

The commander who had ordered the whipping immediately told the soldiers to stop. Paul was a Roman citizen and was therefore protected from being whipped before conviction and had the right to appeal. He asked to have his case heard in Rome, where he was sentenced to death and beheaded.

DISCUSSION

Do you think modern legal systems treat all people equally?

Appeal to the emperor

One way of obtaining justice was to appeal directly to the emperor. Emperors had to deal with a stream of appeals from towns and individuals. We know about the case of a woman called Tryphera from a letter sent by Augustus to the council, magistrates, and people of Cnidus in the province of Asia.

When Tryphera was charged with murder in Cnidus, she appealed to Augustus. The city sent representatives to Rome to petition the Emperor to uphold their decision to charge her. Augustus ordered Asinus Gallus, the proconsul of Asia, to investigate the case by questioning Tryphera's slaves under torture. Gallus reported that a man had repeatedly attacked Tryphera's house. On the third night the man's brother came too. Tryphera told one of her slaves to pour the contents of a chamber pot on the two men. However, the slave let go of the pot, which struck the brother and killed him. The slave, even when tortured, insisted it was an accident. Augustus ends his letter to the council, magistrates, and people of Cnidus by saying:

> You weren't angry with the men who deserved to be punished for three times making a violent attack on someone else's house at night and thus threatening the safety of everyone in your city. Instead you directed your anger at an innocent woman who had suffered misfortune while trying to defend herself. Now I think you should see to it that your public records follow my judgment in this matter. Farewell.

QUESTIONS

1. What steps did Augustus take to find out the truth?
2. Why did he decide that Tryphera should not be punished for the death of the attacker?
3. According to Augustus, who should have been punished, and why?
4. What can you learn from this letter about the relationship between the emperor and the local magistrates in the provinces?
5. Do you think this is a fair way of administering justice?

LANGUAGE PRACTICE

3. Complete each sentence with the **future tense** form of the verb, then translate.

a.	mox līberōs, quī in montibus procul habitant, ...	(servāmus, servābāmus, servābimus)
b.	crās cōnsul rēgī vestrō auxilium	(praebēbit, praebuit, praebet)
c.	iūdex Rūfīnam Rōmam, ubi ea poenās dabit, ...	(mittet, mittit, mīsit)
d.	quantae sunt nāvēs quae hominēs .... ?	(portant, portābant, portābunt)
e.	quālia animālia ex agrīs altīs .... ?	(pellō, pellam, pellēbam)
f.	quō .... sī Rōmānī oppidum oppugnābunt?	(fugiēs, fugis, fūgistī)

Actaeon

After a successful day hunting with his companions, Actaeon came across the goddess Diana bathing with her nymphs.

- Read or listen to the myth of Diana and Actaeon.

An extreme reaction?

Look at Source 1. Why do you think Diana was so angry with Actaeon? Was it simply that he startled her or could there be another reason?

SOURCE 1

A painting of the myth of Diana and Actaeon by Joachim Wtewael.

Divine displeasure

SOURCE 2

'Now you may tell everyone, if you are able to speak, that is, of having seen the goddess Diana naked!' She gave him the antlers of a stag with a long neck, pointed ear-tips, changing feet for hands, long legs for arms, and covering his body with a dappled hide. And then she added fear.

Ovid

- Look at what Diana says at the start of Source 2. What do you think her tone of voice might have been? How would Actaeon have reacted to what he heard?
- As he saw what was happening to him, how do you imagine Actaeon felt? How appropriate was it that Diana chose to change Actaeon into a stag, rather than into another kind of creature?
- 'And then she added fear.' Does this detail add anything to the story, or to the way in which we view the characters?

The death of Actaeon by Jacopo del Sellaio, from 1485.

SOURCE 3

A punishment to fit the crime?

SOURCE 4

While Actaeon hesitates, his dogs catch sight of him. In front is Black-foot and keen-scented Tracker; then others rush at him as fast as the wind – Greedy and Gazelle, Deer-killer, Whirlwind and Hunter ...

Not until his many wounds take his life away is the fury of Diana appeased. Even Chance must be atoned for; to a wounded deity, Chance is no excuse.

Ovid

- Look at Sources 3 and 4. How do you react to Actaeon's death and the way in which Ovid describes it?

In his version of the story Ovid makes it clear that it was completely by chance that Actaeon saw Diana. Did he therefore deserve such a dreadful death? Another version of the story says that Actaeon wanted to marry Diana and that she killed him for being arrogant. Yet another claims that Diana was angered when Actaeon boasted that he was a better hunter than she was.

- To what extent do the other versions justify Diana's reaction?
- Why might Romans have thought that gods were so easily offended by the actions of mortals? Can you think of other myths where the same theme is explored?

Chapter 30: ōmina

auspicia mala

Iānuārius *of January*
augur *augur (interpreter of auspices)*
concidō *I fall down*
Mausōlēum *Mausoleum (tomb of Augustus)*
foris *door, gate*
sponte *of one's own accord, spontaneously*
būbō *horned owl, eagle owl*
clāvis *key*
fulmen *lightning*
tonitrus *thunder*

16 pullārius fīliō pullōs sacrōs ostendit.

17 cūr augurēs pullōs habent?

18 hī pullī sunt sacrī. augurēs eōs intentē spectant.

pullārius *keeper of chickens*

19 crās pullī ab augure līberābuntur ac spectābuntur.

20 sī offa ex ōre pullī pāscentis cadet, bona auspicia ab augure referentur.

21 sed sī pullī nōn pāscentur, auspicia mala ab eō nūntiābuntur.

offa *piece of food*
pāscor *I feed, eat*

Augury

auspiciīs hanc urbem conditam esse, auspiciīs bellō ac pāce, domī mīlitiaeque omnia gerī, quis est, quī ignōret?

This city was founded by consulting auspices; all things, in war and in peace, in the home and on the battlefield, are carried out by consulting auspices. Who is there that does not know this?

Livy

The Romans believed that they could find out the will of the gods by observing birds and other natural phenomena. The practice of interpreting these signs is called augury. Special priests, called augurs, were in charge of reading the signs. Before the state made a decision or before an important event, it was necessary to consult the ***auspicia*** (auspices). For example, elections, the passing of laws, and military campaigns could not go ahead until it was confirmed, through reading the omens, that the gods supported the undertaking. Unlike Greek oracles, which gave advice or warnings, the Roman auspices simply indicated whether the gods approved or not.

auspicia

Omens from the gods appeared in two ways: in answer to a particular request in a ceremonial setting (***auspicia impetrātīva***), or as signs that occurred without being requested (***auspicia oblātīva***). Any apparently significant or unusual occurrence could be considered an auspicium oblativum, for example thunder and lightning during a ceremony. A magistrate could choose to accept these unrequested signs and seek interpretation from an augur or reject them as meaningless.

One way an augur consulted the auspices was by observing the flight of specific kinds of bird: for example, eagles, vultures, or woodpeckers. First, he marked out an area in the sky to watch. He then waited for birds and determined whether the omens were good or bad. The interpretation was based on which types of bird appeared, the direction and pattern of flight, and the height and speed at which they flew. During this time there had to be no interruption; otherwise, the reading was declared void and the process was started again. Once the auspices had been interpreted by an augur, it was up to the magistrate or military commander to decide on the course of action.

The sacred chickens

Another method of divining the will of the gods was by watching sacred chickens to see if they ate the food that was given to them. This form of augury was often used in military campaigns, and the chickens were brought along specifically for this purpose, cared for by the ***pullārius***. If the chickens ate enthusiastically, then the omen was good. If they refused to eat, then the omen was unfavorable and the undertaking for which the reading had been requested was abandoned.

Augurs

Reading the auspices was an important job, since to misinterpret an omen sent by the gods could have dire consequences. Membership in the college of augurs was a great honor and the position was held for life. At the time of our stories there were only sixteen augurs. As symbols of their office, augurs wore a special toga called the ***trabea***, which had red stripes and a purple border. They also carried the ***lituus***, a wooden stick which was curved at the top.

prōdigia

The most serious type of auspicium oblativum was a ***prōdigium***. This was an unnatural phenomenon which represented the extreme displeasure of the gods. It was a Roman citizen's duty to report any prodigium that he witnessed. These reported omens were then referred to a group of officials who presented the most serious cases to the Senate. If a prodigium was deemed to be threatening, the augurs were called to investigate the source of the divine anger and perform a purification to re-establish the ***pāx deōrum*** (peace with the gods). Some examples of prodigia recorded by Roman writers include marble statues sweating blood, sheep becoming goats, comets, and eclipses.

A bronze statue of Jupiter, the god most closely associated with the omens read by augurs. He holds a thunderbolt in his right hand and his symbol was an eagle.

LANGUAGE NOTE 1: FUTURE PASSIVE

1. In Chapter 14 you met the future tense of first and second conjugation verbs. For example:

   crās in thermīs labōrābimus.
   Tomorrow we shall work in the baths.

2. In Chapter 18 you met the future tense of third and fourth conjugation verbs. For example:

   ad salūtātiōnem cōtīdiē veniēs.
   You will come to the salutatio every day.

3. Now look at the following sentences. What do you notice about the words in red?

   crās pullī ab augure līberābuntur.
   Tomorrow the chickens will be set free by the augur.

   nōs pūniēmur.
   We shall be punished.

   līberābuntur and **pūniēmur** are passive forms of the future tense.

4. Look at the future passive of **vocō** (*I call*) and **mittō** (*I send*):

vocābor	*I shall be called*	**mittar**	*I shall be sent*
vocāberis	*you will be called*	**mittēris**	*you will be sent*
vocābitur	*he/she/it will be called*	**mittētur**	*he/she/it will be sent*
vocābimur	*we shall be called*	**mittēmur**	*we shall be sent*
vocābiminī	*you will be called*	**mittēminī**	*you will be sent*
vocābuntur	*they will be called*	**mittentur**	*they will be sent*

Note that the end of the verb (**-r**, **-ris**, **-tur**, **-mur**, **-minī**, **-ntur**) tells us who will receive the action of the verb.

viae Subūrae

in plaustrō, montem Palātīnum ascēnsūrō, captīvī per viās Subūrae vehēbantur. inter eōs sedēbat Rūfīna, fessa atque sordida. medica viās Subūrānās spectābat, aedificia nova vidēns, nēminem agnōscēns. Rūfīnae, mox peritūrae, in mentem vēnērunt frāter et Sabīna, parentēs, coniūnx abhinc longum tempus mortuus.

aedificium *building*
mēns *mind*

Augurs and influence

The augurs held a great amount of power. Without their readings of favorable omens, no important public actions could be undertaken. Although the auspices were sent by the gods, their meaning and validity could be confirmed only by an augur. After the establishment of the Principate, the emperor, as Pontifex Maximus, was also the chief augur.

SOURCE 1

Cicero, writing in the Republic, questions how the readings of the augurs had been manipulated for the benefit of those in power:

> We regard lightning on the left as the most favorable omen for everything except for assemblies of the people. This exception was made, no doubt, for political reasons, so that the leaders of the state would interpret the omens for popular assemblies, whether held to conduct trials judged by the people, or to pass laws, or to elect magistrates.

SOURCE 2

This coin has a portrait of Emperor Vespasian on one side and the signs of the office of augur on the other. The lettering reads AUGUR TRI POT (augur tribunicia potestas), referring to two powerful positions held by the emperor.

SOURCE 3

This altar shows Augustus as an augur, holding the lituus in his right hand. Throughout his rule he promoted the practice of augury.

SOURCE 4

Pliny, who had recently been appointed as an augur, writes to a friend:

> You congratulate me on accepting the office of augur. You do so rightly, first because it is right to obey the judgment of so wise an emperor, and secondly because the priestly office itself is an ancient and sacred one, and its sanctity and dignity is clear from the fact that it is an office that is held for life. For, although other offices are almost equal in dignity, they may be granted one day and taken away the next. But with the augurship, there is no chance of it being taken away.

DISCUSSION

In what ways was the office of the augur a powerful and desirable one?

iūdicium imperātōris

in aulā prīnceps, rēs cīvium iūdicātūrus, in tribūnālī sedēbat. scrībae, cohors Batāvōrum, atque nōnnūllī lībertī circum tribūnal stābant ut imperātōrem adiuvārent. plūrimī cīvēs in aulam vocātī erant ut ā Caesare iūdicārentur. prīnceps nōnnūllōs cīvēs, quī coniūrātiōnis aut parricīdiī accūsātī erant, damnāvit.

Rūfīnā adductā, scrība accūsātiōnem recitābat. dīxit fēminam in prōvinciā Asiā sacerdōtem necāvisse, venēnō ūsam esse. addidit Rūfīnam sāgam esse, dēvōtiōnēs et herbās magicās vēndidisse, hominēs in animālia mūtāvisse, in āere volitantem vīsam esse. contrā quod Rūfīna, quae lacrimātūra esse vidēbātur, respondēbat sē innocentem esse. medicam sīc loquentem subitō agnōvit Indus. prīnceps, Rūfīnam damnātūrus, breviter dubitāvit. eam rogāvit num in venēnīs perīta esset. Rūfīna, haec negātūra et sē dēfēnsūra, vultum Indī, quī eī signum dabat, forte cōnspexit. Rūfīna, maximē mīrāta, respondit sē multa didicisse dē venēnīs, et ab eīs nōnnūllōs hominēs servāvisse.

prīnceps Epaphrodītum gravī vōce sīc adlocūtus est: 'ōmen est! crēdō eam ā deīs missam esse, Epaphrodīte! haec Rūfīna mē servābit!' et maiōre vōce nūntiāvit sē Rūfīnae ignōtūrum esse, et Rūfīnam in Domō Aureā labōrātūram esse.

aula *court, hall*
iūdicō *I judge, pass judgment on*
parricīdium *murder of a relative*
āēr *air*

A bronze eagle with garnet inlays.

LANGUAGE NOTE 2: FUTURE PARTICIPLE AND FUTURE INFINITIVE

1. Study the following sentences. What do you notice about the way in which the words in red are translated?

   prīnceps, Rūfīnam damnātūrus, breviter dubitāvit.
   The emperor, on the point of condemning Rufina, hesitated briefly.

   Rūfīna, sē dēfēnsūra, Indum cōnspexit.
   Rufina, about to defend herself, caught sight of Indus.

2. The words **damnātūrus** and **dēfēnsūra** are future participles. A future participle such as **dēfēnsūra** can be translated in various ways, including *about to defend*, *going to defend*, *intending to defend*, and *on the point of defending*.

3. Compare the form and meaning of the future participles with the perfect passive participles below:

	Future participle		*Perfect passive participle*	
first conjugation	**vocātūrus**	*about to call*	**vocātus**	*having been called*
second conjugation	**tentūrus**	*about to hold*	**tentus**	*having been held*
third conjugation	**missūrus**	*about to send*	**missus**	*having been sent*
fourth conjugation	**audītūrus**	*about to hear*	**audītus**	*having been heard*

4. Now look at the following sentences:

   Rūfīna lacrimātūra esse vidēbātur.
   Rufina seemed to be about to cry.

   pullī cibum cōnsūmptūrī esse dīcuntur.
   The chickens are said to be about to eat the food.

5. When the future participle is combined with **esse** it forms the **future infinitive**. The future infinitives of the four conjugations are therefore as follows:

	Future infinitive	
first conjugation	**vocātūrus esse**	*to be about to call*
second conjugation	**tentūrus esse**	*to be about to hold*
third conjugation	**missūrus esse**	*to be about to send*
fourth conjugation	**audītūrus esse**	*to be about to hear*

6. Finally, note the future participle and future infinitive of **sum**:

future participle	**futūrus**	*about to be*
future infinitive	**futūrus esse** or **fore**	*to be about to be*

in popīnā

Indus Rūfīnam per viās urbis ad popīnam quandam dūxit. Batāvus explicābat sē Giscōnem ibi conventūrum esse; et Giscōnem in urbe nūntium labōrāre. popīnam ingressa, Rūfīna Giscōnem in angulō sedentem statim agnōvit, et lacrimīs fluentibus inter sē complexī sunt amīcī. ambō simul loquī incēpērunt, 'Attō adest?', 'quandō Ephesum relīquistī?' dīcentēs. tum Giscō Rūfīnam hortātus est ut ad mēnsam sedēret et 'Sabīna vīvit,' inquit. 'eam vīdī. in urbe Pompēiīs est cum Quārtillā, Attōne, et marītō suō ... nōmine Alexandrō.'

Rūfīna, Indus, et Giscō, modo rīdentēs, modo lacrimantēs, rēs suās diū nārrābant.

ambō *both*

modo ... modo *sometimes ... sometimes ...*

LANGUAGE PRACTICE

1. Complete the sentence with the correct form of the verb, then translate.

a. sī Rōmānī cōpiās nostrās superābunt, nōs ab eīs .... (regentur, regēminī, regēmur)

b. mox vōs ē nostrā patriā ab exercitū fortī .... (pellēminī, pellētur, pellēris)

c. crās ego cum amīcā meā domum .... (regrediētur, regrediēmur, regrediar)

d. tū ad cēnam .... , quod fābulās optimās nārrās. (invītābuntur, invītābor, invītāberis)

e. crās captīvī īnfēlīcēs in amphitheātrum .... (movēbimur, movēbuntur, movēbitur)

f. haec mātrōna ab omnibus .... , quod amīcōs bene cūrat. (laudāberis, laudābitur, laudābiminī)

2. Choose the most appropriate word to complete each sentence, then translate.

factūra effugitūrus interfectūrum moritūrī ablātūrae raptūrōs

a. puerī sacerdōtem agnum .... spectābant.

b. gladiātōrēs, in harēnā .... , vōs salūtāvērunt.

c. ego patrem virginis cibum .... vocāvī.

d. mīles, ex hostibus .... , subitō cōnstitit et sē vertit.

e. nōs fūrēs nostrum canem .... cēpimus.

f. fēmina, iter longum .... , aquam cibumque parāvit.

coniūrātiō

cēnā cōnsūmptā, Indus tandem Rūfīnam graviter adlocūtus est, 'tibi aliam rem explicāre dēbēmus. Rōmam advēnit Giscō ut coniūrātiōnem facerēmus.' etiam gravius 'contrā Nerōnem' addidit. 'nōbīs auxilium dabis, Rūfīna?' cum tōtam rem cognōvisset, Rūfīna prōmīsit sē eōs adiūtūram esse.

illīs sīc loquentibus, iuvenis vestīmenta sordida gerēns popīnam ingressus est. quem Indus ut cōnspexit, laetē salūtāvit: 'salvē, amīce!' iuvenis cōnsēdit, et rīdēns 'salvē, Inde!' respondit. Giscō, sē ad Rūfīnam vertēns, susurrāvit eum esse Lūcīlium senātōrem, et ūnum ē coniūrātīs. Indus Lūcīliō explicāvit Nerōnem ipsum Rūfīnae crēdere; eam in domō imperātōris labōrātūram esse et coniūrātiōnem adiūtūram esse.

vōcibus gravibus, virī Rūfīnae omnem rem explicābant. Indus nūntiāvit Nerōnem nunc omnia timēre, crēdentem sē mox moritūrum esse. Batāvus rettulit sē malefica in mūrīs cubiculī Nerōnis cēlāvisse; carmina et dēvōtiōnēs, corpora animālium, et nōmen Nerōnis tabulīs īnscrīptum. Giscō tamen Indum vituperāvit, dīcēns eum superstitiōne victum esse. Rūfīnae dīxit sē nūntium esse et illō modō epistulās magnī mōmentī in urbe intercēpisse. Lūcīlius dīcēbat sē astrologum cōnsuluisse, et illum praedīxisse imperātōrem novum ante Īdūs Iūniās fore. omnēs cōnsentiēbant fīnem Nerōnis adesse. diū inter sē loquentēs et rēs in animīs volventēs, cōnsilia capiēbant coniūrātī.

coniūrātus *conspirator*
maleficum *wicked charm*
īnscrībō *I write on, inscribe*
intercipiō *I intercept*
astrologus *astrologer*
praedīcō *I predict*
Iūnius *of June*

A lead curse tablet, pierced by two iron nails.

LANGUAGE NOTE 3: INDIRECT STATEMENTS WITH FUTURE INFINITIVE

1. Compare the way these sentences are translated:

   dīcit Rūfīnam in domō imperātōris labōrātūram esse.
   He says Rufina will work in the emperor's house.
   (lit. *He says Rufina to be going to work in the emperor's house.*)

   dīxit Rūfīnam in domō imperātōris labōrātūram esse.
   He said Rufina would work in the emperor's house.
   (lit. *He said Rufina to be going to work in the emperor's house.*)

2. The tense of the Latin infinitive reflects the tense of the original direct statement. As **labōrātūram esse** is a future infinitive, the original statement was *Rufina will work in the emperor's house.*

LANGUAGE PRACTICE

3. Translate the following sentences.

   a. māter nostra dīcit sē gladiōs libenter redditūram esse.
   b. māter nostra dīxit sē gladiōs libenter redditūram esse.
   c. Giscō prōmīsit sē ad fīlium mox regressūrum esse.
   d. quamquam comitēs procul habitant, spērō mē iterum eōs vīsūram esse.
   e. nōs omnēs prōmīsimus nōs equum per tōtam silvam quaesītūrōs esse.
   f. spērāvistis nēminem dē coniūrātiōne eōrum cognitūrum esse.

4. Translate each sentence into Latin by choosing the correct word or phrase from each pair.

   a. *The doctor said that she had made a journey from Asia.*

medicae	dīxit	sē	iter	ad Asiam	factam esse.
medica	dīcit	eum	itinera	ex Asiā	fēcisse.

   b. *The emperor, however, believed that Rufina had been sent by the gods.*

prīnceps	tuum	crēdidit	Rūfīna	ā deīs	missūram esse.
imperium	tamen	crēdit	Rūfīnam	ad deōs	missam esse.

   c. *Rufina promised that she would give help to them.*

Rūfīna prōmīsit	eōs	eīs	auxiliō	datūram esse.
Rūfīna prōmittit	sē	eōrum	auxilium	datam esse.

   d. *Perhaps Indus hoped that Rufina would make poison.*

saepe	Indus spērat	Rūfīnam	venēnō	factam esse.
fortasse	Indus spērāvit	Rūfīna	venēnum	factūram esse.

   e. *Gisco said that Sabina had sailed to the city of Pompeii.*

Giscō dīcit	Sabīnam	ab urbe Pompēiīs	nāvigāvisse.
Giscō dīxit	Sabīna	ad urbem Pompēiōs	nāvigāre.

   f. *The friends, talking in the bar, did not think that they had been seen.*

amīcōs,	in popīnā loquentēs,	nōn putant	sē	vīsōs esse.
amīcī,	in popīnā loquēns,	nōn putāvērunt	eum	vīsūrōs esse.

Magic

Magic and religion

Humans attempt to understand and control their lives and their environment in various ways. In the Roman world most people believed in the existence of gods and spirits who intervened in and controlled natural processes. They thought that it was possible for humans to influence the actions of these gods and spirits. In Roman religion, people offered prayers, votives, or sacrifices to the gods in the hope of receiving some benefit in return: for example, a cure for an illness or a safe journey. Many people thought they could control events and discover the future by magic, using certain actions, rituals, and spells.

Magic and science

Scientists try to understand natural phenomena by employing observation and reason. By the first century AD there was a long tradition among doctors and medical writers of using the scientific method in the treatment of diseases. Doctors tried to discover the causes of diseases, employed close observation of symptoms, and carried out experiments. Some people, however, continued to employ unscientific, magical remedies. Pliny the Elder records hundreds of remedies, but states that many of them are based on magic rather than science. For instance, he reports these cures for toothache:

- Burn the head of a dog that has died from rabies, mix the ash with cypress oil, then pour this into the ear on the side affected by toothache.
- Place the tooth of a mole on the body.
- Eat a mouse twice a month to prevent toothache.
- Boil earthworms in oil and pour the mixture into the ear on the side of the painful tooth.
- Catch a spider with your left hand, beat it up with oil of roses, and drip the mixture into the ear.

Practicing magic

Magical practices included using potions, spells, incantations, curses, and charms. Magic could be used for good or bad purposes. For example, there were potions and charms for curing an illness or winning someone's love. On the other hand, curses were employed to harm one's enemies. A magician or witch often needed to have an item connected with the person they wanted to control, such as a lock of hair or nail clippings, or a scrap of clothing. Wax images were made, then melted in a fire or pierced with a nail, in the belief that the victim would be melted with love or suffer pain. A person's name could also be used. As you saw in Chapter 10, the name of an enemy could be scratched on a piece of lead, sometimes with a curse or magical formula added, then thrown into a spring or well. Magical formulae often included nonsense words, as in this cure for a bone fracture:

> This charm will cure any kind of fracture. Take a green reed four or five feet long, split it down the middle, and let two men hold it to your hips. Begin to chant:
>
> ***motas vaeta daries dardares astataries dissunapiter***,
>
> until the reeds come together. Brandish a knife over them. When the reeds meet and one is touching the other, grasp the knife with your hand and cut the reeds right and left. Tie them to the fracture and it will heal. Even so, every day chant:
>
> ***huat haut haut istasis tarsis ardannabou dannaustra***.
>
> *Cato*

People at all levels of society used magical practices and spells. Pliny the Elder claimed that Emperor Nero's 'passion for the magic arts was no less than his passion for the lyre and tragic song.' In AD 19 the governor of Syria, Piso, was put on trial for having used magic to kill Germanicus, the nephew and adopted son of Emperor Tiberius. After Germanicus' death, magical objects were found hidden in the walls and floor of his bedroom. These included spells, curse tablets inscribed with Germanicus' name, and the remains of human bodies. Curse tablets, which have been found all over the Roman Empire, provide evidence that many ordinary people also used magic.

Magic and witches in literature

Witches and magical practices feature frequently in Roman literature. Horace described a witch who had the power 'to bring down the stars and the moon from the sky with her incantations.' Feats like this, which disrupt the natural order of the world, were thought to be magical. Witches were associated with the dead and the Underworld, and it was said that they fed on rotting corpses. Apuleius tells a story about witches who steal the noses and ears of corpses before they are buried, and the poet Lucan mentions that witches would bite off the tongue of an unburied corpse. A poem of Horace describes the witch Canidia making a love potion to bring back her lover:

> Canidia, with little snakes twined in her unkempt hair, gives orders: wild fig trees uprooted from tombs, funeral cypresses, the eggs of a foul frog smeared with blood, the feather of a nocturnal owl, herbs imported from Iolcos and poison-rich Thessaly, and the bones snatched from the mouth of a hungry dog – all of these are to be burned in her magic flames.

Canidia and her fellow witches then kill a boy they have kidnapped 'so that his marrow could be cut out and his liver dried to make a love potion.'

The image of the witch presented in literature probably owes a lot to the imagination and does not tell us very much about what people actually believed. However, the epitaph of Iucundus, who died in Rome in about AD 20, suggests that the fear that witches might steal children was not confined to literature:

> As I was coming up to my fourth year I was snatched and killed, when I could have been a delight to my mother and father. A cruel magic hand stole me. While she remains on earth she can bring harm with her arts. You parents, guard your children, lest sorrow fills your hearts.

DISCUSSION

Think of examples of magic and witches in modern fiction, films, and TV. In what ways are they similar to Roman ideas about magic and witches?

Necromancy

One way to find out about the future was to consult a ghost, a procedure known as necromancy. Lucan described a witch raising a ghost from the dead to ask it about the future:

> His thick blood grew warm and heated his dark wounds, and ran into his veins and the extremities of his limbs. In his icy breast the nerves trembled. New life crept into his marrow and mingled with death. Then every limb quivered. His nerves stretched. The corpse all at once was ejected from the earth and stood upright.

The dangers of magic

Despite the widespread use of magic, the authorities often viewed it as dangerous. When Emperor Tiberius discovered a conspiracy against him, he expelled magicians and astrologers from Rome and Italy. He then decreed that any Roman citizen found practicing magic should be exiled, while non-citizens should be put to death.

Pliny the Elder expressed hostility to magic and contrasted it with religion. He condemned Druidism as magic, not religion, on the grounds that the Druids performed human sacrifice. He regarded human sacrifice and drinking human blood as magical practices, which the Romans had outlawed hundreds of years before Pliny's time. He writes:

> The magic arts have been practiced throughout the whole world. It cannot be overestimated how great a debt is owed to the Romans, who have put an end to those monstrous rites in which to kill a man was a most holy act.

The Romans regarded human sacrifice as a perverted form of animal sacrifice. Emperor Claudius forbade Roman citizens to join the Druid cult and then banned it in Gaul.

Thus, magic was seen by some as outside or even opposed to Roman religion. However, throughout the Roman Empire, magic was used by people at all levels of society, coexisting with scientific discovery and traditional religious practices. Often the lines between magic and religion, or magic and medicine, were blurred.

per nocturnās umbrās

ex urbe ēgressus iter fēcit Giscō, agnum in umerīs portāns, in saccō vīnum, lac, atque mel. aberat lūna, sīdera nōn fulgēbant. ille per nocturnās umbrās prōgrediēbātur dum silvam quendam invenīret, quam sāga eī indicāverat. ibi, terrā effossā, et vīnō, lacte, melle effūsīs, agnum necāvit ut sanguis eius in terram effunderet. tum Giscō verba magica, in tabellā ā sāgā scrīpta, recitāvit, ut Mānēs vocāret.

paulisper nihil accidit. tum imāgō ex arboribus prōgrediēbātur, sacrificiō appropinquāns. Giscō Luccum, iuvenem īnfēlīcem Britannicum, agnōvit. quem sequentem, comīs diffūsīs, Aucissam vīdit. tum multae imāginēs Giscōnī appāruērunt: parentēs Aucissae, Antigonus veterānus, hostēs in bellō ab eō occīsī, frāter Rūfīnae in incendiō mortuus. hīs vīsīs, multum movēbātur Giscō, sed vultus quem vidēre māluit eī nōn appāruit.

nocturnus *nocturnal, of night*

lac *milk*

sīdus *star*

diffundō *I disorder, dishevel*

solve cūrās tuās

dēspērābat Giscō, tenebrās adloquēns: 'ubi es, mea coniūnx? adiuvā mē, tē ōrō. fīlium nostrum relīquī, ut coniūrātus fierem, imperātōrem necārem. quālis vīta est Attōnī? vim et perīculum eī sōlum praebēre possum. quōmodo sine tē vītam agere poterō, mea Catia?'

tum ex umbrīs prōcessit uxor, oculīs fulgentibus in marītum fīxīs, et verbīs dūrīs Giscōnem adlocūta est: 'quid iuvat tantō īnsānō dolōrī indulgēre? cūr respōnsa ā mortuīs exspectās dē rēbus vīventium? tūne vītam facilem esse putāvistī? est in tē pietās et industria, summaque virtūs. nunc pelle lacrimās, solve cūrās tuās. vītam longam cum līberīs atque uxōre dūcēs. iamque valē, et fīliī servā nostrī amōrem.'

quae cum dīxisset, Giscōnem lacrimantem et multa dīcere volentem dēseruit, et in tenebrās regressa est coniūnx.

fīgō *I fix*

quid iuvat? *how does it help?*

indulgeō *I give in to, indulge in*

industria *diligence, hard work*

dēserō *I desert, forsake*

A fragment of a Roman charm necklace, with multiple charms in the shape of everyday objects including a pin, a lamp, and a cup. The charm on the far right is a female figurine, perhaps a goddess such as Venus, Fortuna, or Isis.

The everyday objects and the fact that it is made out of a cheap metal indicate that this necklace belonged to an average person. The worn surfaces of the charms, particularly the female figure, suggest the wearer might have rubbed them for luck, or in prayer.

Ghosts

Ghosts are mentioned frequently in Roman literature. Some appear because they want to get revenge or complete unfinished business, while others are deceased ancestors and relatives who offer protection and guidance. Not all Romans believed in the existence of ghosts, but since there was no single view about life after death, ghosts continued to intrigue them.

SOURCE 1

Pliny, writing to a friend, asks:

> I am extremely eager to know whether you think ghosts exist and have their own shape and some sort of divine power, or whether they are false, empty images conjured up by our fear?

He then goes on to relate a ghost story that he has recently heard. He begins by describing an old but grand house which has been left empty because the inhabitants had been haunted each night by the presence of a ghost. The house had been put up for rent or sale and a philosopher, Athenodorus, who was new in town, had rented it, keen to find out more. Pliny continues:

> When it began to get dark, he ordered a couch to be set for him in the front of the house, called for his tablets, pen, and a light, and sent everyone else away. He focused his mind, eyes, and hands on his writing, lest his empty mind and his fear might conjure up imaginary noises and visions. At first the night was silent as usual, then began the clanging of iron and the clinking of chains. He looked around and saw the ghost, as it had been described to him. It was standing and beckoning with a finger. Athenodorus picked up his lamp and followed. The ghost was stumbling slowly as if weighed down by the chains and after it turned into the courtyard of the house, suddenly it vanished leaving Athenodorus alone. He placed some grass and leaves on the spot as a marker and the next day he went to the magistrate and advised that they order that place to be dug up. And they found bones there, caught up and twisted with chains. The bones were collected and buried at public expense. After the ghost had been properly laid to rest, the house was haunted no more.

SOURCE 2

Lucretius, an Epicurean philosopher, explains that visions of ghosts are not to be feared:

> There exist what we call the images of things. Like membranes stripped from the surface of objects, they fly about in the air. When we are awake, they appear in our minds and frighten us. They terrify us too in our sleep, when we often see strange shapes and the images of people who have died and are deprived of light. When we are relaxing in slumber they frequently wake us up in terror. And so, we should not think that souls escape from the Underworld or ghosts flit about among the living, or that some part of us can be left after death, when our body and mind have both been destroyed, and each has been dissolved into its own primary atoms.

SOURCE 3

Ghosts often appear in love poetry. Here Propertius praises the eternal love that continues after death:

> The hero Protesilaus* was not able to forget his darling wife, even in the dark Underworld, but he came as a ghost to his former home, longing to hold his love in his ghostly arms.
>
> *A Greek soldier who died in the Trojan War.

SOURCE 4

Suetonius records that Nero was plagued by visions of his mother Agrippina, who had been murdered on his orders:

> He often confessed that he was haunted by his mother's ghost and by the whips and the burning torches of the vengeful spirits. He even tried to call up her ghost, in a ritual performed by sorcerers, and beg it for forgiveness.

DISCUSSION

1. From these sources what can you tell about the various Roman attitudes towards ghosts?
2. Why are stories about ghosts so popular?

Circe

In Greek mythology, Circe was a minor goddess and an enchantress, the daughter of the sun god Helios; she was able to change humans into animals with spells and potions. The most famous story about Circe is from Homer's poem the *Odyssey*. The Greek hero Odysseus (called Ulysses by the Romans) landed on Circe's island and she changed his men into pigs.

- Read or listen to the story of Odysseus and Circe.

Transformation

Look at Source 1. Transforming people into animals is a common theme in myths, folklore, and fairy tales from all over the world. In the ancient Babylonian poem the *Epic of Gilgamesh*, an angry goddess turns her lovers into animals when she tires of them.

- Can you think of other stories which have this as a theme? Which animals are the characters turned into? Why do you think these animals were chosen?

Circe's family

Circe was not the only female in her family with magical powers. Her sister Pasiphaë was also a sorceress who enchanted her husband, Minos, king of Crete. More deadly still was Circe's niece Medea, who married the hero Jason and used her magical powers to inflict a terrible revenge on him when he left her to marry a young princess.

SOURCE 1

Circe changes Odysseus' men into pigs.

SOURCE 2

This Greek vase shows Odysseus overpowering Circe.

The female enchantress or witch is a familiar figure in mythology, fairy tales, and literature, from the queen in *Snow White* to the witches in *Macbeth*.

- Why do you think this representation of women is so common?

God vs goddess

Look at Sources 2 and 3. Odysseus is able to resist Circe's magic by using an antidote given to him by the god Hermes. Although Circe is able to use poison and magic, her power is limited and Odysseus avoids coming to harm.

In other stories in literature, films, or video games, what elements bring protection or even invincibility to their heroes? Does divine or magical intervention make the achievements of the characters less heroic? Or does divine help enhance their reputations?

SOURCE 3

'Look: here is a drug of real virtue which you must take into Circe's palace; it will make you immune from evil. She will begin by preparing you a mixture into which she will put her drug, but this antidote will rob it of its power.' Then Hermes handed me a herb with a black root and white flower. The gods call it moly.

Homer

RESEARCH

Find out about:

1. Medea and Jason.
2. Gilgamesh and the goddess Ishtar.
3. Telegonus, the son of Circe and Odysseus.

Chapter 31: bellum

A relief of legionaries, from Lugdunum.

I: Vindex

in prōvinciā Galliā Lugdūnēnsī, lēgātus Gāius Iūlius Vindex epistulās scrībēbat. epistulīs nūntiīs trāditīs, Vindex lentē surrēxit et tablīnum vīllae frīgidae circumspectābat. Īdūs Martiae erant. quamquam vir audācissimus atque fortissimus, paulum tamen timēbat. nam Vindex rebelliōnem faciēbat.

timēbat nē epistulae interciperentur. timēbat nē etiam nunc lēgātī prōvinciārum proximārum Nerōnī favērent. timēbat nē legiōnēs Rōmānae bellum cum cōpiīs gentium Gallicārum gererent. spērābat autem sē senātum populumque Rōmānum ab imperiō illīus tyrannī malī līberātūrum esse.

Martius *of March*
Gallicus *Gallic*

II: Galba et Othō

in Hispāniā Tarracōnēnsī, Lūcius Līvius Ocella Sulpicius Galba, lēgātus summae auctōritātis, cum Marcō Salviō Othōne loquēbātur. epistulīs acceptīs, duo virī celeriter rēs ēgerant.

Galba verēbātur nē Nerō rebelliōnem superāre posset. verēbātur quoque ut Othō satis aurī obtinuisset. eundem igitur rogāvit quantum aurī eī esset, et num Rōmae omnia parāta essent.

Othō nōlī timēre, mī amīce! mox legiōnēs tē Caesarem salūtābunt. nōs enim sumus dīvitiōrēs omnibus aliīs lēgātīs. fidēlēs tibi erunt legiōnēs sī eīs aurum dabis.

vereor *I fear*
eundem: īdem *the same, this, that*

III: Verginius

Lūcius Verginius Rūfus, lēgātus superiōris Germāniae, dux trium legiōnum, vir summae virtūtis, in prīncipiīs sedēbat, duās epistulās tenēns. prīma ā Vindice scrīpta erat, altera ā Nerōne missa. ille metuēbat nē, sine auxiliō Verginiī, patria nōn līberārētur. alterā ex parte hic metuēbat nē patria ā Galbā dēlērētur.

diū incertus erat Verginius quōmodo senātum populumque Rōmānum melius servāret. 'loquī quam pugnāre saepe mālō,' sibi dīxit. tandem surrēxit ut mīlitēs nōn longā ōrātiōne hortārētur. tempus erat signa tollere.

superior *upper*
prīncipia *headquarters (of camp)*
ille ... hic ... *the former ... the latter*
metuō *I fear, dread*
signa tollō *I lift up the standards (symbols of a legion), set off*

LANGUAGE NOTE 1: VERBS OF FEARING

1. Look at the following sentences. What do you notice about the use of **nē** and **ut**?

   Vindex timēbat nē lēgātī Nerōnī favērent.
   Vindex was afraid that the commanders would support Nero.

   Galba verēbātur ut Othō satis aurī obtinuisset.
   Galba was afraid that Otho had not obtained enough gold.

2. After verbs of fearing (such as **timeō**, **metuō**, and **vereor**) **nē** is used to mean *that* and either **ut** or **nē nōn** is used to mean *that ... not*.

3. In the first sentence above, notice that **favērent** is translated *they would support*. After verbs of fearing, the imperfect subjunctive is usually translated using *would*.

The legions

A legion was a unit in the Roman army, made up of professional soldiers. A legionary soldier had to be a Roman citizen. During the Republic, armies had been raised for specific campaigns under a particular commander. However, Augustus restructured Rome's military power and regularized the soldiers' length of service, pay, and retirement benefits. The legions formed a single army under the direct control of the emperor, the Commander-in-Chief. There were between twenty-five and thirty legions stationed around the Empire in the first century AD, mostly in frontier provinces. These legionary soldiers were supported by a similar number of auxiliaries (non-citizen soldiers). Each legion was made up of ten cohorts totaling about 5,000 foot soldiers, with an additional 120 cavalrymen. The legions stationed around the Empire had four main purposes: imperial expansion, defending existing frontiers, crushing revolts against Roman rule, and maintaining the peace among the inhabitants of a province.

The legionary fort

Generally a legion had a fortified camp as a permanent base. Although they had basic defensive features, forts were not designed to withstand sieges but rather to house the soldiers, their equipment, and supplies. Across the Empire forts had the same basic layout, although there were slight differences owing to the specific terrain and the number of soldiers housed there. The influence of the legion was not confined to the perimeter of the fort. The legion relied on the surrounding land to provide resources such as timber and stone, and also space for training and parades. The fort might also support smaller camps nearby.

Provisions

> **quī frūmentum necessāriaque nōn praeparat, vincitur sine ferrō.**
> A man who does not prepare grain and other necessities is conquered without fighting.
>
> *Vegetius*

The scale of resources required to maintain a legion was immense. Grain made up the greatest part of a

soldier's diet, and each man received a grain ration (***frūmentum***), about 2 pounds per day. Generally this was made into either bread or a sort of porridge. In addition, the men also received some meat, vegetables (especially lentils and beans), olive oil, and cheese, mostly from the local area. Tombstones provide evidence for there being hunters and butchers in the army. Some soldiers kept their own livestock or hunted wild animals in the surrounding area.

Salt was an important part of a soldier's diet; ancient writers include it as one of the necessities for provisioning an army. Soldiers drank diluted wine and vinegar and also, in the northern provinces, beer.

There was no communal canteen. Soldiers were given their raw rations to cook on campfires with their ***contubernium*** (section of eight soldiers). Some permanent forts had more centralized food preparation, with shared mills and bread ovens.

Supplying a legion

Supplying a legion required a huge amount of organization, and supply lines could be hundreds of miles long. Supplies were moved over water where possible. However, over land pack animals and wagons transported provisions between depots, which were set up along a supply line. In North Africa and the eastern provinces camels were commonly used, and mules or donkeys elsewhere.

Many resources were acquired locally. Soldiers foraged for firewood and food for their animals and themselves – although this was dependent on the season. They also relied on local traders who sold produce to supplement their rations. In a crisis, provisions could be requisitioned from local civilian stores, in which case compensation was given, or looted from enemy territory. The legion also needed a huge supply of wood, for building and for cooking and heating. In some cases ancient writers record almost total deforestation of the area around an army camp.

To prevent food rotting or being stolen, good storage was vital. The Romans knew that, in order to preserve the food, it was necessary to keep the temperature and the moisture level low. Therefore they built granaries with raised floors, to increase ventilation. The grain was stored in sacks, which was an efficient use of space and also made it easy to rotate the stock. Each sack held a pre-measured quantity of grain, ready to be distributed.

On the march

A legion could travel about twenty miles a day and marched in a long line, sometimes stretching miles. Each soldier carried his weapons, tools, personal equipment, and rations. The shared equipment of each contubernium, including their tent, was carried by a mule. Lightly-armed troops went ahead, to scout the area and check for ambushes. Pack animals carried sacks of grain, water in leather pouches, and amphorae. Larger pieces of equipment or heavy items were transported in wagons drawn by oxen or mules. Where necessary a group of soldiers would clear a path by cutting down trees or removing obstacles.

At the front of the column there was a detachment of soldiers, including special engineering units, who carried everything needed to construct a temporary camp. On arriving at the planned resting point, a temporary camp was constructed from earth, turf, and timber. It could be built in three to six hours, and would be burned when the legion left it the next day, to prevent it from being used by their enemies.

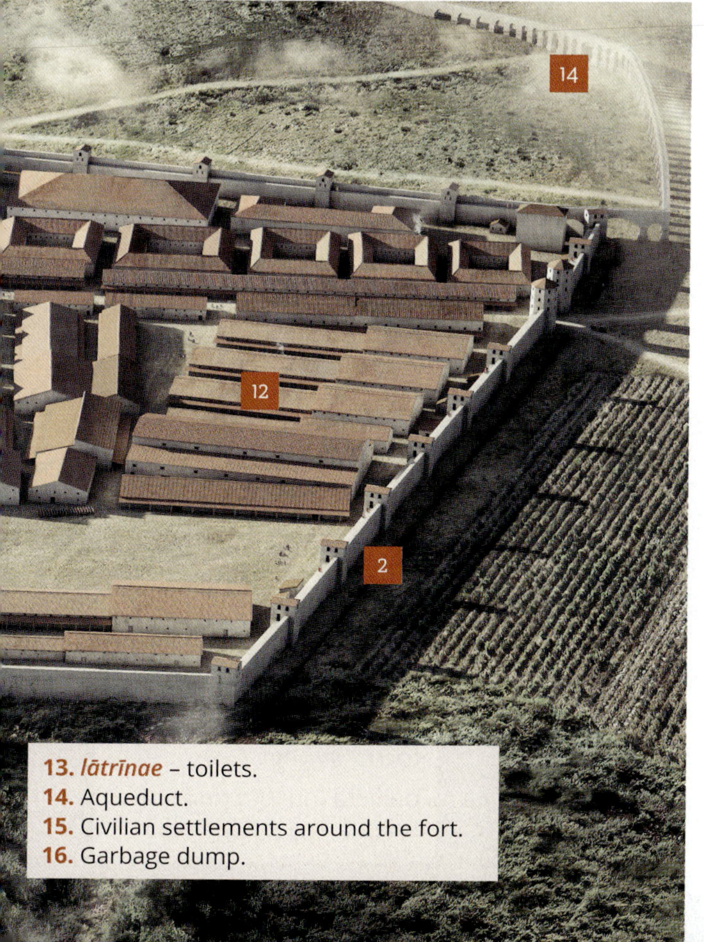

13. ***lātrīnae*** – toilets.
14. Aqueduct.
15. Civilian settlements around the fort.
16. Garbage dump.

The legionary fort at Vindonissa, in modern Switzerland. This digital reconstruction shows the fort as it was in AD *50.*

Vindonissa

prīmā lūce Balbus, mīles in castrīs Vindonissae, in speculā stābat. in mentem veniēbant parentēs quī prope lītus procul habitābant. sōle per nebulās oriente, clāmōrem magnī numerī mīlitum, quī iam ante lūcem sē parāverant ut ē castrīs hodiē discēderent, audīvit. cornibus audītīs, Balbus, veritus nē tardus esset, statim ad contubernium profectus est.

specula *watchtower*
cornū *horn*
veritus *fearing (lit. having feared)*
tardus *late*
contubernium *squad, section*

Balbus, dum per castra prōgrediēbātur, ubīque vidēbat mīlitēs tēla parāre et sarcinās colligere. prope portās centuriōnēs cohortēs īnstruēbant. in prīncipiīs Verginius lēgātus tribūnīs iussa dabat. aquiliferō dūcente, cohors prīma, celerior cēterīs cohortibus, iam per portam proficīscēbātur. Balbus magnum numerum mīlitum arma splendida gerentium breviter spectābat, inter spem metumque suspēnsus.

īnstruō *I draw up, prepare*
iussum *order, command*
aquilifer *standard bearer*

Marius dē officīnā ballistāriōrum Balbum et alium mīlitem vocāvit. illī, Mariō fortiōrēs, ballistam magnā cum difficultāte in plaustrum posuērunt. tum omnēs ad cohortem suam festīnāvērunt.

ballistārius *ballista maker*
fortis *strong*
ballista *ballista (military siege machine)*

centuriōnēs agmen mīlitum per montēs agēbant. Balbus plaustrum ā Mariō āctum sequēbātur. per iter longum Balbō, sarcinās atque arma gravia portantī, cūrae in mentem veniēbant. putābat sē nōn ad bellum satis parātum esse. timēbat nē in proeliō vulnerārētur aut necārētur.

Marius solve metum tuum, Balbe. nōs strēnuē ad bellum parāvimus. summā cum disciplīnā tē saepe exercentem vīdī, et magnā cum fortitūdine pugnantem. in proeliō mēns abest, et metū furōreque magis quam fortitūdine agēris. nōlī cōgitāre, sed pārē optiōnī ac centuriōnī.

tum cornua audīta sunt. per agmen nūntius refertur exercitum ad moenia oppidī Vesontiōnis advēnisse.

agmen *column (of soldiers)*
disciplīna *discipline, training*
fortitūdō *strength, courage*
optiō *optio (second-in-command in a century)*
Vesontiō *Vesontio (Besançon, town in eastern France)*

oppidum Vesontiō

exercitū multōs diēs prōgressō, advēnit Verginius cum tribus legiōnibus ad oppidum Vesontiōnem. cīvēs legiōnibus vīsīs portās statim clausērunt. Verginius, nūntiīs inimīcīs ex oppidō acceptīs, tribūnīs imperāvit ut Vesontiōnem obsidērent.

locō aequō ēlēctō, arboribus ē silvā proximā excīsīs, castra pōnunt mīlitēs. fossās fodiunt et castra vāllō circumdant. centuriōnēs mīlitēs adloquuntur. dīcunt Vindicem hostem mox adventūrum esse, sē proelium commissūrōs esse. Marius ballistās īnspicit. Balbus et aliī mīlitēs scūta, galeās, pīla, et gladiōs parant. magnus est metus.

omnēs oppidum spectant. procul pulveris nūbēs vidētur. cōpiae Vindicis appropinquant.

obsideō *I besiege*
excīdō *I cut down*
fossa *trench*
fodiō *I dig*
vāllum *rampart, earthen wall*
circumdō *I surround*
scūtum *shield*
galea *helmet*
pulvis *dust*

A career in the army

The senior officers were of senatorial or equestrian rank. The legate and senatorial tribune usually served for only a short period in the army as part of a political career, whereas some equestrian tribunes served for several years. The most experienced of the senior officers was often the camp prefect, a man who had spent his whole working life in the army.

Most recruits to the legions came from poor families. If a legionary had talent, worked hard, and survived, he had the chance of retiring with sufficient money and/or land to have a reasonably comfortable life. It was also possible to rise up the ranks and become a person of some social importance in civilian life. In this way, the army was a way of achieving social advancement. Sources 1 and 2 are evidence for the career of the legionary soldier Marcus Helvius Rufus.

SOURCE 1

Helvius Rufus, an ordinary soldier, was honored for saving a citizen's life in battle and was presented with necklaces and a spear by Apronius, the governor of Africa. Emperor Tiberius added the civic crown.*

*The civic crown, necklace, and spear were the equivalent of the medals awarded for bravery today. The civic crown (***cīvica***) was a crown of oak leaves.

Tacitus

SOURCE 2

Inscription from Tibur, near Rome:

MARCUS HELVIUS MARCI
FILIUS CAMILIA RUFUS
CIVICA PRIMUS PILUS
BALNEUM
MUNICIPIBUS ET INCOLIS
DEDIT

Marcus Helvius Rufus Civica, son of Marcus, of the tribe Camilia, chief centurion, gave a set of baths to the citizens and residents.

QUESTION

What do these two sources show about Helvius and his career? Use the table below to help you.

Rank	Description	Number per legion	Pay and duties
lēgātus	Commander of the legion. Member of the Senate.	1	
tribūnus mīlitum (senatorial)	Second-in-command. Young man of senatorial rank embarking on a career in politics. Served for one year.	1	
praefectus castrōrum	Camp prefect. Sometimes a legionary soldier promoted from the ranks.	1	Took command when the legatus and senatorial tribune were away.
tribūnus mīlitum (equestrian)	Equestrian rank.	5	
prīmus pīlus	Chief centurion of the legion.	1	60 times pay. Given equestrian rank on retirement.
centuriō	Centurion, in command of a century (80 men).	59	15 times pay.
optiō	Second-in-command of a century.	60	Double pay.
aquilifer	Carried the legion's standard, the eagle.	1	Double pay.
imāginifer	Carried the image of the emperor.	1	
signifer	Standard bearer of a cohort.	10	
cornicen	Horn player of a cohort.	10	
tesserārius	Organized the night guard and distributed the passwords. One for each cohort.	10	One and a half times pay.
immūnis	Ordinary soldier with special skill, e.g. clerks, blacksmiths, surveyors.	about 4,800	Exempt from general duties. Basic pay.
mīles	Ordinary soldier with no special skills, qualifications, or duties.		General duties. Basic pay.

Each legion also had 120 cavalrymen (***equitēs***), who acted as scouts and messengers.

Vindex et Verginius

castrīs prope oppidum positīs Vindex, veritus nē Verginius Nerōnī favēret, ad eum nūntium mīserat ut sententiam eius cognōsceret. cum nūntius verba ambigua, quae Verginius dīxerat, rettulisset, Vindex ānxiē rem cōgitābat. timēbat enim nē ille exercitum suum facile vinceret. nūntium eundem ad Verginium iterum iterumque mīsit, sed eadem respōnsa semper referēbantur. tandem Vindex lēgātum ad colloquium prīvātum invītāvit. postrīdiē prīmā lūce Vindex cum Verginiō congressus est.

Vindex mī Verginī, tē esse hostem nōlō. exercitus tuus maior est meō. in alium pugnāre mālō: Nerōnem, quī et mihi et tibi et omnibus Rōmānīs hostis est. tē ōrō ut Vesontiōne discēderēs et orbem terrārum līberārēs.

Verginius mī Vindex, verba tua intellegō. ambō spērāmus prīncipem novum futūrum esse.

Vindex verba tua audiēns gaudeō.

Verginius sed quam ob causam Galbae favēs?

Vindex Galba vir nōbilis est atque multō perītior Nerōne ... et multae legiōnēs eī pārēbunt.

Verginius mī Vindex, necesse est senātuī populōque potius quam mīlitibus prīncipem novum ēligere.

Vindex rem nōn intellegis, Verginī. prō certō habeō Galbam imperātōrem novum fore, et senātōrēs cōnsulēsque eī fautūrōs esse. quī hostis Galbae est, hostis imperātōrī erit. nōlī tot vītās frūstrā perdere. pācem facere nōs oportet.

Verginius bene dīcis, amīce.

ambiguus *unclear, uncertain*
prīvātus *private*
congredior *I meet*
in (+ acc.) *against*
nōbilis *noble, renowned*
perītus *experienced*
potius *rather*
ēligō *I choose, elect*
perdō *I destroy, waste*

The tombstone of Lucius Duccius Rufinus was found in York, UK. The inscription reads:

L(VCIVS) DVCCIVS / L(VCI FILIVS) VOLT(INA) RVFI / NVS VIEN(NA) / SIGNIF(ER) LEG(IONIS) VIIII / AN(NORVM) XXIIX / H(IC) S(ITVS) E(ST).

Lucius Duccius Rufinus, son of Lucius, of the Voltinian tribe, from Vienne, a standard bearer of the Ninth Legion, 28 years old. He is laid here.

Rufinus was a signifer, the soldier who carried the standard of his cohort. Each cohort had its own standard (***signum***): several metal discs and crescents representing the honors won by the cohort, mounted on a pole. An ***aquila***, a golden eagle fixed to a pole, was the legionary standard and symbolized the spirit of the legion. There were also standards with an image of the emperor. A legion was identified by its number and title. The title might refer to a region where the legion had served or to a military virtue; in some cases it was a nickname.

LANGUAGE NOTE 2: ABLATIVE OF COMPARISON

1. In Chapter 14 you met sentences like these:

   Sabīna est pulchrior quam aliae fēminae.
   Sabina is more beautiful than other women.

2. You have now met another way in which Latin expresses comparison:

   Balbus erat fortior Mariō.
   Balbus was stronger than Marius.

   cohors prīma, quae erat celerior cēterīs cohortibus, proficīscēbātur.
   The first cohort, which was faster than the other cohorts, was setting out.

3. To express comparison, Latin can use the ablative case rather than **quam**. This use of the ablative is known as the **ablative of comparison**.

LANGUAGE PRACTICE

1. Choose the most appropriate word to complete the sentence, then translate.

   a. Rūfīna metuēbat nē sacerdōs .... (tenēret, perīret, mitteret)
   b. Boudica timēbat nē gentēs ab exercitū hostium .... (portārentur, hortārentur, vincerentur)
   c. Faustus metuēbat nē fīlia ā senātōre .... (adderētur, auferrētur, loquerētur)
   d. Currāx verēbātur nē vir ignōtus mātrem .... (emeret, appārēret, īret)
   e. Mānius timēbat nē nūllum cibum .... (vīveret, invenīret, placēret)
   f. Sabīna verēbātur ut līberōs .... (habēret, pōneret, sedēret)

2. Rewrite the following sentences using the ablative of comparison, rather than **quam**. The words to replace are marked in bold. Then translate. For example:

   imāgō est pulchrior **quam omnēs imāginēs** in Galliā.
   imāgō est pulchrior omnibus imāginibus in Galliā.
   The picture is more beautiful than all the pictures in Gaul.

   a. nōs sumus laetiōrēs **quam amīcī**.
   b. hae vīllae sunt maiōrēs **quam vīllae** in Lūsitāniā.
   c. māter Alexandrī erat laetior **quam soror**.
   d. mātrōna est benignior **quam marītus**.
   e. vīnum Giscōnis est melius **quam vīnum tuum**.

A statuette of Mars, the god of war.

Loyalty and leadership

Roman commanders often had little military experience or training and relied on the higher ranks of the permanent soldiers for advice. Julius Caesar and Corbulo, however, were experienced commanders, who succeeded in winning the loyalty and respect of their troops.

SOURCE 1

Caesar saw that the situation was critical. Snatching a shield from the nearest soldier, he advanced to the front line. Addressing the centurions by name and encouraging the rest, he ordered the soldiers to carry the standards forward. His arrival brought hope to the soldiers and restored their courage, since each man, in the sight of the general, wanted to strive his utmost.

Caesar

SOURCE 2

Corbulo himself, lightly-dressed and bareheaded, regularly marched and toiled alongside his men, praising those who worked hard, consoling the sick, and setting an example to all. Then, because of the harshness of the climate and of military service, many of the men began to desert. Corbulo sought to remedy this by strictness. Any man who deserted the standards was immediately executed. Experience showed that this was more effective than pity, since there were fewer deserters from his army than from armies where forgiveness was shown.

Tacitus

QUESTION

Look at Sources 1 and 2. What qualities are demonstrated by these military leaders?

Commander-in-Chief

Augustus' reorganization of the army had the aim of making the legions loyal to him rather than to their generals. The emperor was Commander-in-Chief (imperator) of the army, and some emperors were experienced military commanders themselves.

SOURCE 3

Titus was the son of Emperor Vespasian and succeeded his father as emperor.

Titus ordered the names of soldiers who had acted bravely in the war to be read out. Summoning each one by name, he applauded them as they came forward. He gave them gold crowns, necklaces, and spears, and silver standards, and promoted each man to a higher rank. Moreover, out of the spoils he generously distributed silver and gold and clothing. When they had all been honored as they deserved, he descended amid tremendous applause, and went on to offer sacrifice for his victory at Jerusalem.

Josephus

SOURCE 4

Augustus introduced a system of salaries and rewards for all soldiers, in accordance with each man's rank, his length of service, and his retirement benefits, so that veterans could not be stirred to revolt in protest over their age or poverty. So that money would always be easily available to maintain them and provide their benefits, he established a military treasury funded by new taxes. In his will he left 1,000 sesterces each to the praetorian guard, 500 to the urban cohorts, and 300* to the legionaries.

*300 sesterces was about four months' pay.

Suetonius

SOURCE 5

The legionaries took an oath of loyalty at the start of each year:

iūrant autem mīlitēs omnia sē strēnuē factūrōs quae praecēperit imperātor, numquam dēsertūrōs mīlitiam nec mortem recūsātūrōs prō Rōmānā rēpūblicā.

The soldiers swear that they will make every effort to do all that the emperor orders, they will never desert their service, and will not refuse death for the sake of the Roman state.

Vegetius

QUESTIONS

Look at Sources 3–5.

1. How did the emperors try to gain the loyalty of the soldiers?
2. Why was this important?

cāsū pugnātur

cāsū *by accident, by chance*

dum Verginius et Vindex loquēbantur, Balbus in speculā castrōrum Rōmānōrum stābat, exercitum Vindicis spectāns. subitō cōnspexit agmen Gallicum prōgrediēns. Balbus timēbat nē Gallī Rōmānōs peterent et statim 'ecce!' clāmāvit, 'hostēs nōbīs appropinquant!' Verginiō absente, tribūnī et praefectī, crēdentēs Gallōs impetum factūrōs esse, mīlitēs celeriter arma capere iussērunt. mox Rōmānī agēbantur ut hostibus resisterent.

Gallī, quī ē castrīs Vindicis discesserant, rē vērā prōcēdēbant ut in templō propinquō vōta nūminibus facerent. ubi Rōmānōs appropinquantēs cōnspexērunt, eques quīdam in castra remissus est ut auxilium ferret. brevī tempore pugna, quam neque Verginius neque Vindex fierī volēbat, cāsū pugnābātur.

propinquus *nearby*
remittō *I send back*
pugna *fight, battle*

Gallī pauciōrēs erant Rōmānīs, sed nihilōminus fortiter pugnābant. Rōmānī tamen erant tam multī ut mox Gallōs superāre coepissent. tandem victōrēs erant et clāmōrem sustulērunt. mīlitibus autem ad castra redeuntibus, Marius hīc corpora Gallōrum, illīc Rōmānōrum cōnspexit. inter quōs Balbum vulnerātum invēnit.

♦ ♦ ♦

Verginius, quī proelium prohibēre nōn potuerat, in castrīs īrātissimus atque trīstissimus erat. cognōscere volēbat quam ob causam suī in Gallōs sine iussū impetum fēcissent. suōs adlocūtus est:

'Rōmānī, Vindex, quī mortēs tot suōrum ferre nōn potuerat, suā manū perīre māluit. longē errāvistis, quod exercitum virī nōbilis dēlēvistis et tot vītae frūstrā perditae sunt. Vindex erat socius. eadem cupiēbāmus. nunc nōs omnēs poenās dabimus.'

prohibeō *I prevent*
iussus *order, command*
socius *ally, colleague*

This Roman shield from the third century AD is the only known surviving example of the semicylindrical shield known as a ***scūtum****. The boss is missing from the center.*

Military engineering

Roman engineers developed sophisticated technology which, combined with their military discipline and training, made the Roman army a formidable opponent. Most of the machinery was based on Greek inventions, which the Romans improved.

Ballista

The ballista was essentially a giant crossbow. It had two horizontal arms which were inserted into two vertical springs, often made of animal sinew. These sinews were tightly wound, and, when released, the torsion force launched a projectile several hundred yards at great speed. Different kinds of ballista were developed to fire either bolts or stones, like these (*right*) from the siege of Masada during the Jewish Revolt. The ballista was a very accurate weapon, which was deployed both to target enemy soldiers and to destroy buildings and fortifications. Ballistae were sometimes used on board ships in naval battles to punch holes in enemy ships.

Onager

The onager, named after a wild donkey with a strong kick, was a small, powerful catapult. It used twisted animal sinews to create a torsion force which, when released, threw forward heavy projectiles from a sling at the end of the main beam. It was less accurate than a ballista, but could fire heavier stones and was generally used for besieging fortified encampments or towns. Sometimes flammable substances were added to the missiles to start fires within the enemy camp. The onager was a heavy weapon, but it could be built easily on site, rather than having to be carried with the army.

Bridge-building

The Romans were skilled civil engineers, frequently building roads, bridges, and camps. These facilitated the swift movement of troops and supplies, and their engineering skills were also employed when attacking the enemy. When Julius Caesar was in Gaul, in 55 BC, he decided to build a bridge across the River Rhine into the territory of the Germanic tribes. He wrote:

> Caesar had resolved to cross the Rhine, but he considered that crossing in boats was neither safe enough, nor in line with his own dignity or that of the Roman people. And so, although the great difficulty of building a bridge had been made clear to him, since the river was wide, deep, and fast-flowing, nevertheless he decided to try.
>
> *Caesar*

He records in detail the construction of the wooden bridge, which sat on top of wooden beams driven into the riverbed at an angle against the current. These beams were bound together and further timbers were added upstream to catch any large logs or obstacles floating down the river, which could damage the supporting beams. The bridge was completed in just ten days, without diverting the river, and under the constant threat of attack. When the army reached the other side, they found the Germanic tribes had fled. The Romans destroyed any settlements they found and soon returned to Gaul, dismantling the bridge behind them. The Rhine had previously been thought of as the limit of Roman power; Caesar's display of engineering proved otherwise.

imperium Urbis et orbis

in Hispāniā, Galba, senex cūrīs paene cōnfectus, nesciēbat quid agere dēbēret.

Galba quanta caedēs nōbīs accidit! cāsibus regimur magis quam regimus cāsūs. vērō putāvī Verginium nōbīs subventūrum esse. quam celeriter cōpiae Gallicae ā legiōnibus eius oppressae sunt! Fortūna omnia mūtāvit.

Othō nōlī dēspērāre, mī amīce! victōrēs erimus. nam cāsū pugnābātur. nōs ac Verginius eadem cupimus: ille suōs etiam nunc pūnit. audī! Rōmae cīvēs iam īrātī sunt, quod cibus dēest, et senātōrēs bellum cīvīle timent. sed tū, cui multum aurum dedī, pānem cīvibus emere, pācem senātōribus reddere potes.

Galba et quid dē Nerōne?

Othō Rōmae mihi sunt nōnnūllī comitēs quī Nerōnem facile necāre possunt. Nerōne occīsō, quis tum imperium Urbis et orbis accipiet? nēminem nisi tē senātōrēs et cōnsulēs ēligere poterunt.

Galba nōnne senātōrēs et cōnsulēs Verginium ēligent?

Othō ha! sī etiam legiōnēs suās regere ille nōn potest, quot senātōrēs eī imperium orbis terrārum committent?

Galba et quid dē cohortibus praetōriānīs?

Othō pff! melius est nōbīs eōs emere quam pugnāre.

Galba bene. Fortūna quidem mihi iterum favet.

dēest *is lacking, running out*
cīvīlis *civil*

praetōriānus *praetorian (bodyguard)*
quidem *indeed, certainly*

LANGUAGE NOTE 3: MĀLŌ, MĀLLE, MĀLUĪ

1. Since Chapter 5 you have met examples of **volō** (*I want, I am willing*) and its compound **nōlō** (*I don't want, I am unwilling*). For example:

   tū Rōmae manēre vīs, Giscō?
   Do you want to stay in Rome, Gisco?

   nōs in īnsulā habitāre nōlumus.
   We don't want to live in an apartment building.

2. Now look at the following sentences:

   loquī quam pugnāre mālō.
   I prefer to talk than to fight.

   tū māvīs pauperēs senēsque quam iuvenēs dīvitēsque.
   You prefer the poor and the old to the young and the wealthy.

3. The verb **mālō**, meaning *I prefer, I would rather*, is a compound of **magis** (*more*) and **volō**. Compare the present tenses of **volō** and **mālō**:

volō	*I want*	**mālō**	*I prefer*
vīs	*you want*	**māvīs**	*you prefer*
vult	*he/she/it wants*	**māvult**	*he/she/it prefers*
volumus	*we want*	**mālumus**	*we prefer*
vultis	*you want*	**māvultis**	*you prefer*
volunt	*they want*	**mālunt**	*they prefer*

LANGUAGE PRACTICE

3. Choose the correct form of **mālō** to complete the sentence, then translate.

   a. tūne abīre aut manēre .... ? (mālumus, māvīs, māvultis)
   b. hī quiētē vīvere quam petere honōrēs .... (mālō, māvult, mālunt)
   c. nōs aquam frīgidam atque calidum cibum .... (māvultis, māvīs, mālumus)
   d. tam fessa erat puella ut dormīre quam loquī .... (māllet, māllēs, māllem)
   e. vōsne ā mē aut ab alterō lēgātō dūcī .... ? (māvīs, māvult, māvultis)
   f. fēminae esse quam vidērī bonae .... (mālēbās, mālēbam, mālēbant)

Succession

The Principate was not a hereditary monarchy, and there was no fixed rule about who should take over when an emperor died. However, the first five emperors all belonged to two families, the Julii and the Claudii, and are known as the Julio-Claudians. The emperors who followed Augustus came to power through adoption, or by winning the support of the army, especially the praetorian guard (the soldiers who formed the emperor's bodyguard), or through the involvement of women in the family.

The concentration of powers in the hands of one man, the system instituted by Augustus, was a protection against civil war. The death of an emperor was a critical time; unless a new princeps was installed quickly, there was a danger that various factions or individuals would vie for power. It was therefore essential that the Senate, the praetorian guard, and the army agreed in conferring powers on a new emperor and swore allegiance to him.

Augustus to Tiberius: adoption

Augustus planned for the peaceful transfer of power by nominating his successor. The family line was very important to the Romans, so Augustus wanted power to pass to a blood relative in the Julian family. However, his only child was a daughter, Julia, and Romans would not accept a woman as ruler. Augustus adopted as his heir Julia's husband, Tiberius. Tiberius was the son of Augustus' wife Livia and was a member of the Claudian family.

Tiberius to Caligula: the praetorians intervene

Tiberius left both his grandson and his great-nephew Caligula as joint heirs. However, Caligula had the advantage of being Augustus' great-grandson. As Tiberius had not designated a clear successor, the commander of the praetorian guard took the initiative and had Caligula hailed emperor by the troops. The Senate followed suit.

Caligula to Claudius: the praetorians again

When Caligula was assassinated, leaving no designated heir, the praetorians acted again. The story goes that some praetorians found Caligula's uncle, Claudius, hiding behind a curtain in the palace and took him to their camp, where they hailed him as emperor. The Senate followed their lead, and conferred the title of emperor on Claudius. He gave each of the praetorians a generous payment. Suetonius commented:

> Claudius was the first of the emperors to have won the loyalty of the soldiers with bribery.

Claudius to Nero: the intrigues of Agrippina

When Claudius died, his son Britannicus was just thirteen years old. However, through his second wife, Agrippina, he also had a stepson, Nero, the great-great-grandson of Augustus. Agrippina had ambitions for her son to be emperor. Under her influence, Claudius adopted Nero, and Nero married Claudius' daughter, Octavia. Agrippina also secured the loyalty of the praetorian guard by persuading Claudius to appoint Burrus, her ally, as commander. When Claudius died suddenly, perhaps poisoned by Agrippina, Burrus took Nero to the praetorian camp. There Nero was hailed as emperor, having promised to make a large payment to each of the praetorians. Then he went to the Senate House and received powers from the Senate.

Nero to Galba: the army

Dissatisfaction with Nero as emperor led governors in several provinces to turn against him. Galba, the governor of Hispania Tarraconensis, declared himself 'Legate of the Senate and Roman People.' His own soldiers hailed him as imperator, and other military commanders joined him. He promised the praetorian guard a large payment, and the praetorians and the Senate then recognized Galba as emperor, even before Nero was dead. Galba's accession was the end of the Julio-Claudian dynasty in Rome and saw the breakdown of the peaceful transition of power.

After Galba: return to civil war

Galba ruled for only six months. AD 69 was a year of civil war, known as 'The Year of the Four Emperors' because there were four rulers in quick succession: Galba, Otho, Vitellius, and Vespasian. All these men were military commanders, backed by armies. The position of emperor was now claimed by military violence and could be conferred on someone outside the Julio-Claudian family, and not even in Rome. As Tacitus wrote:

> The secret of empire was now revealed, that an emperor could be made elsewhere than at Rome.

Vespasian restored stability to Rome. He ruled for almost ten years and founded the Flavian dynasty.

Chapter 32: fīnis

imperium sine fīne

Vergil

tempus est

in Domō Aureā, Indus et Rūfīna quiētē susurrant.

Indus Lūcīlius nūntium ab Othōne accēpit. nunc agere tempus est. Phaōn cōnsentit. esne parāta?

Rūfīna herbās obtinuī. parāta sum.

Indō ēgressō, Rūfīna in officīnam festīnat ad herbās parandās. mox cibum Batāvōrum quaerit ad medicāmenta addenda.

Nerōnī cēnantī intereā nūntiātur cēterōs exercitūs rebelliōnem facere. ille, metū atque furōre ductus, mēnsam subvertit et pōcula ad terram iacit. deinde, prīmum veritus nē ipse vīvus caperētur, venēnum in pyxide aureā ā Lōcustā parātum rapit ad vītam suam exstinguendam. tandem in cubiculum ingreditur ad rem cōgitandam. īdem tamen postrēmō obdormit.

Phaōn *Phaon (freedman of Nero)*
subvertō *I overturn*
pyxis *small box*

nec amīcus nec inimīcus

mediā nocte excitātus, dēsiluit dē lectō vocāvitque amīcōs. nēmō advēnit. īdem ipse igitur cucurrit sōlus ad Batāvōs petendōs. iānuīs tamen omnium clausīs, nūllō respondente, ad cubiculum rediit, unde iam et custōdēs effūgerant, eādem aureā venēnī pyxide ablātā. statim Spīculum gladiātōrem, cuius manū perīret, petīvit. nēmine tamen inventō 'ergō ego,' inquit, 'nec amīcum habeō, nec inimīcum?' itaque ex aulā cucurrit, quasi iactūrus sē in Tiberim.

perīret *he might die*

LANGUAGE NOTE 1: AD + GERUNDIVE

1. Look at the following sentences. What do you notice about the phrases in red?

   Rūfīna in officīnam festīnāvit ad herbās parandās.
   Rufina hurried into her workshop to prepare some herbs.

   tandem in cubiculum ingreditur ad rem cōgitandam.
   At last he enters his bedroom to consider the situation.

   Nerō cucurrit ad Batāvōs petendōs.
   Nero ran to look for the Batavians.

2. Each of the phrases in red starts with **ad** and contains a form of the verb known as the **gerundive** (e.g. **parandās**, **cōgitandam**, **petendōs**). Latin uses **ad** followed by a noun and gerundive in the accusative case to explain the purpose of an action.

3. Note the gerundives of the four conjugations:

first conjugation	**vocandus, a, um**
second conjugation	**tenendus, a, um**
third conjugation	**mittendus, a, um**
fourth conjugation	**audiendus, a, um**

4. As adjectives, gerundives change their endings to agree (in case, number, and gender) with the nouns they describe.

LANGUAGE PRACTICE

1. Complete each sentence with the appropriate form of the gerundive, then translate.

a.	Celer currit ad mūrem	(petendōs, petendās, petendum)
b.	Aucissa ad forum vēnit ad gladiōs	(vēndendās, vēndendōs, vēndenda)
c.	Lūcriō per flammās ruit ad virginēs Vestālēs	(servandās, servandam, servandum)
d.	Faustus ad cellam ascendit ad tēctum	(reficiendōs, reficiendum, reficiendam)
e.	illa āream intrābit ad Rūfīnam	(salūtandum, salūtandam, salūtandās)
f.	Sōrānos per viās currēbat ad eam	(inveniendam, inveniendās, inveniendōs)

Guarding the emperor

The praetorian guard

The praetorian guard protected the emperor and his family. The praetorians were elite soldiers, with better conditions of service than legionaries: they had higher pay, served for a shorter term, and received more generous pensions and bonuses. Originally, when they were established by Augustus, they numbered about 4,500 men (nine cohorts of 500), although later the number was increased. Praetorians guarded the emperor's residence, provided an escort for him in Rome, and accompanied him on journeys outside the city. When the emperor, or a member of his family, was on a military campaign, the praetorians joined him. They also had a wider role in the city, putting down plots against the emperor and suppressing disturbances (although this was mainly the job of the urban cohorts). Sometimes they were sent to other parts of Italy to deal with civil unrest. When Galba became emperor after the death of Nero, the legionaries in Germania turned against him:

> They decided to send a delegation to the praetorians with these instructions: they did not like the emperor who had been chosen in Hispania and the praetorians themselves should choose another who would be approved of by all the armies.
>
> *Suetonius*

Usually the praetorians were commanded by two ***praefectī***, although occasionally there was a single praefectus. The praefectus was chosen by the emperor. He was a man of equestrian rank, who had often begun his career as an officer in the army. The praefectus was close to the emperor: he was a member of the emperor's council and the emperor would confide in him. Burrus, for example, had been the sole praefectus under Claudius and continued in this position when Nero became emperor. Along with the philosopher Seneca, he was Nero's adviser for the first eight years of his reign.

The Batavians

Our character Indus is one of the Batavians (***Batāvī***), the cohort who formed the emperor's personal bodyguard. There were 500 Batavians, most of whom were recruited from the Batavi, a Germanic people who lived in what is now the Netherlands. Suetonius calls them ***cohors fidēlissima*** and Tacitus says that Nero trusted them because they were foreigners:

Germānīs, quibus fīdēbat quasi externīs.

On becoming emperor, Galba disbanded the Batavians because, as Suetonius tells us, he thought that they did not support him.

INDVS
NERONISCLAVDI
CAESARISAVG
CORPOR CVSTOS
DEC SECVNDI
NATIONE BATAVVS
VIXANN XXXVI H S E
POSVIT
EVMENES FRATER
ETHERES EIVS EX COLLEGIO
GERMANORVM

This is a drawing of the tombstone of a man named Indus who was one of Nero's Batavian bodyguards.

This marble relief from the Arch of Claudius in Rome shows soldiers of the praetorian guard. The eagle with folded wings carried by the standard bearer was the emblem of the praetorian guard.

locus dēsertus

sed Nerō, impetū iterum revocātō, locum dēsertum ad colligendum animum cupīvit. lībertō Phaonte suam vīllam suburbānam offerente, nūdō pede et ante faciem sūdāriō, equum ascendit ad eandem vīllam petendam, quattuor sōlīs comitantibus, inter quōs erat Indus.

tremōre tamen terrae et in caelō fulmine perterritus erat prīnceps. sūdārium, cum equus ex odōre corporis in viā iactī cōnsternārētur, cecidit et Nerō ā quōdam praetōriānō agnitus est et salūtātus. dīmissīs equīs, inter veprēs dēnsōs veste sub pedibus strātā, per sēmitam rēpsit dum ad mūrum vīllae clam pervenīret.

ibi Phaōn īdem eum hortātus est ut, dum aditus per mūrum fūrtim parārētur, sē in antrō cēlāret. Nerō tamen negāvit sē vīvum sub terram itūrum esse, ac dum aditus parātur, aquam ē lacūnā hausit. deinde quadrupēs per angustam cavernam effossam in proximam cellam rēpsit atque in lectō sordidō recubuit. intereā Indus nūntium aequō animō exspectābat.

impetus *impulse, purpose*
suburbānus *near the city*
nūdus *bare, naked*
sūdārium *handkerchief*
cōnsternō *I alarm, terrify*
veprēs *bramble, thorn bush*
vestis *item of clothing*
sternō *I spread out*
sēmita *footpath, track*
aditus *entrance, access*
caverna *hole*
lacūna *ditch, pond*
hauriō *I drink*
quadrupēs *on all fours*

verbō aut gladiō

in cūriā tantus clāmor fīēbat ut senātōrēs ōrātiōnēs vix audīrent. aliī clāmābant Galbam hostem reī pūblicae esse, aliī Nerōnem. aliī monēbant ut vītae prīncipis, ā populō amātī, parcerent.

Lūcīlius ē cūriā discēdit ad Giscōnem quaerendum. quem in forō invēnit.

Giscō quid tibi vidētur?

Lūcīlius incertus sum. quamquam multī senātōrēs Nerōnem ōdērunt, nōn crēdō senātum eum hostem iūdicātūrum esse. tibi necesse est aliquid ad eum ferre.

Giscō oculōs ad gladium, ā parentibus Catiae factum, vertit.

Lūcīlius et hanc epistulam.

LANGUAGE NOTE 2: ĪDEM, EADEM, IDEM

1. Since Chapter 31, you have met forms of **īdem**, **eadem**, **idem** meaning *the same*. For example:

    īdem postrēmō obdormit.
    The same man finally falls asleep.

    nūntium eundem ad Verginium mīsit.
    He sent the same messenger to Verginius.

    eandem vīllam petīvit.
    He headed to the same villa.

    eadem respōnsa semper referēbantur.
    The same replies were always brought back.

    nōs ac Verginius eadem volumus.
    We and Verginius want the same things.

2. **īdem**, **eadem**, **idem** is a compound of **is**, **ea**, **id** with the suffix -**dem**. Note that before -**dem**, an -**m** becomes -**n**. For example, **eam** becomes **eandem**, and **eum** becomes **eundem**.

3. There is a chart of all the forms of **īdem**, **eadem**, **idem** on page 277.

ultima hōra

intereā, comitibus hortantibus ut quam prīmum impendentia perīcula fugeret, Nerō sepulcrum fierī imperābat, lacrimāns atque identidem dīcēns 'quālis artifex pereō!'

tunc nūntius Giscō advēnit, epistulam tenēns. Nerō eam rapuit lēgitque sē hostem ā senātū iūdicātum esse et quaerī; senātum eum mōre maiōrum pūnītūrum esse. ille rogāvit quālis esset is modus poenae; et cum cognōvisset caput nūdī hominis furcā retinērī et corpus usque ad mortem verberārī, multō magis perterritus erat quam anteā. eōdem tamen clāmante nōndum adesse suam ultimam hōram, Giscō Indō gladium trādidit.

ac modo Nerō aliōs hortābātur ut lāmentārī inciperent, modo ōrābat ut aliquis exemplō sē iuvāret ad mortem petendam. eōdem tempore equitēs appropinquābant, quibus imperātum erat ut vīvum eum extraherent. quod ut Nerō sēnsit, Indus eī gladium obtulit. iuvante Epaphrodītō gladium iugulō adēgit prīnceps. centuriōnī irrumpentī et simulantī in auxilium sē vēnisse nōn aliud respondit quam 'sērō' et 'haec est fidēs'. atque in eā vōce mortuus est, exstantibus oculīs usque ad horrōrem metumque videntium. sīc periit Nerō.

Indus eandem epistulam cēpit et ad Epaphrodītum sē vertit. 'haec in animō dīligenter volve, amīce: quōmodo tū hanc rem referēs? nunc enim Nerō ad rēgnum Dītis trānsit. mox imperātor novus Rōmam reget.'

impendēns *imminent*
sepulcrum *grave*
tunc *then*
furca *two-pronged fork*
usque ad *right up to*
lāmentor *I weep*
exemplum *example*
adigō *I drive, thrust*
irrumpō *I burst in*
sērō *too late*
fidēs *loyalty*
exstō *I stand out, bulge out*
horror *horror*
Dīs *Dis (god of the Underworld)*

LANGUAGE PRACTICE

2. Use the chart of **īdem**, **eadem**, **idem** on page 277 to translate the words in bold into Latin.

- **a.** The following day we saw the **same** girl in front of the temple.
- **b.** The **same** boy was selling rooms in the apartment building.
- **c.** We were watching the **same** soldiers.
- **d.** Rufina gave help **to the same** priestess.
- **e.** You must wait for the decision **of the same** senators.
- **f.** We worship the **same** goddesses.
- **g.** The **same** freedwomen were selling garum throughout the city.
- **h.** You were sending weapons **to the same** tribes.

Nero: post mortem

Reaction to Nero's death

Nero's death was received at first with joy. However, it also roused other emotions, not only in Rome among the senators, people, and the soldiers stationed in the city, but also among the legions and generals; for the secret of empire was now revealed, that an emperor could be made outside of Rome. The senators rejoiced and immediately made use of their freedom of speech while the new emperor was not in Rome. The leading equestrians were almost as happy. The most respectable common people, who were connected to the great houses, and the clients and freedmen of men who had been condemned and exiled, were hopeful. The lowest classes, who spent their time in the circus and theaters, as well as the worst of the slaves, or men who had wasted their property and depended on Nero's disgraceful handouts, were in mourning and listened eagerly to rumors.

Tacitus

Emperors needed to win the favor of three main groups: the upper classes, the army, and the urban population.

Nero and the upper classes

Nero had little support among the upper classes. Many disapproved of his public performances. He had raised taxes on the rich, confiscated property, and even had some members of the Senate exiled or killed. In AD 65 a group of senators plotted to assassinate him, but the conspiracy was uncovered and the conspirators were executed.

Nero and the army

Nero never proved himself as a strong military leader; however, he did achieve some diplomatic success. Although he gave each soldier a large payment when he became emperor, he neglected to sustain the goodwill of the army.

Nero and the people

Among the common people, especially in Rome, Nero was generally popular. He positioned himself as a patron of the people and gave out food and gifts. He paid for shows in the circus, theater, and his own palace. He constructed a grand bathing complex which was open to everyone, along with an amphitheater and a food market. He also started to build a canal connecting Naples and Ostia, Rome's harbor, which would secure the city's food supply. Some viewed Nero's extravagant building programs as self-promotion, but others benefited from the employment they created. Suetonius reports that after Nero's death people continued to place flowers on his tomb for a number of years.

Look at these five sources. What different views of Nero do they show?

SOURCE 1

Most of all, he craved popularity, and he envied anyone else who in any way inspired the enthusiasm of the common people.

Suetonius

SOURCE 2

quid Nerōne peius?
quid thermīs melius Nerōniānīs?

What is worse than Nero?
What is better than Nero's baths?

Martial

SOURCE 3

By putting on the mask of an actor, he discarded the dignity of a ruler.

Cassius Dio

SOURCE 4

On every day of the games all kinds of presents were thrown to the people: a thousand birds of every kind each day, various types of food, tokens for grain, clothing, gold, silver, precious stones, pearls, paintings, slaves, pack animals, and even tame wild animals, and finally ships, apartment buildings, and farms.

Suetonius

SOURCE 5

Tacitus describes the reaction to Nero's announcement that he has decided to stay in Rome rather than go abroad:

Nero's words pleased the common people, who wanted entertainment and – their main concern – were afraid that there might be a shortage of corn if he were away from Rome. The Senate and the upper classes could not decide whether Nero was worse at a distance or nearby.

Tacitus

damnātiō memoriae

Upon his death, Nero was declared an enemy of the state by the Senate, and images of him were attacked or removed. Sometimes statues of Nero were recycled and carved to look like more popular emperors or private individuals.

The term ***damnātiō memoriae*** (condemnation of memory) is a modern phrase used to describe the process of removing someone from official accounts.

Right: two portraits of Nero recarved after his death. Image 1 was recarved into a likeness of another man, Image 2 into a portrait of Emperor Vespasian. Features such as the receding lower lip and famous curled hairstyle help identify these heads as belonging originally to statues of Nero.

Below: a coin of Nero which has been cut and scratched.

IMAGE 1

IMAGE 2

The philosopher Epictetus jokingly wrote:

> Whose image is on this coin? Trajan's? Give it to me. Nero's? Throw it away. It's unacceptable, it's worthless.

A new dynasty

The death of Nero brought an end to the Julio-Claudian dynasty, which started with the first emperor Augustus. After a year of civil war, Emperor Vespasian established a new dynasty, the Flavians. They had to justify overthrowing imperial power to legitimize their authority. They did this by destroying any favorable representations of Nero and discrediting his memory. Authors writing under Nero's successors were encouraged to paint his reign in a bad light.

The ancient sources

The surviving accounts of Nero's rule come primarily from three historians:

- Tacitus, c.AD 56–120, a senator.
- Suetonius, c.AD 70–130, a member of the equestrian class.
- Cassius Dio, c.AD 164–230, a senator.

The historian Josephus (c.AD 37–100), however, writes that these were not the only written accounts of Nero's reign:

> Many men have written the history of Nero. Some, who had been treated well by him, were biased in his favor and neglected the truth. Others, because of hatred and enmity, have shamelessly abused him with their lies, so that they deserve to be condemned.

Nero's reputation

Nero has the reputation of being one of Rome's worst emperors – selfish, greedy, and cruel. As a young man under Seneca's counsel, he initally showed promise, maintaining peace across the Empire, economic stability, and good relations with the Senate. However, his Domus Aurea was criticized for its extravagance and cost, particularly in the wake of the Great Fire of Rome. He is guilty of murdering and exiling those who opposed him – even ordering the murder of his own mother – but he was not the only emperor who got rid of enemies in this way.

QUESTIONS

1. Look at the written sources on these two pages.
    a. Whose version of events is recorded?
    b. How reliable do you think these accounts are?
    c. What reasons might they have for being biased?
2. What evidence can we use along with literary sources?

nova initia

postrīdiē, sōle suprā montēs oriente, coniūrātī in ponte stābant, flūmen spectantēs. cinerēs epistulae incēnsae in Tiberim ē manibus Indī cadēbant.

Giscō	fīnis est.
Lūcīlius	initium quoque est. quid nunc vōs pecūniā acceptā faciētis?
Giscō	ex urbe discēdere ad fundum emendum volō. nam urbēs nimium perīculōsae sunt. Catia Attōnī vītam rūsticam et sēcūram māluit.
Indus	nōlīte procul abīre, amīcī. ego popīnam in Subūrā tenēre cōnstituī. mē iuvābis, Rūfīna?
Rūfīna	ha! minimē! prīmum meam Sabīnam vīsitābō. tum servō ēmptō auxilium atque medicāmenta aegrīs offeram. sed fortasse tibi dōnum quoddam parvum dabō.

initium *beginning*

suprā *over, above*

Homecoming

In ancient Greek literature, the term ***nostos*** (homecoming) was used to describe the return of a hero. The greatest example of this is the story of Odysseus, who came back home to Ithaca after fighting in the Trojan War. His journey took ten years and he faced many trials and dangers along the way, one of them being his encounter with the Cyclops, Polyphemus.

- Read or listen to the story of Odysseus and Polyphemus.

Hero or villain?

Look at Sources 1 and 2. Odysseus lied to the Cyclops, he and his men blinded him, and they eventually escaped from his cave. From what you know of the story, do you think that Odysseus comes across as heroic? Do you think Polyphemus is justified in cursing Odysseus?

- Are deceit and violence acceptable in order to overcome an enemy?
- What other stories do you know where the hero or heroine acts in a similar way to Odysseus?

This Greek vase shows Odysseus blinding the Cyclops.

SOURCE 1

SOURCE 2

After Odysseus escapes and taunts him, Polyphemus appeals to his father:

'Hear me, Poseidon. If I really am your son, if you say you are my father, grant that Odysseus, destroyer of cities, does not return home to Ithaca. But if he is fated to see his loved ones, let him arrive late and in distress, having lost all of his companions, on another man's ship, and may he find trouble at home.'

Homer

Death or glory?

On his way back home, Odysseus visited the Underworld where he met the great hero Achilles. Achilles had been given the choice of having a short but glorious life or one that was long and unremarkable, and he chose the former. He died in the Trojan War. He said this to Odysseus: 'My homecoming was not to be, but my glory will be never-ending.'

- If you were given the same choice as Achilles, what would you choose?
- Some people want to be famous. Why do you think this might be?

SOURCE 3

Penelope's words stirred up Odysseus' tears, and he wept as he held his beloved, loyal wife. She was happy to see her husband, and her white arms around his neck did not quite let go.

Homer

Reunited

Look at Source 3. Odysseus was eventually reunited with his wife Penelope, their son Telemachus, and Odysseus' father Laertes.

- Should a good story always have a happy ending?

RESEARCH

Find out about:

1. Achilles and Thetis.
2. The death of Agamemnon.
3. Other adventures of Odysseus, such as those with the Sirens and the Laestrygonians.

Urbs aeterna

imperium sine fīne dedī.
I have given an empire without end.

Jupiter's promise to Aeneas was not fulfilled. The Roman Empire did not last, but its buildings and literature have had a strong hold on the imaginations of people for centuries.

Rome's changing face

Throughout Rome's history leading men and emperors made their mark on the city by paying for buildings which the ordinary people could use and enjoy. The greatest transformation probably took place under Augustus, but the emperors who followed also left their legacies. Nero built public facilities, such as baths, as well as a new imperial palace, the Domus Aurea. However, some of the most impressive and famous buildings of ancient Rome that are visible today were not yet built in AD 68.

Pantheon

The Pantheon was first built during the reign of Augustus, but burned down twice, the second time after a lightning strike. It was rebuilt in its current form during the reign of Emperor Hadrian. It was dedicated in around AD 126, and Hadrian chose to keep the original dedication to Agrippa, rather than replacing it with his own name. The building is circular, covered by a large concrete dome. In the center of the dome is an ***oculus*** (eye) which is open to the sky.

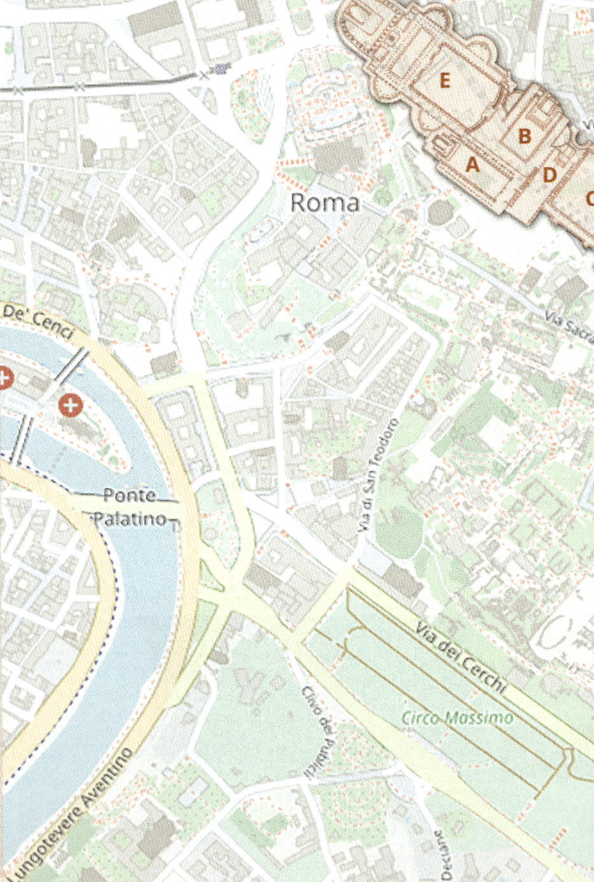

Monuments

The English word 'monument' comes from the Latin ***monumentum***. The Latin word is related to the verb ***moneō***, which can mean 'I remind' as well as 'I advise, warn'.

- What do you think is the difference between a monument and a building?
- Which people or events are memorialized now by monuments? Who makes the choice?

Horace described his poems as a monument to himself:

exēgī monumentum aere perennius.
I have built a monument more lasting than bronze.

- What various forms might monuments take?

Baths of Caracalla

The bathing complex was inaugurated in AD 216 and contained two libraries, one for Latin language texts and one for Greek. The baths themselves consisted of a frigidarium, tepidarium, caldarium, laconica, two palaestrae, and a natatio. They were built on a vast scale; the swimming pool alone measured 55 yards (the same length as a modern Olympic-sized pool). The baths were heated by an underground hypocaust system, and also by the use of glass windows and bronze mirrors, which took advantage of the sunlight. They were decorated lavishly and housed many marble statues.

This painting by Thorald Læssøe shows the Baths of Caracalla as they were in 1845.

Imperial fora

A. Julius Caesar was the first to build a forum in his name. The Forum of Caesar stands next to the Forum Romanum and was inaugurated in 46 BC. It houses the Temple of Venus Genetrix, from whom the Julian family claimed to be descended.

B. Augustus built the Forum of Augustus next to the Forum of Caesar. It was inaugurated in 2 BC and includes the Temple of Mars Ultor (Avenger), marking Augustus' revenge for his adoptive father's assassination.

C. The Forum of Vespasian, also called the Temple of Peace, was inaugurated in AD 75. It was built to celebrate the successful conquest of Jerusalem and had a garden at its center.

D. The Forum of Nerva was started by Emperor Domitian, but completed and inaugurated in AD 97 by his successor, Nerva, who gave it his own name. It filled the space between the existing fora.

E. The Forum of Trajan was inaugurated in AD 112 and celebrated the conquest of Dacia. It included a temple, a basilica, and two libraries. Between the libraries stood Trajan's column (see coin, *right*). It was over 115 feet high and was decorated with a continuous frieze which depicts scenes from the Dacian war.

Martial wrote this poem to celebrate the dedication of the Amphitheatrum by Emperor Titus in AD 80:

hīc ubi sīdereus propius videt astra Colossus
et crēscunt mediā pēgmata celsa viā,
invidiōsa ferī radiābant ātria rēgis
ūnaque iam tōtā stābat in urbe domus;
hīc ubi cōnspicuī venerābilis Amphitheātrī
ērigitur mōlēs, stāgna Nerōnis erant;
hīc ubi mīrāmur vēlōcia mūnera thermās,
abstulerat miserīs tēcta superbus ager;
reddita Rōma sibi est et sunt tē prēside, Caesar,
dēliciae populī, quae fuerant dominī.

Here, where the blazing Colossus sees the nearby stars, and in the middle of the road tall scaffolding rises, the hateful palace of a cruel king used to gleam, and in the entire city a single dwelling now stood. Here, where the honored mass of the amphitheater, visible from afar, is being built, was Nero's lake. Here, where we gaze in wonder at the baths of Emperor Titus, a gift quickly built, an arrogant estate had stolen from the wretched poor their homes. Rome has been given back to herself, and under your rule, Caesar, the master's pleasures belong to the people.

QUESTIONS

1. According to Martial, how has Rome changed since the time of Nero?
2. Pick out some words and phrases that show Martial's disapproval of Nero.

The Colosseum

The Colosseum was inaugurated in AD 80 under Emperor Titus and could hold an estimated 50,000 spectators. Gladiatorial fights, animal hunts, and other spectacles were held there. Emperor Domitian ordered the construction of a series of passages and cages under the arena floor. These were connected to access points on the outside of the amphitheater, where animals and gladiators could be brought in, then taken up into the arena.

In Roman times it was known simply as the Amphitheatrum. The name Colosseum did not appear until much later, and is believed to come from the Colossus, the giant bronze statue of Nero, which stood nearby. After Nero's death the statue was remodeled as the god Apollo.

Left: a coin from AD 80.
Right: the Colosseum painted by John Richards in 1776.

RESEARCH

Find out how some of these buildings look now.

1. To what extent have they been preserved or reconstructed?
2. What are they used for today?

Subūrānī

1 ego sum Sabīna. in Subūrā nāta sum, et, quamquam nōn semper hīc habitābam, nunc in eōdem locō iterum vīvō.
2 vīcīnus mihi est Indus, Batāvus quī popīnam tenet. quī Subūrānīs ibi bibentibus semper fābulās mīrābilēs nārrat.
3 meminī fēminam Britannicam, ferōciōrem Medūsā, quae in Subūrā habitābat. eī crīnēs ut flammae erant. ōlim sōla octo aurīgās necāvit gladiō ...
crīnis *hair*
4 tū es mendāx!

MEDICA
6 Rūfīna, labōre occupāris?
7 minimē, mī lepus, nōn labōrō! tempus semper habeō ad līberōs meae Sabīnae indulgendōs.
5 taberna proxima amitae Rūfīnae est. illīc medicāmenta vēndit ad aegrōs cūrandōs, et deum quiētē colit.
8 marītus in officīnā labōrat. ibi emblēmata facimus quae sunt in aedificiīs pūblicīs, in domibus dīvitum, etiam in aulā imperātōris ipsīus.

9 saepe ego et fīlia in cellā legere temptāmus ...
10 Sabīna? ubi estis? mē adiuvāre potestis?
11 māter! ubi es?
12 ... sed Subūra numquam est quiēt

ō quid solūtīs est beātius cūrīs,
cum mēns onus repōnit, ac peregrīnō
labōre fessī vēnimus larem ad nostrum
dēsīderātōque acquiēscimus lectō?
hoc est quod ūnumst prō labōribus tantīs.

What is more joyful than forgetting cares,
when the mind lays down its burden, and, exhausted
from working abroad, we have come home,
and rest in the bed we longed for?
It is this alone which makes up for such great labors.

Catullus

ohē, iam satis est, ohē, libelle!
iam pervēnimus usque ad umbilīcōs.

Hey, that's enough for now, hey, little book!
Now we have come right to the very end.

Martial

Reference

VOCABULARY FOR LEARNING

Chapter 17

appāreō, appārēre, appāruī	*appear*
benignus, benigna, benignum	*kind, generous*
dūrus, dūra, dūrum	*hard, harsh*
emō, emere, ēmī, ēmptus	*buy*
et	*even, also; and*
hūc	*here, to this place*
igitur	*therefore, and so*
is, ea, id	*this, that; he, she, it, them*
lentus, lenta, lentum	*slow*
libenter	*willingly, gladly*
līberō, līberāre, līberāvī, līberātus	*free, set free*
oppugnō, oppugnāre, oppugnāvī, oppugnātus	*attack*
paene	*almost, nearly*
plēnus, plēna, plēnum	*full*
praebeō, praebēre, praebuī, praebitus	*provide*
prō + *abl.*	*for, in return for; in front of*
quam + *superlative*	*as ... as possible*
relinquō, relinquere, relīquī, relictus	*leave, leave behind*
sōl, sōlis, *m.*	*sun*
unda, undae, *f.*	*wave*

Chapter 18

abeō, abīre, abiī	*go away, depart*
animus, animī, *m.*	*spirit, soul, mind*
aut ... aut ...	*either ... or ...*
crēdō, crēdere, crēdidī, crēditus + *dat.*	*believe, trust, have faith in*
eques, equitis, *m.*	*horseman; pl. = cavalry*
exeō, exīre, exiī	*come out of*
fēlīx, fēlīcis	*lucky, fortunate; happy*
heri	*yesterday*
legiō, legiōnis, *f.*	*legion*
licet, licēre, licuit	*it is allowed, one may*
malus, mala, malum	*bad, evil*
nam	*for*
necesse	*necessary*
perveniō, pervenīre, pervēnī	*arrive, reach*
placeō, placēre, placuī + *dat.*	*please*
prōmittō, prōmittere, prōmīsī, prōmissus	*promise*
quam	*than; how ...? how ...!*
scrībō, scrībere, scrīpsī, scrīptus	*write*
umbra, umbrae, *f.*	*shadow, shade; ghost*
vetus, veteris	*old*

Chapter 19

adferō, adferre, attulī, adlātus	*bring*
gerō, gerere, gessī, gestus	*wage (war); wear (clothes)*
lacrima, lacrimae, *f.*	*tear*
lentē	*slowly*
maximus, maxima, maximum	*very big, huge; biggest, greatest*
melior, melior, melius	*better*
mortuus, mortua, mortuum	*dead*
multō	*much, by much*
neque	*and not, nor, neither*
neque ... neque ...	*neither ... nor ...*
oculus, oculī, *m.*	*eye*
optimus, optima, optimum	*very good, excellent; best*
pōnō, pōnere, posuī, positus	*put, place, put up*
referō, referre, rettulī, relātus	*bring back, carry back; report, tell*
sīc	*so, in this way*
sīcut	*just as, like*
ut	*as*
vestīmentum, vestīmentī, *n.*	*item of clothing, garment; pl. = clothes*
vōtum, vōtī, *n.*	*prayer*
vulnus, vulneris, *n.*	*wound*

Chapter 20

ā, ab + *abl.*	*by; from, away from*
adeō, adīre, adiī	*go to, approach*
agō, agere, ēgī, āctus	*act; drive, lead; do*
alter, altera, alterum	*the other, another, one of two, the second of two*
āmittō, āmittere, āmīsī, āmissus	*lose*
atque	*and*
audāx, audācis	*bold, daring*
dēbeō, dēbēre, dēbuī, dēbitus	*ought, should, must; owe*
enim	*for, because*
facilis, facilis, facile	*easy*
fuga, fugae, *f.*	*escape*
graviter	*heavily; seriously*
hīc	*here*
lībertās, lībertātis, *f.*	*freedom*
persuādeō, persuādēre, persuāsī, persuāsus + *dat.*	*persuade*
tēlum, tēlī, *n.*	*missile, weapon, spear*
vix	*scarcely, hardly, with difficulty*
ūnus, ūna, ūnum	*one*
duo, duae, duo	*two*
trēs, trēs, tria	*three*

Chapter 21

alius, alia, aliud	*else; other, another*
auris, auris, *f.*	*ear*
cōgō, cōgere, coēgī, coāctus	*force, compel*
forte	*by chance*
gaudium, gaudiī, *n.*	*joy, pleasure*
ignis, ignis, *m.*	*fire*
longē	*far off*
pēs, pedis, *m.*	*foot*
petō, petere, petīvī, petītus	*make for; attack; seek; beg, ask for*
poena, poenae, *f.*	*punishment*
poenās dō, dare, dedī, datus	*pay the penalty, am punished*
postrīdiē	*on the following day*
propter + *acc.*	*on account of, because of*
quot?	*how many?*
Rōmae	*at/in Rome*
tēctum, tēctī, *n.*	*roof*
tūtus, tūta, tūtum	*safe*
unde	*from where*
ventus, ventī, *m.*	*wind*
vester, vestra, vestrum	*your (plural), yours*

Chapter 22

adiuvō, adiuvāre, adiūvī, adiūtus	*help*
aliquis, aliquid	*someone, something*
aperiō, aperīre, aperuī, apertus	*open*
canis, canis, *m.*	*dog*
cōnor, cōnārī, cōnātus sum	*try*
cūra, cūrae, *f.*	*care, worry*
dīves, dīvitis	*rich*
ēgredior, ēgredī, ēgressus sum	*go out, leave*
hortor, hortārī, hortātus sum	*encourage, urge*
ingredior, ingredī, ingressus sum	*go into, enter*
loquor, loquī, locūtus sum	*speak, talk*
mīror, mīrārī, mīrātus sum	*wonder at, admire*
morior, morī, mortuus sum	*die*
patior, patī, passus sum	*suffer, endure*
precor, precārī, precātus sum	*pray, pray to*
proficīscor, proficīscī, profectus sum	*set out*
prōgredior, prōgredī, prōgressus sum	*go forward, advance*
proximus, proxima, proximum	*nearest, next to*
regredior, regredī, regressus sum	*go back, return*
sequor, sequī, secūtus sum	*follow*

Chapter 23

apud + *acc.*	*among, with, at the house of*
aurum, aurī, *n.*	*gold*
cārus, cāra, cārum	*dear; expensive*
celer, celeris, celere	*quick, fast*
cōnficiō, cōnficere, cōnfēcī, cōnfectus	*wear out, exhaust; finish*
cum + *subj.*	*when, since*
cūrō, cūrāre, cūrāvī, cūrātus	*look after, care for, supervise*
dum	*while*
maximē	*very much, a lot, very greatly*
minor, minor, minus	*smaller, less; younger*
num?	*surely not?*
parātus, parāta, parātum	*ready*
parēns, parentis, *m.f.*	*parent*
plūs, plūris	*more*
posteā	*afterwards*
quālis, quālis, quāle	*what sort of?*
quantus, quanta, quantum	*how big? how much?*
signum, signī, *n.*	*sign, signal; seal*
soror, sorōris, *f.*	*sister*
validus, valida, validum	*strong*

Chapter 24

addūcō, addūcere, addūxī, adductus	*lead to*
adeō	*so much, so greatly, to such an extent*
conveniō, convenīre, convēnī	*come together, gather, meet*
dēspērō, dēspērāre, dēspērāvī	*despair*
exercitus, exercitūs, *m.*	*army*
ita	*so, in this way*
manus, manūs, *f.*	*hand; group of people*
minimē	*very little, least; no*
mūtō, mūtāre, mūtāvī, mūtātus	*change*
opus, operis, *n.*	*work*
reddō, reddere, reddidī, redditus	*give back, restore*
saxum, saxī, *n.*	*rock*
spērō, spērāre, spērāvī, spērātus	*hope, expect*
tālis, tālis, tāle	*such, of such a kind*
tam	*so*
tantus, tanta, tantum	*so great, such a great, so much*
tot	*so many*
ut	*(+ subj.) that, so that, in order that; (+ indic.) as*
vērus, vēra, vērum	*true, real*
vultus, vultūs, *m.*	*expression, face*

Chapter 25

ante + *acc.*	*before, in front of*
domī	*at home*
faciēs, faciēī, *f.*	*face, appearance*
frangō, frangere, frēgī, frāctus	*break*
imperium, imperiī, *n.*	*command; empire; power*
imperō, imperāre, imperāvī, imperātus + *dat.*	*order, command*
lēgātus, lēgātī, *m.*	*commander, governor*
maior, maior, maius	*bigger, larger, greater*
mīlle, *pl.* mīlia	*thousand*
minimus, minima, minimum	*very small, tiny*
nē + *subj.*	*that … not, so that … not*
num	*whether; surely not?*
pāreō, pārēre, pāruī + *dat.*	*obey*
postulō, postulāre, postulāvī, postulātus	*demand*
rēs, reī, *f.*	*business, matter, event; thing; story*
scelestus, scelesta, scelestum	*wicked*
spēs, speī, *f.*	*hope*
trādō, trādere, trādidī, trāditus	*hand down; hand over*
umquam	*ever*
victōria, victōriae, *f.*	*victory*

Chapter 26

canō, canere, cecinī	*sing; play (an instrument)*
carmen, carminis, *n.*	*poem, song*
circum + *acc.*	*around*
fātum, fātī, *n.*	*fate, destiny; death*
īra, īrae, *f.*	*anger*
lātus, lāta, lātum	*wide, broad*
magnopere	*greatly, very much*
modus, modī, *m.*	*manner, way, kind, style*
peior, peior, peius	*worse*
pessimus, pessima, pessimum	*very bad, worst*
simulac	*as soon as*
vīvus, vīva, vīvum	*alive, living*
quattuor	*four*
quīnque	*five*
sex	*six*
septem	*seven*
octo	*eight*
novem	*nine*
decem	*ten*
centum	*a hundred*

Chapter 27

arbor, arboris, *f.*	*tree*
ars, artis, *f.*	*art, skill*
compōnō, compōnere, composuī, compositus	*arrange*
dexter, dextra, dextrum	*right*
doceō, docēre, docuī, doctus	*teach*
dolor, dolōris, *m.*	*pain*
dum	*(+ subj.) until; (+ indic.) while*
gaudeō, gaudēre, gāvīsus sum	*am pleased, rejoice*
impōnō, impōnere, imposuī, impositus	*put, put on*
ipse, ipsa, ipsum	*himself, herself, itself, themselves*
liber, librī, *m.*	*book*
metus, metūs, *m.*	*fear*
modo	*only*
moneō, monēre, monuī, monitus	*warn, advise*
pectus, pectoris, *n.*	*chest, breast*
prīmō	*at first*
soleō, solēre, solitus sum	*am accustomed, used*
tempestās, tempestātis, *f.*	*storm*
vīs, vim, *f.*	*force*
vulnerō, vulnerāre, vulnerāvī, vulnerātus	*wound, injure*

Chapter 28

adhūc	*still, until now*
ager, agrī , *m.*	*field*
ascendō, ascendere, ascendī	*climb*
autem	*but, however*
beātus, beāta, beātum	*happy, blessed*
cōpiae, cōpiārum, *f. pl.*	*forces, troops*
dēscendō, dēscendere, dēscendī	*go down, come down*
dulcis, dulcis, dulce	*sweet*
ergō	*therefore*
errō, errāre, errāvī	*make a mistake; wander*
incipiō, incipere, incēpī, inceptus	*begin, start*
nōnnūllī, nōnnūllae, nōnnūlla	*some, several*
quīdam, quaedam, quoddam	*one, a certain; pl. = some*
sapiēns, sapientis	*wise*
scelus, sceleris , *n.*	*crime*
super + *acc.*	*over*
temptō, temptāre, temptāvī, temptātus	*try*
terra, terrae, *f.*	*country; land, ground*
videor, vidērī, vīsus sum	*seem, appear*
virgō, virginis, *f.*	*virgin, girl, young woman*

Chapter 29

aedificō, aedificāre, aedificāvī, aedificātus	*build*
audeō, audēre, ausus sum	*dare*
clārus, clāra, clārum	*clear; famous, distinguished*
custōdiō, custōdīre, custōdīvī, custōdītus	*guard*
decet, decēre, decuit	*it is right for, it is proper for*
dēfendō, dēfendere, dēfendī, dēfēnsus	*defend*
dubitō, dubitāre, dubitāvī, dubitātus	*hesitate, doubt*
gēns, gentis, *f.*	*people, race, family, tribe*
honor, honōris, *m.*	*honor*
ingenium, ingeniī, *n.*	*nature, character*
interficiō, interficere, interfēcī, interfectus	*kill*
līber, lībera, līberum	*free*
moveō, movēre, mōvī, mōtus	*move*
nisi	*unless, except*
orbis, orbis, *m.*	*globe, sphere*
poscō, poscere, poposcī	*ask for, demand*
regō, regere, rēxī, rēctus	*rule*
similis, similis, simile	*similar, alike*
somnus, somnī, *m.*	*sleep*
ut	*(+ indic.) when, as soon as; as; (+ subj.) that, so that, in order that*

Chapter 30

addō, addere, addidī, additus	*add*
āra, ārae, *f.*	*altar*
captīvus, captīvī, *m.*	*captive, prisoner*
coma, comae, *f.*	*hair*
crās	*tomorrow*
discō, discere, didicī	*learn*
fīō, fierī, factus sum	*become*
iuvō, iuvāre, iūvī, iūtus	*help, assist*
negō, negāre, negāvī, negātus	*deny, say that ... not*
nūmen, nūminis, *n.*	*deity, divine power*
opprimō, opprimere, oppressī, oppressus	*crush, overwhelm*
ōs, ōris, *n.*	*mouth*
pellō, pellere, pepulī, pulsus	*drive, push*
pūniō, pūnīre, pūnīvī, pūnītus	*punish*
quandō?	*when?*
simul	*at the same time*
solvō, solvere, solvī, solūtus	*undo, let go*
ūtor, ūtī, ūsus sum + *abl.*	*use, employ*
vertō, vertere, vertī, versus	*turn*
virtūs, virtūtis, *f.*	*courage, virtue*

Chapter 31

arma, armōrum, *n. pl.*	*arms, weapons*
caedēs, caedis, *f.*	*killing, slaughter*
castra, castrōrum, *n. pl.*	*camp*
cāsus, cāsūs, *m.*	*accident, chance*
causa, causae, *f.*	*reason*
cōnsul, cōnsulis, *m.*	*consul*
faveō, favere, fāvī, fautus + *dat.*	*favor, support*
illīc	*there*
impetus, impetūs, *m.*	*charge, assault*
inimīcus, inimīcī, *m.*	*enemy*
invītō, invītāre, invītāvī, invītātus	*invite*
lītus, lītoris, *n.*	*shore, beach*
magis	*more; rather*
mālō, mālle, māluī	*prefer*
mēns, mentis, *f.*	*mind*
numerus, numerī, *m.*	*number*
patria, patriae, *f.*	*country, homeland*
proelium, proeliī, *n.*	*battle*
rēgnum, rēgnī, *n.*	*kingdom*
victor, victōris, *m.*	*winner*

Chapter 32

auxilium, auxiliī, *n.*	*help*
claudō, claudere, clausī, clausus	*close*
colō, colere, coluī, cultus	*worship*
diligēns, diligentis	*careful*
ecce!	*look! see!*
fīnis, fīnis, *m.*	*end*
flamma, flammae, *f.*	*flame; pl. = fire*
fortūna, fortūnae, *f.*	*fortune*
īdem, eadem, idem	*the same*
mōs, mōris, *m.*	*way, fashion, custom*
nōndum	*not yet*
populus, populī, *m.*	*people*
prīmum	*for the first time*
procul	*far off*
pūblicus, pūblica, pūblicum	*public*
Rōmānī, Rōmānōrum, *m. pl.*	*Romans*
satis	*enough*
senātus, senātūs, *m.*	*Senate*
ultimus, ultima, ultimum	*final; furthest*
valē!	*goodbye, farewell*

ORDER OF INFORMATION IN LATIN SENTENCES

1. In a Latin sentence information tends to come in a standard order. Familiarity with that order can help you to read and understand Latin.

2. In general, expect the nominative first, then accusative, and then verb. For example:

sorōrēs	**gladiōs**	**vēndēbant.**
sisters	*swords*	*they were selling*

The sisters were selling swords.

3. If the nominative does not need to be stated, expect accusative, verb:

gladiōs	**vēndēbant.**
swords	*they were selling*

They were selling swords.

4. If there is no accusative, then expect nominative, verb:

sorōrēs	**currēbant.**
sisters	*they were running*

The sisters were running.

5. Adverbs, and phrases describing the action, are usually immediately before the verb:

sorōrēs	**gladiōs**	**in forō**	**vēndēbant.**
sisters	*swords*	*in the forum*	*they were selling*

The sisters were selling swords in the forum.

6. A dative noun is usually between the nominative and accusative:

sorōrēs	**cīvibus**	**gladiōs**	**in forō**	**vēndēbant.**
sisters	*to the citizens*	*swords*	*in the forum*	*they were selling*

The sisters were selling swords to the citizens in the forum.

However, a sentence may begin with a dative noun:

Alexandrō	**Sabīna**	**respondit,**	**'omnia**	**temptāvimus.'**
to Alexander	*Sabina*	*replied*	*all things*	*we have tried*

Sabina replied to Alexander, 'We have tried everything.'

7. Adjectives may appear before or after the nouns they describe:

sorōrēs	**cīvibus**	**gladiōs**	**pulchrōs**	**in forō**	**vēndēbant.**
sisters	*to the citizens*	*swords*	*beautiful ones*	*in the forum*	*they were selling*

The sisters were selling beautiful swords to the citizens in the forum.

Adjectives of size or number are usually before the noun they describe:

sorōrēs	**cīvibus**	**multōs**	**gladiōs**	**in forō**	**vēndēbant.**
sisters	*to the citizens*	*many*	*swords*	*in the forum*	*they were selling*

The sisters were selling many swords to the citizens in the forum.

8. Genitives usually follow the nouns they describe:

sorōrēs	**cīvibus**	**gladiōs**	**parentum**	**in forō**	**vēndēbant.**
sisters	*to the citizens*	*swords*	*of their parents*	*in the forum*	*they were selling*

The sisters were selling their parents' swords to the citizens in the forum.

9. Relative clauses also often follow the nouns they describe:

Sabīna,	**quae**	**paene**	**rīdēbat,**	**Alexandrō**	**appropinquāvit.**
Sabina	*who*	*almost*	*was laughing*	*to Alexander*	*drew near*

Sabina, who was almost laughing, drew near to/approached Alexander.

10. Indirect statements use an accusative and infinitive construction. The accusative usually comes immediately after the verb of saying, thinking, or perceiving. The infinitive often comes at the end of the sentence:

puellae	**dīcunt**	**hominēs**	**plaustra**	**custōdīre.**
girls	*say*	*men*	*carts*	*to guard*

The girls say that men are guarding the carts.

11. Where a participle describes a noun, further information relating to the noun - participle phrase is usually placed between the noun and the participle:

Giscō	**Iūliam**	**in hortō**	**stantem**	**relīquit.**
Gisco	*Julia*	*in the garden*	*standing*	*left*

Gisco left Julia standing in the garden.

12. As you become familiar with the usual word order, you may notice when the author departs from that order to emphasize a particular word or point:

Mānium	**in viā**	**invēnimus**	**mortuum.**
Manius	*in the street*	*we found*	*dead*

We found Manius in the street. He was dead.

amīcam	**Rūfīna**	**videt.**
friend	*Rufina*	*sees*

It's her friend that Rufina sees.

Sometimes Latin authors used a symmetrical order of words:

clāmōrēs	**hominum**	**et**	**equōrum**	**hinnītus**
shouts	*of men*	*and*	*of horses*	*neighing*

the shouts of men and the neighing of horses

Latin authors were also fond of using three parallel examples, as well as removing words such as **et**:

vigilēs,	**cīvēs,**	**servī**	**servāre**	**temptābant**	**virginēs**
firemen	*citizens*	*slaves*	*to save*	*were trying*	*young women*

The firemen, citizens, and enslaved people were trying to save the young women.

Latin verbs are sometimes omitted if they can be understood from elsewhere in the sentence:

mīles erat nimium gravis, puella nōn valida, glaciēs nōn firma.
The soldier was too heavy, the girl (was) not strong, the ice (was) not firm.

NOUNS

	First declension	Second declension			Third declension			
	feminine	*masculine*	*masculine*	*neuter*	*masculine*	*feminine*	*feminine*	*neuter*
SINGULAR	*girl*	*friend*	*boy*	*gift*	*thief*	*night*	*city*	*head*
nominative	puella	amīcus	puer	dōnum	fūr	nox	urbs	caput
genitive	puellae	amīcī	puerī	dōnī	fūris	noctis	urbis	capitis
dative	puellae	amīcō	puerō	dōnō	fūrī	noctī	urbī	capitī
accusative	puellam	amīcum	puerum	dōnum	fūrem	noctem	urbem	caput
ablative	puellā	amīcō	puerō	dōnō	fūre	nocte	urbe	capite*
PLURAL								
nominative	puellae	amīcī	puerī	dōna	fūrēs	noctēs	urbēs	capita
genitive	puellārum	amīcōrum	puerōrum	dōnōrum	fūrum	noctium	urbium	capitum
dative	puellīs	amīcīs	puerīs	dōnīs	fūribus	noctibus	urbibus	capitibus
accusative	puellās	amīcōs	puerōs	dōna	fūrēs	noctēs	urbēs	capita
ablative	puellīs	amīcīs	puerīs	dōnīs	fūribus	noctibus	urbibus	capitibus

* The ablative singular of **mare** (*sea*) ends -ī: **marī**.

	Fourth declension		Fifth declension	
	masculine	*neuter*	*feminine*	*masculine*
SINGULAR	*hand; group*	*horn*	*thing*	*day*
nominative	manus	cornū	rēs	diēs
genitive	manūs	cornūs	reī	diēī
dative	manuī	cornū	reī	diēi
accusative	manum	cornū	rem	diem
ablative	manū	cornū	rē	diē
PLURAL				
nominative	manūs	cornua	rēs	diēs
genitive	manuum	cornuum	rērum	diērum
dative	manibus	cornibus	rēbus	diēbus
accusative	manūs	cornua	rēs	diēs
ablative	manibus	cornibus	rēbus	diēbus

The vocative case has exactly the same form as the nominative case, except in the singular of the second declension, where -**us** becomes -**e** and -**ius** becomes -ī. For examples see Book 1, page 190.

The locative case endings (singular and plural) are as follows: first declension -**ae** and -**īs**; second declension -ī and -**īs**; third declension -ī or -**e** and -**ibus**. In the fourth declension **domus** has the locative **domī**.

USES OF THE CASES

nominative	**amīcus** labōrat.	The **friend** is working.	The noun carrying out the action.
genitive	nōmen **amīcī**	the **friend's** name the name **of the friend**	Possession: of, 's.
	satis **aurī**; plūs **cibī**	enough **gold**; more **food**	Quantity.
	vir **magnae auctōritātis**	a man **of great authority**; a very **authoritative** man	Quality.
dative	puella **amīcō** dōnum dat.	The girl gives a present **to her friend**.	to
	necesse est **amīcō** labōrāre.	It is necessary **for the friend** to work.	for
	puella semper **amīcō** crēdit.	The girl always trusts her **friend**.	Some verbs are used with a noun in the dative case.
accusative	puella **amīcum** laudat.	The girl praises her **friend**.	The noun receiving the action.
	puella ad **amīcum** ambulat.	The girl walks towards her **friend**.	With some prepositions, e.g. **ad**, **per**, **trāns**, **in**
	puella **multās hōrās** dormiēbat.	The girl was sleeping **for many hours**.	How long something lasts for.
	Lūcriō dīxit **Rūfīnam** labōrāre.	Lucrio said **Rufina** was working.	Noun carrying out the action in an indirect statement.
ablative	puella cum **amīcō** in **forō** ambulat.	The girl is walking with her **friend** in the **forum**.	in, on, by, with, from, at Often with a preposition, e.g. **cum**, **ā/ab**, **ē/ex**, **in**
	mediā nocte canis lātrāvit.	**In the middle of the night** the dog barked.	The time when something happens.
	Sabīna ab **Alexandrō** salūtātur.	Sabina is greeted by **Alexander**.	Agent of a passive verb.
	senex **venēnō** necātus est.	The old man was killed **by poison**.	Instrument of a passive verb.
	Sōrānos altior **amīcō** est.	Soranos is taller **than his friend**.	In comparisons.
	vīnum **magnō pretiō** vēndit.	He sells the wine **at a high price**.	The price of something.
	pecūniā trāditā	after the money was handed over	Ablative absolute.
vocative	salvē, **Fauste**!	Hello, **Faustus**!	Speaking to someone.
locative	**Rōmae** manēbāmus. **Athēnīs** habitābam.	We remained **in/at Rome**. I was living **in Athens**.	Indicating location.

ADJECTIVES

	First and second declension			Third declension			
	masculine	*feminine*	*neuter*	*masculine/ feminine*	*neuter*	*masculine/ feminine*	*neuter*
SINGULAR	*good*			*sad*		*huge*	
nominative	bonus	bona	bonum	trīstis	trīste	ingēns	
genitive	bonī	bonae	bonī	trīstis		ingentis	
dative	bonō	bonae	bonō	trīstī		ingentī	
accusative	bonum	bonam	bonum	trīstem	trīste	ingentem	ingēns
ablative	bonō	bonā	bonō	trīstī		ingentī	
PLURAL							
nominative	bonī	bonae	bona	trīstēs	trīstia	ingentēs	ingentia
genitive	bonōrum	bonārum	bonōrum	trīstium		ingentium	
dative	bonīs			trīstibus		ingentibus	
accusative	bonōs	bonās	bona	trīstēs	trīstia	ingentēs	ingentia
ablative	bonīs			trīstibus		ingentibus	

COMPARATIVE AND SUPERLATIVE ADJECTIVES

Positive		Comparative		Superlative	
laetus	*happy*	laetior	*happier*	laetissimus	*happiest, very happy*
pulcher	*beautiful*	pulchrior	*more beautiful*	pulcherrimus	*most beautiful, very beautiful*
trīstis	*sad*	trīstior	*sadder*	trīstissimus	*saddest, very sad*
dīves	*rich*	dīvitior	*richer*	dīvitissimus	*richest, very rich*
facilis	*easy*	facilior	*easier*	facillimus	*easiest, very easy*

IRREGULAR FORMS OF ADJECTIVES

Positive		Comparative		Superlative	
bonus	*good*	melior	*better*	optimus	*best, very good*
magnus	*big*	maior	*bigger*	maximus	*biggest, very big*
malus	*bad*	pēior	*worse*	pessimus	*worst, very bad*
multus	*much*	plūs	*more*	plūrimus	*most, very much*
parvus	*small*	minor	*smaller*	minimus	*smallest, very small*

ADVERBS

Many adverbs are formed from adjectives:

Adjective		Adverb	
First and second declension			
laetus	*happy*	laetē	*happily*
cautus	*cautious*	cautē	*cautiously*
Third declension			
celer	*quick*	celeriter	*quickly*
facilis	*easy*	facile	*easily*

For more information on the formation of adverbs from adjectives, see page 16.

There are many other adverbs, such as **nunc** (*now*), **saepe** (*often*), **diū** (*for a long time*), **nimium** (*too much*), and **vix** (*hardly*).

A mosaic from Daphne, a holiday resort near Antioch.

COMPARATIVE AND SUPERLATIVE ADVERBS

Positive		Comparative		Superlative	
laetē	*happily*	laetius	*more happily*	laetissimē	*very happily*
cautē	*cautiously*	cautius	*more cautiously*	cautissimē	*very cautiously*
facile	*easily*	facilius	*more easily*	facillimē	*very easily*
celeriter	*quickly*	celerius	*more quickly*	celerrimē	*very quickly*

IRREGULAR FORMS OF ADVERBS

Positive		Comparative		Superlative	
bene	*well*	melius	*better*	optimē	*best, very well*
magnopere	*greatly*	magis	*more, more greatly*	maximē	*most, very greatly*
male	*badly*	peius	*worse*	pessimē	*worst, very badly*
multum	*much*	plūs	*more*	plūrimum	*most*
paulum	*little*	minus	*less*	minimē	*least, not at all; no*
diū	*for a long time*	diūtius	*for a longer time*	diūtissimē	*for a very long time*

ADJECTIVES/PRONOUNS

	masculine	feminine	neuter
SINGULAR	*this; he, she, it*		
nominative	hic	haec	hoc
genitive	huius		
dative	huic		
accusative	hunc	hanc	hoc
ablative	hōc	hāc	hōc
PLURAL			
nominative	hī	hae	haec
genitive	hōrum	hārum	hōrum
dative	hīs		
accusative	hōs	hās	haec
ablative	hīs		

	masculine	feminine	neuter
SINGULAR	*that; he, she, it*		
nominative	ille	illa	illud
genitive	illius		
dative	illī		
accusative	illum	illam	illud
ablative	illō	illā	illō
PLURAL			
nominative	illī	illae	illa
genitive	illōrum	illārum	illōrum
dative	illīs		
accusative	illōs	illās	illa
ablative	illīs		

	masculine	feminine	neuter
SINGULAR	*himself, herself, itself*		
nominative	ipse	ipsa	ipsum
genitive	ipsīus		
dative	ipsī		
accusative	ipsum	ipsam	ipsum
ablative	ipsō	ipsā	ipsō
PLURAL			
nominative	ipsī	ipsae	ipsa
genitive	ipsōrum	ipsārum	ipsōrum
dative	ipsīs		
accusative	ipsōs	ipsās	ipsa
ablative	ipsīs		

	masculine	feminine	neuter
SINGULAR	*who, which*		
nominative	quī	quae	quod
genitive	cuius		
dative	cui		
accusative	quem	quam	quod
ablative	quō	quā	quō
PLURAL			
nominative	quī	quae	quae
genitive	quōrum	quārum	quōrum
dative	quibus		
accusative	quōs	quās	quae
ablative	quibus		

Note that the forms of **quis? quid?** (*who? what?*) differ from **quī**, **quae**, **quod** (*who, which*) only in the nominative and accusative singular:

	masculine	feminine	neuter
SINGULAR	*who? what?*		
nominative	quis?	quis?	quid?
accusative	quem?	quam?	quid?

	masculine	feminine	neuter
SINGULAR	*he, she, it; this; that*		
nominative	is	ea	id
genitive	eius		
dative	eī		
accusative	eum	eam	id
ablative	eō	eā	eō
PLURAL			
nominative	eī	eae	ea
genitive	eōrum	eārum	eōrum
dative	eīs		
accusative	eōs	eās	ea
ablative	eīs		

	masculine	feminine	neuter
SINGULAR	*the same; this; that*		
nominative	īdem	eadem	idem
genitive	eiusdem		
dative	eīdem		
accusative	eundem	eandem	idem
ablative	eōdem	eādem	eōdem
PLURAL			
nominative	īdem	eaedem	eadem
genitive	eōrundem	eārundem	eōrundem
dative	eīsdem *or* īsdem		
accusative	eōsdem	eāsdem	eadem
ablative	eīsdem *or* īsdem		

PERSONAL PRONOUNS

SINGULAR	*I*	*you (sing.)*
nominative	ego	tū
genitive	meī	tuī
dative	mihi	tibi
accusative	mē	tē
ablative	mē	tē

PLURAL	*we*	*you (pl.)*
nominative	nōs	vōs
genitive	nostrum	vestrum
dative	nōbīs	vōbīs
accusative	nōs	vōs
ablative	nōbīs	vōbīs

SINGULAR/ PLURAL	*himself, herself, themselves*
nominative	–
genitive	suī
dative	sibi
accusative	sē
ablative	sē

A marble relief of an elephant.

NUMBERS

1	I	ūnus, ūna, ūnum
2	II	duo, duae, duo
3	III	trēs, trēs, tria
4	IIII or IV	quattuor
5	V	quīnque
6	VI	sex
7	VII	septem
8	VIII	octo
9	VIIII or IX	novem
10	X	decem
50	L	quīnquāgintā
100	C	centum
500	D	quīngentī
1,000	M	mīlle

1st	prīmus, a, um
2nd	secundus, a, um
3rd	tertius, a, um
4th	quārtus, a, um
5th	quīntus, a, um
6th	sextus, a, um
7th	septimus, a, um
8th	octāvus, a, um
9th	nōnus, a, um
10th	decimus, a, um

The numbers 4–10, 50, and 100 do not change their endings.

The numbers 1–3 change their endings as follows:

	masculine	*feminine*	*neuter*	*masculine*	*feminine*	*neuter*	*masculine/ feminine*	*neuter*
nominative	ūnus	ūna	ūnum	duo	duae	duo	trēs	tria
genitive	ūnīus			duōrum	duārum	duōrum	trium	
dative	ūnī			duōbus	duābus	duōbus	tribus	
accusative	ūnum	ūnam	ūnum	duōs	duās	duo	trēs	tria
ablative	ūnō	ūnā	ūnō	duōbus	duābus	duōbus	tribus	

A mosaic from near Rome.

EXPRESSIONS, MOTTOES, AND ABBREVIATIONS

A.D.	annō dominī	*in the year of the Lord*
a.m.	ante merīdiem	*before midday*
ad lib	ad libitum	*as you desire*
c.	circā	*about, approximately*
cf.	confer	*compare (with)*
C.V.	curriculum vītae	*course of life*
e.g.	exemplī grātiā	*as an example*
et al.	et aliī	*and the other people*
etc.	et cētera	*and the other things*
ibid.	ibidem	*in the same place (in a book)*
i.e.	id est	*that is*
n.b.	notā bene	*note well*
p.m.	post merīdiem	*after midday*
p.s.	post scrīptum	*after what has been written*
Q.E.D.	quod erat demonstrandum	*(that) which had to be proved*
R.I.P.	requiēscat in pāce	*rest in peace*
S.P.Q.R.	Senātus Populusque Rōmānus	*the Senate and the People of Rome*
v. or vs.	versus	*against, facing*

ad hoc	*as necessary; temporary*
ālea iacta est. (*Julius Caesar*)	*The die has been thrown.*
alibī	*in another place*
bonā fidē	*genuine; in good faith*
carpe diem! (*Horace*)	*Seize the day!*
cōgitō ergō sum.	*I think, therefore I am.*
cui bonō?	*to whose benefit?*
dē factō	*in reality*
dē iūre	*according to the law, in theory*
ē plūribus ūnum	*out of many, one*
fortibus Fortūna favet.	*Fortune favors the brave.*
in sitū	*in (the original) place*
mea culpa	*my own fault*
mēns sāna in corpore sānō. (*Juvenal*)	*A healthy mind in a healthy body.*
modus operandī	*a way of doing something*
pecūnia nōn olet.	*Money doesn't stink.*
per capita	*each person*
per sē	*in/by itself*
prīmus inter parēs	*a first among equals*
prō bonō (pūblicō)	*for the public good*
quid prō quō	*one favor in return for another*
quis custōdiet ipsōs custōdēs? (*Juvenal*)	*Who will guard the guards?*
rēs pūblica	*the public situation, the state*
status quō	*the existing situation*
summā cum laude	*with great glory*
vēnī, vīdī, vīcī. (*Julius Caesar*)	*I came, I saw, I conquered.*
viā	*by way of*
vice versā	*the other way around*
vōx populī	*the voice of the people*

VERBS: ACTIVE INDICATIVE

	1st conjugation	2nd conjugation	3rd conjugation	4th conjugation	3rd/4th conjugation
	call	*hold*	*send*	*hear*	*take*
PRESENT (*I call, am calling, etc.*)					
I	vocō	teneō	mittō	audiō	capiō
you (sing.)	vocās	tenēs	mittis	audīs	capis
he, she, it	vocat	tenet	mittit	audit	capit
we	vocāmus	tenēmus	mittimus	audīmus	capimus
you (pl.)	vocātis	tenētis	mittitis	audītis	capitis
they	vocant	tenent	mittunt	audiunt	capiunt
FUTURE (*I shall call, etc.*)					
I	vocābō	tenēbō	mittam	audiam	capiam
you (sing.)	vocābis	tenēbis	mittēs	audiēs	capiēs
he, she, it	vocābit	tenēbit	mittet	audiet	capiet
we	vocābimus	tenēbimus	mittēmus	audiēmus	capiēmus
you (pl.)	vocābitis	tenēbitis	mittētis	audiētis	capiētis
they	vocābunt	tenēbunt	mittent	audient	capient
IMPERFECT (*I was calling, used to call, etc.*)					
I	vocābam	tenēbam	mittēbam	audiēbam	capiēbam
you (sing.)	vocābās	tenēbās	mittēbās	audiēbās	capiēbās
he, she, it	vocābat	tenēbat	mittēbat	audiēbat	capiēbat
we	vocābāmus	tenēbāmus	mittēbāmus	audiēbāmus	capiēbāmus
you (pl.)	vocābātis	tenēbātis	mittēbātis	audiēbātis	capiēbātis
they	vocābant	tenēbant	mittēbant	audiēbant	capiēbant
PERFECT (*I called, have called, etc.*)					
I	vocāvī	tenuī	mīsī	audīvī	cēpī
you (sing.)	vocāvistī	tenuistī	mīsistī	audīvistī	cēpistī
he, she, it	vocāvit	tenuit	mīsit	audīvit	cēpit
we	vocāvimus	tenuimus	mīsimus	audīvimus	cēpimus
you (pl.)	vocāvistis	tenuistis	mīsistis	audīvistis	cēpistis
they	vocāvērunt	tenuērunt	mīsērunt	audīvērunt	cēpērunt
* **FUTURE PERFECT** (*I shall have called, etc.*)					
I	vocāverō	tenuerō	mīserō	audīverō	cēperō
you (sing.)	vocāveris	tenueris	mīseris	audīveris	cēperis
he, she, it	vocāverit	tenuerit	mīserit	audīverit	cēperit
we	vocāverimus	tenuerimus	mīserimus	audīverimus	cēperimus
you (pl.)	vocāveritis	tenueritis	mīseritis	audīveritis	cēperitis
they	vocāverint	tenuerint	mīserint	audīverint	cēperint
PLUPERFECT (*I had called, etc.*)					
I	vocāveram	tenueram	mīseram	audīveram	cēperam
you (sing.)	vocāverās	tenuerās	mīserās	audīverās	cēperās
he, she, it	vocāverat	tenuerat	mīserat	audīverat	cēperat
we	vocāverāmus	tenuerāmus	mīserāmus	audīverāmus	cēperāmus
you (pl.)	vocāverātis	tenuerātis	mīserātis	audīverātis	cēperātis
they	vocāverant	tenuerant	mīserant	audīverant	cēperant

* Charts in grey show forms which are not covered in the **Language notes**. These forms do not appear in the stories.

VERBS: PASSIVE INDICATIVE

	1st conjugation	2nd conjugation	3rd conjugation	4th conjugation	3rd/4th conjugation
	call	*hold*	*send*	*hear*	*take*
PRESENT (*I am called, am being called, etc.*)					
I	vocor	teneor	mittor	audior	capior
you (sing.)	vocāris	tenēris	mitteris	audīris	caperis
he, she, it	vocātur	tenētur	mittitur	audītur	capitur
we	vocāmur	tenēmur	mittimur	audīmur	capimur
you (pl.)	vocāminī	tenēminī	mittiminī	audīminī	capiminī
they	vocantur	tenentur	mittuntur	audiuntur	capiuntur
FUTURE (*I shall be called, etc.*)					
I	vocābor	tenēbor	mittar	audiar	capiar
you (sing.)	vocāberis	tenēberis	mittēris	audiēris	capiēris
he, she, it	vocābitur	tenēbitur	mittētur	audiētur	capiētur
we	vocābimur	tenēbimur	mittēmur	audiēmur	capiēmur
you (pl.)	vocābiminī	tenēbiminī	mittēminī	audiēminī	capiēminī
they	vocābuntur	tenēbuntur	mittentur	audientur	capientur
IMPERFECT (*I was being called, used to be called, etc.*)					
I	vocābar	tenēbar	mittēbar	audiēbar	capiēbar
you (sing.)	vocābāris	tenēbāris	mittēbāris	audiēbāris	capiēbāris
he, she, it	vocābātur	tenēbātur	mittēbātur	audiēbātur	capiēbātur
we	vocābāmur	tenēbāmur	mittēbāmur	audiēbāmur	capiēbāmur
you (pl.)	vocābāminī	tenēbāminī	mittēbāminī	audiēbāminī	capiēbāminī
they	vocābantur	tenēbantur	mittēbantur	audiēbantur	capiēbantur
PERFECT (*I was called, have been called, etc.*)					
I	vocātus sum	tentus sum	missus sum	audītus sum	captus sum
you (sing.)	vocātus es	tentus es	missus es	audītus es	captus es
he, she, it	vocātus est	tentus est	missus est	audītus est	captus est
we	vocātī sumus	tentī sumus	missī sumus	audītī sumus	captī sumus
you (pl.)	vocātī estis	tentī estis	missī estis	audītī estis	captī estis
they	vocātī sunt	tentī sunt	missī sunt	audītī sunt	captī sunt
FUTURE PERFECT (*I shall have been called, etc.*)					
I	vocātus erō	tentus erō	missus erō	audītus erō	captus erō
you (sing.)	vocātus eris	tentus eris	missus eris	audītus eris	captus eris
he, she, it	vocātus erit	tentus erit	missus erit	audītus erit	captus erit
we	vocātī erimus	tentī erimus	missī erimus	audītī erimus	captī erimus
you (pl.)	vocātī eritis	tentī eritis	missī eritis	audītī eritis	captī eritis
they	vocātī erunt	tentī erunt	missī erunt	audītī erunt	captī erunt
PLUPERFECT (*I had been called, etc.*)					
I	vocātus eram	tentus eram	missus eram	audītus eram	captus eram
you (sing.)	vocātus erās	tentus erās	missus erās	audītus erās	captus erās
he, she, it	vocātus erat	tentus erat	missus erat	audītus erat	captus erat
we	vocātī erāmus	tentī erāmus	missī erāmus	audītī erāmus	captī erāmus
you (pl.)	vocātī erātis	tentī erātis	missī erātis	audītī erātis	captī erātis
they	vocātī erant	tentī erant	missī erant	audītī erant	captī erant

VERBS: ACTIVE SUBJUNCTIVE

	1st conjugation	2nd conjugation	3rd conjugation	4th conjugation	3rd/4th conjugation
	call	*hold*	*send*	*hear*	*take*
PRESENT (*I call, am calling, etc.*)					
I	vocem	teneam	mittam	audiam	capiam
you (sing.)	vocēs	teneās	mittās	audiās	capiās
he, she, it	vocet	teneat	mittat	audiat	capiat
we	vocēmus	teneāmus	mittāmus	audiāmus	capiāmus
you (pl.)	vocētis	teneātis	mittātis	audiātis	capiātis
they	vocent	teneant	mittant	audiant	capiant

Latin does not have a future subjunctive.

	1st conjugation	2nd conjugation	3rd conjugation	4th conjugation	3rd/4th conjugation
IMPERFECT (*I was calling, used to call, etc.*)					
I	vocārem	tenērem	mitterem	audīrem	caperem
you (sing.)	vocārēs	tenērēs	mitterēs	audīrēs	caperēs
he, she, it	vocāret	tenēret	mitteret	audīret	caperet
we	vocārēmus	tenērēmus	mitterēmus	audīrēmus	caperēmus
you (pl.)	vocārētis	tenērētis	mitterētis	audīrētis	caperētis
they	vocārent	tenērent	mitterent	audīrent	caperent
PERFECT (*I called, have called, etc.*)					
I	vocāverim	tenuerim	mīserim	audīverim	cēperim
you (sing.)	vocāverīs	tenuerīs	mīserīs	audīverīs	cēperīs
he, she, it	vocāverit	tenuerit	mīserit	audīverit	cēperit
we	vocāverīmus	tenuerīmus	mīserīmus	audīverīmus	cēperīmus
you (pl.)	vocāverītis	tenuerītis	mīserītis	audīverītis	cēperītis
they	vocāverint	tenuerint	mīserint	audīverint	cēperint

Latin does not have a future perfect subjunctive.

	1st conjugation	2nd conjugation	3rd conjugation	4th conjugation	3rd/4th conjugation
PLUPERFECT (*I had called, etc.*)					
I	vocāvissem	tenuissem	mīsissem	audīvissem	cēpissem
you (sing.)	vocāvissēs	tenuissēs	mīsissēs	audīvissēs	cēpissēs
he, she, it	vocāvisset	tenuisset	mīsisset	audīvisset	cēpisset
we	vocāvissēmus	tenuissēmus	mīsissēmus	audīvissēmus	cēpissēmus
you (pl.)	vocāvissētis	tenuissētis	mīsissētis	audīvissētis	cēpissētis
they	vocāvissent	tenuissent	mīsissent	audīvissent	cēpissent

VERBS: PASSIVE SUBJUNCTIVE

	1st conjugation	2nd conjugation	3rd conjugation	4th conjugation	3rd/4th conjugation
	call	*hold*	*send*	*hear*	*take*
PRESENT (*I am called, am being called, etc.*)					
I	vocer	tenear	mittar	audiar	capiar
you (sing.)	vocēris	teneāris	mittāris	audiāris	capiāris
he, she, it	vocētur	teneātur	mittātur	audiātur	capiātur
we	vocēmur	teneāmur	mittāmur	audiāmur	capiāmur
you (pl.)	vocēminī	teneāminī	mittāminī	audiāminī	capiāminī
they	vocentur	teneantur	mittantur	audiantur	capiantur

Latin does not have a future subjunctive.

IMPERFECT (*I was being called, used to be called, etc.*)					
I	vocārer	tenērer	mitterer	audīrer	caperer
you (sing.)	vocārēris	tenērēris	mitterēris	audīrēris	caperēris
he, she, it	vocārētur	tenērētur	mitterētur	audīrētur	caperētur
we	vocārēmur	tenērēmur	mitterēmur	audīrēmur	caperēmur
you (pl.)	vocārēminī	tenērēminī	mitterēminī	audīrēminī	caperēminī
they	vocārentur	tenērentur	mitterentur	audīrentur	caperentur
PERFECT (*I was called, have been called, etc.*)					
I	vocātus sim	tentus sim	missus sim	audītus sim	captus sim
you (sing.)	vocātus sīs	tentus sīs	missus sīs	audītus sīs	captus sīs
he, she, it	vocātus sit	tentus sit	missus sit	audītus sit	captus sit
we	vocātī sīmus	tentī sīmus	missī sīmus	audītī sīmus	captī sīmus
you (pl.)	vocātī sītis	tentī sītis	missī sītis	audītī sītis	captī sītis
they	vocātī sint	tentī sint	missī sint	audītī sint	captī sint

Latin does not have a future perfect subjunctive.

PLUPERFECT (*I had been called, etc.*)					
I	vocātus essem	tentus essem	missus essem	audītus essem	captus essem
you (sing.)	vocātus essēs	tentus essēs	missus essēs	audītus essēs	captus essēs
he, she, it	vocātus esset	tentus esset	missus esset	audītus esset	captus esset
we	vocātī essēmus	tentī essēmus	missī essēmus	audītī essēmus	captī essēmus
you (pl.)	vocātī essētis	tentī essētis	missī essētis	audītī essētis	captī essētis
they	vocātī essent	tentī essent	missī essent	audītī essent	captī essent

OTHER PARTS OF THE VERB

	1st conjugation	2nd conjugation	3rd conjugation	4th conjugation	3rd/4th conjugation
INFINITIVES					
Present Active Infinitive	*to call*	*to hold*	*to send*	*to hear*	*to take*
	vocāre	tenēre	mittere	audīre	capere
Present Passive Infinitive	*to be called*	*to be held*	*to be sent*	*to be heard*	*to be taken*
	vocārī	tenērī	mittī	audīrī	capī
Future Active Infinitive	*to be going to call*	*to be going to hold*	*to be going to send*	*to be going to hear*	*to be going to take*
	vocātūrus esse	tentūrus esse	missūrus esse	audītūrus esse	captūrus esse
Future Passive Infinitive	*to be going to be called*	*to be going to be held*	*to be going to be sent*	*to be going to be heard*	*to be going to be taken*
	vocātum īrī	tentum īrī	missum īrī	audītum īrī	captum īrī
Perfect Active Infinitive	*to have called*	*to have held*	*to have sent*	*to have heard*	*to have taken*
	vocāvisse	tenuisse	mīsisse	audīvisse	cēpisse
Perfect Passive Infinitive	*to have been called*	*to have been held*	*to have been sent*	*to have been heard*	*to have been taken*
	vocātus esse	tentus esse	missus esse	audītus esse	captus esse
IMPERATIVES					
	call!	*hold!*	*send!*	*listen!*	*take!*
singular	vocā	tenē	mitte	audī	cape
plural	vocāte	tenēte	mittite	audīte	capite
PARTICIPLES					
Present Participle	*calling*	*holding*	*sending*	*hearing*	*taking*
	vocāns	tenēns	mittēns	audiēns	capiēns
Future Participle	*about to call*	*about to hold*	*about to send*	*about to hear*	*about to take*
	vocātūrus	tentūrus	missūrus	audītūrus	captūrus
Perfect Passive Participle	*(having been) called*	*(having been) held*	*(having been) sent*	*(having been) heard*	*(having been) taken*
	vocātus	tentus	missus	audītus	captus
GERUNDIVE					
	vocandus	tenendus	mittendus	audiendus	capiendus

IRREGULAR VERBS: INDICATIVE

PRESENT	*I am*	*I am able*	*I go*	*I want*	*I don't want*	*I prefer*
I	sum	possum	eō	volō	nōlō	mālō
you (sing.)	es	potes	īs	vīs	nōn vīs	māvīs
he, she, it	est	potest	it	vult	nōn vult	māvult
we	sumus	possumus	īmus	volumus	nōlumus	mālumus
you (pl.)	estis	potestis	ītis	vultis	nōn vultis	māvultis
they	sunt	possunt	eunt	volunt	nōlunt	mālunt
FUTURE	*I shall be, etc.*					
I	erō	poterō	ībō	volam	nōlam	mālam
you (sing.)	eris	poteris	ībis	volēs	nōlēs	mālēs
he, she, it	erit	poterit	ībit	volet	nōlet	mālet
we	erimus	poterimus	ībimus	volēmus	nōlēmus	mālēmus
you (pl.)	eritis	poteritis	ībitis	volētis	nōlētis	mālētis
they	erunt	poterunt	ībunt	volent	nōlent	mālent
IMPERFECT	*I was, etc.*					
I	eram	poteram	ībam	volēbam	nōlēbam	mālēbam
you (sing.)	erās	poterās	ībās	volēbās	nōlēbās	mālēbās
he, she, it	erat	poterat	ībat	volēbat	nōlēbat	mālēbat
we	erāmus	poterāmus	ībāmus	volēbāmus	nōlēbāmus	mālēbāmus
you (pl.)	erātis	poterātis	ībātis	volēbātis	nōlēbātis	mālēbātis
they	erant	poterant	ībant	volēbant	nōlēbant	mālēbant

Forms based on perfect stems are regular:

PERFECT	*I was, have been, etc.*					
I	fuī	potuī	iī	voluī	nōluī	māluī
you (sing.)	fuistī	potuistī	iistī	voluistī	nōluistī	māluistī
	etc.					
FUTURE PERFECT	*I shall have been, etc.*					
I	fuerō	potuerō	ierō	voluerō	nōluerō	māluerō
you (sing.)	fueris	potueris	ieris	volueris	nōlueris	mālueris
	etc.					
PLUPERFECT	*I had been, etc.*					
I	fueram	potueram	ieram	volueram	nōlueram	mālueram
you (sing.)	fuerās	potuerās	ierās	voluerās	nōluerās	māluerās
	etc.					

IRREGULAR VERBS: SUBJUNCTIVE

PRESENT	*I am*	*I am able*	*I go*	*I want*	*I don't want*	*I prefer*
I	sim	possim	eam	velim	nōlim	mālim
you (sing.)	sīs	possīs	eās	velīs	nōlīs	mālīs
he, she, it	sit	possit	eat	velit	nōlit	mālit
we	sīmus	possīmus	eāmus	velīmus	nōlīmus	mālīmus
you (pl.)	sītis	possītis	eātis	velītis	nōlītis	mālītis
they	sint	possint	eant	velint	nōlint	mālint
IMPERFECT	*I was, etc.*					
I	essem	possem	īrem	vellem	nollem	māllem
you (sing.)	essēs	possēs	īrēs	vellēs	nollēs	māllēs
he, she, it	esset	posset	īret	vellet	nollet	māllet
we	essēmus	possēmus	īrēmus	vellēmus	nollēmus	māllēmus
you (pl.)	essētis	possētis	īrētis	vellētis	nollētis	māllētis
they	essent	possent	īrent	vellent	nollent	māllent
PERFECT	*I was, have been, etc.*					
I	fuerim	potuerim	ierim	voluerim	nōluerim	māluerim
you (sing.)	fuerīs	potuerīs	ierīs	voluerīs	nōluerīs	māluerīs
			etc.			
PLUPERFECT	*I had been, etc.*					
I	fuissem	potuissem	īssem	voluissem	nōluissem	māluissem
you (sing.)	fuissēs	potuissēs	īssēs	voluissēs	nōluissēs	māluissēs
			etc.			

FERŌ, FERRE, TULĪ, LĀTUS (I CARRY, BEAR)

	Indicative		Subjunctive	
PRESENT	*Active*	*Passive*	*Active*	*Passive*
I	ferō	feror	feram	ferar
you (sing.)	fers	ferris	ferās	ferāris
he, she, it	fert	fertur	ferat	ferātur
we	ferimus	ferimur	ferāmus	ferāmur
you (pl.)	fertis	feriminī	ferātis	ferāminī
they	ferunt	feruntur	ferant	ferantur
FUTURE	*Active*	*Passive*		
I	feram	ferar	*Latin does not have a future subjunctive.*	
you (sing.)	ferēs	ferēris		
he, she, it	feret	ferētur		
we	ferēmus	ferēmur		
you (pl.)	ferētis	ferēminī		
they	ferent	ferentur		
IMPERFECT	*Active*	*Passive*	*Active*	*Passive*
I	ferēbam	ferēbar	ferrem	ferrer
you (sing.)	ferēbās	ferēbāris	ferrēs	ferrēris
		etc.		

Forms based on the perfect (**tulī**) and the perfect passive participle (**lātus**) are regular.

FĪŌ, FĪERĪ, FACTUS SUM (I BECOME, AM MADE)

	Indicative	Subjunctive
PRESENT		
I	fīō	fīam
you (sing.)	fīs	fīās
he, she, it	fit	fīat
we	fīmus	fīāmus
you (pl.)	fītis	fīātis
they	fīunt	fīant
FUTURE		
I	fīam	*Latin does not have a future subjunctive.*
you (sing.)	fīēs	
he, she, it	fīet	
we	fīēmus	
you (pl.)	fīētis	
they	fīent	
IMPERFECT		
I	fīēbam	fierem
you (sing.)	fīēbās	fierēs
	etc.	

fīō is used as the passive of **faciō** in the present, future, and imperfect tenses. In the perfect, future perfect, and pluperfect tenses, the passive forms of **faciō** (e.g. **factus sum**) are used.

A bronze statuette of a Roman official. He wears his toga to cover his head suggesting he may be taking part in a religious ceremony.

OTHER PARTS OF IRREGULAR VERBS

INFINITIVES								
Present Active	*to be*	*to be able*	*to go*	*to want*	*to not want*	*to prefer*	*to bring*	*to become*
	esse	posse	īre	velle	nōlle	mālle	ferre	fierī
Perfect Active	*to have been*	*to have been able*	*to have gone*	*to have wanted*	*to have not wanted*	*to have preferred*	*to have brought*	*to have become*
	fuisse	potuisse	īsse	voluisse	nōluisse	māluisse	tulisse	factus esse

IMPERATIVES								
	be!		*go!*		*be unwilling! don't!*		*bring!*	
singular	es		ī		nōlī		fer	
plural	este		īte		nōlīte		ferte	

sum has the future active infinitive **fore / futūrus esse** (*to be going to be*) and the future participle **futūrus** (*about to be*). Some compounds of **sum** have a present participle, for example **absēns**, *gen.* **absentis**.

eō and its compounds have the future active infinitive **itūrus esse** (*to be going to go*), the present participle **iēns**, *gen.* **euntis** (*going*), the future participle **itūrus** (*about to go*), and the gerundive **eundus**.

volō has the present participle **volēns**, *gen.* **volentis** (*wanting*).

USES OF THE SUBJUNCTIVE

1. After **ut** or **ut nōn** in clauses expressing the **result** of a situation:

    Athēna eōs adeō amābat ut eīs oleam daret.

    Athena loved them so much that she gave the olive tree to them.

2. After **ut** or **nē** in clauses expressing the **purpose** of an action:

    lyram in terrā dēposuī, ut saltārem.

    I put down my lyre on the ground, so that I might dance.

3. After **ut** or **nē** in **indirect commands**:

    medica eum monuit nē bracchium movēret.

    The doctor warned him not to move his arm.

4. After **ut** or **nē** with **verbs of fearing**:

    Balbus timēbat nē in proeliō vulnerārētur.

    Balbus was afraid that he might be wounded in battle.

5. In indirect questions:

    pater senem rogāvit quās imāginēs fēcisset.

    My father asked the old man which sculptures he had made.

6. After **cum** meaning *when*, *since*, or *because*:

    Lūcīlius et parentēs tacēbant, cum nūntius advēnisset.

    Lucilius and his parents were silent, because the messenger had arrived.

7. After **dum** meaning *until*:

    mē diū cēlābam dum fūrēs obdormīrent.

    I hid for a long time until the thieves fell asleep.

A wall painting from the villa of Publius Fannius Synistor, near Pompeii.

ANCIENT AUTHORS

Antipater: Antipater (2nd century BC) came from Sidon in Phoenicia and spent the last years of his life in Rome. He was a poet who wrote epigrams in Greek.

Apuleius: Lucius Apuleius (*c.*AD 155) was born in the Roman province of Africa and lived in Carthage. He was the author of the *Metamorphoses*, also known as *The Golden Ass*, a novel about the adventures of a young man who is turned into an ass.

Augustus: Augustus (63 BC–AD 14) was born Gaius Octavius and became Gaius Iulius Caesar Octavianus when he was adopted by his great-uncle, Julius Caesar. He was known by the title Augustus after 27 BC when he became Rome's first emperor. The *Res Gestae Divi Augusti* (*Deeds of the Divine Augustus*) is an account of the career of Augustus written in the first person. Augustus left the document with his will, with instructions to the Senate to set up the text as an inscription. It was engraved on a pair of bronze pillars in front of Augustus' tomb in the Campus Martius. The original has not survived, but copies were carved in stone on monuments and temples all over the Roman Empire, and parts of these have survived.

Cassius Dio (also **Dio Cassius**): Cassius Dio Cocceianus (*c.*AD 164–after 229) was born in Bithynia. He had a political career as a consul in Rome and as governor of the provinces of Africa and Dalmatia. His history of Rome, written in Greek, covers the period from Aeneas' arrival in Italy to AD 229.

Cato: Marcus Porcius Cato (234–149 BC) was born at Tusculum, a town about sixteen miles from Rome. He had a distinguished military and political career, reaching the consulship and the office of censor, despite not being born into a senatorial family. He wrote a book on farming, *De Agricultura* (*On Agriculture*). Cato was famous for his strictness and his criticism of contemporary morality. He wanted to return to the old Roman values of frugality and simplicity.

Catullus: Gaius Valerius Catullus (*c.*84–*c.*54 BC) was born in Verona, in northern Italy, to a wealthy family. Very little is known about his life. He came to Rome as a young man and spent some time in the province of Bithynia on the staff of the governor. He is best known for his love poems.

Celsus: Aulus Cornelius Celsus (first century AD), who lived in the reign of Tiberius (AD 14–37), wrote a treatise on medicine, *De Medicina*.

Cicero: Marcus Tullius Cicero (106–43 BC) was a politician and lawyer, who was a leading figure in events at the end of the Roman Republic. He was born in a town not far from Rome and came to Rome to study. Although not born into the senatorial class, he reached the highest office of state, the consulship. He was executed on the orders of Mark Anthony during the unrest following the assassination of Julius Caesar in 44 BC. His surviving writings include speeches for the law courts, political speeches, philosophical essays, and personal letters to friends and family.

Epictetus: Epictetus (mid–1st to 2nd century AD) was born in Hierapolis in Phrygia and came to Rome when he was enslaved. His owner was Epaphroditus, Nero's freedman. After gaining his freedom, Epictetus studied Stoic philosophy and taught in Rome until he was banished by Emperor Domitian in AD 89. A summary of his ideas, the *Manual*, has survived along with records of his oral teachings (*Discourses*).

Euripides: Euripides (*c.*480–*c.*407/6 BC) was a Greek playwright from Athens. He wrote tragedies, of which eighteen have survived, including *Bacchae* and *Medea*.

Homer: Homer is traditionally the author of the Greek epic poems the *Iliad* and the *Odyssey*, which were composed about 750–700 BC. Nothing is known about his life. Both poems deal with the Trojan War, a ten-year war between the Greeks and the Trojans, and its aftermath. The subject of the *Iliad* is the anger of the hero Achilles and its effects, an episode in the final year of the war. The *Odyssey* tells of the adventures and sufferings of Odysseus after the war, and his return home from Troy to Ithaca.

Horace: Quintus Horatius Flaccus (65–8 BC) was born in Apulia, in the south of Italy. He was of humble origins, the son of a freedman who worked as a collector of payments at auctions. His father sent him to Rome and Athens to be educated, and he became one of the most celebrated poets of his day. Maecenas, the friend and adviser of Emperor Augustus, was his patron. His most famous works are the *Odes*, short poems on a variety of subjects, but he also wrote *Epodes*, *Satires*, and *Epistles*.

Josephus: Flavius Iosephus (AD 37– *c.*100) was born in Jerusalem, in the Roman province of Judaea, to a wealthy, aristocratic family. His Hebrew name was Yosef ben Matityahu. He was captured in the Jewish Revolt against the Romans (AD 66–70), then, after the fall of Jerusalem, he lived in Rome and was given Roman citizenship. His history of the Jewish War (*Bellum Iudaicum*) was originally written in Aramaic, then translated into Greek. His other works were written in Greek: they include a history of the Jews, *Antiquitates Iudaicae* (*Jewish Antiquities*).

Julius Caesar: Gaius Iulius Caesar (100–44 BC), the general, politician, and dictator, belonged to an aristocratic Roman family. He was assassinated on the Ides (15th) of March 44 BC, by a group of senators who feared that he intended to put an end to the republican system of government and keep supreme power for himself and his family. Caesar wrote an account of his campaigns in Gaul and Britain (58-52 BC), the *Commentaries* (also known as the *Gallic Wars*). They are written in the third person, as if to give an objective account of events.

Juvenal: Decius Iunius Iuvenalis (early 2nd century AD) was born in a town in Italy, but lived in Rome. He was the author of sixteen *Satires*, long poems criticizing and attacking the vices of his fellow Romans. The *Satires* have a bitter humor and pessimistic attitude, and there is much exaggeration. Nevertheless, Juvenal sheds light on contemporary Roman society and provides lots of detail about everyday life.

Livy: Titus Livius (59 BC–AD 17) was born at Patavium (modern Padua) in north-east Italy. Little is known about his life, but he probably came to Rome as an adult. He wrote *A History of Rome*, starting with its foundation and going up to his own lifetime. Originally there were 142 books, of which about twenty-five have survived.

Lucan: Annaeus Lucanus Marcus (AD 39–65) was born in Corduba (modern Cordoba), in Spain. He was from a well-connected equestrian family; his uncle was Nero's adviser, Seneca. After studying rhetoric and philosophy in Rome and Athens, he became a friend of Nero, who made him a quaestor. However, he lost the favor of the emperor and joined the Pisonian conspiracy against Nero. When the conspiracy was discovered, Lucan was forced to kill himself. He is the author of the *Pharsalia*, an epic poem about the civil war between Julius Caesar and Pompey.

Lucillius: (1st century AD) lived during the reign of Nero, but nothing more is known about his life. He wrote satirical epigrams in Greek.

Lucretius: Titus Lucretius Carus (*c.*94–*c.*55 BC) was the author of *De Rerum Natura* (*On the Nature of Things*), a long poem about Epicureanism. Very little is known about his life.

Martial: Marcus Valerius Martialis (*c.*AD 40–*c.*104) was born at Bilbilis in Spain and came to live in Rome in about AD 64. He is best known for his short poems, known as *Epigrams*, which often criticize and mock the faults and vices of his fellow Romans. His *De Spectaculis* (*On the Spectacles*) is a collection of epigrams written to celebrate the opening of the Colosseum in AD 80, in the reign of Emperor Titus.

Ovid: Publius Ovidius Naso (43 BC–AD 17) was born in a town near Rome and educated in the city. He abandoned a public career to become a poet. Emperor Augustus banished him to Tomis on the Black Sea (in modern Romania). According to Ovid, there were two reasons for his exile, **carmen** (a poem) and **error** (a mistake). The poem was *Ars Amatoria* (*The Art of Love*) which fell foul of laws introduced by Augustus to improve the morals of contemporary society. The mistake was probably connected to the love affairs of Augustus' granddaughter, Julia. Among his other works are love poems such as the *Amores* (*Loves*) and a long epic poem, the *Metamorphoses*, which is a collection of stories from mythology bound together by the theme of transformation.

Petronius: Petronius Arbiter (died AD 66) was a provincial governor and consul. He then became Emperor Nero's **arbiter ēlegentiae** (arbiter of taste), a play on his name; this meant he advised Nero on what was tasteful or elegant. He was falsely accused of being involved in a plot to kill Nero and committed suicide. Petronius was probably the author of the *Satyricon*, a novel about the adventures of three young men traveling in southern Italy. The main episode is the *Cena Trimalchionis* (*Trimalchio's Dinner Party*). Trimalchio is a wealthy freedman to whose dinner party the three main characters are invited. Petronius mocks and grotesquely exaggerates the vulgar extravagance and bad taste of Trimalchio, and his ostentatious display of wealth.

Pliny the Elder: Gaius Plinius Secundus (AD 23/24–79) was born at Comum (modern Como) in northern Italy. He is known as Pliny the Elder to distinguish him from his nephew, known as Pliny the Younger. He had a career in military and government service, serving as procurator in several provinces before his final post as commander of the fleet at Misenum in Italy. He dedicated his spare time to research and writing, and among his many learned works is his *Natural History*, an encyclopaedic collection of facts and stories about a huge variety of subjects. It is a very useful source of information on many aspects of Roman life. In *Suburani* 'Pliny' refers to Pliny the Younger.

Pliny the Younger: Gaius Caecilius Plinius Secundus (AD 61/2–*c.*112) was the nephew of Pliny the Elder. He was born at Comum (modern Como) in northern Italy. He had a successful career as a lawyer, politician, and administrator, and his final post was as governor of Bithynia. His letters to friends, family, and colleagues include an exchange with Emperor Trajan when he was governor of Bithynia. The letters offer a glimpse into the lives, attitudes, and politics of the society of his time. Pliny wrote with the intention of publishing his letters, and at regular intervals during his lifetime he published collections of them. Although they are real personal letters, many of them resemble short essays on various themes. In *Suburani* 'Pliny' refers to Pliny the Younger.

Plutarch: Ploutarchos (*c.*AD 46–after 120) was a Greek biographer, historian, and philosopher. He took the name Lucius Mercius Plutarchus when he became a Roman citizen. Plutarch visited Rome, where he taught and gave lectures, but spent most of his life in his native Greece. Among his many works are biographies of famous Greek and Roman politicians and soldiers, the *Parallel Lives*, so called because they are arranged in pairs of Greek and Roman so that the subjects can be compared. He also wrote biographies of the Roman emperors. His biographies of Galba and Otho survive in full, and there are fragments of his lives of Tiberius and Nero.

Procopius: Procopios (*c.*AD 500–after 540) was a Greek historian, born in Caesarea, in the Roman province of Syria Palaestina.

Propertius: Sextus Propertius (*c.*50– before 2 BC) was born at Assisium (modern Assisi) in central Italy and educated at Rome. He wrote poems known as *Elegies*, many of them love poems.

Quintilian: Marcus Fabius Quintilianus (*c.*AD 35– *c.*96) was born at Calagurris in Spain. He was a famous teacher of rhetoric in Rome; Pliny the Younger was one of his pupils, and he was tutor to the two great-nephews of Emperor Domitian. He was the author of a book on rhetoric, *Institutio Oratoria* (*Training in Oratory*).

Seneca the Elder: Lucius Annaeus Seneca (*c.*50 BC– *c.*AD 40) was born in Corduba (modern Cordoba) in Spain. He is known as Seneca the Elder to distinguish him from his son of the same name. He was the author of a book on rhetoric, parts of which survive. In *Suburani* 'Seneca' refers to Seneca the Younger.

Seneca the Younger: Lucius Annaeus Seneca (*c.*4 BC–AD 65) is sometimes known as Seneca the Younger to distinguish him from his father of the same name, who was also a writer. He was born in Corduba (modern Cordoba) in Spain and came to Rome to be educated. He was Nero's tutor and, after Nero became emperor, his political adviser. In AD 65, after he had retired from public life, he was implicated in a conspiracy to overthrow Nero and was forced to commit suicide. Seneca was a philosopher, politician, and dramatist. Among his many writings are several works of moral philosophy which contain interesting details about life in Rome in the first century AD. Some of these are in the form of letters to friends and family. In *Suburani* 'Seneca' refers to Seneca the Younger.

Soranos: Soranos (late 1st century AD –*c.*138) was born in Ephesus, in the province of Asia. He studied medicine in Alexandria and practiced in Rome. He wrote several works on medical subjects in Greek, including *On the Art of Surgery* (now lost) and *Gynaecology*.

Statius: Publius Papinius Statius (*c.*AD 45–*c.*96) was born in Neapolis (modern Naples) in Italy. His father was a poet and teacher of literature. He wrote an epic poem, the *Thebaid*, and a collection of shorter poems, the *Silvae*.

Strabo: Strabo (64 BC– after AD 21) was a Greek from Pontus who came to Rome in 44 BC to finish his education, then visited the city several times afterwards. His *Geography*, written in Greek, is a description of the main countries in the Roman world, including physical geography, history, and economic development. There is also much incidental detail about customs, animals, and plants.

Suetonius: Gaius Suetonius Tranquillus (*c.*AD 70–*c.*130) was a secretary at the imperial palace. He wrote biographies of Julius Caesar and the first eleven emperors, *Lives of the Caesars*. Although his position gave him access to the state archives, he is not very reliable in his use of sources, and his work relies heavily on uncritical reporting of gossip and anecdote.

Tacitus: Publius (or Gaius) Cornelius Tacitus (*c.*AD 56– after 117) may have been born in Gaul. He had a successful political career in Rome and wrote two major works of history. *Annals* covered the period AD 14-68, from the death of Augustus to the death of Nero, and *Histories* continued with the years AD 69-96. Only parts of these works survive. Tacitus used as his sources the writings of earlier historians, official records, and his own experience. He was a supporter of the republican system of government and a harsh critic of the emperors and the imperial system. He claims to write without prejudice, but his bias is often evident.

Vegetius: Publius Flavius Vegetius Renatus (late 4th to 5th century AD) was the author of *De Re Militari* (*On Military Matters*), which describes the training and organization of a Roman legion. Vegetius was not himself a soldier, and his work is a collection of material from various periods and sources.

Vergil (also **Virgil**): Publius Vergilius Maro (70–19 BC) was born at Mantua in Cisalpine Gaul and educated at Cremona, Mediolanum (modern Milan), and Rome. Maecenas, the friend and adviser of Emperor Augustus, was his patron, and he became the most celebrated poet of his day. His greatest work is the *Aeneid*, an epic poem which tells the story of the founding of the Roman race by the Trojan hero Aeneas. The poem is a celebration of the origin and growth of the Roman Empire and of the achievements of Augustus. Vergil also wrote the *Eclogues*, pastoral poems about the lives of shepherds, and the *Georgics*, a poem about farming.

ENGLISH TO LATIN

able, I am *possum, posse, potuī*
across *trāns + acc.*
adopt (a plan) *capiō, capere, cēpī, captus*
advice *cōnsilium, cōnsiliī, n.*
afraid, I am *timeō, timēre, timuī*
against *contrā + acc.*
alive *vīvus, vīva, vīvum*
alone *sōlus, sōla, sōlum*
along *per + acc.*
always *semper*
am, I *sum, esse, fuī*
among *inter + acc.*
and *et, -que*
anger *īra, īrae, f.*
angry *īrātus, īrāta, īrātum*
announce *nūntiō, nūntiāre, nūntiāvī, nūntiātus*
arms *arma, armōrum, n. pl.*
arrive *adveniō, advenīre, advēnī*
ask *rogō, rogāre, rogāvī, rogātus*
ask for *petō, petere, petīvī, petītus; rogō, rogāre, rogāvī, rogātus*
at *ad + acc.*
at last *tandem*
at once *statim*
attack *oppugnō, oppugnāre, oppugnāvī, oppugnātus; petō, petere, petīvī, petītus*
away from *ā, ab + abl.*
bad *malus, mala, malum*
bear (carry) *portō, portāre, portāvī, portātus*
beautiful *pulcher, pulchra, pulchrum*
beg (someone) *petō, petere, petīvī, petītus*
between *inter + acc.*
big *magnus, magna, magnum*
boy *puer, puerī, m.*
build *aedificō, aedificāre, aedificāvī, aedificātus*
by *ā, ab + abl.*
call *vocō, vocāre, vocāvī, vocātus*
can *possum, posse, potuī*
capture *capiō, capere, cēpī, captus*
care for *cūrō, cūrāre, cūrāvī, cūrātus*
carry *portō, portāre, portāvī, portātus*
catch *capiō, capere, cēpī, captus*
catch sight of *cōnspiciō, cōnspicere, cōnspexī, cōnspectus*
children *līberī, līberōrum, m. pl.*
come *veniō, venīre, vēnī*
command *imperium, imperiī, n.*
commander *lēgātus, lēgātī, m.*
conquer *vincō, vincere, vīcī, victus*
country (homeland) *patria, patriae, f.*
country (land) *terra, terrae, f.*
country house *vīlla, vīllae, f.*
crowd *turba, turbae, f.*
cruel *saevus, saeva, saevum*
cry *lacrimō, lacrimāre, lacrimāvī*
danger *perīculum, perīculī, n.*
daughter *fīlia, fīliae, f.*
dear *cārus, cāra, cārum*
decide *cōnstituō, cōnstituere, cōnstituī, cōnstitūtus*
deep *altus, alta, altum*
defend *dēfendō, dēfendere, dēfendī, dēfēnsus*
demand *postulō, postulāre, postulāvī, postulātus*
despair *dēspērō, dēspērāre, dēspērāvī*
dinner *cēna, cēnae, f.*
do *faciō, facere, fēcī, factus*
drag, draw *trahō, trahere, trāxī, tractus*
dreadful *dīrus, dīra, dīrum*
drink *bibō, bibere, bibī*
empire *imperium, imperiī, n.*
enter *intrō, intrāre, intrāvī, intrātus*
even *et*
evil *malus, mala, malum*
expect *exspectō, exspectāre, exspectāvī, exspectātus*
ex-slave *lībertus, lībertī, m.*
fall *cadō, cadere, cecidī*
fear *timeō, timēre, timuī*
few, a few *paucī, paucae, pauca*
field *ager, agrī, m.*
fight *pugnō, pugnāre, pugnāvī*
finally *tandem*
find *inveniō, invenīre, invēnī, inventus*
first *prīmus, prīma, prīmum*
flee *fugiō, fugere, fūgī*
food *cibus, cibī, m.*
for a long time *diū*
forum *forum, forī, n.*
freedman *lībertus, lībertī, m.*
friend *amīcus, amīcī, m.*
frighten *terreō, terrēre, terruī, territus*
from (away from) *ā, ab + abl.*
from (out of) *ē, ex + abl.*
garden *hortus, hortī, m.*
gate *porta, portae, f.*
generous *benignus, benigna, benignum*
gift *dōnum, dōnī, n.*
girl *puella, puellae, f.*
give *dō, dare, dedī, datus*
god *deus, deī, m.*
goddess *dea, deae, f.*
good *bonus, bona, bonum*
great *magnus, magna, magnum*
greet *salūtō, salūtāre, salūtāvī, salūtātus*
ground *terra, terrae, f.*
guard *custōdiō, custōdīre, custōdīvī, custōdītus*
hand over, hand down *trādō, trādere, trādidī, trāditus*
handsome *pulcher, pulchra, pulchrum*
happy *laetus, laeta, laetum*
hard *dūrus, dūra, dūrum*
have *habeō, habēre, habuī, habitus*
hear *audiō, audīre, audīvī, audītus*
help *auxilium, auxiliī, n.*
help *adiuvō, adiuvāre, adiūvī, adiūtus*
hide *cēlō, cēlāre, cēlāvī, cēlātus*
high *altus, alta, altum*
hold (have) *habeō, habēre, habuī, habitus*
hold (keep) *teneō, tenēre, tenuī, tentus*
homeland *patria, patriae, f.*
hour *hōra, hōrae, f.*
house *vīlla, vīllae, f.*
hurry *festīnō, festīnāre, festīnāvī*
husband *marītus, marītī, m.*
idea *cōnsilium, cōnsiliī, n.*
immediately *statim*
in *in + abl.*
inn *taberna, tabernae, f.*
into *in + acc.*
invite *invītō, invītāre, invītāvī, invītātus*
keep (possess) *teneō, tenēre, tenuī, tentus*
keep (protect) *servō, servāre, servāvī, servātus*

kill	*necō, necāre, necāvī, necātus*
kind	*benignus, benigna, benignum*
kingdom	*rēgnum, rēgnī, n.*
land	*terra, terrae, f.*
large	*magnus, magna, magnum*
lead	*dūcō, dūcere, dūxī, ductus*
leave, leave behind	*relinquō, relinquere, relīquī, relictus*
letter	*epistula, epistulae, f.*
life	*vīta, vītae, f.*
like	*amō, amāre, amāvī, amātus*
listen to	*audiō, audīre, audīvī, audītus*
live	*habitō, habitāre, habitāvī*
living	*vīvus, vīva, vīvum*
lonely	*sōlus, sōla, sōlum*
long	*longus, longa, longum*
look after	*cūrō, cūrāre, cūrāvī, cūrātus; servō, servāre, servāvī, servātus*
look at	*spectō, spectāre, spectāvī, spectātus*
love	*amō, amāre, amāvī, amātus*
maid	*ancilla, ancillae, f.*
make	*faciō, facere, fēcī, factus*
make for	*petō, petere, petīvī, petītus*
man	*vir, virī, m.*
many	*multus, multa, multum*
marketplace	*forum, forī, n.*
master	*dominus, dominī, m.*
meal	*cēna, cēnae, f.*
messenger	*nūntius, nūntiī, m.*
miserable	*miser, misera, miserum*
mistress	*domina, dominae, f.*
money	*pecūnia, pecūniae, f.*
much	*multus, multa, multum*
my	*meus, mea, meum*
near	*prope + acc.*
new	*novus, nova, novum*
news	*nūntius, nūntiī, m.*
no (not any)	*nūllus, nūlla, nūllum*
not	*nōn*
not any	*nūllus, nūlla, nūllum*
notice	*cōnspiciō, cōnspicere, cōnspexī, cōnspectus*
often	*saepe*
on	*in + abl.*
only	*sōlus, sōla, sōlum*
onto	*in + acc.*
out of	*ē, ex + abl.*
overcome, overpower	*superō, superāre, superāvī, superātus*
place	*pōnō, pōnere, posuī, positus*
plan	*cōnsilium, cōnsiliī, n.*
possess	*teneō, tenēre, tenuī, tentus*
power	*imperium, imperiī, n.*
praise	*laudō, laudāre, laudāvī, laudātus*
prepare	*parō, parāre, parāvī, parātus*
present	*dōnum, dōnī, n.*
prize	*praemium, praemiī, n.*
profit	*praemium, praemiī, n.*
protect	*servō, servāre, servāvī, servātus*
pull	*trahō, trahere, trāxī, tractus*
put, put up	*pōnō, pōnere, posuī, positus*
queen	*rēgīna, rēgīnae, f.*
quiet, I am	*taceō, tacēre, tacuī*
real	*vērus, vēra, vērum*
relate	*nārrō, nārrāre, nārrāvī, nārrātus*
report	*nūntiō, nūntiāre, nūntiāvī, nūntiātus*
reward	*praemium, praemiī, n.*
road	*via, viae, f.*
Roman	*Rōmānus, Rōmāna, Rōmānum*
rule	*regō, regere, rēxī, rēctus*
run	*currō, currere, cucurrī*
run away	*fugiō, fugere, fūgī*
sad	*miser, misera, miserum*
safe	*tūtus, tūta, tūtum*
sail	*nāvigō, nāvigāre, nāvigāvī*
sailor	*nauta, nautae, m.*
savage	*saevus, saeva, saevum*
save	*servō, servāre, servāvī, servātus*
say	*dīcō, dīcere, dīxī, dictus*
seal	*signum, signī, n.*
seek	*petō, petere, petīvī, petītus*
send	*mittō, mittere, mīsī, missus*
shop	*taberna, tabernae, f.*
shout	*clāmō, clāmāre, clāmāvī, clāmātus*
sign	*signum, signī, n.*
silent, I am	*taceō, tacēre, tacuī*
slave (female)	*ancilla, ancillae, f.*
slave (male)	*servus, servī, m.*
sleep	*dormiō, dormīre, dormīvī*
small	*parvus, parva, parvum*
son	*fīlius, fīliī, m.*
speak	*dīcō, dīcere, dīxī, dictus*
stand	*stō, stāre, stetī*
story	*fābula, fābulae, f.*
street	*via, viae, f.*
stupid	*stultus, stulta, stultum*
suddenly	*subitō*
supervise	*cūrō, cūrāre, cūrāvī, cūrātus*
sword	*gladius, gladiī, m.*
take (capture)	*capiō, capere, cēpī, captus*
take (carry)	*portō, portāre, portāvī, portātus*
take (lead)	*dūcō, dūcere, dūxī, ductus*
tell (relate)	*nārrō, nārrāre, nārrāvī, nārrātus*
tell (speak)	*dīcō, dīcere, dīxī, dictus*
temple	*templum, templī, n.*
terrified	*perterritus, perterrita, perterritum*
through	*per + acc.*
to, towards	*ad + acc.*
true	*vērus, vēra, vērum*
victorious, I am	*vincō, vincere, vīcī, victus*
wait for	*exspectō, exspectāre, exspectāvī, exspectātus*
walk	*ambulō, ambulāre, ambulāvī*
wall	*mūrus, mūrī, m.*
watch	*spectō, spectāre, spectāvī, spectātus*
water	*aqua, aquae, f.*
way (street)	*via, viae, f.*
weapons	*arma, armōrum, n. pl.*
weep	*lacrimō, lacrimāre, lacrimāvī*
well	*bene*
when?	*quandō?*
why?	*cūr?*
wide	*lātus, lāta, lātum*
win	*vincō, vincere, vīcī, victus*
wine	*vīnum, vīnī, n.*
with	*cum + abl.*
woman	*fēmina, fēminae, f.*
wood	*silva, silvae, f.*
word	*verbum, verbī, n.*
work	*labōrō, labōrāre, labōrāvī, labōrātus*
wretched	*miser, misera, miserum*
write	*scrībō, scrībere, scrīpsī, scrīptus*
year	*annus, annī, m.*
your (sing.), yours	*tuus, tua, tuum*

HOW TO USE THE DICTIONARY

Numbers before words

A number before a word means the word appears in the **Vocabulary for learning** list for that chapter.

For example: 19 **oculus, oculī**, *m.* *eye*

means that **oculus** appears in the Chapter 19 **Vocabulary for learning** list.

Nouns

The information given is: nominative, genitive, gender.

For example: **gēns**, **gentis**, *f.* *people, race, family, tribe*

- **gēns** is the nominative form (used for the subject of the sentence);
- **gentis** is the genitive form (meaning 'of the people');
- **gēns** is a feminine word.

m. stands for masculine; *f.* stands for feminine; *n.* stands for neuter.

m.f. is used for a word which can sometimes be masculine, sometimes feminine. For example, the word **familiāris** (*relative*) can be either masculine or feminine, depending on the gender of the relative.

Verbs

The forms given are: 1st person present tense, infinitive, 1st person perfect tense, perfect passive participle.

You might prefer to think of this as: *I do something, to do something, I did/have done something, having been somethinged*.

For example: **laudō**, **laudāre**, **laudāvī**, **laudātus** *praise, admire*

- **laudō** means *I praise*
- **laudāre** means *to praise*
- **laudāvī** means *I (have) praised*
- **laudātus** means *having been praised*

Adjectives

Most adjectives are given with the following forms: masculine, feminine, neuter (all nominative singular).

For example: **plēnus**, **plēna**, **plēnum** *full*
trīstis, **trīstis**, **trīste** *sad*

Some third declension adjectives, such as **ferōx** and **vetus**, change their stems. For these adjectives, the forms given are: nominative, genitive.

For example: **vetus**, *gen.* **veteris** *old*

See page 274 of the Reference, and pages 157 and 160 of Book 1 for more information on adjectives.

LATIN TO ENGLISH DICTIONARY

A

6, 20	ā, ab + *abl.*	*from, away from; by*
18	abeō, abīre, abiī	*go away, depart*
	abhinc	*ago*
	ablātus	see auferō
	abstulī	see auferō
11	absum, abesse, āfuī	*am out, am absent, am away*
16	ac	*and*
11	accidō, accidere, accidī	*happen*
10	accipiō, accipere, accēpī, acceptus	*accept, take in, receive*
	accūsātiō, accūsātiōnis, *f.*	*accusation*
	accūsō, accūsāre, accūsāvī, accūsātus	*accuse*
	acētum, acētī, *n.*	*vinegar*
	Achaea, Achaeae, *f.*	*Achaea*
	āctus	see agō
4	ad + *acc.*	*to, towards; at*
	usque ad	*right up to*
30	addō, addere, addidī, additus	*add*
24	addūcō, addūcere, addūxī, adductus	*lead to*
24	adeō	*so much, so greatly, to such an extent*
20	adeō, adīre, adiī	*go to, approach*
19	adferō, adferre, attulī, adlātus	*bring*
28	adhūc	*still, until now*
	adigō, adigere, adēgī, adactus	*drive, thrust*
	adiī	see adeō
	aditus, aditūs, *m.*	*entrance, access*
22	adiuvō, adiuvāre, adiūvī, adiūtus	*help*
	adloquor, adloquī, adlocūtus sum	*speak to, address*
	administrō, administrāre, administrāvī, administrātus	*manage, administer*
	adolēscō, adolēscere, adolēvī, adultus	*grow up*
	adōrō, adōrāre, adōrāvī, adōrātus	*worship*
	adstō, adstāre, adstitī	*stand by, stand near*
4	adsum, adesse, adfuī	*am here, am present*
	adulēscentia, adulēscentiae, *f.*	*youth*
9	adveniō, advenīre, advēnī, adventus	*arrive*
	adytum, adytī, *n.*	*innermost chamber*
	aedificium, aedificiī, *n.*	*building*
29	aedificō, aedificāre, aedificāvī, aedificātus	*build*
	aedīlis, aedīlis, *m.*	*aedile*
	aeger, aegra, aegrum	*sick, ill*
	Aegyptius, Aegyptia, Aegyptium	*Egyptian*
	Aegyptus, Aegyptī, *f.*	*Egypt*
	Aenēās, Aenēae, *m.*	*Aeneas*
	aēneus, aēnea, aēneum	*bronze*
	aequus, aequa, aequum	*calm; level, flat*
	āēr, āeris, *m.*	*air*
	aestus, aestūs, *m.*	*heat*
	affīgō, affīgere, affīxī, affīxus	*fasten*
	Āfrica, Āfricae, *f.*	*Africa (Roman province in what is now North Africa)*
28	ager, agrī, *m.*	*field*
	agitō, agitāre, agitāvī, agitātus	*drive, drive on, chase*
	agmen, agminis, *n.*	*column (of soldiers)*
	agnōscō, agnōscere, agnōvī, agnitus	*recognize*
	agnus, agnī, *m.*	*lamb*
8, 20	agō, agere, ēgī, āctus	*do; act; spend (time); drive, lead*
	grātiās ago	*give thanks*
	āh!	*ah!*
	ai!	*ai!*
	ālea, āleae, *f.*	*game of dice, a die*
	Alexander, Alexandrī, *m.*	*Alexander*
22	aliquis, aliquid	*someone, something*
10, 21	alius, alia, aliud	*another, other; else*
	aliī ... aliī ...	*some ... others ...*
20	alter, altera, alterum	*the other, another, one of two, the second of two*
11	altus, alta, altum	*high, deep*
	amanter	*lovingly*
	amātor, amātōris, *m.*	*lover*
	ambāgēs, ambāgis, *f.*	*riddle, utterance*
	ambiguus, ambigua, ambiguum	*unclear, uncertain*
	ambō, ambae, ambō	*both*
3	ambulō, ambulāre, ambulāvī, ambulātus	*walk*
	amīca, amīcae, *f.*	*friend (female)*
	amīcitia, amīcitiae, *f.*	*friendship*
3	amīcus, amīcī, *m.*	*friend (male)*
	amita, amitae, *f.*	*aunt*
20	āmittō, āmittere, āmīsī, āmissus	*lose*
14	amō, amāre, amāvī, amātus	*love, like*
14	amor, amōris, *m.*	*love*
	amphitheātrum, amphitheātrī, *n.*	*amphitheater*

	Latin	English
	amphora, amphorae, *f.*	*amphora, jar*
	amplector, amplectī, amplexus sum	*embrace*
	Ampliātus, Ampliātī, *m.*	*Ampliatus*
3	ancilla, ancillae, *f.*	*slave, enslaved person (female)*
	angulus, angulī, *m.*	*corner*
	angustus, angusta, angustum	*narrow*
	anhēlus, anhēla, anhēlum	*breathless, panting*
	animadvertō, animadvertere, animadvertī, animadversus	*notice*
	animal, animālis, *n.*	*animal*
18	animus, animī, *m.*	*mind, spirit*
10	annus, annī, *m.*	*year*
25	ante + *acc.*	*before; in front of*
15	anteā	*before*
	Antigonus, Antigonī, *m.*	*Antigonus*
	antīquus, antīqua, antīquum	*old, ancient*
	antrum, antrī, *n.*	*cave*
	ānxiē	*anxiously, worriedly*
	ānxius, ānxia, ānxium	*worried, concerned*
	Apelles, Apellis, *m.*	*Apelles*
22	aperiō, aperīre, aperuī, apertus	*open*
	Aphrodīsias, Aphrodīsiadis, *f.*	*Aphrodisias*
	Apiōn, Apiōnis, *m.*	*Apion*
	Apollō, Apollinis, *m.*	*Apollo (god of music and prophecy)*
	Aponia, Aponiae, *f.*	*Aponia*
	Aponius, Aponiī, *m.*	*Aponius*
17	appāreō, appārēre, appāruī	*appear*
7	appropinquō, appropinquāre, appropinquāvī + *dat.*	*approach, come near to*
	Aprōniānus, Aprōniānī, *m.*	*Apronianus*
23	apud + *acc.*	*at the house of; with; among*
5	aqua, aquae, *f.*	*water*
	aquilifer, aquiliferī, *m.*	*standard bearer*
30	āra, ārae, *f.*	*altar*
	Arabia, Arabiae, *f.*	*Arabia*
	arānea, arāneae, *f.*	*cobweb*
27	arbor, arboris, *f.*	*tree*
	arca, arcae, *f.*	*crate, strongbox*
	architectus, architectī, *m.*	*architect*
	ardenter	*eagerly*
	ārea, āreae, *f.*	*square, courtyard*
	Arēopagus, Arēopagī, *m.*	*Areopagus (hill in Athens)*
	argentārius, argentāriī, *m.*	*silversmith*
	argenteus, argentea, argenteum	*silver, made of silver*
	Ariadna, Ariadnae, *f.*	*Ariadne (Cretan princess)*
31	arma, armōrum, *n. pl.*	*arms, weapons*
	arō, arāre, arāvī, arātus	*plow*
	arōma, arōmatis, *n.*	*spice*
27	ars, artis, *f.*	*art, skill*
	Artemis, Artemidis, *f.*	*Artemis (Greek goddess of hunting and the moon)*
	artifex, artificis, *m.f.*	*artist*
	artificium, artificiī, *n.*	*business*
	artus, artūs, *m.*	*limb*
	as, assis, *m.*	*as (copper coin of small value)*
28	ascendō, ascendere, ascendī, ascēnsus	*climb*
	Asia, Asiae, *f.*	*Asia*
	asinus, asinī, *m.*	*stupid person, fool; donkey*
	astrologus, astrologī, *m.*	*astrologer*
	astrum, astrī, *n.*	*star*
	āter, ātra, ātrum	*dark*
	Athēna, Athēnae, *f.*	*Athena*
	Athēnae, Athēnārum, *f. pl.*	*Athens*
	Athēniēnsis, Athēniēnsis, Athēniēnse	*Athenian*
	āthlēta, āthlētae, *m.*	*athlete*
20	atque	*and*
	ātrium, ātriī, *n.*	*reception room, entrance hall*
	Attalicus, Attalica, Attalicum	*of Attalus*
	Attō, Attōnis, *m.*	*Atto*
	attonitus, attonita, attonitum	*shocked, astonished*
	attulī	see adferō
	Aucissa, Aucissae, *f.*	*Aucissa*
	auctōritās, auctōritātis, *f.*	*power, importance*
20	audāx, audācis	*bold, daring*
29	audeō, audēre, ausus sum	*dare*
5	audiō, audīre, audīvī, audītus	*hear, listen to*
16	auferō, auferre, abstulī, ablātus	*steal, take away, carry off*
	augur, auguris, *m.*	*augur*
	Augustus, Augusta, Augustum	*August*
	aula, aulae, *f.*	*court, hall*
	aureus, aurea, aureum	*golden*
	aureus, aureī, *m.*	*gold coin*
	aurīga, aurīgae, *m.*	*charioteer*
21	auris, auris, *f.*	*ear*
23	aurum, aurī, *n.*	*gold*
	auspicium, auspiciī, *n.*	*auspices, sign*
	ausus	see audeō
18	aut	*or*
18	aut ... aut ...	*either ... or ...*
28	autem	*but, however*
32	auxilium, auxiliī, *n.*	*help*
	avis, avis, *f.*	*bird*

B

	Latin	English
	Balbus, Balbī, *m.*	*Balbus*
	ballista, ballistae, *f.*	*ballista, military siege machine*
	ballistārius, ballistāriī, *m.*	*ballista maker*
	bālō, bālāre, bālāvī	*bleat*
	barba, barbae, *f.*	*beard*
	barbarus, barbarī, *m.*	*foreigner; barbarian*
	Barca, Barcae, *m.*	*Barca*
	basilica, basilicae, *f.*	*hall*
	Bastiza, Bastizae, *m.*	*Bastiza*
	Batāvus, Batāvī, *m.*	*Batavian*
28	beātus, beāta, beātum	*happy, blessed*
15	bellum, bellī, *n.*	*war*
11	bene	*well*
17	benignus, benigna, benignum	*kind, generous*
	bēstia, bēstiae, *f.*	*beast, wild animal*
8	bibō, bibere, bibī	*drink*
	blandus, blanda, blandum	*flattering*
10	bonus, bona, bonum	*good*
	bracchium, bracchiī, *n.*	*arm*
16	brevis, brevis, breve	*short, brief*
	breviter	*briefly*
	Britannia, Britanniae, *f.*	*Britannia, Britain*
	Britannicus, Britannica, Britannicum	*British*
	būbō, būbōnis, *m.*	*horned owl, eagle owl*

C

	Latin	English
2	cadō, cadere, cecidī, cāsus	*fall*
31	caedēs, caedis, *f.*	*killing, slaughter*
	Caelius, Caelia, Caelium	*Caelian (hill in Rome)*
12	caelum, caelī, *n.*	*sky, heaven*
	Caesar, Caesaris, *m.*	*Caesar (title of emperor)*
	calcō, calcāre, calcāvī, calcātus	*tread*
	calidus, calida, calidum	*hot*
	callidus, callida, callidum	*clever*
	Calvia, Calviae, *f.*	*Calvia*
	camēlopardalis, camēlopardalis, *f.*	*giraffe*
	camēlus, camēlī, *m.*	*camel*
22	canis, canis, *m.*	*dog*
26	canō, canere, cecinī	*sing; play (an instrument)*
6	capiō, capere, cēpī, captus	*take, catch, capture*
	cōnsilium capiō	*adopt a plan*
	Capitōlium, Capitōliī, *n.*	*the Capitoline Hill*
30	captīvus, captīvī, *m.*	*captive, prisoner*
12	caput, capitis, *n.*	*head*
26	carmen, carminis, *n.*	*poem, song*
	Carthāgō, Carthāginis, *f.*	*Carthage (city in North Africa)*
23	cārus, cāra, cārum	*expensive; dear*
	Caryātides, Caryātidum, *f.*	*Caryatids (female statues)*
	casa, casae, *f.*	*hut, cottage*
	Castalius, Castalia, Castalium	*Castalian*
	Castor, Castoris, *m.*	*Castor*
3	castra, castrōrum, *n. pl.*	*camp*
31	cāsus, cāsūs, *m.*	*accident; chance*
	Catia, Catiae, *f.*	*Catia*
31	causa, causae, *f.*	*reason*
	cautē	*cautiously*
	caveō, cavēre, cāvī, cautus	*beware, look out (for), watch out (for)*
	caverna, cavernae, *f.*	*hole*
	cecidī	see cadō
	celebrō, celebrāre, celebrāvī, celebrātus	*celebrate*
	Celer, Celeris, *m.*	*Celer*
23	celer, celeris, celere	*quick, fast*
	celeriter	*quickly*
	celerius	*more quickly, faster*
	celerrimē	*very quickly*
	quam celerrimē	*as quickly as possible*
	cella, cellae, *f.*	*room*
16	cēlō, cēlāre, cēlāvī, cēlātus	*hide*
	Celsa, Celsae, *f.*	*Celsa*
15	cēna, cēnae, *f.*	*dinner, meal*
	cēnō, cēnāre, cēnāvī, cēnātus	*dine*
26	centum	*hundred*
	centuriō, centuriōnis, *m.*	*centurion (officer in the army)*
	cēpī	see capiō
	certē	*certainly, clearly*
	certus, certa, certum	*certain, sure*
	prō certō habeō	*know for certain, am sure*
15	cēterī, cēterae, cētera *pl.*	*the rest, the others*
	charta, chartae, *f.*	*sheet of papyrus*
	Christiānus, Christiāna, Christiānum	*Christian*
2	cibus, cibī, *m.*	*food*
	cicātrīx, cicātrīcis, *f.*	*scar*
	cinis, cineris, *m.f.*	*ashes*
	circēnsēs, circēnsium, *m. pl.*	*circuses, races*
26	circum + *acc.*	*around*
	circumdō, circumdare, circumdedī, circumdatus	*surround*
	circumspectō, circumspectāre, circumspectāvī	*look around*
	cīvīlis, cīvīlis, cīvīle	*civil*
9	cīvis, cīvis, *m.f.*	*citizen*
	clam	*secretly*

	Latin	English
3	clāmō, clāmāre, clāmāvī, clāmātus	*shout*
3	clāmor, clāmōris, *m.*	*noise, shouting, shout*
	clāmōsus, clāmōsa, clāmōsum	*noisy, rowdy*
29	clārus, clāra, clārum	*clear; famous, distinguished*
	Claudius, Claudiī, *m.*	*Claudius*
32	claudō, claudere, clausī, clausus	*close*
	claustrum, claustrī, *n.*	*lock*
	clāvis, clāvis, *f.*	*key*
	cliēns, clientis, *m.*	*client*
	Clōdius, Clōdiī, *m.*	*Clodius*
	coēgī	see cōgō
13	coepī, coepisse, coeptus	*began*
14	cōgitō, cōgitāre, cōgitāvī, cōgitātus	*think, consider*
15	cognōscō, cognōscere, cognōvī, cognitus	*get to know, find out, learn*
21	cōgō, cōgere, coēgī, coāctus	*force, compel*
	cohors, cohortis, *f.*	*cohort*
	colligō, colligere, collēgī, collēctus	*collect, gather*
	colloquium, colloquiī, *n.*	*conversation*
32	colō, colere, coluī, cultus	*worship*
	columba, columbae, *f.*	*dove; darling*
30	coma, comae, *f.*	*hair*
15	comes, comitis, *m.*	*comrade, companion, friend*
	comitor, comitārī, comitātus sum	*accompany*
	commisceō, commiscēre, commiscuī, commixtus	*mix together*
	committō, committere, commīsī, commissus	*join; commit*
	complector, complectī, complexus sum	*hug, embrace*
	complūrēs, complūrium *pl.*	*many, very many*
27	compōnō, compōnere, composuī, compositus	*arrange*
	concidō, concidere, concidī	*fall down*
	concipiō, concipere, concēpī, conceptus	*conceive, become pregnant*
	condiciō, condiciōnis, *f.*	*proposal*
	condō, condere, condidī, conditus	*found, establish; hide*
	cōnfectus, cōnfecta, cōnfectum	*worn out, exhausted*
14, 23	cōnficiō, cōnficere, cōnfēcī, cōnfectus	*finish; wear out, exhaust*
	cōnfringō, cōnfringere, cōnfrēgī, cōnfrāctus	*break, smash*
	cōnfūsus, cōnfūsa, cōnfūsum	*confused*
	congredior, congredī, congressus sum	*meet*
	coniciō, conicere, coniēcī, coniectus	*throw*
	coniector, coniectōris, *m.*	*fortune teller*
	coniūnx, coniugis, *m.f.*	*wife, partner*
	coniūrātiō, coniūrātiōnis, *f.*	*plot*
	coniūrātus, coniūrātī, *m.*	*conspirator*
	conlābor, conlābī, conlāpsus sum	*collapse, fall down*
22	cōnor, cōnārī, cōnātus sum	*try*
	cōnsentiō, cōnsentīre, cōnsēnsī, cōnsēnsus	*agree*
	cōnsīderō, cōnsīderāre, cōnsīderāvī, cōnsīderātus	*consider, think about*
	cōnsīdō, cōnsīdere, cōnsēdī	*sit down*
14	cōnsilium, cōnsiliī, *n.*	*plan, idea, advice*
	cōnsilium capiō	*adopt a plan*
	cōnsistō, cōnsistere, cōnstitī	*stop, stand*
8	cōnspiciō, cōnspicere, cōnspexī, cōnspectus	*catch sight of, notice*
	cōnsternō, cōnsternāre, cōnsternavī, cōnsternātus	*alarm, terrify*
14	cōnstituō, cōnstituere, cōnstituī, cōnstitūtus	*decide*
31	cōnsul, cōnsulis, *m.*	*consul*
	cōnsulō, cōnsulere, cōnsuluī, cōnsultus	*consult*
13	cōnsūmō, cōnsūmere, cōnsūmpsī, cōnsūmptus	*consume, eat*
	contendō, contendere, contendī, contentus	*compete*
	contentus, contenta, contentum	*happy, contented*
	conterō, conterere, contrīvī, contrītus	*grind, crush*
10	contrā + *acc.*	*against*
	contrahō, contrahere, contrāxī, contractus	*draw together, wrinkle*
	contrōversia, contrōversiae, *f.*	*argument, dispute*
	contubernium, contuberniī, *n.*	*squad, section*
24	conveniō, convenīre, convēnī, conventus	*come together, gather, meet*
	convocō, convocāre, convocavī, convocātus	*call together*
28	cōpiae, cōpiārum, *f. pl.*	*forces, troops*
	corbis, corbis, *m.*	*basket*
	corbula, corbulae, *f.*	*little basket*
	Corēlia, Corēliae, *f.*	*Corelia*
	Corinthus, Corinthī, *f.*	*Corinth*
	cornū, cornūs, *n.*	*horn*
	corōna, corōnae, *f.*	*garland, crown*
12	corpus, corporis, *n.*	*body*
	corrumpō, corrumpere, corrūpī, corruptus	*spoil, ruin*
	Cosmus, Cosmī, *m.*	*Cosmus*
	cōtīdiē	*every day*
30	crās	*tomorrow*
18	crēdō, crēdere, crēdidī, crēditus + *dat.*	*believe, trust, have faith in*

	Latin	English
	cremō, cremāre, cremāvī, cremātus	*cremate*
	creō, creāre, creāvī, creātus	*create, make*
	crīnis, crīnis, *f.*	*hair*
	Crīspinilla, Crīspinillae, *f.*	*Crispinilla (adviser to Nero)*
	Crītō, Crītōnis, *m.*	*Crito*
	crocodīlus, crocodīlī, *m.*	*crocodile*
	cruciō, cruciāre, cruciāvī, cruciātus	*torture*
12	crūdēlis, crūdēlis, crūdēle	*cruel*
	cubiculum, cubiculī, *n.*	*bedroom*
	cucurrī	see currō
	cui	*to whom, to which*
	cuius	*of whom, of which, whose*
	culīna, culīnae, *f.*	*kitchen*
3	cum + *abl.*	*with*
23	cum + *subj.*	*when, since*
	cupiditās, cupiditātis, *f.*	*greed*
	Cupīdō, Cupīdinis, *m.*	*Cupid*
5	cupiō, cupere, cupīvī, cupītus	*want, desire*
7	cūr?	*why?*
22	cūra, cūrae, *f.*	*care, worry*
	cūria, cūriae, *f.*	*Senate House*
23	cūrō, cūrāre, cūrāvī, cūrātus	*care about, am bothered about, look after, supervise*
	Currāx, Currācis, *m.*	*Currax*
3	currō, currere, cucurrī, cursus	*run*
	currus, currūs, *m.*	*chariot*
29	custōdiō, custōdīre, custōdīvī, custōdītus	*guard*
5	custōs, custōdis, *m.*	*guard*
	Cynisca, Cyniscae, *f.*	*Cynisca*

D

	Latin	English
	damnō, damnāre, damnāvī, damnātus	*condemn*
	Dāmōn, Dāmōnis, *m.*	*Damon*
8	dē + *abl.*	*from, down from; about*
	dē industriā	*on purpose*
10	dea, deae, *f.*	*goddess*
5, 20	dēbeō, dēbēre, dēbuī, dēbitus	*owe; ought, should, must*
26	decem	*ten*
	dēcernō, dēcernere, dēcrēvī, dēcrētus	*decide, settle*
	dēcerpō, dēcerpere, dēcerpsī, dēcerptus	*pull off*
29	decet, decēre, decuit	*it is right for, it is proper for*
	dēcidō, dēcidere, dēcidī	*fall down*
	dēcipiō, dēcipere, dēcēpī, dēceptus	*deceive, trick*
	dedī	see dō
	dēdūcō, dēdūcere, dēdūxī, dēductus	*lead, escort*
29	dēfendō, dēfendere, dēfendī, dēfēnsus	*defend*
	dēfēnsiō, dēfēnsiōnis, *f.*	*defense*
	dēiciō, dēicere, dēiēcī, dēiectus	*throw down*
10	deinde	*then*
	dēlectō, dēlectāre, dēlectāvī, dēlectātus	*please, delight*
12	dēleō, dēlēre, dēlēvī, dēlētus	*destroy*
	Delphī, Delphōrum, *m. pl.*	*Delphi (town in Greece)*
	Delphicus, Delphica, Delphicum	*Delphic*
	Dēmētrius, Dēmētriī, *m.*	*Demetrius*
	dēmōnstrō, dēmōnstrāre, dēmōnstrāvī, dēmōnstrātus	*show, point out*
	dēnsus, dēnsa, dēnsum	*thick*
	dēpōnō, dēpōnere, dēposuī, dēpositus	*take off, put down*
28	dēscendō, dēscendere, dēscendī, dēscēnsus	*go down, come down*
	dēscrībō, dēscrībere, dēscrīpsī, dēscrīptus	*draw, sketch*
	dēserō, dēserere, dēseruī, dēsertus	*desert, forsake*
	dēsertus, dēserta, dēsertum	*deserted*
	dēsiliō, dēsilīre, dēsiluī	*jump, jump down*
24	dēspērō, dēspērāre, dēspērāvī, dēspērātus	*despair*
	dēstruō, dēstruere, dēstrūxī, dēstrūctus	*destroy*
	dēsum, dēesse, dēfuī	*am wanting, am lacking*
	dētrahō, dētrahere, dētrāxī, dētractus	*pull down*
4	deus, deī, *m.*	*god*
	dēvōtiō, dēvōtiōnis, *f.*	*curse*
	dēvoveō, dēvovēre, dēvōvī, dēvōtus	*curse*
27	dexter, dextra, dextrum	*right*
3	dīcō, dīcere, dīxī, dictus	*say, speak, tell*
	didicī	see discō
	Dīdō, Dīdōnis, *f.*	*Dido*
6	diēs, diēī, *m.*	*day*
9	difficilis, difficilis, difficile	*difficult*
	difficilius	*with more difficulty*
	difficultās, difficultātis, *f.*	*difficulty*
	diffundō, diffundere, diffūdī, diffūsus	*scatter, dishevel*
	digitus, digitī, *m.*	*finger*
	dīligēns, dīligentis	*careful, hard-working*
	dīligenter	*carefully*
	dīmittō, dīmittere, dīmīsī, dīmissus	*release*
	dīmoveō, dīmovēre, dīmōvī, dīmōtus	*remove*
14	dīrus, dīra, dīrum	*dreadful*

	Latin	English
	Dīs, Dītis, *m.*	*Dis (god of the Underworld)*
6	discēdō, discēdere, discessī	*depart, leave*
	disciplīna, disciplīnae, *f.*	*discipline, training*
	discipulus, discipulī, *m.*	*student*
30	discō, discere, didicī	*learn*
	discus, discī, *m.*	*discus*
	dispēnsātor, dispēnsātōris, *m.*	*housekeeper, supervisor*
	dissentiō, dissentīre, dissensī, dissensus	*disagree, dissent*
12	diū	*for a long time*
	diūtius	*longer, for a longer time*
22	dīves, dīvitis	*rich*
	dīvortium, dīvortiī, *n.*	*divorce*
	dīvus, dīva, dīvum	*divine*
	dīxī	see dīcō
5	dō, dare, dedī, datus	*give*
	poenās dō	*pay the penalty, am punished*
27	doceō, docēre, docuī, doctus	*teach*
	doleō, dolēre, doluī, dolitus	*feel pain, suffer*
	dōlium, dōliī, *n.*	*very large jar*
27	dolor, dolōris, *m.*	*pain*
9	domina, dominae, *f.*	*mistress, lady*
4	dominus, dominī, *m.*	*master*
8	domus, domūs, *f.*	*house, home*
	domī	*at home*
4	dōnum, dōnī, *n.*	*gift, present*
1	dormiō, dormīre, dormīvī	*sleep*
29	dubitō, dubitāre, dubitāvī, dubitātus	*hesitate, doubt*
	dubium, dubiī, *n.*	*doubt*
2	dūcō, dūcere, dūxī, ductus	*lead, guide, take*
	in matrimōnium dūcō	*marry*
	dulce	*sweetly*
28	dulcis, dulcis, dulce	*sweet*
	dulcius	*more sweetly*
23	dum + *indic.*	*while*
27	dum + *subj.*	*until*
20	duo, duae, duo	*two*
17	dūrus, dūra, dūrum	*hard, harsh*
11	dux, ducis, *m.*	*leader*
	dūxī	see dūcō

E

	Latin	English
6	ē, ex + *abl.*	*from, out of*
	ēbrius, ēbria, ēbrium	*drunk*
32	ecce!	*look! see!*
	ēditor, ēditōris, *m.*	*sponsor (of gladiator shows)*
	effluō, effluere, efflūxī	*flow*
	effodiō, effodere, effōdī, effossus	*dig, dig out*
5	effugiō, effugere, effūgī	*flee, escape*
	effundō, effundere, effūdī, effūsus	*pour out*
	ēgī	see agō
1	ego, meī	*I, me*
22	ēgredior, ēgredī, ēgressus sum	*go out, leave*
	ēheu!	*ah! oh no!*
	Eirēnē, Eirēnēs, *f.*	*Eirene*
	ēlābor, ēlābī, ēlāpsus sum	*slip out, glide out*
	elephantus, elephantī, *m.*	*elephant*
	ēligō, ēligere, ēlēgī, ēlēctus	*choose, elect*
	emblēma, emblēmatis, *n.*	*mosaic*
17	emō, emere, ēmī, ēmptus	*buy*
20	enim	*for, because*
15	eō, īre, iī	*go*
	Epaphrodītus, Epaphrodītī, *m.*	*Epaphroditus*
	Ephesius, Ephesia, Ephesium	*Ephesian, from Ephesus*
	Ephesus, Ephesī, *f.*	*Ephesus (city in what is now Turkey)*
7	epistula, epistulae, *f.*	*letter*
18	eques, equitis, *m.*	*horseman, pl. = cavalry; member of equestrian class*
3	equus, equī, *m.*	*horse*
28	ergō	*therefore*
28	errō, errāre, errāvī, errātus	*make a mistake; wander*
	ērubēscō, ērubēscere, ērubuī	*blush*
	ērumpō, ērumpere, ērūpī, ēruptus	*burst out, shoot out*
	Esquiliae, Esquiliārum, *f. pl.*	*Esquiline Hill (area in Rome)*
2, 17	et	*and; even, also*
	et ... et ...	*both ... and ...*
15	etiam	*even, also*
	eugē!	*hurray!*
	eurīpus, eurīpī, *m.*	*canal, channel*
	ēvānēscō, ēvānēscere, ēvānuī	*disappear*
	ēveniō, ēvenīre, ēvēnī	*happen; come out*
6	ex, ē + *abl.*	*out of*
	ex lēge	*according to law*
	exanimātus, exanimāta, exanimātum	*unconscious*
	excīdō, excīdere, excīdī, excīsus	*cut down*
	excitō, excitāre, excitāvī, excitātus	*wake someone up*
	exclāmō, exclāmāre, exclāmāvī, exclāmātus	*exclaim*
	exemplum, exemplī, *n.*	*example*
18	exeō, exīre, exiī	*come out of*
	exerceō, exercēre, exercuī, exercitus	*exercise, train*

	Latin	English
24	exercitus, exercitūs, *m.*	*army*
	exhauriō, exhaurīre, exhausī, exhaustus	*finish, empty*
	exiī	see exeō
	explicō, explicāre, explicāvī, explicātus	*explain*
	expōnō, expōnere, exposuī, expositus	*reveal*
6	exspectō, exspectāre, exspectāvī, exspectātus	*wait for; expect*
	exspīrō, exspīrāre, exspīrāvī, exspīrātus	*die*
	exspuō, exspuere, exspuī, exspūtus	*spit*
	exstinguō, exstinguere, exstīnxī, exstīnctus	*put out, extinguish*
	exstō, exstāre	*stand out, bulge out*
	extrā + *acc.*	*outside*
	extrahō, extrahere, extrāxī, extractus	*take out, extract*

F

	Latin	English
	faber, fabrī, *m.*	*craftsman*
	Fabius, Fabiī, *m.*	*Fabius*
	fābula, fābulae, *f.*	*story; play; pl. = nonsense!*
25	faciēs, faciēī, *f.*	*face, appearance*
	facile	*easily*
20	facilis, facilis, facile	*easy*
6	faciō, facere, fēcī, factus	*do; make*
	factus sum	see fīō
	Falernum, Falernī, *n.*	*Falernian wine*
	fāma, fāmae, *f.*	*rumor*
	familia, familiae, *f.*	*family, household*
	familiāris, familiāris, *m.f.*	*relative; member of household*
	fascia, fasciae, *f.*	*bandage*
	fatīgō, fatīgāre, fatīgāvī, fatīgātus	*tire, tire out*
26	fātum, fātī, *n.*	*fate, destiny; death*
	faucēs, faucium, *f. pl.*	*entrance, entry passage*
31	faveō, favere, fāvī, fautus + *dat.*	*favor, support*
	fax, facis, *f.*	*torch*
	febris, febris, *f.*	*fever*
	fēcī	see faciō
	fēlēs, fēlis, *f.*	*cat*
	Fēlīx, Fēlīcis, *m.*	*Felix*
18	fēlīx, fēlīcis	*lucky, fortunate; happy*
14	fēmina, fēminae, *f.*	*woman*
	fenestra, fenestrae, *f.*	*window*
10	ferō, ferre, tulī, lātus	*bring, carry, bear*
	ferōciter	*fiercely*
15	ferōx, ferōcis	*fierce, ferocious*
	fervidus, fervida, fervidum	*boiling hot, fiery*
	fessus, fessa, fessum	*tired*
3	festīnō, festīnāre, festīnāvī, festīnātus	*hurry, rush*
	fēstus, fēsta, fēstum	*festival*
	fībula, fībulae, *f.*	*brooch, pin*
	fīcus, fīcī, *f.*	*fig*
10	fidēlis, fidēlis, fidēle	*loyal, faithful; trustworthy*
	fidēs, fideī, *f.*	*loyalty*
	fīgō, fīgere, fīxī, fīxus	*fix*
	figūra, figūrae, *f.*	*shape, form*
2	fīlia, fīliae, *f.*	*daughter*
2	fīlius, fīliī, *m.*	*son*
	fingō, fingere, fīnxī, fictus	*form, shape*
32	fīnis, fīnis, *m.*	*end*
30	fīō, fierī, factus sum	*become*
	fistula, fistulae, *f.*	*pipe*
	fīxus	see fīgō
32	flamma, flammae, *f.*	*flame; pl. = fire*
11	flūmen, flūminis, *n.*	*river*
	fluō, fluere, flūxī, flūxus	*flow*
	fodiō, fodere, fōdī, fossus	*dig*
	fōns, fontis, *m.*	*fountain*
	foris, foris, *f.*	*door, gate*
	formīca, formīcae, *f.*	*ant*
	fortasse	*perhaps*
21	forte	*by chance*
11	fortis, fortis, forte	*brave; strong*
	fortiter	*bravely*
	fortitūdō, fortitūdinis, *f.*	*strength, courage*
32	Fortūna, Fortūnae, *f.*	*Fortune (goddess)*
	fortūna, fortūnae, *f.*	*fortune*
	Fortūnāta, Fortūnātae, *f.*	*Fortunata*
2	forum, forī, *n.*	*forum, market, meeting place*
	fossa, fossae, *f.*	*trench*
	fragmentum, fragmentī, *n.*	*fragment*
25	frangō, frangere, frēgī, frāctus	*break*
1	frāter, frātris, *m.*	*brother*
	fremō, fremere, fremuī	*roar*
	frīgēscō, frīgēscere, frīxī	*get cold, chill*
	frīgidus, frīgida, frīgidum	*cold*
	frīgus, frīgoris, *n.*	*cold*
	frōns, frontis, *f.*	*facade; forehead, brow*
	frūmentum, frūmentī, *n.*	*corn, grain*
11	frūstrā	*in vain, without success*
11	fugiō, fugere, fūgī	*run away, flee*
	fugitīvus, fugitīva, fugitīvum	*runaway*
	fugitīvus, fugitīvī, *m.*	*runaway*
	fuī	see sum
	fulgeō, fulgēre, fulsī	*flash with lightning*
	fullō, fullōnis, *m.*	*fuller, laundry manager*

	Latin	English
	fullōnica, fullōnicae, *f.*	*fullery, laundry*
	fulmen, fulminis, *n.*	*lightning*
	fundō, fundere, fūdī, fūsus	*pour out*
	fundus, fundī, *m.*	*farm*
	fūnis, fūnis, *m.*	*rope*
	fūr, fūris, *m.*	*thief*
	furca, furcae, *f.*	*two-pronged fork*
	furor, furōris, *m.*	*rage, fury*
	fūrtim	*secretly, like a thief*

G

	Latin	English
	Gāius, Gāiī, *m.*	*Gaius*
	Galba, Galbae, *m.*	*Galba*
	galea, galeae, *f.*	*helmet*
	Gallia, Galliae, *f.*	*Gaul*
	Gallicus, Gallica, Gallicum	*Gallic*
	Gallus, Gallī, *m.*	*a Gaul*
	garum, garī, *n.*	*garum (fish sauce)*
27	gaudeō, gaudēre, gāvīsus sum	*am pleased, rejoice*
21	gaudium, gaudiī, *n.*	*joy, pleasure*
	geminus, gemina, geminum	*twin*
	gemitus, gemitūs, *m.*	*groan*
	gemma, gemmae, *f.*	*jewel, stone*
	gemō, gemere, gemuī	*moan, groan*
29	gēns, gentis, *f.*	*people, race, family, tribe*
	Germānia, Germāniae, *f.*	*Germania*
8, 19	gerō, gerere, gessī, gestus	*wear (clothes); wage (war)*
	Giscō, Giscōnis, *m.*	*Gisco*
	gladiātor, gladiātōris, *m.*	*gladiator*
3	gladius, gladiī, *m.*	*sword*
	glis, glīris, *m.*	*dormouse, rodent*
	glōria, glōriae, *f.*	*glory, fame*
	Graecia, Graeciae, *f.*	*Greece*
	Graecus, Graeca, Graecum	*Greek*
	Graecus, Graecī, *m.*	*Greek*
	grammatica, grammaticae, *f.*	*school teacher*
19	grātiae, grātiārum, *f. pl.*	*thanks*
	grātiās ago	*give thanks*
	gravidus, gravida, gravidum	*pregnant*
9	gravis, gravis, grave	*heavy; serious*
20	graviter	*heavily; seriously*
	grundiō, grundīre, grundīvī	*grunt*
	gustō, gustāre, gustāvī, gustātus	*taste*

H

	Latin	English
	ha!	*ha!*
2	habeō, habēre, habuī, habitus	*have, hold*
	prō certō habeō	*know for certain, am sure*
2	habitō, habitāre, habitāvī, habitātus	*live*
	haedus, haedī, *m.*	*goat*
	hahae!	*ha ha!*
	harēna, harēnae, *f.*	*sand; arena*
	hauriō, haurīre, hausī, haustus	*drink*
	Hector, Hectoris, *m.*	*Hector*
	herba, herbae, *f.*	*herb*
	hercle!	*oh no! oh dear!*
	hērēs, hērēdis, *m.*	*heir*
18	heri	*yesterday*
	Hermionē, Hermionēs, *f.*	*Hermione*
	hērōs, hērōis, *m.*	*hero*
	hesternus, hesterna, hesternum	*yesterday's*
	heus!	*hey! hey there!*
20	hīc	*here*
16	hic, haec, hoc	*this, he, she, it*
	ille ... hic ...	*the former ... the latter ...*
	hiems, hiemis, *f.*	*winter*
	Hierosolyma, Hierosolymōrum, *n. pl.*	*Jerusalem*
	hinc	*from here*
	Hispānia, Hispāniae, *f.*	*Hispania*
11	hodiē	*today*
7	homō, hominis, *m.*	*man, person, human being*
29	honor, honōris, *m.*	*honor*
1	hōra, hōrae, *f.*	*hour*
	horreō, horrēre, horruī	*shiver, shudder*
	horror, horrōris, *m.*	*horror*
22	hortor, hortārī, hortātus sum	*encourage, urge*
15	hortus, hortī, *m.*	*garden*
	hospes, hospitis, *m.*	*guest*
9	hostis, hostis, *m.*	*enemy*
17	hūc	*here, to this place*
	humus, humī, *f.*	*earth, soil*

I

	Latin	English
8	iaceō, iacēre, iacuī	*lie down*
10	iaciō, iacere, iēcī, iactus	*throw*
6	iam	*now, already, at this/that time*
	iānitor, iānitōris, *m.*	*doorkeeper*
12	iānua, iānuae, *f.*	*door, doorway*
	Iānuārius, Iānuāria, Iānuārium	*of January*
11	ibi	*there*
32	īdem, eadem, idem	*the same, this, that*
	identidem	*repeatedly*
	Īdūs, Īduum, *f.*	*Ides (15th day of March, May, July, October, 13th day of other months)*

	Latin	English
	iēcī	see iaciō
	ientāculum, ientāculi, *n.*	*breakfast*
17	igitur	*so, therefore*
21	ignis, ignis, *m.*	*fire*
	ignōrō, ignōrāre, ignōravī, ignōrātus	*be unaware of*
	ignōscō, ignōscere, ignōvī, ignōtus	*forgive*
	ignōtus, ignōta, ignōtum	*unknown*
	iī	see eō
16	ille, illa, illud	*that, he, she, it*
	ille ... hic ...	*the former ... the latter ...*
31	illīc	*there*
	imāgō, imāginis, *f.*	*image, picture*
	imber, imbris, *m.*	*rain*
	immortālis, immortālis, immortāle	*immortal*
	immōtus, immōta, immōtum	*motionless*
	impedīmenta, impedīmentōrum, *n. pl.*	*baggage*
	impendeō, impendēre	*am near, am imminent*
9	imperātor, imperātōris, *m.*	*emperor; general, commander, leader*
16, 25	imperium, imperiī, *n.*	*power; empire; command*
25	imperō, imperāre, imperāvī, imperātus + *dat.*	*command; order*
31	impetus, impetūs, *m.*	*charge, assault; impulse, purpose*
	impleō, implēre, implēvī, implētus	*fill*
	impluvium, impluviī, *n.*	*impluvium (pool for rainwater)*
27	impōnō, impōnere, imposuī, impositus	*put, put on*
	imprimō, imprimere, impressī, impressus	*press*
6	in + *acc.*	*into, onto; against*
1	in + *abl.*	*in, on*
	incantātiō, incantātiōnis, *f.*	*enchantment, spell*
	incendium, incendiī, *n.*	*fire*
8	incendō, incendere, incendī, incēnsus	*burn, set on fire*
	incertus, incerta, incertum	*uncertain*
28	incipiō, incipere, incēpī, inceptus	*begin, start*
	increpō, increpāre, increpuī, increpitus	*play, pluck*
	indicō, indicāre, indicāvī, indicātus	*point out, show*
	indulgeō, indulgēre, indulsī, indultus	*give in to, indulge in*
	induō, induere, induī, indūtus	*put on*
	Indus, Indī, *m.*	*Indus*
	industria, industriae, *f.*	*diligence, hard work*
	dē industriā	*on purpose*
	ineō, inīre, iniī	*go into, enter*
	īnfāns, īnfantis, *m.*	*baby*
3	īnfēlīx, īnfēlīcis	*unlucky; unhappy*
	īnferō, īnferre, intulī, inlātus	*carry in, carry into*
	īnfirmus, īnfirma, īnfirmum	*weak*
29	ingenium, ingeniī, *n.*	*nature, character*
7	ingēns, ingentis	*huge*
22	ingredior, ingredī, ingressus sum	*go into, enter*
	iniī	see ineō
31	inimīcus, inimīcī, *m.*	*enemy*
	inīquē	*unjustly, unfairly*
	inīquus, inīqua, inīquum	*unfair*
	initium, initiī, *n.*	*beginning*
	innocēns, innocentis	*innocent*
	innocenter	*blamelessly, innocently*
6	inquit	*says, said*
	īnsānia, īnsāniae, *f.*	*madness*
	īnsānus, īnsāna, īnsānum	*mad, insane*
	īnscrībō, īnscrībere, īnscrīpsī, īnscrīptus	*write on, inscribe*
	īnsignis, īnsignis, īnsigne	*distinguished, eminent*
	īnspiciō, īnspicere, īnspexī, īnspectus	*inspect*
	īnstrūmentum, īnstrūmentī, *n.*	*instrument, tool*
	īnstruō, īnstruere, īnstrūxī, īnstrūctus	*draw up, prepare*
1,7	īnsula, īnsulae, *f.*	*apartment building; island*
	īnsum, inesse	*am in*
	īnsuper	*moreover, besides*
13	intellegō, intellegere, intellēxī, intellēctus	*understand, realize*
	intentē	*intently, closely, carefully*
13	inter + *acc.*	*among, between*
	intercipiō, intercipere, intercēpī, interceptus	*intercept*
15	intereā	*meanwhile*
29	interficiō, interficere, interfēcī, interfectus	*kill*
	interpellō, interpellāre, interpellāvī, interpellātus	*interrupt*
	interrogō, interrogāre, interrogāvī, interrogātus	*question*
	interrumpō, interrumpere, interrūpī, interruptus	*interrupt*
2	intrō, intrāre, intrāvī, intrātus	*come in, enter*
	intulī	see īnferō
	inūtilis, inūtilis, inūtile	*useless*
11	inveniō, invenīre, invēnī, inventus	*find*
	invideō, invidēre, invīdī, invīsus	*envy*
	invītātiō, invītātiōnis, *f.*	*invitation*
31	invītō, invītāre, invītāvī, invītātus	*invite*

	Latin	English
27	ipse, ipsa, ipsum	*himself, herself, itself, themselves*
26	īra, īrae, *f.*	*anger*
	īrātē	*angrily*
9	īrātus, īrāta, īrātum	*angry*
	irrumpō, irrumpere, irrūpī	*burst in*
17	is, ea, id	*he, she, it; this, that*
	Īsis, Īsidis, *f.*	*Isis (Egyptian goddess)*
	Isthmus, Isthmī, *m.*	*Isthmus, strip of land between two seas*
24	ita	*so, in this way*
11	itaque	*and so, therefore*
9	iter, itineris, *n.*	*journey, route, way*
12	iterum	*again*
15	iubeō, iubēre, iussī, iussus	*order*
	Iūdaea, Iūdaeae, *f.*	*Judea*
	Iūdaeus, Iūdaea, Iūdaeum	*Jewish*
	iūdex, iūdicis, *m.*	*judge*
	iūdicium, iūdiciī, *n.*	*court, trial, judgment*
	iūdicō, iūdicāre, iūdicāvī, iūdicātus	*judge, pass judgment on*
	iugulum, iugulī, *n.*	*throat*
	Iūlia, Iūliae, *f.*	*Julia*
	Iūlius, Iūliī, *m.*	*Julius*
	iungō, iungere, iūnxī, iūnctus	*join, link*
	iūnior, iūnior, iūnius	*younger*
	Iūnius, Iūnia, Iūnium	*of June*
	Iūnō, Iūnōnis, *f.*	*Juno (queen of the gods)*
	Iuppiter, Iovis, *m.*	*Jupiter (king of the gods)*
	iussī	see iubeō
	iussum, iussī, *n.*	*order, command*
	iussus, iussūs, *m.*	*order, command*
	iussus	see iubeō
	iūstitia, iūstitiae, *f.*	*justice*
	iūstus, iūsta, iūstum	*right, proper*
5	iuvenis, iuvenis, *m.f.*	*young person*
	iuventūs, iuventūtis, *f.*	*youth*
30	iuvō, iuvāre, iūvī, iūtus	*help, assist*
	iuxtā + *acc.*	*near, close to*

K

	Latin	English
	Kalendae, Kalendārum, *f. pl.*	*Kalends, first day of the month*

L

	Latin	English
	lābor, lābī, lāpsus sum	*slip*
13	labor, labōris, *m.*	*work*
1	labōrō, labōrāre, labōrāvī, labōrātus	*work*
	lac, lactis, *n.*	*milk*
19	lacrima, lacrimae, *f.*	*tear*
9	lacrimō, lacrimāre, lacrimāvī, lacrimātus	*cry, weep*
	lacūna, lacūnae, *f.*	*ditch, pond*
	lacus, lacūs, *m.*	*tub, basin*
	laetē	*happily, gladly*
	laetitia, laetitiae, *f.*	*joy, happiness*
3	laetus, laeta, laetum	*happy*
	lambō, lambere, lambī	*lick, lap*
	lāmentor, lāmentārī, lāmentātus sum	*wail, weep*
	lanista, lanistae, *m.*	*trainer (of gladiators)*
	lapicīdīnae, lapicīdīnārum, *f. pl.*	*stone quarries*
	Lar, Laris, *m.*	*household god, Lar*
	larārium, larāriī, *n.*	*lararium (shrine to the household gods)*
	larva, larvae, *f.*	*skeleton*
	lātrō, lātrāre, lātrāvī	*bark*
	latrō, latrōnis, *m.*	*bandit, robber*
26	lātus, lāta, lātum	*wide, broad*
	lātus	see ferō
4	laudō, laudāre, laudāvī, laudātus	*praise, admire*
	laurus, laurī, *f.*	*laurel, bay*
	lavō, lavāre, lāvī, lautus	*wash, soak*
	Lēander, Lēandrī, *m.*	*Leander*
	lectīca, lectīcae, *f.*	*litter (portable couch)*
	lectus, lectī, *m.*	*bed*
25	lēgātus, lēgātī, *m.*	*governor; commander*
18	legiō, legiōnis, *f.*	*legion*
1,16	legō, legere, lēgī, lēctus	*read; choose*
	lēniter	*gently*
19	lentē	*slowly*
	lentius	*more slowly*
17	lentus, lenta, lentum	*slow*
	leō, leōnis, *m.*	*lion*
	lepus, leporis, *m.*	*hare; darling*
	lēx, lēgis, *f.*	*law*
	ex lēge	*according to law*
17	libenter	*willingly, gladly*
29	līber, lībera, līberum	*free*
27	liber, librī, *m.*	*book*
9	līberī, līberōrum, *m. pl.*	*children*
17	līberō, līberāre, līberāvī, līberātus	*free, set free*
	līberta, lībertae, *f.*	*freedwoman, former slave*
20	lībertās, lībertātis, *f.*	*freedom*
15	lībertus, lībertī, *m.*	*freedman, former slave*
18	licet, licēre, licuit, licitum est	*it is allowed, one may*
	ligō, ligāre, ligāvī, ligātus	*tie, bind*
	līnea, līneae, *f.*	*line, string, thread*
	lingua, linguae, *f.*	*language, tongue*
	littera, litterae, *f.*	*letter*
31	lītus, lītoris, *n.*	*shore, beach*

	Līvius, Līviī, *m.*	*Livius*
10	locus, locī, *m.*	*place*
	Lōcusta, Lōcustae, *f.*	*Locusta*
	locūtus	see loquor
21	longē	*far off*
13	longus, longa, longum	*long*
	loquāx, loquācis	*talkative, chatty*
22	loquor, loquī, locūtus sum	*speak, talk*
	Luccus, Luccī, *m.*	*Luccus*
	lūceō, lūcēre, lūxī	*shine*
	Lūcīlius, Lūcīliī, *m.*	*Lucilius*
	Lūcius, Lūciī, *m.*	*Lucius*
	Lūcriō, Lūcriōnis, *m.*	*Lucrio*
	lucrum, lucrī, *n.*	*money, profit*
	luctor, luctārī, luctātus sum	*wrestle*
	lūdō, lūdere, lūsī, lūsus	*play, am at leisure*
	lūdus, lūdī, *m.*	*game; pl. = races; gladiator training ground*
	Lugdūnēnsis, Lugdūnēnsis, Lugdūnēnse	*Lugdunensis, of Lugdunum (modern Lyon)*
	lūna, lūnae, *f.*	*moon*
16	lūx, lūcis, *f.*	*light, daylight*
	lyra, lyrae, *f.*	*lyre*

M

	magicus, magica, magicum	*magic*
31	magis	*more, rather*
	magister, magistrī, *m.*	*employer*
	magistra, magistrae, *f.*	*teacher*
	magnificus, magnifica, magnificum	*magnificent, wonderful, amazing*
26	magnopere	*greatly, very much*
2	magnus, magna, magnum	*big, large, great*
	maiestās, maiestātis, *f.*	*majesty, authority*
25	maior, maior, maius	*bigger, larger, greater*
	maleficum, maleficī, *n.*	*wicked charm*
31	mālō, mālle, māluī	*prefer*
	mālum, mālī, *n.*	*apple*
18	malus, mala, malum	*bad, evil*
	māne	*in the morning*
5	maneō, manēre, mānsī	*remain, stay*
	Mānēs, Mānium, *m. pl.*	*Manes (spirits of the dead)*
24	manus, manūs, *f.*	*hand; group (of people), gang, crew*
	Marcus, Marcī, *m.*	*Marcus*
11	mare, maris, *n.*	*sea*
	marīnus, marīna, marīnum	*of the sea, marine*
6	marītus, marītī, *m.*	*husband*
	Marius, Mariī, *m.*	*Marius*
	Martius, Martia, Martium	*of March*
	Marus, Marī, *m.*	*Marus*
6	māter, mātris, *f.*	*mother*
	mātrimōnium, mātrimōniī, *n.*	*marriage*
	in matrimōnium dūcō	*marry*
	mātrōna, mātrōnae, *f.*	*lady, married woman*
	Mausōlēum, Mausōlēī, *n.*	*Mausoleum, tomb of Augustus*
23	maximē	*very much, a lot, very greatly*
19	maximus, maxima, maximum	*very big, huge; biggest, greatest*
	medica, medicae, *f.*	*doctor (female)*
	medicāmentum, medicāmentī, *n.*	*medicine, drug*
	medicīnus, medicīna, medicīnum	*of medicine*
	medicus, medicī, *m.*	*doctor (male)*
9	medius, media, medium	*middle, middle of*
	Medūsa, Medūsae, *f.*	*Medusa*
	mehercle!	*good heavens! by Hercules!*
	mel, mellis, *n.*	*honey*
19	melior, melior, melius	*better*
	meminī, meminisse	*remember*
	memorō, memorāre, memorāvī, memorātus	*bring to mind, recall*
	Menander, Menandrī, *m.*	*Menander*
	mendāx, mendācis, *m.f.*	*liar*
	mendīcus, mendīcī, *m.*	*beggar*
31	mēns, mentis, *f.*	*mind*
	mēnsa, mēnsae, *f.*	*table*
	mēnsis, mēnsis, *m.*	*month*
	mercātor, mercātōris, *m.*	*merchant*
	mercēs, mercum, *f. pl.*	*trade, goods*
	mereō, merēre, meruī, meritus	*serve; deserve, earn*
	metuō, metuere, metuī, metūtus	*fear, dread*
27	metus, metūs, *m.*	*fear*
1	meus, mea, meum	*my*
7	mīles, mīlitis, *m.*	*soldier*
	mille, pl. mīlia, *n.*	*thousand*
7, 24	minimē	*no; not at all, very little*
25	minimus, minima, minimum	*very small, tiny*
23	minor, minor, minus	*smaller; younger; less*
	mīrābilis, mīrābilis, mīrābile	*strange, wonderful*
22	mīror, mīrārī, mīrātus sum	*wonder at, admire; be amazed*
10	miser, misera, miserum	*poor, unfortunate, sad*
	misereor, miserērī, miseritus sum	*pity, feel sorry for*
12	mittō, mittere, mīsī, missus	*send*
	mixtus, mixta, mixtum	*mixed*

27 modo — *only*
  modo ... modo ... — *sometimes ... sometimes ...*
  nōn modo ... sed etiam ... — *not only ... but also ...*
26 modus, modī, *m.* — *way, manner, style*
moenia, moenium, *n. pl.* — *town walls*
Moesia, Moesiae, *f.* — *Moesia*
molestus, molesta, molestum — *annoying*
mōmentum, mōmentī, *n.* — *importance*
27 moneō, monēre, monuī, monitus — *advise, warn*
14 mōns, montis, *m.* — *mountain*
morbus, morbī, *m.* — *illness*
22 morior, morī, mortuus sum — *die*
14 mors, mortis, *f.* — *death*
19 mortuus, mortua, mortuum — *dead*
mōrus, mōrī, *f.* — *mulberry tree*
32 mōs, mōris, *m.* — *way, fashion, custom*
29 moveō, movēre, mōvī, mōtus — *move*
8 mox — *soon*
mulceō, mulcēre, mulsī, mulsus — *stroke*
mulier, mulieris, *f.* — *woman*
multitūdō, multitūdinis, *f.* — *large number, crowd*
19 multō — *much, by much*
15 multum — *much*
3 multus, multa, multum — *much; pl. = many, a lot of*
mūnus, mūneris, *n.* — *gladiatorial show*
murmillō, murmillōnis, *m.* — *murmillo (type of gladiator)*
murmurō, murmurāre, murmurāvī, murmurātus — *mutter*
13 mūrus, mūrī, *m.* — *wall*
mūs, mūris, *m.* — *mouse; rat*
mūsica, mūsicae, *f.* — *music*
mūsicus, mūsicī, *m.f.* — *musician*
mustum, mustī, *n.* — *must (unfermented grape juice)*
24 mūtō, mūtāre, mūtāvī, mūtātus — *change*

N

18 nam — *for, because*
7 nārrō, nārrāre, nārrāvī, nārrātus — *tell, relate*
nascor, nascī, nātus sum — *am born*
nāsus, nāsī, *m.* — *nose*
nātūra, nātūrae, *f.* — *nature*
nātus — see nascor
7 nauta, nautae, *m.* — *sailor*
11 nāvigō, nāvigāre, nāvigāvī, nāvigātus — *sail*
11 nāvis, nāvis, *f.* — *ship*
25 nē + *subj.* — *so that ... not, that ... not*
nebula, nebulae, *f.* — *mist*
14 nec — *and not, nor, neither*
14 nec ... nec ... — *neither ... nor ...*
18 necesse — *necessary*
14 necō, necāre, necāvī, necātus — *kill*
30 negō, negāre, negāvī, negātus — *deny, say that ... not*
negōtium, negōtiī, *n.* — *business*
5 nēmō, nēminis, *m.f.* — *no one, nobody*
Neptūnus, Neptūnī, *m.* — *Neptune (god of the sea)*
19 neque — *and not, nor, neither*
19 neque ... neque ... — *neither ... nor ...*
Nerō, Nerōnis, *m.* — *Nero*
14 nesciō, nescīre, nescīvī — *don't know*
8 nihil — *nothing*
nihilōminus — *nevertheless*
nimium — *too (much)*
29 nisi — *unless, except*
nōbilis, nōbilis, nōbile — *noble, renowned*
noceō, nocēre, nocuī, nocitus — *harm*
nocturnus, nocturna, nocturnum — *of night*
5 nōlō, nōlle, nōluī — *don't want, refuse*
13 nōmen, nōminis, *n.* — *name*
nōminō, nōmināre, nōmināvī, nōminātus — *name, nominate*
1 nōn — *not*
  nōn modo ... sed etiam ... — *not only ... but also ...*
32 nōndum — *not yet*
15 nōnne? — *surely?*
28 nōnnūllī, nōnnūllae, nōnnūlla *pl.* — *some, several*
4 nōs, nostrum — *we, us*
8 noster, nostra, nostrum — *our*
nōtus, nōta, nōtum — *known, familiar*
26 novem — *nine*
10 novus, nova, novum — *new*
5 nox, noctis, *f.* — *night*
nūbēs, nūbis, *f.* — *cloud*
nūdus, nūda, nūdum — *bare, naked*
10 nūllus, nūlla, nūllum — *no, not any*
23 num? — *surely not?*
25 num — *whether*
30 nūmen, nūminis, *n.* — *deity, divine power*
Numerius, Numeriī, *m.* — *Numerius*
numerō, numerāre, numerāvī, numerātus — *count*
31 numerus, numerī, *m.* — *number*
14 numquam — *never*
7 nunc — *now*

	Latin	English
15	nūntiō, nūntiāre, nūntiāvī, nūntiātus	*announce, report*
9	nūntius, nūntiī, *m.*	*messenger; message, news*
	nūper	*recently, not long ago*
	nusquam	*nowhere*
	nūtō, nūtāre, nūtāvī	*nod*
	Nymphius, Nymphiī, *m.*	*Nymphius*

O

	Latin	English
	ō!	*o!*
	ob + *acc.*	*because of*
	obdormiō, obdormīre, obdormīvī	*go to sleep, fall asleep*
	oblātus	see offerō
	obrēpō, obrēpere, obrēpsī, obrēptus	*creep up on*
	obscūrus, obscūra, obscūrum	*dark*
	obsideō, obsidēre, obsēdī, obsessus	*besiege*
	obstetrīx, obstetrīcis, *f.*	*midwife*
	obstupefaciō, obstupefacere, obstupefēcī, obstupefactus	*astonish, amaze*
	obtineō, obtinēre, obtinuī, obtentus	*gain, obtain*
	obtulī	see offerō
	Ocar, Ocaris, *m.*	*Ocar*
10	occīdō, occīdere, occīdī, occīsus	*kill*
	occupātus, occupāta, occupātum	*busy*
	occupō, occupāre, occupāvī, occupātus	*occupy, keep busy*
	Ocella, Ocellae, *m.*	*Ocella*
	octo	*eight*
	Oculātius, Oculātiī, *m.*	*Oculatius*
19	oculus, oculī, *m.*	*eye*
	ōdī, ōdisse	*hate*
	odor, odōris, *m.*	*smell, scent*
	offa, offae, *f.*	*piece of food*
	offendō, offendere, offendī, offēnsus	*offend, displease*
12	offerō, offerre, obtulī, oblātus	*offer*
	officīna, officīnae, *f.*	*workshop*
	ohē!	*hey!*
	olea, oleae, *f.*	*olive tree*
	olfaciō, olfacere, olfēcī, olfactus	*smell*
7	ōlim	*once, some time ago*
	Olympia, Olympiae, *f.*	*Olympia (town in Greece)*
	Olympiacus, Olympiaca, Olympiacum	*Olympic*
	ōmen, ōminis, *n.*	*omen, sign*
3	omnis, omnis, omne	*all, every*
	operārius, operāriī, *m.*	*workman*
	oportet, oportēre, oportuit	*it is necessary for, it is proper for*
	oppidum, oppidī, *n.*	*town*
30	opprimō, opprimere, oppressī, oppressus	*crush, overwhelm*
17	oppugnō, oppugnāre, oppugnāvī, oppugnātus	*attack*
	optimē	*very well*
19	optimus, optima, optimum	*very good, excellent; best*
	optiō, optiōnis, *m.*	*optio (army officer, second-in-command in a century)*
24	opus, operis, *n.*	*work*
	opus est mihi	*I need*
	ōrāculum, ōrāculī, *n.*	*oracle*
	ōrātiō, ōrātiōnis, *f.*	*speech*
29	orbis, orbis, *m.*	*globe, sphere*
	orbis terrārum	*world*
	orior, orīrī, ortus sum	*rise, arise*
16	ōrō, ōrāre, ōrāvī, ōrātus	*beg, beg for*
	oryx, orygis, *m.*	*gazelle*
30	ōs, ōris, *n.*	*mouth*
	os, ossis, *n.*	*bone*
	ōsculum, ōsculī, *n.*	*kiss*
14	ostendō, ostendere, ostendī, ostentus	*show*
	Othō, Othōnis, *m.*	*Otho*

P

	Latin	English
	paedagōgus, paedagōgī, *m.*	*paedagogus (enslaved person who took child to school)*
17	paene	*almost, nearly*
	paenitet, paenitēre	*am sorry, regret*
	mē paenitet	*I am sorry*
	pah!	*pah! pff!*
	palaestra, palaestrae, *f.*	*exercise ground*
	Palātīnus, Palātīna, Palātīnum	*Palatine (hill in Rome)*
	palla, pallae, *f.*	*robe*
	Palmȳra, Palmȳrae, *f.*	*Palmyra*
	pānis, pānis, *m.*	*bread*
23	parātus, parāta, parātum	*ready*
	parcō, parcere, pepercī + *dat.*	*spare, am sparing of*
	pardus, pardī, *m.*	*leopard*
23	parēns, parentis, *m.f.*	*parent*
25	pāreō, pārēre, pāruī + *dat.*	*obey*
	pariō, parere, peperī, partus	*give birth*
	Parnāsus, Parnāsī, *m.*	*Parnassus (mountain at Delphi)*
13	parō, parāre, parāvī, parātus	*prepare*
	parricīdium, parricīdiī, *n.*	*murder of a relative*
7	pars, partis, *f.*	*part*

	Latin	English
	Parthenōn, Parthenōnis, *m.*	*Parthenon (temple to Athena)*
	partus, partūs, *m.*	*birth*
4	parvus, parva, parvum	*small*
	pāscor, pāscī, pāstus sum	*feed, eat*
1	pater, patris, *m.*	*father*
22	patior, patī, passus sum	*suffer, endure*
31	patria, patriae, *f.*	*homeland*
	patrōnus, patrōnī, *m.*	*patron*
9	paucī, paucae, pauca *pl.*	*few, a few*
	paulātim	*gradually*
	paulisper	*for a short time, for a little while*
	paulum, paulī, *n.*	*a little bit*
	pauper, pauperis	*poor*
	pauper, pauperis, *m.f.*	*poor person*
	pavīmentum, pavīmentī, *n.*	*floor*
10	pāx, pācis, *f.*	*peace*
27	pectus, pectoris, *n.*	*chest, breast*
2	pecūnia, pecūniae, *f.*	*money, sum of money*
26	peior, peior, peius	*worse*
30	pellō, pellere, pepulī, pulsus	*drive, push*
	peperī	see pariō
3	per + *acc.*	*through, along*
	perdō, perdere, perdidī, perditus	*destroy, waste*
10	pereō, perīre, periī, peritus	*die, perish*
	perfodiō, perfodere, perfōdī, perfossus	*dig, dig through*
	perīculōsus, perīculōsa, perīculōsum	*dangerous*
4	perīculum, perīculī, *n.*	*danger*
	Perilla, Perillae, *f.*	*Perilla*
	peristȳlium, peristȳliī, *n.*	*peristyle (courtyard surrounded by columns)*
	perītē	*skillfully*
	perītus, perīta, perītum	*skillful*
	perrumpō, perrumpere, perrūpī, perruptus	*break through*
	Persa, Persae, *m.*	*Persian*
	persevērō, persevērāre, persevērāvī, persevērātus	*carry on*
20	persuādeō, persuādēre, persuāsī, persuāsus + *dat.*	*persuade*
4	perterritus, perterrita, perterritum	*terrified*
18	perveniō, pervenīre, pervēnī, perventus	*arrive, reach*
21	pēs, pedis, *m.*	*foot*
	pessimē	*very badly*
26	pessimus, pessima, pessimum	*very bad, worst*
9, 21	petō, petere, petīvī, petītus	*attack; beg, ask for; make for; seek*
	pff!	*pff!*
	Phaōn, Phaontis, *m.*	*Phaon (freedman of Nero)*
	Pherenīcē, Pherenīcēs, *f.*	*Pherenice*
	Philō, Philōnis, *m.*	*Philo*
	philosophia, philosophiae, *f.*	*philosophy*
	philosophus, philosophī, *m.*	*philosopher*
	philtrum, philtrī, *n.*	*potion*
	Phoebē, Phoebēs, *f.*	*Phoebe*
	phoenicopterus, phoenicopterī, *m.*	*flamingo*
	pietās, pietātis, *f.*	*sense of duty, piety*
	pigmentum, pigmentī, *n.*	*paint, pigment*
	pila, pilae, *f.*	*ball*
	pīlum, pīlī, *n.*	*javelin*
	piscis, piscis, *m.*	*fish*
	pistor, pistōris, *m.*	*baker*
	pistrīnum, pistrīnī, *n.*	*bakery*
	pittacium, pittaciī, *n.*	*label*
18	placeō, placēre, placuī + *dat.*	*please*
	mihi placet	*I like*
	placidus, placida, placidum	*gentle, peaceful*
	plaudō, plaudere, plausī, plausus	*clap, applaud*
	plaustrum, plaustrī, *n.*	*wagon, cart*
17	plēnus, plēna, plēnum	*full*
	plumbārius, plumbārius, *m.*	*plumber*
	pluō, pluere, plūvī	*rain*
	plūrēs, plūrium *pl.*	*more*
	plūrimī, plūrimae, plūrima *pl.*	*very many*
	plūrimum	*very much, most of all*
23	plūs, plūris, *n.*	*more*
	pōculum, pōculī, *n.*	*cup*
21	poena, poenae, *f.*	*penalty, punishment*
21	poenās dō	*pay the penalty, am punished*
	poēta, poētae, *m.*	*poet*
	pollex, pollicis, *m.*	*thumb*
	pompa, pompae, *f.*	*procession*
	Pompēiānus, Pompēiānī, *m.*	*Pompeian*
	Pompēiī, Pompēiōrum, *m. pl.*	*Pompeii (town in Italy)*
19	pōnō, pōnere, posuī, positus	*put, place*
	pōns, pontis, *m.*	*bridge*
	Popidius, Popidiī, *m.*	*Popidius*
	popīna, popīnae, *f.*	*bar*
	popīnāria, popīnāriae, *f.*	*barkeeper, bar owner*
32	populus, populī, *m.*	*people*
8	porta, portae, *f.*	*gate, grate*
	porticus, porticūs, *f.*	*portico, colonnade, arcade*
5	portō, portāre, portāvī, portātus	*carry, bear, take*

	portus, portūs, *m.*	*harbor*
29	poscō, poscere, poposcī	*ask for, demand*
	positus	see pōnō
5	possum, posse, potuī	*am able, can*
13	post + *acc.*	*after, behind*
23	posteā	*afterwards*
8	postquam	*after, when*
	postrēmō	*at last*
	postrēmus, postrēma, postrēmum	*last, final*
21	postrīdiē	*on the following day*
25	postulō, postulāre, postulāvī, postulātus	*demand*
	Postumus, Postumī, *m.*	*Postumus*
	posuī	see pōnō
	potēns, potentis	*powerful*
	pōtiō, pōtiōnis, *f.*	*potion*
	potius	*rather*
	potuī	see possum
17	praebeō, praebēre, praebuī, praebitus	*provide*
	praecō, praecōnis, *m.*	*town crier, herald*
	praedīcō, praedīcere, praedīxī, praedictus	*predict*
	praedium, praediī, *n.*	*land, estate*
	praefectus, praefectī, *m.*	*commander*
13	praemium, praemiī, *n.*	*prize, reward, profit*
	praescrīptum, praescrīptī, *n.*	*recipe*
	praesum, praeesse, praefuī	*am in charge*
	praeter + *acc.*	*except, apart from*
	praetereā	*besides, furthermore*
	praetor, praetōris, *m.*	*praetor*
	praetōriānus, praetōriāna, praetōriānum	*praetorian, bodyguard*
22	precor, precārī, precātus sum	*pray, pray to*
	prehendō, prehendere, prehendī, prehēnsus	*grab, seize*
	premō, premere, pressī, pressus	*press*
	pretium, pretiī, *n.*	*price*
	prīdiē	*the day before, on the previous day*
27	prīmō	*at first*
32	prīmum	*for the first time*
	quam prīmum	*as soon as possible*
3	prīmus, prīma, prīmum	*first*
16	prīnceps, prīncipis, *m.*	*chief; emperor*
	prīncipia, prīncipiōrum, *n. pl.*	*headquarters (of camp)*
	priusquam	*before*
	prīvātus, prīvāta, prīvātum	*private*
11, 17	prō + *abl.*	*in front of; for, in return for; on behalf of, in the name of*
	prō certō habeō	*know for certain, am sure*
8	prōcēdō, prōcēdere, prōcessī	*go along, advance, proceed*
	prōcōnsul, prōcōnsulis, *m.*	*governor*
32	procul	*far off*
	prōcūrātor, prōcūrātōris, *m.*	*procurator (province's finance officer)*
31	proelium, proeliī, *n.*	*battle*
22	proficīscor, proficīscī, profectus sum	*set out*
22	prōgredior, prōgredī, prōgressus sum	*go forward, advance*
	prohibeō, prohibēre, prohibuī, prohibitus	*prevent*
	Promētheus, Promētheī, *m.*	*Prometheus (mythical sculptor, created mankind)*
18	prōmittō, prōmittere, prōmīsī, prōmissus	*promise*
6	prope + *acc.*	*near*
	propinquitās, propinquitātis, *f.*	*closeness, proximity*
	propinquus, propinqua, propinquum	*nearby*
	propius	*nearer*
21	propter + *acc.*	*on account of, because of*
	Propylaea, Propylaeōrum, *n. pl.*	*Propylaea (gateway to the Acropolis)*
	prōspectus, prōspectūs, *m.*	*view*
	prōtegō, prōtegere, prōtēxī, prōtēctus	*protect*
	prōvincia, prōvinciae, *f.*	*province*
	prōvocātiō, prōvocātiōnis, *f.*	*challenge, appeal*
22	proximus, proxima, proximum	*nearest; next to*
	psittacus, psittacī, *m.*	*parrot*
32	pūblicus, pūblica, pūblicum	*public*
	rēs pūblica, reī pūblicae, *f.*	*state*
4	puella, puellae, *f.*	*girl*
7	puer, puerī, *m.*	*boy*
	pugiō, pugiōnis, *m.*	*dagger*
	pugna, pugnae, *f.*	*fight, battle*
7	pugnō, pugnāre, pugnāvī, pugnātus	*fight*
5	pulcher, pulchra, pulchrum	*beautiful, handsome*
	pullārius, pullāriī, *m.*	*keeper of chickens*
	pullus, pullī, *m.*	*chicken*
	pulsō, pulsāre, pulsāvī, pulsātus	*beat*
	pulvis, pulveris, *m.*	*dust*
	Pūnicus, Pūnica, Pūnicum	*Punic, Carthaginian*
30	pūniō, pūnīre, pūnīvī, pūnītus	*punish*
	puppis, puppis, *m.*	*stern*
15	putō, putāre, putāvī, putātus	*think*
	Pȳthia, Pȳthiae, *f.*	*Pythia (priestess of Apollo)*
	pyxis, pyxidis, *f.*	*small box*

Q

	Latin	English
	quadrīga, quadrīgae, *f.*	*chariot*
	quadrupēs, quadrupedis	*on all fours*
2	quaerō, quaerere, quaesīvī, quaesītus	*look for, search for; ask*
	quaestor, quaestōris, *m.*	*quaestor*
23	quālis, quālis, quāle?	*what sort of?*
10	quam	*(1) how ... ! how ... ?*
18	quam	*(2) than*
17	quam + *superlative*	*(3) as ... as possible*
	quam celerrimē	*as quickly as possible*
	quam prīmum	*as soon as possible*
13	quamquam	*although*
30	quandō?	*when?*
23	quantus, quanta, quantum?	*how big? how much?*
	Quārtilla, Quārtillae, *f.*	*Quartilla*
	quārtus, quārta, quārtum	*fourth*
	quasi	*as if*
26	quattuor	*four*
13	quī, quae, quod	*who, which*
28	quīdam, quaedam, quoddam	*one, a certain, pl. = some*
	quidem	*indeed, certainly*
	quiēscō, quiēscere, quiēvi, quiētus	*rest*
	quiētē	*quietly*
	quiētus, quiēta, quiētum	*quiet*
	quīnquāgintā	*fifty*
26	quīnque	*five*
	quīntus, quīnta, quīntum	*fifth*
12	quis? quid?	*who? what?*
	quid?	*how?*
16	quō?	*to where?*
4	quod	*because*
13	quōmodo?	*how? in what way?*
2	quoque	*also, too*
21	quot?	*how many?*

R

	Latin	English
	rādix, rādīcis, *f.*	*foothill*
16	rapiō, rapere, rapuī, raptus	*seize, grab*
	rastellus, rastellī, *m.*	*hoe, mattock*
	raucus, rauca, raucum	*hoarse*
	rebelliō, rebelliōnis, *f.*	*rebellion*
	recitātiō, recitātiōnis, *f.*	*recitation, public reading*
	recitō, recitāre, recitāvī, recitātus	*recite*
	rēctē	*rightly, correctly*
	recumbō, recumbere, recubuī	*recline, lie down*
	redargūtiō, redargūtiōnis, *f.*	*contempt*
24	reddō, reddere, reddidī, redditus	*give back, restore*
12	redeō, redīre, rediī, reditus	*go back, come back, return*
19	referō, referre, rettulī, relātus	*carry back; report*
	reficiō, reficere, refēcī, refectus	*fix, mend, repair*
16	rēgīna, rēgīnae, *f.*	*queen*
	regiō, regiōnis, *f.*	*region, area*
31	rēgnum, rēgnī, *n.*	*kingdom*
29	regō, regere, rēxī, rēctus	*rule*
22	regredior, regredī, regressus sum	*go back, return*
	relātus	see referō
17	relinquō, relinquere, relīquī, relictus	*leave, leave behind*
	remittō, remittere, remīsī, remissus	*send back*
	rēmus, rēmī, *m.*	*oar*
	repente	*suddenly*
	rēpō, rēpere, rēpsī	*crawl*
	repōnō, repōnere, reposuī, repositus	*put back*
	reprimō, reprimere, repressī, repressus	*suppress*
	reputō, reputāre, reputāvī, reputātus	*consider*
	requīrō, requīrere, requīsīvī, requīsītus	*require, need*
7, 25	rēs, reī, *f.*	*story; thing, business, matter, event*
	rēs pūblica, reī pūblicae, *f.*	*state*
16	resistō, resistere, restitī + *dat.*	*resist*
	resonō, resonāre, resonāvī, resonātus	*resound*
	respiciō, respicere, respexī, respectus	*look back at*
5	respondeō, respondēre, respondī, respōnsus	*reply*
	retineō, retinēre, retinuī, retentus	*hold back, restrain*
	rettulī	see referō
16	reveniō, revenīre, revēnī, reventus	*come back, return*
	revocō, revocāre, revocāvī, revocātus	*call back*
4	rēx, rēgis, *m.*	*king*
	rhētor, rhētoris, *m.*	*teacher of oratory*
1	rīdeō, rīdēre, rīsī	*laugh; smile*
	rīdiculus, rīdicula, rīdiculum	*laughable*
	rīsī	see rīdeō
6	rogō, rogāre, rogāvī, rogātus	*ask, ask for*
	rogus, rogī, *m.*	*funeral pyre*
12	Rōma, Rōmae, *f.*	*Rome*
	Rōmae	*in/at Rome*
32	Rōmānī, Rōmānōrum, *m. pl.*	*Romans*
4	Rōmānus, Rōmāna, Rōmānum	*Roman*
	rōstrum, rōstrī, *n.*	*beak*

	rota, rotae, *f.*	*wheel*
	rudis, rudis, *f.*	*wooden sword*
	Rūfīna, Rūfīnae, *f.*	*Rufina*
	Rūfus, Rūfī, *m.*	*Rufus*
	rumpō, rumpere, rūpī, ruptus	*break*
	ruō, ruere, ruī, rutus	*rush*
	rūpēs, rūpis, *f.*	*cliff*
	rūsticus, rūstica, rūsticum	*in the country*

S

	Sabīna, Sabīnae, *f.*	*Sabina*
	sacculus, sacculī, *m.*	*purse*
	saccus, saccī, *m.*	*sack, bag*
10	sacer, sacra, sacrum	*sacred, holy*
	sacerdōs, sacerdōtis, *m.f.*	*priest*
	sacrificium, sacrificiī, *n.*	*sacrifice, offering*
7	saepe	*often*
11	saevus, saeva, saevum	*savage, cruel*
	sāga, sāgae, *f.*	*witch*
	saliō, salīre, saluī	*jump*
	saltem	*at least, in any case*
	saltō, saltāre, saltāvī, saltātus	*dance*
	salūs, salūtis, *f.*	*safety; greeting*
	salūtātiō, salūtātiōnis, *f.*	*morning greeting*
2	salūtō, salūtāre, salūtāvī, salūtātus	*greet*
	salvē! salvēte!	*hello! hi!*
	Salvius, Salviī, *m.*	*Salvius*
	sanguineus, sanguinea, sanguineum	*bloody*
9	sanguis, sanguinis, *m.*	*blood*
	sānō, sānāre, sānāvī, sānātus	*heal*
28	sapiēns, sapientis	*wise*
	sapientia, sapientiae, *f.*	*wisdom*
	sarcina, sarcinae, *f.*	*large bag*
	Sarnus, Sarnī, *m.*	*Sarno (river near Pompeii)*
32	satis	*enough*
24	saxum, saxī, *n.*	*rock*
	scaena, scaenae, *f.*	*stage*
	scālae, scālārum, *f. pl.*	*ladder*
	Scaurus, Scaurī, *m.*	*Scaurus*
25	scelestus, scelesta, scelestum	*wicked*
28	scelus, sceleris, *n.*	*crime*
16	sciō, scīre, scīvī, scītus	*know*
	scrība, scrībae, *m.*	*local official*
18	scrībō, scrībere, scrīpsī, scrīptus	*write*
	sculpō, sculpere, sculpsī, sculptus	*carve, sculpt*
	scūtum, scūtī, *n.*	*shield*
15	sē, suī	*himself, herself, itself, themselves*
	Sebastēion, Sebastēiī, *n.*	*Sebasteion (temple dedicated to Augustus)*
	sēcūrus, sēcūra, sēcūrum	*safe*
	secūtus	see sequor
2	sed	*but*
6	sedeō, sedēre, sēdī	*sit, sit down*
	sēditiōsus, sēditiōsa, sēditiōsum	*seditious, treasonous*
	sēdō, sēdāre, sēdāvī, sēdātus	*settle, calm down*
	sella, sellae, *f.*	*chair*
	sēmita, sēmitae, *f.*	*footpath, track*
13	semper	*always*
3	senātor, senātōris, *m.*	*senator*
32	senātus, senātūs, *m.*	*Senate*
	senex, senis	*old*
8	senex, senis, *m.f.*	*old person*
	sententia, sententiae, *f.*	*opinion*
16	sentiō, sentīre, sēnsī, sēnsus	*feel, notice*
26	septem	*seven*
	sepulcrum, sepulcrī, *n.*	*tomb; grave*
22	sequor, sequī, secūtus sum	*follow*
	sermō, sermōnis, *m.*	*conversation, talk*
	sērō	*too late*
12	servō, servāre, servāvī, servātus	*save, protect, keep, look after*
1	servus, servī, *m.*	*slave, enslaved person (male)*
	sextus, sexta, sextum	*sixth*
16	sī	*if*
19	sīc	*so, in this way*
	siccō, siccāre, siccāvī, siccātus	*dry*
	Sicilia, Siciliae, *f.*	*Sicily*
19	sīcut	*just as, like*
	sīdus, sīderis, *n.*	*star*
23	signum, signī, *n.*	*sign, signal; seal; military standard*
	silentium, silentiī, *n.*	*silence*
7	silva, silvae, *f.*	*wood, forest*
	sīmia, sīmiae, *f.*	*ape, monkey*
29	similis, similis, simile	*similar, alike*
30	simul	*at the same time*
26	simulac	*as soon as*
15	simulatque	*as soon as*
	simulō, simulāre, simulāvī, simulātus	*pretend*
16	sine + *abl.*	*without*
	societās, societātis, *f.*	*company*
	socius, sociī, *m.*	*ally, colleague*
17	sōl, sōlis, *m.*	*sun*
	sōlārium, sōlāriī, *n.*	*sundial*
27	soleō, solēre, solitus sum	*am accustomed, used*
	sōlitūdō, sōlitūdinis, *f.*	*solitude, pl. = desert*

	Latin	English
	sollicitus, sollicita, sollicitum	*worried, anxious*
	sōlum	*only*
11	sōlus, sōla, sōlum	*alone, only, lonely, on one's own*
30	solvō, solvere, solvī, solūtus	*undo, let go*
	somnium, somniī, *n.*	*dream*
29	somnus, somnī, *m.*	*sleep*
	sonitus, sonitūs, *m.*	*sound, noise*
	Sōrānos, Sōrānī, *m.*	*Soranos*
	sordidus, sordida, sordidum	*dirty*
23	soror, sorōris, *f.*	*sister*
	spargō, spargere, sparsī, sparsus	*shower, spray*
	speciēs, speciēī, *f.*	*appearance*
	spectāculum, spectāculī, *n.*	*sight, spectacle*
	spectātor, spectātōris, *m.*	*spectator*
2	spectō, spectāre, spectāvī, spectātus	*look at, watch*
	specula, speculae, *f.*	*watchtower*
	speculum, speculī, *n.*	*mirror*
24	spērō, spērāre, spērāvī, spērātus	*hope, expect*
25	spēs, speī, *f.*	*hope*
	Spīculus, Spīculī, *m.*	*Spiculus*
	spīrō, spīrāre, spīrāvī, spīrātus	*breathe*
	splendidus, splendida, splendidum	*splendid, sumptuous*
	sponte	*of one's own accord, spontaneously*
	sportula, sportulae, *f.*	*little basket, money*
	spūma, spūmae, *f.*	*foam, froth*
	st!	*hey!*
	stabulum, stabulī, *n.*	*stable*
	stāgnum, stāgnī, *n.*	*pool*
	Stalliānus, Stalliānī, *m.*	*Stallianus*
9	statim	*at once, immediately*
	statua, statuae, *f.*	*statue*
	stercus, stercoris, *n.*	*dung, filth*
	sternō, sternere, strāvī, strātus	*spread out*
6	stō, stāre, stetī	*stand*
	stola, stolae, *f.*	*dress*
	strangulātus, strangulāta, strangulātum	*strangled*
	strēnuē	*strenuously, energetically, hard*
	strūthocamēlus, strūthocamēli, *m.*	*ostrich*
	studeō, studēre, studuī	*study, concentrate on*
12	stultus, stulta, stultum	*stupid, foolish*
10	sub + *acc.* or *abl.*	*under, below, beneath*
4	subitō	*suddenly*
	sublātus	see tollō
	Subūra, Subūrae, *f.*	*the Subura*
	Subūrānus, Subūrāna, Subūrānum	*from the Subura*
	Subūrānus, Subūrānī, *m.*	*inhabitant of the Subura*
	suburbānus, suburbāna, suburbānum	*near the city*
	subveniō, subvenīre, subvēnī, subventus + *dat.*	*help*
	subvertō, subvertere, subvertī, subversus	*overturn*
	sūdārium, sūdāriī, *n.*	*handkerchief*
	sūdor, sūdōris, *m.*	*sweat*
	Sulpicius, Sulpiciī, *m.*	*Sulpicius*
1	sum, esse, fuī	*I am, to be, I was*
13	summus, summa, summum	*highest, greatest, top (of)*
28	super + *acc.*	*over*
	superbus, superba, superbum	*proud, arrogant*
	superior, superior, superius	*upper*
12	superō, superāre, superāvī, superātus	*overcome, overpower*
	superstitiō, superstitiōnis, *f.*	*superstition*
	supersum, superesse, superfuī	*survive, stay alive*
	supplicō, supplicāre, supplicāvī, supplicātus	*pray to*
	suppūrō, suppūrāre, suppūrāvī, suppūrātus	*be infected, suppurate*
	suprā + *acc.*	*over, above*
8	surgō, surgere, surrēxī, surrēctus	*get up, stand up, rise*
	suspendō, suspendere, suspendī, suspēnsus	*hang, suspend*
	sustulī	see tollō
	susurrō, susurrāre, susurrāvī	*whisper*
13	suus, sua, suum	*her, his, its, their (own)*
	Syrācūsae, Syrācūsārum, *f. pl.*	*Syracuse (city in Sicily)*
	Syria, Syriae, *f.*	*Syria*

T

	Latin	English
	tabella, tabellae, *f.*	*writing tablet*
12	taberna, tabernae, *f.*	*shop, inn*
	tablīnum, tablīnī, *n.*	*tablinum (room next to the atrium)*
	tabula, tabulae, *f.*	*curse tablet*
5	taceō, tacēre, tacuī, tacitus	*am silent, am quiet*
	tacitē	*quietly, silently*
24	tālis, tālis, tāle	*such, of such a kind*
24	tam	*so*
13	tamen	*however*
8	tandem	*at last, finally*
	tangō, tangere, tetigī, tāctus	*touch*
24	tantus, tanta, tantum	*so great, such a great, so much*
	tardus, tarda, tardum	*late*
	Tarracōnēnsis, Tarracōnēnsis, Tarracōnēnse	*of Tarraconensis*
21	tēctum, tēctī, *n.*	*roof*

A B C D E F G H I K L M N O P Q R S T U V X Z

	Latin	English
	tēgula, tēgulae, *f.*	*roof tile*
20	tēlum, tēlī, *n.*	*missile, weapon, spear*
	temere	*rashly*
27	tempestās, tempestātis, *f.*	*storm*
4	templum, templī, *n.*	*temple*
28	temptō, temptāre, temptāvī, temptātus	*try*
14	tempus, temporis, *n.*	*time*
	tenebrae, tenebrārum, *f. pl.*	*darkness*
4	teneō, tenēre, tenuī, tentus	*hold, keep, possess*
	tentōrium, tentōriī, *n.*	*tent*
12, 28	terra, terrae, *f.*	*ground, land, country*
	orbis terrārum	*world*
14	terreō, terrēre, terruī, territus	*frighten*
	terribilis, terribilis, terribile	*terrible*
	tertius, tertia, tertium	*third*
	testis, testis, *m.f.*	*witness*
	tetigī	see tangō
	theātrum, theātrī, *n.*	*theater*
	thermae, thermārum, *f. pl.*	*baths*
	Thēseus, Thēseī, *m.*	*Theseus (Athenian hero)*
	Tiberis, Tiberis, *m.*	*Tiber (river)*
	Tiberius, Tiberiī, *m.*	*Tiberius*
	tībiae, tībiārum, *f. pl.*	*pipes*
	tībīcen, tībīcinis, *m.*	*pipe-player*
5	timeō, timēre, timuī	*fear, am afraid*
	Tīrō, Tīrōnis, *m.*	*Tiro*
	titulus, titulī, *m.*	*description*
	toga, togae, *f.*	*toga (formal garment)*
4	tollō, tollere, sustulī, sublātus	*raise, lift up, hold up*
	tondeō, tondēre, totondī, tōnsus	*cut, shave*
	tonitrus, tonitrūs, *m.*	*thunder*
	tōnsor, tōnsōris, *m.f.*	*barber*
	torculum, torculī, *n.*	*wine press*
24	tot	*so many*
6	tōtus, tōta, tōtum	*whole*
	tractō, tractāre, tractāvī, tractātus	*handle, manipulate*
9, 25	trādō, trādere, trādidī, trāditus	*hand over; hand down*
12	trahō, trahere, trāxī, tractus	*drag, draw, pull*
8	trāns + *acc.*	*across*
	trānseō, trānsīre, trānsiī, trānsitus	*go across*
	tremō, tremere, tremuī	*tremble, shake*
	tremor, tremōris, *m.*	*tremor, earthquake*
20	trēs, trēs, tria	*three*
	tribūnal, tribūnālis, *n.*	*platform (for judge or magistrate)*
	tribūnus, tribūnī, *m.*	*tribune (officer in the army)*
	trīclīnium, trīclīniī, *n.*	*dining room*
	trīgintā	*thirty*
	trīste	*sadly*
6	trīstis, trīstis, trīste	*sad*
	triumphus, triumphī, *m.*	*military parade, triumph*
	Trogus, Trogī, *m.*	*Trogus*
1	tū, tuī	*you (s.)*
	tuba, tubae, *f.*	*trumpet*
	tulī	see ferō
7	tum	*then*
	tumultus, tumultūs, *m.*	*riot*
	tunc	*then*
1	turba, turbae, *f.*	*crowd*
	turbulentus, turbulenta, turbulentum	*troublesome*
	tūs, tūris, *n.*	*frankincense*
21	tūtus, tūta, tūtum	*safe*
6	tuus, tua, tuum	*your (s.), yours*
	tyrannus, tyrannī, *m.*	*ruler, sovereign, tyrant*

U

	Latin	English
	ūber, ūberis	*plentiful*
1, 11	ubi?	*where? where; when*
	ubīque	*everywhere*
32	ultimus, ultima, ultimum	*final; furthest*
	ululō, ululāre, ululāvī, ululātus	*howl, yell*
18	umbra, umbrae, *f.*	*shadow, shade; ghost*
	Umbricia, Umbriciae, *f.*	*Umbricia*
	Umbricius, Umbriciī, *m.*	*Umbricius*
	umerus, umerī, *m.*	*shoulder*
	ūmidus, ūmida, ūmidum	*damp, wet*
25	umquam	*ever*
	ūnā	*together*
17	unda, undae, *f.*	*wave*
21	unde	*from where*
	undique	*everywhere*
	ungō, ungere, ūnxī, ūnctus	*smear, rub*
	unguentum, unguentī, *n.*	*perfume*
20	ūnus, ūna, ūnum	*one*
3	urbs, urbis, *f.*	*city*
	ūrīna, ūrīnae, *f.*	*urine*
	urna, urnae, *f.*	*jug, urn*
	ursa, ursae, *f.*	*bear*
	usque	*continuously*
	usque ad	*right up to*
19, 29	ut + *indic.*	*as; when, as soon as*
24	ut + *subj.*	*that, so that, in order that*
	ūtilis, ūtilis, ūtile	*useful*
30	ūtor, ūtī, ūsus sum + *abl.*	*use, employ*
	ūvae, ūvārum, *f. pl.*	*grapes*
6	uxor, uxōris, *f.*	*wife*

V

	vacca, vaccae, *f.*	*cow*
	vacuus, vacua, vacuum	*empty*
	vae!	*woe!*
	vah!	*ha! huh!*
	valdē	*very, very much*
32	valē! valēte!	*goodbye! farewell!*
23	validus, valida, validum	*strong*
	vāllum, vāllī, *n.*	*rampart, earthen wall*
	vātēs, vātis, *f.*	*priestess*
7	vehementer	*loudly, powerfully, forcefully*
	vehō, vehere, vēxī, vectus	*carry, convey*
	vēlum, vēlī, *n.*	*cloth, sheet*
	vēnālicius, vēnāliciī, *m.*	*slave dealer*
	vēnātor, vēnātōris, *m.*	*hunter*
5	vēndō, vēndere, vēndidī, vēnditus	*sell*
	venēnum, venēnī, *n.*	*poison*
4	veniō, venīre, vēnī	*come*
	venter, ventris, *m.*	*stomach*
21	ventus, ventī, *m.*	*wind*
	veprēs, vepris, *m.*	*bramble, thorn bush*
	vēr, vēris, *n.*	*spring*
	verberō, verberāre, verberāvī, verberātus	*hit, beat*
14	verbum, verbī, *n.*	*word*
	vereor, verērī, veritus sum	*fear*
	Vergilius, Vergiliī, *m.*	*Vergil*
	Verginius, Verginiī, *m.*	*Verginius*
	vēritās, vēritātis, *f.*	*truth*
13	vērō	*indeed, truly, certainly*
30	vertō, vertere, vertī, versus	*turn*
	vērum, vērī, *n.*	*truth*
24	vērus, vēra, vērum	*true, real*
	Vesontiō, Vesontiōnis, *m.*	*Vesontio (Besançon, town in eastern France)*
	Vespasiānus, Vespasiānī, *m.*	*Vespasian*
	vesper, vesperī, *m.*	*evening*
21	vester, vestra, vestrum	*your (pl.), yours*
19	vestīmentum, vestīmentī, *n.*	*item of clothing, garment; pl. = clothes*
	vestis, vestis, *f.*	*item of clothing*
	Vesuvius, Vesuviī, *m.*	*Vesuvius (mountain near Pompeii)*
	veterānus, veterānī, *m.*	*veteran, retired soldier*
18	vetus, veteris	*old*
	vexō, vexāre, vexāvī, vexātus	*annoy*
1	via, viae, *f.*	*street, road, way*
	vīcī	see vincō
	vīcīnus, vīcīnī, *m.*	*neighbor*
	Victor, Victōris, *m.*	*Victor*
31	victor, victōris, *m.*	*winner*
25	victōria, victōriae, *f.*	*victory*
	victus	see vincō
	vīcus, vīcī, *m.*	*settlement*
2	videō, vidēre, vīdī, vīsus	*see*
28	videor, vidērī, vīsus sum	*appear, seem*
	vīlis, vīlis, vīle	*low, cheap*
15	vīlla, vīllae, *f.*	*country house, house*
	vīnārius, vīnāria, vīnārium	*wine (adjective)*
3	vincō, vincere, vīcī, victus	*win, am victorious; conquer*
	vinculum, vinculī, *n.*	*chain*
	vīndēmia, vīndēmiae, *f.*	*grape harvest*
	Vindex, Vindicis, *m.*	*Vindex*
	Vindonissa, Vindonissae, *f.*	*Vindonissa*
	vīnea, vīneae, *f.*	*vine, vines*
2	vīnum, vīnī, *n.*	*wine*
9	vir, virī, *m.*	*man*
28	virgō, virginis, *f.*	*virgin, girl, young woman*
30	virtūs, virtūtis, *f.*	*courage; virtue*
27	vīs, vim, *f.*	*force*
	vīsitō, vīsitāre, vīsitāvī	*visit*
	vīsus	see videō
9	vīta, vītae, *f.*	*life*
	vītō, vītāre, vītāvī, vītātus	*avoid*
	vituperō, vituperāre, vituperāvī, vituperātus	*criticize, complain about*
13	vīvō, vīvere, vīxī	*live, am alive*
26	vīvus, vīva, vīvum	*alive, living*
20	vix	*scarcely, hardly, with difficulty*
2	vocō, vocāre, vocāvī, vocātus	*call*
	volitō, volitāre, volitāvī	*fly*
5	volō, velle, voluī	*want, wish, am willing*
	volvō, volvere, volvī, volūtus	*roll, turn*
4	vōs, vestrum	*you (pl.)*
19	vōtum, vōtī, *n.*	*prayer*
12	vōx, vōcis, *f.*	*voice; shout*
	vulnerātus, vulnerāta, vulnerātum	*wounded*
27	vulnerō, vulnerāre, vulnerāvī, vulnerātus	*wound, injure*
19	vulnus, vulneris, *n.*	*wound*
	vultur, vulturis, *m.*	*vulture*
24	vultus, vultūs, *m.*	*expression; face*

X

	Xerxēs, Xerxis, *m.*	*Xerxes*

Z

	Zabdela, Zabdelae, *m.*	*Zabdela*
	zingiberī	*ginger*

ACKNOWLEDGEMENTS

Thanks are due to the following for permission to reproduce images:

p.10, Pearl earrings, The Metropolitan Museum of Art, New York; p.11, Mosaic, 'Cave Canem', Su concessione del Ministero della Cultura–Parco Archeologico di Pompei, House of the Tragic Poet; p.13, Fullonica, Su concessione del Ministero della Cultura–Parco Archeologico di Pompei, photography by Carole Raddato; p.15, Pomegranate, Alamy; p.15, Cinnamon, Alamy; p.15, Myrrh and frankincense, Alamy; p.15, Marjoram, Alamy; p.15, Rose, Alamy; p.15, Iris, Alamy; p.15, Wall painting of perfume makers, Su concessione del Ministero della Cultura–Parco Archeologico di Pompei, House of the Vetii; p.18, Mosaic, 'Salve Lucrum', Su concessione del Ministero della Cultura–Parco Archeologico di Pompei; p.18, Wall painting of Vesuvius and Bacchus, Su concessione del Ministero della Cultura–Museo Archeologico Nazionale di Napoli.; p.19, Via Mercurio, Su concessione del Ministero della Cultura–Parco Archeologico di Pompei; p.19, Lamp, The Metropolitan Museum of Art, New York; p.20, Wall painting of fullers, Bridgeman Images, Su concessione del Ministero della Cultura–Museo Archeologico Nazionale di Napoli; p.21, Alexander mosaic, Su concessione del Ministero della Cultura–Museo Archeologico Nazionale di Napoli.; p.22, Etching of Pompeii, Wellcome Collection, London, (CC BY 4.0); p.24, House of Menander, Su concessione del Ministero della Cultura–Parco Archeologico di Pompei; p.25, Eumachia, Su concessione del Ministero della Cultura–Parco Archeologico di Pompei; p.26, Togatus Barberini statue, Roma, Musei Capitolini, Centrale Montemartini © Roma, Sovrintendenza Capitolina ai Beni Culturali; p.29, Sundial, Su concessione del Ministero della Cultura–Parco Archeologico di Pompei; p.31, Mosaic of garum, Su concessione del Ministero della Cultura–Parco Archeologico di Pompei; p.33, Wall painting, The Metropolitan Museum of Art, New York; p.37, Dolia, Su concessione del Ministero della Cultura–Parco Archeologico di Pompei; p.37, Mosaic of treading grapes, Con agradecimiento al Departamento de Documentación del Museo Nacional de Arte Romano; p.38, Silenus holding Bacchus, © Musée du Louvre, Dist. RMN-Grand Palais / Thierry Ollivier; p.38, Ariadne and Bacchus, Titian, © The National Gallery, London.; p.38, Cup with Bacchae, © RMN-Grand Palais (musée du Louvre)/ Stéphane Maréchalle; p.43, Columbaria, Su concessione del Ministero della Cultura–Parco Archeoloico di Ostia Antica; p.43, Columellae, ©Jackie and Bob Dunn www.pompeiiinpictures.com, Su concessione del Ministero della Cultura–Parco Archeologico di Pompei; pp.44-45, Mosaic of Nile, Su concessione del Ministero della Cultura–Museo Archeologico Nazionale di Napoli.; p.46, Sistrum, The Metropolitan Museum of Art, New York; p.46, Statue of Isis, Su concessione del Ministero della Cultura–Museo Archeologico Nazionale di Napoli.; p.47, Fresco of Isis and Io, Su concessione del Ministero della Cultura–Museo Archeologico Nazionale di Napoli.; p.47, Temple of Isis, Su concessione del Ministero della Cultura–Parco Archeologico di Pompei; p.47, Inscription of Popidius, Su concessione del Ministero della Cultura–Museo Archeologico Nazionale di Napoli.; p.48, Goblet with skeletons, © RMN-Grand Palais (musée du Louvre) / Hervé Lewandowski; p.49, Bronze skeleton, Digital image courtesy of the Getty's Open Content Program; p.49, Grave top, Wellcome Collection, London, (CC BY 4.0); p.50, Portrait of elderly woman, The Metropolitan Museum of Art, New York; p.50, Portrait of woman, The Metropolitan Museum of Art, New York; p.50, Portrait of Eutyches, The Metropolitan Museum of Art, New York; p.50, Portrait of man with mole, The Metropolitan Museum of Art, New York; p.50, Portrait of woman with garland, The Metropolitan Museum of Art, New York; p.50, Portrait of man with garland, The Metropolitan Museum of Art, New York; p.54, Mosaic of Orpheus, Su concessione del Museo Archeologico Regionale "Antonino Salinas" di Palermo; p.54, Orpheus sculpture by Rodin, The Metropolitan Museum of Art, New York; p.57, El Djem amphitheatre, Diego Delso (https://commons.wikimedia.org/wiki/File: Anfiteatro,_El_Jem,_Túnez,_2016-09-04,_DD_55-66_HDR_PAN.jpg), https://creativecommons.org/licenses/by-sa/4.0/legalcode; p.63, Bestiarii and musicians from the Zliten mosaic, Alamy; p.64, Femal gladiators, © The Trustees of the British Museum; p.65, Symmachius mosaic, Museo Arqueológico Nacional, Madrid. Inv. 3601. Foto: José Barea; p.67, Lamp, The Metropolitan Museum of Art, New York; p.69, Magerius mosaic, Alamy; p.74, Mosaic of peacock, Alamy; p.74, Seated camel relief, Courtesy of the Virtual Museum Of Palmyra | Mirath Initiative All rights reserved.; p.75, Altar of Anthus, The Metropolitan Museum of Art, New York; p.75, Lod mosaic, Photo Nicky Davidov, Courtesy of the Israel Antiquities Authority; p.77, Mosaic of cat and bird, Su concessione del Ministero della Cultura–Museo Archeologico Nazionale di Napoli.; p.79, Brooch, Gallo-Roman Museum, Tongeren; p.79, Snake bracelet, The Metropolitan Museum of Art, New York; p.79, Crescent Amulet, The Metropolitan Museum of Art, New York; p.79, Wall painting of Sappho, Su concessione del Ministero della Cultura–Museo Archeologico Nazionale di Napoli.; p.79, Portrait of woman, AGF/Bridgeman Images, National Museums of Scotland; p.79, Carnelian ring from above and side, The Metropolitan Museum of Art, New York; p.81, Mirror front and back, The Metropolitan Museum of Art, New York; p.83, Bust of woman front and back, Digital image courtesy of the Getty's Open Content Program; p.83, Portrait of woman, The Metropolitan Museum of Art, New York; p.86, Meroe head of Augustus, © Trustees of the British Museum; p.86, Plaque with meroitic text, The Walters Art Museum; p.86, Coin of Massinissa, Classical Numismatics Group, LLC, (www.cngcoins.com); pp.87, 92, Mask of Claudia Victoria, Death mask of Claudia Victoria, © photo: Jean-Michel Degueule, Christian Thioc / Lugdunum; p.90, Hermione Grammatike, Reproduced by permission of the Mistress and Fellows of Girton College, Cambridge; p.91, Wax tablet with Greek, © British Library Board, Shelfmark: Add MS 34186; p.94, Votive offering, Wellcome Collection, London, (CC BY 4.0); p.95, Child with Bulla, Yale University Art Gallery; p.96, Carthaginian coin, Classical Numismatics Group, LLC, (www.cngcoins.com); p.97, Gold bulla, JHAM 487, Image courtesy of the Johns Hopkins Archaeological Museum. Photograph by James T. VanRensselaer; p.98, Tombstone of child miner, Museo Arqueológico Nacional Madrid. Inv. 16744. Foto: Miguel Angel Otero; p.99, Rattle, The Metropolitan Museum of Art, New York; p.99, Terracotta doll, JHAM HT787, Image courtesy of the Johns Hopkins Archaeological Museum. Photograph by James T. VanRensselaer; p.102, Low Ham mosaic, Somerset Museum; p.102, Dido and Aeneas, Digital image courtesy of the Getty's Open Content Program; p.109, Coin of Vespasian, The Metropolitan Museum of Art, New York; p.113, Coin 'aeqypto capta', Classical Numismatics Group, LLC, (www.cngcoins.com); p.116, Poppy, Alamy; p.116, Monkshood, Alamy; p.116, Belladonna, Alamy; p.122, Acropolis, Alamy; p.123, Reconstruction of Erechtheum, © 2021. 3D Artist: John Goodinson. Reconstruction of the Erechtheion porch of the maidens in antiquity; p.123, Parthenon frieze, © Trustees of the British Museum; p.129, Stoa of Attalos, Alamy; p.130, Mosaic of philosophers, Su concessione del Ministero della Cultura–Museo Archeologico Nazionale di Napoli.; p.130, Intaglio of Socrates, The Metropolitan Museum of Art, New York; p.131, Epicurus, The Metropolitan Museum of Art, New York; p.131, Zeno, Ny Carlsberg Glyptotek, Copenhagen; p.132, Corinth canal, Alamy; p.134, Head of Alexander, © Trustees of the British Museum; p.138, Vase showing pankration, The Metropolitan Museum of Art, New York; p.140, Stadium at Olympia, Alamy; p.141, Athletic trophies, The Metropolitan Museum of Art, New York; p.142, Figurines of boxers, © The Trustees of the British Museum; p.143, Mosaic of women in bikinis, su concessione del Parco Archeologico di Mw-igantina e della Villa Romana del Casale di Piazza Armerina; p.143, Leather bikini bottoms, © Museum of London; p.147, Diadoumenos, The Metropolitan Museum of Art, New York; p.147, Hercules, Digital image courtesy of the Getty's Open Content Program; p.150, Echo and Narcissus, Waterhouse, Walker Art Gallery © National Museums Liverpool /Bridgeman Images; p.150, Metamorphosis, © Salvador Dali, Fundació Gala-Salvador Dalí, DACS 2022; p.150, Narcissus flower, Alamy; p.148, Cymbal, Museo Arqueológico Nacional Madrid. Inv. 38417. Foto: Ángel Martínez Levas.; p.151, Mosaic of musicians, Su concessione del Ministero della Cultura–Museo Archeologico Nazionale di Napoli.; p.155, Tile with musicians, The Cleveland Museum of Art; p.156, Seiklos epitaph, Nationalmuseets fotograf (https://commons.wikimedia.org/wiki/File:Seikilos1.tif), https://creativecommons.org/licenses/by-sa/3.0/legalcode; p.156, Seikilos notation, SVG by David W. (https://commons.wikimedia.org/wiki/File:Seikilos.svg), https://creativecommons.org/licenses/by-sa/3.0/legalcode; p.157, Cithara player, The Metropolitan Museum of Art, New York; p.157, Horn player, Museo Arqueológico Nacional Madrid. Inv. 1973/36/1819. Foto: Fernando Velasco Mora.; p.158, Coin of Nero, Classical Numismatics Group, LLC, (www.cngcoins.com); p.161, Sarcophagus of Muses, © RMN-Grand Palais (musée du Louvre) / Stéphane Maréchalle; p.163, Apollo with cithara, Digital image courtesy of the Getty's Open Content Program; p.164, Temple at Dephi, Alamy; p.165, Cave at cumae, Alamy; p.166, Krater of apollo, © The Trustees of the British Museum; p.166, Apollo flaying Marsyas, Sarah Campbell Blaffer Foundation, Houston; p.171, Votive offerings or viscera, foot, and hands, Wellcome Collection, London, (CC BY 4.0); p.172, Tombstone of Athenian doctor, © Trustees of the British Museum; p.173, Relief of childbirth scene, Wellcome Collection, London, (CC BY 4.0); p.173, Cupping vessel, Wellcome Collection, London, (CC BY 4.0); p.175, Ephesus, Alamy; p.176, Achilles and telephus, Su concessione del Ministero della Cultura–Museo Archeologico Nazionale di Napoli; p.177, Artificial leg, Wellcome Collection, London, (CC BY 4.0); p.177, Surgical instruments, Wellcome Collection, London, (CC BY 4.0); p.179, Tombstone of medica, © Laurianne Kieffer–Musée de La Cour d'Or–Metz Métropole; p.180, Page of Dioscorides, The Metropolitan Museum of Art, New York; p.182, Head of Constantine, The Metropolitan Museum of Art, New York; p.182, Court of Justinian, The Metropolitan Museum of Art, New York; p.183, Roman road, Petra, Alamy; p.184, Coin of Claudius, Classical Numismatics Group, LLC, (www.cngcoins.com); p.185, Beautiful Artemus, T.C. Culture and Ministry of Tourism, KVMGM, DÖSİMM, Ephesus Museum Directorate; p.186, Tower tomb in Palmyra, Alamy; p.190, Temple of Bel, Alamy; p.191, Relief with camel and men, Photos are courtesy of the Virtual Museum Of Palmyra | Mirath Initiative All rights reserved.; p.193, Beauty of Palmyra, Ny Carlsberg Glyptotek, Copenhagen/Anders Sune Berg; p.194, Milestone, Alamy; p.195, Relief of ox-drawn cart, Kunstsammlungen und Museen Augsburg; p.196, Modern Bulgaria, Alamy; p.198, Relief of griffins from Hatra, The Metropolitan Museum of Art, New York; p.203, Flight from Troy, New York University Excavations at Aphrodisias (G. Petruccioli); p.205, Agrippina crowning Nero, New York University Excavations at Aphrodisias (G. Petruccioli); p.206, Painted cast of Augustus Prima Porta, ©Ashmolean Museum, University of Oxford/Bridgeman Images; p.207, Hadrian's wall, Alamy; p.207, Coin of Galba, Classical Numismatics Group, LLC, (www.cngcoins.com); p.208, Coin from Gamla, Classical Numismatics Group, LLC, (www.cngcoins.com); p.210, Lex Ursonensis, Museo Arqueológico Nacional. Inv. 16736. Foto: Ángel Martínez Levas.; p.211, Zliten mosaic, Alamy; p.214, Diana and Actaeon, Public domain; p.214, Actaeon, Yale University Art Gallery; p.218, Bronze statue of Jupiter, The Metropolitan Museum of Art, New York; p.220, Altar of the Lares Augusti, Morehead State University. Camden-Carroll Library, Metropolitan Museum of Art Cast Collection, 37.https://scholarworks.moreheadstate.edu/metropolitan_art_collection /37; p.220, Coin of Vespasian, Classical Numismatics Group, LLC, (www.cngcoins.com); p.221, Bronze eagle, The Cleveland Museum of Art; p.224, Curse tablet, Digital image courtesy of the Getty's Open Content Program; p.226, Worms, Alamy; p.226, Spider, Alamy; p.226, Mouse, Alamy; p.228, Charm bracelet, JHAM HT1194, Image courtesy of the Johns Hopkins Archaeological Museum. Photograph by James T. VanRensselaer; p.230, Cup with Circe, The Metropolitan Museum of Art, New York; p.230, Etching of Circe and swine, Alamy; p.231, Relief of legionaries, Collection de Lugdunum, musée & théâtres romains, num.inv.:2001.0.308 ©photo : Jean-Michel Degueule, Christian Thioc/Lugdunum; pp.234-235, Vindonissa, View of the Roman legion camp Vindonissa in 50 AD, ikonaut, 2017; p.239, Standard bearer, Image courtesy of York Museums Trust, https://yorkmuseumstrust.org.uk; p.240, Mars Ultor, The Walters Art Museum; p.242, Roman shielf, Yale University Art Gallery; p.243, Onager, Alamy; p.243, Ballista, Alamy; p.243, Ballista balls, Alamy; p.247, Modern Rome, J M W Turner, Digital image courtesy of the Getty's Open Content Program; p.250, Relief of praetorians, © RMN-Grand Palais (musée du Louvre) / Hervé Lewandowski; p.255, Head of unknown man, Yale University Art Gallery; p.255, Head of Vespasian, The Cleveland Museum of Art; p.255, Coin of Nero, Classical Numismatics Group, LLC, (www.cngcoins.com); p.257, Cup of Polyphemus, © RMN-Grand Palais (musée du Louvre) / Maurice et Pierre Chuzeville; pp.258-260, Map of Rome, © OpenStreetMap contributors, CC BY-SA, openstreetmap.org; p.258, Baths of Caracalla, Public domain; p.259, Coin of column of Trajan, Classical Numismatics Group, LLC, (www.cngcoins.com); p.259, Coin of Colosseum, Classical Numismatics Group, LLC, (www.cngcoins.com); p.259, Painting of Colosseum, Yale Center for British Art; p.265, wall painting, The Metropolitan Museum of Art, New York; p.275, mosaic from Daphne, The Metropolitan Museum of Art, New York; p.277, relief of elephant, Digital image courtesy of the Getty's Open Content Program; p.278, mosaic , The Metropolitan Museum of Art, New York; p.287, statuette of official, The Walters Art Museum; p.288, wall painting from the villa of Fannius Synistor, The Metropolitan Museum of Art, New York.

While every effort has been made to contact copyright-holders of images, the author and publisher would be grateful for information about any illustrations where they have been unable to trace them, and would be glad to make amends in further editions.

TIMELINE

Ruler of Rome

- Romulus (753–715 BC)
- King Numa Pompilius (715–673 BC)
- King Tullus Hostilius (673–642 BC)
- King Ancus Marcius (642–616 BC)
- King Lucius Tarquinius Priscus (616–579 BC)
- King Servius Tullius (579–534 BC)
- King Lucius Tarquinius Superbus (534–509 BC)
- Roman Republic (509–27 BC)
- Emperor Augustus (27 BC–AD 14)
- Emperor Tiberius (AD 14–37)
- Emperor Gaius (Caligula) (AD 37–41)
- Emperor Claudius (AD 41–54)
- Emperor Nero (AD 54–68)
- Emperors Galba, Otho, Vitellius, and Vespasian (AD 68–69)

Events in Roman history

753 BC Traditional date of the foundation of Rome. According to legend, Romulus was the first ruler of Rome.
753-509 BC Rome was ruled by seven legendary kings.

C.600 BC Construction of the Cloaca Maxima in Rome.
C.534–509 BC Sibylline Books brought to Rome.
509 BC King Lucius Tarquinius Superbus (Tarquin the Proud) is expelled and the Roman Republic established.

451–449 BC Rome's laws written down on Twelve Tables.

387 BC Gauls capture Rome.

334–264 BC Rome expands to control Italy.
264–241 BC First Punic War, Rome against Carthage.
218–201 BC Hannibal crosses Alps, invading Italy; Second Punic War.
202 BC Scipio Africanus defeats Hannibal at Battle of Zama.
149–146 BC Third Punic War; Rome defeats Carthage; Africa becomes a province of the Roman Empire.
135–132 BC First Slave War, in Sicily.
104–100 BC Second Slave War, in Sicily.
73–71 BC Third Slave War, in mainland Italy, led by Spartacus.
67 BC Pompey's campaign against the pirates.
53 BC Parthia defeats Rome at Battle of Carrhae.
52 BC Vercingetorix leads Gallic revolt against Rome; Battle of Alesia.
44 BC Assassination of Julius Caesar.
31 BC Battle of Actium; Octavian (later Augustus) defeats Mark Antony.

27 BC Augustus becomes sole ruler of the Roman Empire: Rome's first emperor.
25 BC Baths of Agrippa, in Rome, are completed.
20 BC Peace treaty between Rome and Kingdom of Kush.
19 BC Aqua Virgo completed.

9 BC Consecration of the Ara Pacis.

2 BC Julia, daughter of Augustus, exiled.

AD 14 Pantheon is built on Field of Mars, in Rome.
AD 17–24 Tacfarinas leads rebellion against Roman rule in North Africa.

AD 20–60 Sebasteion built in Aphrodisias, Asia.

C.AD 30 Crucifixion of Jesus.
AD 32 Temple of Bel dedicated in Palmyra, Syria.

AD 43 Emperor Claudius invades Britain.

AD 52 Aqua Claudia completed.
AD 58–68 Otho governor of Lusitania.
AD 60 Boudica's revolt in Britannia; Londinium destroyed by fire.
AD 64 Great Fire of Rome.
AD 66–67 Nero visits Greece.
AD 66–73 The Jewish population of Judaea revolts against Roman rule.
AD 68 Revolt of Vindex in Gaul.
AD 69 Year of the Four Emperors.
AD 70 Destruction of the Temple in Jerusalem.

Events in the rest of the world

776 BC First Olympic Games, in Olympia, Greece.
C.750–700 BC *Iliad* and *Odyssey*.

660 BC According to legend, Jimmu becomes the first emperor of Japan.

563 BC Buddha, the religious leader, is born.
551–479 BC Confucius, Chinese philosopher.
550 BC Foundation of the Achaemenid (First Persian) Empire by Cyrus the Great.
508 BC Democracy is instituted at Athens.
480 BC Persians, led by Xerxes, invade Greece; Persians are defeated at Battle of Salamis.
C.431–404 BC Peloponnesian War between Athens and Sparta.
333 BC Battle of Issos. Alexander defeats Persian king, Darius.
331 BC Alexander the Great founds Alexandria, in Egypt.
C.324/21–185/80 BC Mauryan Empire in India.
323 BC Death of Alexander the Great, at Babylon.
261 BC Kalinga War between the Mauryan Empire and the state of Kalinga, in India.
C.247 BC King Arshak ousts the Seleucids from Parthia.
221–206 BC King Zheng unifies China as the first emperor of the Qin dynasty.
206 BC–AD 220 Han dynasty in China.
179 BC The earliest evidence for papermaking, in China.
141–87 BC reign of Emperor Wu in China.
69–30 BC Cleopatra VIII, the last Ptolemaic ruler of Egypt.
C.57 BC Three Kingdoms period begins in Korea.
30 BC Egypt becomes part of the Roman Empire.

C.AD 10–70 Hero of Alexandria, inventor of the fire engine.

C.AD 68 The Dead Sea scrolls are hidden in caves, to save them from the Romans.

Emperor Vespasian (AD 69–79)

Emperor Titus (AD 79–81)

Emperor Domitian (AD 81–96)

Emperor Nerva (AD 96–98)

Emperor Trajan (AD 98–117)

Emperor Hadrian (AD 117–138)

Western Empire (AD 395–476)

Eastern (Byzantine) Empire (AD 395–1453)

AD 73–74 The last of the Jewish rebels are besieged by the Romans in the fortress of Masada.

AD 79 Volcano Vesuvius erupts, destroying Pompeii and nearby towns.
AD 80 The Colosseum is completed in Rome.
AD 86 Capitoline Games instituted by Emperor Domitian.

AD 100 Londinium replaces Camulodunum as capital of Britannia.

AD 113 Trajan's column, celebrating Roman victory over the Dacians.

AD 122 Emperor Hadrian visits Britannia and orders construction of a wall: Hadrian's Wall.
C.AD 126 Pantheon rebuilt in final form.

AD 161–180 Emperor Marcus Aurelius.

AD 212 Emperor Caracalla grants citizenship to virtually all the free people of the Empire.
AD 216 Baths of Caracalla inaugurated.

AD 306–337 Emperor Constantine.
AD 313 All religions, including Christianity, tolerated in the Empire.
AD 324 Byzantium (modern Istanbul) becomes capital of the Empire.
AD 330 Byzantium renamed Constantinople.
AD 380 Christianity becomes the official religion of the Empire.
AD 395 The Roman Empire splits into two empires.
AD 408 Visigoths besiege Rome, the capital of the Western Empire.
AD 410 Visigoths sack Rome.
AD 410 Traditional date for the end of Roman rule in Britain.
AD 455 Vandals sack Rome.
AD 476 Fall of the Western Roman Empire. The Eastern Empire (renamed the Byzantium Empire) survives, with its capital at Constantinople.
AD 610–641 Byzantine Empire's official language changes to Greek.
AD 674–678 First Arab siege of Constantinople is unsuccessful.
AD 717–718 Second Arab attack on Constantinople, ending in failure.

AD 1054 the Christian Church breaks up into two parts, the Western section (Roman Catholic) and the eastern section (Greek Orthodox).
AD 1096–1099 The First Crusade.

AD 1453 The Ottomans capture Constantinople. Fall of the Byzantine Empire.

AD 127 Kanishka becomes king of the Kushan Empire of Afghanistan and northern India.

AD 166 First recorded Roman envoy arrives in China.

AD 224 The Parthian Empire falls and is succeeded by the Sasanian Empire, in modern Iran.

C.AD 360–415 Hypatia, female philosopher and mathematician, in Alexandria, in Egypt.

AD 570 The prophet Muhammad is born.
AD 581–618 Sui dynasty in China.
AD 619–907 Tang dynasty in China.
AD 632 Abu Bakr succeeds Muhammad as leader of the Muslim community.
AD 681 The Bulgarian Empire is established.
AD 750 The Abbasid Caliphate begins its rule in what is now Iraq.
C.AD 780–850 al-Khwarizmi, Persian mathematician.
AD 800 Charlemagne is crowned Holy Roman Emperor.

AD 827–902 Arab conquest of Sicily and parts of southern Italy.
AD 866 Viking army arrives in England.
AD 868 First known printed book, in China.
AD 886 Alfred the Great becomes the first king of England.
AD 904 Gunpowder first used in warfare, in China.

AD 1037 The Great Seljuk Empire is founded in what is now Kazakhstan.
AD 1066 William the Conqueror, Duke of Normandy, invades England and becomes king.

C. AD 1150 City of Angkor and temple of Angkor Wat created by the Khmer dynasty in Southeast Asia.
AD 1206 Genghis Khan is elected as Khagan of the Mongols and the Mongol Empire is established.
AD 1215 Magna Carta.
C.AD 1271–1275 Marco Polo travels to China.
C.AD 1299 The Ottoman Empire is founded by Osman I.
C.AD 1325 Aztecs found Tenochtitlan (now Mexico City).
AD 1347 The Black Death ravages Europe for the first time.
AD 1415 Portugal captures Ceuta, in North Africa.
AD 1431 Trial and execution of Joan of Arc.
C.AD 1440 Gutenberg printing press invented.
AD 1485 Henry Tudor becomes King of England.
AD 1452–1519 Leonardo da Vinci.
AD 1492 Christopher Columbus reaches the New World.

GRAMMAR INDEX

Key: 20.58 means Chapter 20, page 58.